The Child's View of the Third Reich in German Literature

The Eye among the Blind

DEBBIE PINFOLD

CLARENDON PRESS · OXFORD

OXFORD

UNIVERSITY PRESS

Great Clarendon Street, Oxford OX2 6DP

Oxford University Press is a department of the University of Oxford.
It furthers the University's objective of excellence in research, scholarship,
and education by publishing worldwide in

Oxford New York

Athens Auckland Bangkok Bogotá Buenos Aires Cape Town
Chennai Dar es Salaam Delhi Florence Hong Kong Istanbul Karachi
Kolkata Kuala Lumpur Madrid Melbourne Mexico City Mumbai Nairobi
Paris São Paulo Shanghai Singapore Taipei Tokyo Toronto Warsaw
with associated companies in Berlin Ibadan

Oxford is a registered trade mark of Oxford University Press
in the UK and in certain other countries

Published in the United States
By Oxford University Press Inc., New York

British Library Cataloguing in Publication Data

Data available
Library of Congress Cataloging in publication Data
Data available
ISBN 0-19-924565-7

1 3 5 7 9 10 8 6 4 2

Typeset in Baskerville
by Newgen Imaging Systems (P) Ltd.
Printed in Great Britain
on acid-free paper by
Biddles Ltd
Guildford and King's Lynn

This book is dedicated to the memory of my mother, to my Dad, and to my nephew Matthew— who provides me with my favourite examples of the child's perspective.

ACKNOWLEDGEMENTS

This book is based on a D.Phil thesis submitted to the Faculty of Medieval and Modern Languages at the University of Oxford in the summer of 1996. For support during the writing of this thesis I am grateful to the British Academy; St Hugh's College, Oxford; and the F.v.S. Stiftung in Hamburg. I would also like to acknowledge the friendly cooperation of the staff at the Taylorian and Bodleian Libraries, Oxford; the Staatsbibliothek, Hamburg; and the Deutsches Literaturarchiv in Marbach am Neckar. Thanks are also due to many colleagues and friends for suggestions and encouragement: in particular my supervisor Jim Reed, who has been generous with his time and support well beyond the completion of the thesis; Michael Butler, David Constantine, Osman Durrani, Margaret Jacobs, Tom Kuhn, Karen Leeder, and Ray Ockenden.

I would also like to thank my colleagues at Brasenose for their support and encouragement, and especially Sos Eltis and Nick Barber for keeping me away from my work when it mattered. I am grateful to my students, past and present, both for their interest in this project and for offering me a highly enjoyable alternative to working on it. Special thanks go to Chris Cairns, Katherine Dennis, Julie Smith, and Alexandra Stein for putting up with me and my work at different times; their friendship, support, and willingness to join me in extended lunch, tea, and supper breaks often eased my progress. And my greatest debt is to my family, which has always supported me in everything I have done. Nothing I could say here would be adequate to express my gratitude to them.

DMP

PERMISSIONS

CONTENTS

ABBREVIATIONS

AA	*Antike und Abendland: Beiträge zum Verständnis der Griechen und Römer und ihres Nachlebens*
AB	*Amsterdamer Beiträge zur neueren Germanistik*
BdM	*Bund deutscher Mädel*
Deutschunterricht	*Der Deutschunterricht: Beiträge zu seiner Praxis und wissenschaftlichen Begründung*
DVjs	*Deutsche Vierteljahresschrift für Literaturwissenschaft und Geistesgeschichte*
Ef	*Exilforschung: Ein internationales Jahrbuch*
GDR	*German Democratic Republic (East Germany)*
GLL	*German Life and Letters*
GM	*German Monitor*
GQ	*German Quarterly*
GR	*The Germanic Review*
GSR	*Germanic Studies Review*
HJ	*Hitler Jugend*
JM	*Jungmädel-Bund*
KLV	*Kinderlandverschickung*
NS	*Neue Sammlung: Vierteljahres-Zeitschrift für Erziehung und Gesellschaft*
NSDAP	*Nationalsozialistische Deutsche Arbeiterpartei*
NSLB	*Nationalsozialistischer Lehrerbund*
OGS	*Oxford German Studies*
Seminar	*Seminar: A Journal of Germanic Studies*
SSAWL	*Sitzungsberichte der Sächsischen Akademie der Wissenschaften zu Leipzig: Philologisch-Historische Klasse*
WB	*Weimarer Beiträge: Zeitschrift für Literaturwissenschaft, Ästhetik und Kulturwissenschaften*

WORKS CITED

Reference to the following works appear in the text.

Ilse Aichinger — *Die größere Hoffnung: Roman* (repr. Frankfurt, 1994).

Jurek Becker — *Jakob der Lügner: Roman* (repr. Frankfurt, 1982).

— *Die Mauer*, in id., *Nach der ersten Zukunft: Erzählungen* (Frankfurt, 1980).

Hubert Fichte — *Das Waisenhaus: Roman* (Reinbek, 1965).

Anna Gmeyner — *Manja. Ein Roman um fünf Kinder*, mit einem Vorwort von Heike Klapdor-Kops (repr. Mannheim, 1987).

Günter Grass — *Werkausgabe*, ed. Volker Neuhaus, 10 vols. (Darmstadt and Neuwied, 1987).

— *Die Blechtrommel: Roman*, in *Werkausgabe*, ii.

— *Hundejahre: Roman*, in *Werkausgabe*, iii.

Ludwig Harig — *Weh dem, der aus der Reihe tanzt* (Frankfurt, 1994).

Gert Hofmann — *Unsere Eroberung: Roman* (Darmstadt and Neuwied, 1984).

— *Veilchenfeld: Erzählung* (Darmstadt and Neuwied, 1986).

Hanna Johansen — *Die Analphabetin: Eine Erzählung* (Munich and Vienna, 1982).

Gudrun von Le Fort — *Die Unschuldigen*, in Gudrun von Le Fort, *Erzählende Schriften*, 3 vols. (Munich and Wiesbaden, 1956), vol. iii.

Siegfried Lenz — *Deutschstunde: Roman* (repr. Hamburg, 1969).

Thomas Mann — *Gesammelte Werke*, 12 vols (Frankfurt, 1960).

— *Buddenbrooks: Verfall einer Familie*, in *Gesammelte Werke*, i.

— *Doktor Faustus: Das Leben des deutschen Tonsetzers Adrian Leverkühn erzählt von einem Freunde*, in *Gesammelle Werke*, vi.

Helga M. Novak — *Die Eisheiligen: Roman* (Darmstadt and Neuwied, 1979).

Friedrich von Schiller — *Werke: Nationalausgabe*, ed. Julius Petersen (Weimar, 1943—).

Anna Seghers — *Der Ausflug der toten Mädchen und andere Erzählungen* (Berlin, 1948).

Christa Wolf — *Kindheitsmuster*, in *Werkausgabe*, 12 vols., ed. Sonja Hilzinger, v (Munich, 2000).

Thou, whose exterior semblance doth belie
Thy soul's immensity;
Thou best Philosopher, who yet dost keep
Thy heritage, thou Eye among the blind

William Wordsworth, 'Ode: Intimations of
Immortality from Recollections of Early Childhood'

INTRODUCTION

In his 1917 essay 'Art as Technique', Victor Shklovsky describes the purpose of art as follows: 'art exists that one may recover the sensation of life; it exists to make one feel things, to make the stone *stony*. The purpose of art is to impart the sensation of things as they are perceived and not as they are known'.[1] According to Shklovsky writers achieve this aim by using a range of aesthetic devices to defamiliarize our familiar world. In the first instance he describes this process as a way of making the reader re-experience physical sensations (i.e. making the stone *stony*). But his subsequent analyses of two passages by Tolstoy, one from 'Shame', which depicts a flogging without naming it, and one from 'Kholstomer', which considers the notion of human property from a horse's perspective, suggest that defamiliarization also has a moral purpose; the flogging example is described as 'typical of Tolstoy's way of pricking the conscience'.[2] According to Shklovsky, we need art to provide this defamiliarization because we are creatures of habit and 'Habitualization devours works, clothes, furniture, one's wife and the fear of war'.[3] To borrow an image from Kafka, we might say that most human beings resemble the narrator here:

Ich bin gewohnt in allem meinem Kutscher zu vertrauen. Als wir an eine hohe weiße seitwärts und oben sich langsam wölbende Mauer kamen, die Vorwärtsfahrt einstellten, die Mauer entlang fahrend sie betasteten und schließlich der Kutscher sagte: Es ist eine Stirn.[4]

We travel through life unconsciously, trusting to our habitual guides, and our perceptions are confined by the boundaries of our own mental world as surely as if by a physical obstacle; this idea is perfectly expressed in the pejorative 'engstirnig'. But art exists to break down Kafka's wall, whether by presenting us with events and sensations that we have not experienced personally or by

---

[1] In Lee T. Lemon and Marion J. Rees (eds. and trans.), *Russian Formalist Criticism: Four Essays* (Lincoln, Nebr. 1965), 12.　　　　　　　　　　　　　　[2] Ibid. 13.

[3] Ibid. 12.

[4] 'Oktavheft F', in id., *Beim Bau der chinesischen Mauer und andere Schriften aus dem Nachlaß* (Frankfurt, 1994), 128.

offering us new perspectives on our routine existence. Ultimately art may be the only means of breaking out of the prison of our limited perceptions so as to 'see oursels [and the society that has helped to form us] as others see us'.[5]

One of the principal literary devices for achieving a defamiliarization effect has always been to adopt an outsider's perspective, like that of Tolstoy's equine narrator, whose view of human mores leaves them very much open to question. But this is an extreme example; there are many instances of the outsider perspective coming from human beings who are on the margins of society. The literary outsider figure and his viewpoint have a long history; one of the earliest examples is Wolfram von Eschenbach's *Parzival* (*c.*1210), whose eponymous hero is brought up in the wilderness with the result that when he is first introduced to courtly society he is a 'reiner Tor' with a highly distinctive perspective on his new environment. Grimmelshausen uses a similar perspective in the early chapters of *Der Abenteuerliche Simplicissimus Teutsch* (1668) and in both of these texts the unsocialized outsider's view of his new society clearly has a moral and didactic function. European literature abounds in such figures: as representative examples we could cite Voltaire's *Candide* (1759), where the protagonist's unclouded moral perspective is used to satirical effect; the Wise Fools of Shakespeare, whose apparent eccentricity is paradoxically institutionalized, since their comments contain much truth and their *Narrenfreiheit* acts as a kind of social safety valve; and even the character who appears metaphysically estranged from the human race, like Meursault in Camus's *L'Étranger* (1942). Just as the paradoxical position of the Wise Fool suggests society's need for an alternative perspective upon itself, so the survival of the outsider figure and his viewpoint into more modern literature suggests the continuation of that need.

The wilderness that creates and shelters the 'reiner Tor' and the hermit is not often to be found in twentieth-century literature; nor is the court that is both refuge and butt to the Wise Fool. But all societies have margins, even if they are not quite as physically identifiable as the wilderness, and twentieth-century literature has

---

[5] 'To a Louse', in Robert Burns, *Selected Poems*, ed. Carol McGuirk (Harmondsworth, 1993), 86.

more than its fair share of 'outsider' figures, many of them with recognizable literary ancestors amongst the Wise Fools and hermits of the past. Some of these more recent literary figures are still physically segregated from the societies to which they nominally belong, incarcerated in prisons, borstals, and mental institutions that could be seen as sinister modern equivalents of the wilderness; we might mention the eponymous heroes of Thomas Mann's *Bekenntnisse des Hochstaplers Felix Krull* (1954) and Max Frisch's *Stiller* (1954); Oskar Matzerath in Günter Grass's *Die Blechtrommel* (1959); and Siggi Jepsen in Siegfried Lenz's *Deutschstunde* (1968) amongst others. Nor should we be misled by the overtly negative associations of these modern-day wildernesses, which might suggest a far more negative perception of those who inhabit them than of the likes of Parzival and Simplicissimus. Not all the modern outsiders mentioned above are entirely victims of social exclusion; paradoxically they are often seen as having taken refuge from a mad world and so the ostensible madman's viewpoint is in fact the sane perspective.[6]

These obvious outsiders are not the only such figures to be found in twentieth-century literature. There are also those who are in the world but not of it: clowns like the protagonist of Heinrich Böll's *Ansichten eines Clowns* (1963) or nonconformists like the protagonist of Christa Wolf's *Nachdenken über Christa T.* (1968). There are descendants of Rousseau's Noble Savage as in Aldous Huxley's *Brave New World* (1932), and the nineteenth-century foundling Kaspar Hauser has also seen a remarkable resurgence of interest in recent years, with his completely unsocialized perspective being put to various literary uses.[7] These modern literary outsiders tend to suffer a hard fate; they are either forced to conform to or else destroyed by the societies of which they form a reluctant part. This may be a consequence of our modern, pessimistic belief in the power of the mass over the individual, but it can also form a devastating critique of the society juxtaposed with that individual; we may recall Marcel Reich-Ranicki's comment on Christa T.: 'Christa T. stirbt an Leukämie, aber sie leidet an der

---

[6] For a more detailed discussion of this motif, see Theodor Ziolkowski, 'The View from the Madhouse', in id., *Dimensions of the Modern Novel: German Texts and European Contexts* (Princeton, 1969), 332–61.

[7] See Ursula Sampath, *Kaspar Hauser: A Modern Metaphor* (Columbia, 1991).

DDR'.[8] It is significant that post-war authors are still convinced of our need for such nonconformist characters and their perspective—a need which is clearly evoked in the narrator's admonition to the reader when she refers to her attempt to summon up the memory of Christa T., significantly using the first-person plural: 'Und bloß nicht vorgeben, wir täten es ihretwegen. Ein für allemal: Sie braucht uns nicht. Halten wir also fest, es ist unseretwegen, denn es scheint, wir brauchen sie'.[9]

The tensions that inform the presentation of Christa T., who is both a product of her society and a rebel against it, show how difficult it is for a modern author to create a plausible outsider figure and perspective. Characters are shaped by their society and so presenting an outsider perspective always leaves us with the question as to how this deviant viewpoint was acquired. In this respect Wolfram von Eschenbach and Grimmelshausen had a slightly easier task; not only was keeping their characters in the extra-social space of the wilderness a more plausible option than it is in our own time, but the societies they depicted had quite straightforward, unambiguous social and moral structures, and so the outsider position was also more clearly defined.

Given the difficulties of creating a plausible outsider figure and viewpoint it is small wonder that modern authors have often adopted a perspective that has so far only been mentioned in my epigraph from Wordsworth's 'Ode': that of the child. The child may be born into a specific social and cultural context, but it takes some time before the values of that society become its own; while it is still being socialized it may be considered as existing on the margins of adult society, and its perspective, however provisionally, is that of an outsider. Using the child's viewpoint is a particularly effective defamiliarizing device, for a child has not had time to become jaded by the process of habitualization that Shklovsky describes; to use Wordsworth's words, it has not yet been weighed down by 'custom', but instead experiences the world with the kind of intensity evoked by the phrase the 'Eye among the

<hr />

[8] 'Christa Wolfs unruhige Elegie', 1st pub. *Die Zeit* (23 May 1969), repr. in Manfred Behn (ed.), *Wirkungsgeschichte von Christa Wolfs 'Nachdenken über Christa T.'* (Königstein, 1978), 62.

[9] *Nachdenken über Christa T.* (Frankfurt, 1971), 10.

blind'.[10] The child who is experiencing something for the very first time perceives it in the way that Shklovsky believes art should make us experience the world; adopting this point of view might therefore be the most direct means of achieving the defamiliarization effect. Moreover, just as Shklovsky describes art as having the dual purpose of restoring physical sensation and moral vision, so the untainted vision of Wordsworth's child is not simply a physical attribute. This vision has been brought from his heavenly home and the fact that he remains in touch with this heritage gives him understanding beyond that of other human beings; his intuitive wisdom is more valuable than the acquired knowledge of adults, for he is a 'Philosopher' whose pure gaze can see 'truths' that adults have to search for all their lives.[11] This puts the intuitive wisdom of the child above the acquired knowledge of the adults; the child's state might best be described as an aesthetic innocence that has moral implications.[12]

However, the child's perspective that I shall deal with in this study is not quite as clear-cut as Wordsworth's harmonious image of the child in the midst of nature might suggest, for I shall focus on the way German authors have used the child's perspective to describe the Third Reich. There are obvious reasons, both moral and aesthetic, for adopting the child's point of view on this era; these are summed up by Walter Jens when he describes the modern novelist's perception of childhood:

Kindheit: das heißt für den modernen Romancier vollkommene Unschuld, Bei-Sich-Sein, mythische Allmacht. Kindheit heißt: Antithese (nicht Vergröberung!) der Erwachsenen-Welt; Kindheit: das ist die wahre Idealität, deren Existenz die Heillosigkeit unserer Gesellschaft

[10] *Selected Poems*, 109. Wordsworth's importance to the literary history of childhood is well documented. See esp. Peter Coveney, *The Image of Childhood, The Individual and Society: A Study of the Theme in English Literature* (rev. edn., Harmondsworth, 1967), 68–83; Aleida Assmann, 'Werden was wir waren: Anmerkungen zur Geschichte der Kindheitsidee', *AA* 24 (1978), 116–20; and Tony Tanner, *The Reign of Wonder: Naivety and Reality in American Literature* (Cambridge, 1965), 4–5. Also Robert Pattison, *The Child Figure in English Literature* (Athens, Ga., 1978), 56–66 and George Boas, *The Cult of Childhood* (London, 1966), 49-52. Coveney discusses the 'Ode' in detail, *Image of Childhood*, 75–81. Assmann discusses the implications of the phrase 'the Eye among the blind', 'Werden was wir waren', 116–18; Tanner also focuses on this phrase.

[11] *Selected Poems*, 108–9.

[12] Boas questions the validity of the term 'aesthetic innocence' when used to describe art produced by a child *(Cult of Childhood*, 100–1). I use the term to describe the quality of the child's vision rather than anything it might produce as a result.

spiegelt. Am Kind entscheidet sich alles; Kindheit, das ist gleichsam der klärende Zusatz, der die Welt zwingt, sich zu entlarven.[13]

The terms 'vollkommene Unschuld', 'Bei-Sich-Sein', and 'mythische Allmacht' suggest an image of childhood very close to that expressed in the 'Ode', but while authors might find the idea of juxtaposing childhood innocence with a depiction of the Third Reich attractive, it is difficult to reconcile this image of childhood with the probable psychological reality of a child brought up in this era. Children were the first casualties of the vigorously waged Nazi propaganda war, and those who were born into this era tended to regard it as the 'Normalität, in die sie [meine Generation] hineingeboren, in der sie aufgewachsen, für die sie erzogen war'.[14] Any child will unconsciously adopt the values of the society it is born into, as Georg Hensel suggests when he writes of his childhood in the Third Reich: 'Die Lebensbedingungen mußten nicht einmal bewußt gelernt werden, sie wuchsen uns zu, wir wuchsen in sie hinein'.[15] Moreover, in the Third Reich this normal socialization process was accelerated and emphasized by systematic indoctrination from a very early age. Contemporary reports by Erika Mann and Gregor Ziemer suggest that children were parroting Nazi ideology practically as soon as they could talk, and in the light of this it is difficult to see at what stage the child might be seen as offering a morally independent, naive viewpoint.[16] If anything, a realistic depiction of a child growing up in this era will tend to show it identifying itself with the value system of the time rather than coming to its society with the fresh

---

[13] 'Erwachsene Kinder: Das Bild der Jugendlichen in der modernen Literatur', in: id., Statt einer Literaturgeschichte (5th expanded edn., Pfullingen, 1962), 149.

[14] Josef Ippers, Zacharias Zachary, in Heinrich Böll (ed.), Niemands Land: Kindheitserinnerungen an die Jahre 1945 bis 1949 (Munich, 1988), 113.

[15] Der Sack überm Kopf, in Marcel Reich-Ranicki (ed.), Meine Schulzeit im Dritten Reich: Erinnerungen deutscher Schriftsteller (4th expanded edn., Munich, 1993), 117.

[16] In Education for Death: The Making of the Nazi (London, 1942), 21, Gregor Ziemer quotes a conversation with an official in the office of Baldur von Schirach, the Reichsjugendführer, who tells him that the Nazi state's interest in the child pre-dates its conception. This point is amply proved by Ziemer's investigations, for conversations with pre-school children demonstrate the extent to which Nazi ideology has already been drummed into them (ibid. 39–48). See also Erika Mann, Zehn Millionen Kinder: Die Erziehung der Jugend im Dritten Reich (Amsterdam, 1938), 32, for an example of the confusion caused in very young children's minds by the ideology imposed on them. Ch. 2, below will discuss to what extent the child's vision and thought processes are in fact corrupted by the ideology it is forced to parrot.

eyes of the outsider. The identification with a pernicious era makes it highly problematic to talk about childhood innocence in this context.

However, the child narrator or focalizer is first and foremost a literary device, and therefore the child behind the perspective need not necessarily be a psychologically plausible construct. For an early example, witness Grimmelshausen's *Simplicissimus*, where the way the lad's home is looted and laid waste by marauding soldiers during the Thirty Years War is clearly described in retrospect, as suggested by the adult conceptual framework: the narrator refers to the soldiers ransacking the house as though they expected to find 'das gülden Fell von Kolchis'.[17] But Grimmelshausen nonetheless uses the child's original perceptions of the scene to good satirical effect so as to highlight the irrational madness of the soldiers' savage destruction: for instance, he comments 'Bettladen, Tisch, Stühl und Bänk verbrannten sie, da doch viel Klafter dürr Holz im Hof lag'.[18] This use of the supposedly unknowing perspective of the child looks forward to such twentieth-century scenes as Oskar Matzerath's depiction of the *Kristallnacht*.[19] And even when authors aim to create more psychologically convincing children than Oskar, they still find ways of incorporating powerful myths about childhood, notably the idea of the child's unsullied vision. Wolf's Christa T. is a case in point. She has had an overwhelmingly positive reception as a nonconformist figure who somehow came through the Third Reich with her spirit and moral vision intact, while her counterpart in *Kindheitsmuster* (1976), Nelly Jordan, is generally regarded as having been corrupted and psychologically crippled by the regime.[20] And yet the intertextual links between the two books

---

[17] *Der Abenteuerliche Simplicissimus Teutsch* (repr. Munich, 1990), 16. [18] Ibid. 17.

[19] Grass's work was frequently compared with that of Grimmelshausen when *Die Blechtrommel* first appeared. See Franz Josef Görtz (ed.), *Die Blechtrommel; Attraktion und Ärgernis; Ein Kapitel deutscher Literaturkritik* (Darmstadt and Neuwied, 1984) for some of the earliest reviews. The comparison between Oskar and Simplicissimus is developed in detail in G. Richard Dimler SJ, 'Simplicius Simplicissimus and Oskar Matzerath as Alienated Heroes: Comparison and Contrast', *AB* 4 (1975), 113–34.

[20] See e.g. Pamela R. Barnett, 'Perceptions of Childhood', in Ian Wallace (ed.), 30, *Christa Wolf in Perspective* (GM 30, Amsterdam and Atlanta, Ga., 1994), 60, 63–4, and 70. Barnett draws too stark a distinction between Nelly Jordan and Christa T., for she sees Nelly as emotionally crippled by Nazism whereas Christa is presented as coming through the era unscathed. The effects of Nazi ideology on Nelly will be discussed in more detail in Chs. 1 and 2, below.

make it clear that Christa and Nelly receive a basically similar upbringing; Christa, like Nelly, is a member of the Nazi youth organization and it is only after the war that Christa too realizes the full extent of the ideology to which she has unwittingly subscribed:

Der Reiter, hinter dem nichts lag als ein zufällig fest gefrorener See, fiel tot vom Pferd, als er erfuhr, was er hinter sich hatte. Sie schrie nur, das ist nicht zuviel. Sie verbrannte ihre alten Tagebücher, da gingen die Schwüre in Rauch auf und die Begeisterungen, deren man sich nun schämte, die Sprüche und Lieder.[21]

Interestingly however, although Christa has been subjected to, and to some extent believed in, the same indoctrination as her contemporaries, she is nonetheless presented as seeing things differently herself and as being able to make other people adopt her point of view. A conversation with Christa in the playground prompts the narrator to reflect:

ich fühlte, ich sah die Dinge, wie sie waren. Sie hatte recht. Sie kam von Gott weiß woher, denn Eichholz kann jeder sagen, . . . setzte sich auf den Rand des Brunnens, der den Namen unserer Lehrerin trug, denn sie stammte aus einer der einflußreichsten Familien der Stadt–hielt ihre Hand in das Wasser und sah sich mit ihrem gründlichen Blick um. Und ich mußte auf einmal denken, daß dieses Wasser da vielleicht doch nicht das Wasser des Lebens war, und die Marienkirche nicht das erhabenste Bauwerk und unsere Stadt nicht die einzige Stadt der Welt.[22]

There is a tension between Christa's apparently privileged vision and her sheer ordinariness; when she first arrives at her new school the narrator is irritated by her superior manner, since there seems to be little to justify it:

Kraucht aus einem Dorfschullehrerhaus, keine fünfzig Kilometer von hier, und dann dieser Blick. Ja, wenn einer ein paar Dutzend rauchende Zechenschornsteine hinter sich hat, oder wenigstens den Schlesischen Bahnhof und den Kurfürstendamm... Aber Kiefern und Ginster und Heidekraut, denselben Sommergeruch, den auch wir bis zum Überdruß

---

[21] *Nachdenken über Christa T.*, 34–5.
[22] Ibid. 19. Quernheim points to the importance of Christa T.'s 'gründlicher Blick' and of the 'Erkenntnisprinzip' associated with it. Mechthild Quernheim, *Das moralische Ich: Kritische Studien zur Subjektwerdung in der Erzählprosa Christa Wolfs* (Würzburg, 1990), 29 and 53.

und fürs Leben in der Nase hatten, breite Backenknochen und bräunliche Haut, und dieses Benehmen?[23]

However, these dismissive comments are somewhat undermined by the way the narrator had previously introduced Christa's first day at her school, for this description has a touch of the miraculous about it, summed up in the self-conscious use of the verb *erscheinen* ('als sie bei uns erschien, anders möchte ich es nicht nennen').[24] The case of Christa T. encapsulates neatly the difficulties faced by a twentieth-century author writing about an outsider or specifically a child figure, especially in the Third Reich context. While there is a long literary history that follows the Wordsworth line of seeing the child as a miraculous being whose clarity of vision is part of its heavenly inheritance, more recent insights from the field of child psychology would have given us a less mystical view of the child, even without seeing the kind of perversion of childhood innocence that could be brought about by the Nazis.

THE CHILD FIGURE IN GERMAN LITERATURE:
A BRIEF OVERVIEW

Both the real and the literary child have had a much more chequered history than the other outsider figures mentioned in the previous section; there have been centuries of debate over the nature of the child and thus the significance of its literary representative has changed accordingly. The child figure is therefore rich in potential meanings and extends an open invitation to writers with very different agendas. It is obviously impossible to give a very detailed account of the shifting perceptions of childhood here, but what follows is a broad outline of the main developments in thought on the subject as they affect this study.

It is possible to divide perceptions of childhood into, broadly speaking, two groups which might be labelled Old and New Testament.[25] The perception of the child inherited from the Old

---

[23] *Nachdenken über Christa T.*, 13–14.   [24] Ibid. 13.

[25] This is the understanding that informs Pattison's study of the child figure in English literature. He comments that after the Reformation the child emerged as 'a literary figure around whom ideas of our original nature, our fallen condition, and our hopes for salvation cluster' (*Child Figure*, 20).

Testament was that it was the principal inheritor of Original Sin and condemned to hell in the event of it dying before it was baptized. This view of childhood was popularized by St Augustine amongst others and it had a profound and lasting impact on child-rearing methods.[26] This seems rather odd, for as Pattison points out, if the Old Testament seemed to sanction a decidedly negative view of childhood one would have thought that the value ascribed to children and the childlike mentality by Jesus would have had some impact on adult perceptions of childhood;[27] we think especially of the famous statement 'Except ye be converted and become as little children ye shall not enter the kingdom of heaven' (Matthew 18: 3) which has influenced many writers' presentation of the child.[28] Yet it was the Old Testament perception that prevailed until the advent of Jean-Jacques Rousseau and his seminal educational treatise *Émile* (1762); before this turning point in the history of childhood it seems the best the real life child could hope for was to be regarded as a tabula rasa who, with time and patience on the part of the educator, could be made a responsible citizen.[29]

The ideas put forward in *Émile* continue to influence our perception of childhood today.[30] Rousseau's work presented two

---

[26] For the Old Testament origins of the perception of the child, see ibid., 10. For an account of the debate regarding the necessity for infant baptism, ibid. 11–20.

[27] Ibid. 9–10. See also Lloyd deMause (ed.), *The History of Childhood: The Untold Story of Child Abuse* (London, 1991), 16–17. DeMause suggests that the positive images of childhood in the New Testament are not all they might seem: 'Even the well-known saying, "Suffer little children, and forbid them not, to come unto me" turns out to be the customary Near Eastern practice of exorcising by laying on of hands, which many holy men did to remove the evil inherent in children . . .', (*History of Childhood*, 17).

[28] In *Le Génie Enfant: Die Kategorie des Kindlichen bei Clemens Brentano* (Berlin and New York, 1973), 4, Gerhard Schaub points out the importance of these words for both Hamann and Goethe and suggests that the fact both writers drew on this religious source indicates that there was no specifically literary precedent for idealizing childhood at the time when they were writing. That these words have enduring significance for the literary depiction of childhood is clear from the work of Ilse Aichinger amongst others (see the discussion of her work in Ch. 2, below).

[29] See John Locke, *Some Thoughts concerning Education* (1693).

[30] *Émile* is generally seen as the work that heralds a new conception of childhood and most studies of the literary treatment of this theme take it as their starting point. For a more detailed discussion see esp. Coveney, *Image of Childhood*, 37–51 and Hans-Heino Ewers, *Kindheit als poetische Daseinsform; Studien zur Entstehung der romantischen Kindheitsutopie im 18. Jahrhundert: Herder, Jean Paul, Novalis und Tieck* (Munich, 1989), 39–58. Also Boas, *Cult of Childhood*, 29–33; Pattison, *Child Figure*, 50–56; and David Grylls, *Guardians and Angels: Parents and Children in Nineteenth-Century Literature* (London, 1978), 32–5.

revolutionary theses. The first was summed up in the words 'On ne connaît point l'enfance', intended to suggest that hitherto children had been treated as miniature adults rather than childhood being seen as a stage of development in its own right.[31] The second thesis was closely linked to the first, and was summed up in the programmatic opening sentence of the work: 'Tout est bien en sortant des mains de l'Auteur des choses; tout dégénère entre les mains de l'homme';[32] that is, the child was distinct from the adult because it arrived in the world in a state of original innocence. This was a complete reversal of the Augustinian position and heralded new childrearing methods based on the etymological definition of education provided many years later by Miss Jean Brodie: 'a leading out of what is already there in the pupil's soul'.[33] While the educator was still supposed to guide the child, he was to follow the child's own inclinations, which were assumed to be positive.

Émile was translated into German in the year of its publication and had a profound influence on contemporary German writers, who were deeply affected by the idea of the child's original innocence. They were also struck by the presentation of the child's upbringing, for to avoid sullying social influences, Rousseau's fictional tutor insists on bringing up his pupil in idyllic rural seclusion. These ideas of original innocence and a close association with the natural world are two elements taken up by Romantic writers in the image of childhood they went on to create. But the German Romantic perception of childhood includes more than this; namely, an identification between the child and the saviour (largely indebted to the cult of the Virgin and Child at this time) and, importantly for my context, between the child and the artist.[34] When examining this key aspect of the German myth of childhood we have to look a little closer to home for the principal influence; namely, to Schiller and his aesthetic treatise *Über naive und sentimentalische Dichtung* (1795/6).[35]

[31] Jean-Jacques Rousseau, *Émile ou de l'éducation*, ed. François and Pierre Richard (Paris, 1992), 2.   [32] Ibid. 5.

[33] Muriel Spark, *The Prime of Miss Jean Brodie* (1961; Harmondsworth, 1965), 36.

[34] This idea can be traced back to Hamann and Herder. Herder's role in creating the Romantic image of childhood is discussed in Ewers, *Kindheit*, 59–96. For a discussion of the topos of the child as artist and artist as child see Schaub, *Génie Enfant*, 11–17 and Boas, *Cult of Childhood*, 79–102.

[35] The significance of *Über naive und sentimentalische Dichtung* to a new conception of childhood is well documented. See Hansgeorg Kind, *Das Kind in der Ideologie und der*

Schiller clearly wrote this treatise as a celebration of the intellectual or 'sentimental' poet, but some of its most moving passages are those devoted to an evocation of childhood and the childlike mentality. Perhaps most important of all is his statement that the 'Kultur' of the 'sentimental' poet should actually aim to return us to a higher form of that naive state from whence we came:

Sie *sind*, was wir *waren*; sie sind, was wir wieder *werden sollen.* Wir waren Natur, wie sie, und unsere Kultur soll uns, auf dem Wege der Vernunft und der Freyheit, zur Natur zurückführen. Sie sind also zugleich Darstellung unserer verlornen Kindheit, die uns ewig das theuerste bleibt; daher sie uns mit einer gewissen Wehmuth erfüllen. Zugleich sind sie Darstellungen unserer höchsten Vollendung im Ideale, daher sie uns in eine erhabene Rührung versetzen. (*Werke*, xx. 414)

This statement opened up new ways of seeing childhood for, while Schiller's treatise does not see naivety as a property of real children ('Das Naive ist eine *Kindlichkeit, wo sie nicht mehr erwartet wird,* und kann eben deßwegen der wirklichen Kindheit in strengster Bedeutung nicht zugeschrieben werden', xx. 419), nonetheless the idea of childhood as a lost ideal which should be reattained, albeit on a higher level, was a revolutionary one which was taken up with great enthusiasm by the Romantics. *Über naive und sentimentalische Dichtung* suggests the idea of the child's vision as a model for that of the artist, an idea we find in the work of authors such as Wordsworth and Novalis. In Novalis's *Die Lehrlinge zu Sais* (post-1802) for example, children's intuitive wisdom and its implications for the artist are described as follows:

Oft erfahren diese liebenden Kinder in seligen Stunden herrliche Dinge aus den Geheimnissen der Natur, und tun sie in unbewußter Einfalt kund. Ihren Tritten folgt der Forscher, um jedes Kleinod zu sammeln, was sie in ihrer Unschuld und Freude haben fallen lassen, ihrer Liebe huldigt der mitfühlende Dichter und sucht durch seine Gesänge diese Liebe, diesen Keim des goldenen Alters, in andre Zeiten und Länder zu verplanzen.[36]

Dichtung der deutschen Romantik (Diss. Leipzig; Dresden, 1936), 9; Boas, *Cult of Childhood*, 72–4; Rainer Hagen, *Kinder, wie sie im Buche stehen* (Munich, 1967), 24; Schaub, *Génie Enfant*, 10 and 13–14; Assmann, 'Werden was wir waren', 99 and 124; and Dieter Richter, *Das fremde Kind: Zur Entstehung der Kindheitsbilder des bürgerlichen Zeitalters* (Frankfurt, 1987), 254.

[36] In, *Schriften*, ed. Paul Kluckhorn and Richard H. Samuel, 5 vols. (2nd rev. and expanded edn., Stuttgart, 1960–88), i. 103–4.

The child's vision was frequently thought to have heavenly origins as in Wordsworth's 'Ode', and the obvious associations between any child and the infant Christ meant that the ideas of child, saviour, and artist became closely intertwined.[37] There is a powerful example of this in Novalis's *Heinrich von Ofterdingen* (post-1802) where Heinrich's father reports a dream he has had:

ich sah deine Mutter mit freundlichem, verschämten Blick vor mir; sie hielt ein glänzendes Kind in den Armen, und reichte mir es hin, als auf einmal das Kind zusehends wuchs, immer heller und glänzender ward, und sich endlich mit blendendweißen Flügeln über uns erhob, uns beide in seinen Arm nahm, und so hoch mit uns flog, daß die Erde nur wie eine goldene Schüssel mit den saubersten Schnitzwerk aussah.[38]

Mähl points out that this dream is a reference both to Heinrich's poetic vocation and his 'messianischen Erlösungsauftrag'; it is one of a number of examples in Novalis's work where the child is used to symbolize a future golden age corresponding to an earlier era of prelapsarian innocence and primal harmony.[39]

For the Romantics the child's status is best described by the title of E. T. A. Hoffmann's story *Das fremde Kind* (1817).[40] The children who appear in the literature of this period are rarely plausible psychological constructs; while Kind notes some moves towards psychologizing Felix and Christlieb, especially in the gender differentiation that runs through Hoffmann's work, the children's names already suggest their symbolic purpose. Moreover, the

---

[37] The idea that literary child figures often have a redemptive function is highlighted in Reinhard Kuhn, *Corruption in Paradise: The Child in Western Literature* (Hanover, NH and London, 1982), 44–56. Kuhn points out that the idea of the child as saviour actually pre-dates Christianity, for it is also central to the classical tradition (ibid. 44).

[38] In *Schriften*, i.202.

[39] Hans-Joachim Mähl, *Die Idee des goldenen Zeitalters im Werk des Novalis: Studien zur Wesensbestimmung der frühromantischen Utopie und zu ihren ideengeschichtlichen Voraussetzungen* (Heidelberg, 1965), 367. See esp. Mähl's deliberations on 'Die Gestalt des "Kindes" als Repräsentation des goldenen Zeitalters', ibid. 362–71. Both Mähl and Kuhn indicate that the presentation of the child figure in *Die Lehrlinge zu Sais* derives from the Christian mystical tradition and point to the significance of its second coming (Mähl, *Idee des goldenen Zeitalters*, 362–3 and Kuhn, *Corruption in Paradise*, 19).

[40] This story is discussed by Kind, *Kind*, 66–70; Richter, *Fremde Kind*, 261–80; and Kuhn in *Corruption in Paradise*, 162–5. It is accorded special significance by Ueding in 'Verstoßen in ein fremdes Land: Kinderbilder der deutschen Literatur; *NS* 17 (1977), 350 and by Richter in *Fremde Kind*, 277–80. Both Ueding and Richter interpret the story as demonstrating a new perception of childhood as an alien state.

eponymous 'fremde Kind' who appears both genderless and age-less represents a dimension beyond the real children in any case. This is typical of literary children of this time, who tend to stand apart from society, representing both a former ideal state and one that might be reattained were there to be some kind of apoca-lypse;[41] they are an ideal standard against which to measure social mores.

But for the Romantics the child did not merely offer a means of evoking an ideal state beyond society or the ideal artistic vision; it also provided them with an image for their own status. In Romantic works the child represents all the qualities required to both produce and appreciate art: spontaneity, closeness to nature, and imagination. As Kind points out, these qualities were utterly opposed to what the Romantics saw as the sterile rational values of the *Aufklärung*, and to the beginnings of a more industrialized age, where the individual was less important.[42] These intellectual and social trends were inimical to the Romantics' conception of art, and it may be that, like English writers of the late eighteenth and early nineteenth centuries, their own sense of alienation and vulnerability and their dissatisfaction with society were expressed by their obsessive use of the child figure.[43] This would also account for their almost equally insistent repetition of the adjective *kindlich* to describe adults who had not succumbed to the baser forces of the age, for it is significant that the word *kindlich* seems to appear more frequently than do real children in the works of the Romantic era; Schaub points out that for an author to refer to one of his characters as 'kindlich' is the highest compliment he can pay.[44] Artists are frequently credited with characteristics of child-hood or with striving for them; both Schaub and Ewers point to

[41] See esp. Mähl, *Idee des goldenen Zeitalters,* 362–71. This reattainment of childhood has both individual and social implications. Assmann points out that literary presenta-tions of childhood do not always spring from a regressive impulse but have socio-critical potential ('Werden was wir waren', 121–2) and Richter both concurs with this and suggests the utopian vision that can be achieved through the child (*Fremde Kind,* 27 and 249–61).

[42] For a discussion of the ideology of childhood as it permeated esp. the 'Frühro-mantik', see Kind, *Kind,* 20–5.

[43] Coveney, *Image of Childhood,* 31–2. See also Ueding, 'Verstoßen in ein fremdes Land', 349–50, where the child in Novalis's poem 'An Tieck' is taken to suggest the new perception of the artist and his sense of social alienation in the 19th cent.

[44] *Génie Enfant,* 14.

the example of Ludwig Tieck's *Franz Sternbalds Wanderungen* (1798) where, although Franz and Sebastian have actually grown beyond a childlike mentality, they promise each other 'immer ein Kind [zu] bleiben'.[45] Writers of this time are less concerned with childhood itself than with what childhood represents.

Clearly this description of children in the Romantic era as depicting symbols of purity, spontaneity, closeness to nature and imagination is a rather one-sided one, and critics are quick to point out that it is not the whole story. Certainly not every child who appears in the literature of this time is an ethereal ideal who speaks to us of a poetic dimension beyond our humdrum reality. Ewers concedes that his study of the utopian aspect of the eighteenth-century's childhood discourse does not do justice to the wide range of different images of childhood during the period;[46] Simonis points out that there was a pluralistic image of childhood at this time, and that criticism of the idealization of childhood was actually inherent in the Romantic era.[47] However, the fact remains that idealization of childhood and what it represents is a significant phenomenon during this period, and my study focuses specifically on this idealistic aspect and its survival against all the odds into the post-war era. Hereafter, for convenience, the term 'Romantic' will be used to refer to this idealistic presentation of the child.

The idealization of childhood and what it represents has been interpreted as a particularly German phenomenon, notably by Rainer Hagen, who believes that different nationalities have distinct literary images of childhood.[48] He regards German writers and readers as fascinated to the point of delusion by Goethe's Mignon, and concludes his chapter on the German image of childhood with the comment: 'Die deutschen Leser scheinen sich auch heute noch mit unretuschierten Kinderbildern nicht befreunden zu wollen. Mignon verstellt ihnen immer noch den Blick auf die Wirklichkeit'.[49] He explains the attraction of this figure by saying that she is a symbol of innocence, who has to die in order to preserve that innocence and 'dem Leser eine liebe Idee'.[50] She is the 'fremde Kind' par excellence, the child who initially is

---

[45] Ibid. 14; Ewers, *Kindheit*, 238.

[47] *Kindheit in Romanen um 1800* (Bielefeld, 1993), 265-7.

[49] Ibid. 35.

[46] *Kindheit*, 8.

[48] *Kinder*, 8-9.

[50] Ibid. 26.

unable to communicate with the adult world and who seems to point to a mysterious other realm beyond the adults' ken, even if the mystery surrounding her is resolved by entirely rational explanations at the end of the text.[51] She is a perfect example of the Romantic child who embodies an alternative to mainstream society, but one that appears unattainable.

But even when Goethe was writing, the days of Mignon's type were numbered. The beginnings of a new perception of child-hood are obvious if we compare the two versions of the Wilhelm Meister text, for the later version anticipates a more widespread change in attitude towards childhood.[52] In *Wilhelm Meisters The-atralische Sendung* (written 1777–85) Wilhelm's childhood is pre-sented as an important formative period. Not only do his activities with the puppet theatre anticipate his involvement with the real theatre, but Goethe also privileges the childhood chapters by using an omniscient narrator, an implied value judgement. Yet by the time we reach the *Lehrjahre* (1795/6) Goethe's ideas about the importance of childhood have changed in line with his different conception of his hero. Not only is Wilhlem's 'Sendung' now sub-jected to amused irony, the fact that he indulges *himself* with a lengthy and detailed description of his childhood while Mariane tries in vain to stay awake, powerfully suggests what had already been implicit in the *Sendung*; namely, that while childhood can be a delightful time it must be left behind at the appropriate juncture and transmuted into something else. In this sense the *Sendung* is closer to the Romantic conception of childhood as suggested in Wordsworth's 'Ode', for it allows for a certain inner continuity between Wilhelm's child and adult, artist self: the latter stage and its theatrical activities are merely a *Steigerung* of the earlier phase. The *Lehrjahre* on the other hand offers a more sober view of child-hood as a transitory stage that Wilhelm has to go through in order to attain more mature qualities,[53] and this aspect of the novels pre-figures the work of the poetic realists.

---

[51] Kuhn calls her the 'quintessential child' because she is 'a pure enigma' (*Corruption in Paradise*, 186–7).

[52] This contrast is discussed by Joachim Müller, 'Die Gestalt des Kindes und des Jugendlichen in der deutschen Literatur von Goethe bis Thomas Mann', *SSAWL* 116/1 (1971), 6–7. Müller does not, however, point out the implications of the different narrative modes (see below).

[53] Ueding, 'Verstoßen in ein fremdes Land', 348.

Goethe's *Bildungsroman* was very much a product of its time in that there was an ever-increasing emphasis on education and the development of the individual, caused partly by the influence of Rousseau. By the early years of the nineteenth century Rousseau's ideas had been taken up in German-speaking countries by Johann Heinrich Pestalozzi and Jean Paul amongst others, and the increasing emphasis on education and bringing the child into a mature adulthood contributed to a more realistic literary representation of the child figure. It was now less likely to be presented as quasi-divine or a potential model for others, and more likely to be perceived as the object of adult attentions as the influence of writers such as Rousseau, Pestalozzi, and Jean Paul made itself felt in many works of poetic realism.[54] And yet even amongst these writers we find child figures whose Romantic heritage is clear. Hagen points out, for example, that Keller's *Der grüne Heinrich* (1854/5), for all its much trumpeted realism, cannot do without its Mignon figure, Meretlein.[55] She is another embodiment of the 'fremdes Kind' who stands outside society, but she receives far less sympathetic treatment than her literary ancestor, having had the misfortune to fall into the hands of a pastor with very Old Testament views on the nature of childhood and the proper means of childrearing. It might of course be possible to explain away Meretlein's presence by saying that her story belongs quite explicitly to an earlier time; the 'real' child of the story, Heinrich, is treated in a manner entirely consistent with the *Bildungsroman*, whose motto is that 'the Child is father of the Man'.[56] Indeed, Heinrich notes: 'Wenn ich nicht überzeugt wäre, daß die Kindheit schon ein Vorspiel des ganzen Lebens ist und bis zu ihrem Abschlusse schon die Hauptzüge der menschlichen Zerwürfnisse im kleinen abspiegele, . . . so würde ich mich nicht so weitläufig mit den kleinen Dingen jener Zeit beschäftigen.'[57]

---

[54] See A. C. F. Scherer, 'Formative Influences in the Life of the Child in German Prose Fiction of the Nineteenth Century' (unpublished doctoral thesis, University of Ilinois, 1939). I have only been able to consult the abstract of this thesis.

[55] *Kinder*, 32. On the nature of 'symbolische Kinder' see ibid., 26; also Kuhn, *Corruption in Paradise*, 193 on Mignon and Thomas Mann's Echo.

[56] Wordsworth, 'My heart leaps up', in id., *Selected Poems*, 106. Kuhn indicates the different treatments of Heinrich and Meretlein and points out that the *Bildungsroman* assumes a consistent, undelineated development from childhood to adulthood (*Corruption in Paradise*, 25–6 and 129).

[57] *Der grüne Heinrich*, i. *Fassung*, in Gottfried Keller, *Sämtliche Werke*, ed. Thomas Böning et al., 7 vols. (Frankfurt, 1985–1996), ii. 205.

And yet while Meretlein's somewhat incongruous presence in *Der grüne Heinrich* can be explained away by suggesting that she is an anachronistic character, in fact she is not such an exceptional figure as she may at first appear. Even the more development-conscious writers of the later nineteenth century still seem to have been powerfully influenced by the myth of childhood inherited from the Romantics, and to some extent this can be explained by the way Rousseau's ideas were understood and adapted in Germany. In *Émile* the child was deemed pure when he left his creator God and his unspoilt nature was mirrored by the natural environment in which he grew up. But while Émile's potential is basically positive, he still needs adult guidance in order to develop it. The German tradition that grew out of this belief in original innocence is rather different, since it supposed rather more of a ready-made personality within the child: Herder, for example, rejected the idea of the tabula rasa[58] and in *Levana oder Erziehlehre* (1807 and 1813) Jean Paul refers to the need to develop the 'idealen Preismenschen in sich'.[59] The child is thus assumed to come into the world with all the potential required to become a specific adult, but as yet untainted by experience. To this extent the German tradition apparently echoes the more mystical English tradition of childhood represented by Wordsworth's 'Ode' and its belief in the child's intuitive wisdom. This may explain why even the more sober-minded writers of the mid- to late nineteenth century often presented children in such a way that poetry more than held the balance with realism. These children are portrayed as socially integrated and as flesh-and-blood characters rather than the personifications of abstract ideas; nonetheless they suggest a dimension beyond their various social environments.

We find a prime example of this in Konrad and Sanna in Stifter's *Bergkristall* (1845), who appear more realistically childlike than characters like Novalis's self-sufficient and obviously symbolic child in *Die Lehrlinge zu Sais* simply because of their vulnerability when they are lost on the mountainside. This experience is presented in a realistic manner with due emphasis on Konrad's common sense in forcing both children to stay awake by drinking

---

[58] Ewers, *Kindheit*, 66.
[59] In *Werke*, ed. Norbert Miller (Munich, 1959—), v. 560–1.

coffee.[60] However, there is also something miraculous in the children's survival, for not only is there a reference to 'die Natur in ihrer Größe' supporting them, but unusually in such a snowstorm there was no wind; had there been, the children would undoubtedly have been 'verloren'.[61] The alien environment is beyond the reach even of religion, for although it is 'Heiliger Abend' in the valley where all the church bells are ringing, 'nur zu den Kindern herauf kam kein Laut, hier wurde nichts vernommen; denn hier war nichts zu verkündigen'.[62] And yet the children experience the wonder of Christmas in a much more profound way than the adults, for they witness daybreak on the mountain, a privileged moment which, as Blackall suggests, reveals to them 'the great mystery of creation';[63] thus when Sanna tells her mother Mutter, ich habe heute nachts, als wir auf dem Berge saßen, den heiligen Christ gesehen[64] she is expressing her recognition of the 'beauty and wonder of all creation . . . the mystic meaning of Christmas'.[65] Sanna's comments suggest that the unknowing child has access to knowledge beyond the everyday and this closeness to God and nature suggests the pre-socialized Romantic child even within a social context. The child's capacity for wonder results from that pre-socialized vision celebrated by Wordsworth which, even when it is not factually accurate, may bring us nearer the truth than adult rationalizations.

This combination of the realistic and the poetic can also be seen in Lütt Agnes in Theodor Fontane's *Der Stechlin* (1897/8). She is a mysterious child, rumoured to be a natural relation of Dubslav von Stechlin himself, and although shown in a social context she appears to exist on the very fringes of it.[66] While she is obviously a more 'real' child than the ethereal constructs of the Romantic era, nonetheless she represents an alternative dimension, rooted in the natural environment and thus far removed from the politics

---

[60] Müller emphasizes the realistic presentation of these children by stressing the role played by their 'besonnenes Verhalten' as well as the protective force of nature in allowing them to survive ('Gestalt des Kindes', 23).

[61] In *Gesammelte Werke*, ed. Konrad Steffen, 14 vols. (Basle and Stuttgart 1962–72), iv. 227 and 239.   [62] Ibid. 227.

[63] Eric A. Blackall, *Adalbert Stifter: A Critical Study* (Cambridge, 1948), 268–9.

[64] Ibid.   [65] Ibid. 268–9.

[66] Patricia Howe suggests that this is where her real value lies ('The Child as Metaphor in the Novels of Fontane', *OGS* 10 (1979), 134).

of the novel. Bance suggests that she, like Dubslav himself, represents a conjunction of old and new, for while she is rooted in the
past through her grandmother, a herbalist regarded as a witch by
the local population, her youth is strikingly evident, even down
to her scarlet stockings.[67] Bance refers to her expressing youth's
'unconscious revolutionary function'[68] and this ambivalent position between past and future embodies the novel's motto as pro-
nounced by Melusine: 'Alles Alte, soweit es Anspruch darauf hat,
sollen wir lieben, aber für das Neue sollen wir recht eigentlich
leben'.[69] Bance calls Agnes 'a perfect poetic symbol of all that is
best in old Stechlin'[70] and thus, as in the Romantic era, we have a
sense of the child standing beyond the social context, embodying
values which have not yet been realized and the hope that they
will one day be achieved, since she is presented realistically
enough for us to envisage her growing up (unlike Novalis's more
obviously symbolic children) and there is no indication of an
early death. She thus combines the positive features of the
Romantic child with a realistic presentation.

    But by the time Lütt Agnes appeared on the scene the difficul-
ties of presenting a child as though it inhabited a separate domain
from adults were about to become very much more substantial.
The most radical change in the perception of childhood since
Rousseau was on the horizon: the work of Sigmund Freud and
especially the *Drei Abhandlungen zur Sexualtheorie* (1905). Since
Rousseau's emphatic statement that childhood and adulthood
were separate states, the boundary between them had been very
clearly defined as the sexual Rubicon.[71] But this perception of the
boundary was already under attack by the end of the nineteenth
century; Frank Wedekind's *Frühlings Erwachen* (1891), specifically
subtitled a *Kindertragödie*, presents the adolescents as having
the same sexual impulses as adults. The presentation of their
sexual awakening is entirely consistent with Freud's ideas on the
subject, for there is no moral judgement made on the young

---

[67] *Theodor Fontane: The Major Novels* (Cambridge, 1982), 218–19.
[68] Ibid. 219.
[69] In Fontane, *Werke*, ed. Hans-Heinrich Reuter, 5 vols. (Berlin and Weimar,
1964), v. 294–5.   [70] *Theodor Fontane*, 220.
[71] James R. Kincaid notes that the 'definitional base' for distinguishing children
from adults for the past two centuries has been erotic (*Child-Loving: The Erotic Child and
Victorian Culture* (New York and London, 1992), 6–7).

protagonists; they are portrayed as following natural impulses whose consequences are so tragic only because of their ignorance. This suggests, as Freud was to do, that children and adults are in fact subject to the same physical impulses, an idea that went some way towards eliding the traditional boundary between childhood and adulthood. But while Freud may not have made any moral issue out of children's sexual potential, commentators have tended to interpret the physical phenomena he suggested in moral terms, using words like 'innocence' and 'guilt' rather loosely when discussing his work. As Coveney suggests, while the *Drei Abhandlungen zur Sexualtheorie* caused a scandal when they were first published, in fact the Augustinian doctrine of Original Sin was a much more total denial of the child's essential innocence than the ideas contained in Freud's work.[72] After all, as Kuhn points out, we can hardly say the child's innocence is affected by the involuntary stirring of a bodily impulse.[73] So while Freud's theories and various distortions of them clearly survive in our literature until the present, the extent to which they have affected our view of childhood innocence is open to question. Hagen goes so far as to claim that they have only ever been given a very lukewarm reception in German writing about the child because they do not fit with the German perception of childhood as an intrinsically pure and innocent state, distinct from adulthood.[74] And even less idealistic authors might accept the physical implications of Freud's theories without this affecting their view that intellectually, emotionally, spiritually, and morally the child is quite different from the adult.

There is clearly some reluctance in our modern culture to see children as anything but innocent. This reluctance now appears in heightened form because the traditional image of children as unaware of sex and therefore as pure is under attack from various quarters, not least the advertising industry. But as Higonnet points

---

[72] *Image of Childhood,* 301. Coveney attributes our acceptance of the religious idea of the child's fallen nature to a long cultural conditioning on the subject of Original Sin and the 'emotional counter-balance provided by the ritual of baptism and the whole concept of Man's "redemption"'.

[73] *Corruption in Paradise,* 133.

[74] Hagen makes this point with reference to Carl Ludwig Schleich's *Besonnte Vergangenheit,* suggesting that although Schleich, a surgeon, probably knew Freud's writings he did not incorporate them into his idealizing autobiography of childhood (*Kinder,* 19).

out, our treasured image of innocent childhood is simply a cultural construct invented in the eighteenth century and inherited by us; we are simply in the process of exchanging one cultural construct for another, albeit with some trepidation.[75] And if we are reluctant to see our image of childhood innocence challenged now, this is nothing to the resistance to this idea at the beginning of the twentieth century when Freud's ideas caused such an uproar. Writers tended to cling to an image of childhood unknowing and innocence, untainted by any hint of sexuality. How were they able to maintain this image of childhood?

In literary terms there are, broadly speaking, two methods of preserving the child's innocence. One is for the writer to stop writing about the child before what Kuhn regards as the inevitable intrusion of Thanatos and Eros can destroy the paradise of childhood.[76] The other is the method adduced by Hagen; namely, rather than the text stopping, the child stops instead. This is what happens to Mignon in order for her symbolic value to be preserved, but this technique is certainly not reserved for her and her brethren of the Romantic era.[77] Hagen goes on to instance examples of dying children from nineteenth- and twentieth-century literature, and while he concedes that this might simply be realistic, given higher child mortality rates in earlier times or that it might be motivated by a desire for social critique, especially of oldfashioned repressive academic institutions, nonetheless he considers it more likely that authors are taking up the Romantic tradition of the innocent child who has to die so that the reader's perception of its innocence remains unchallenged.[78] Barbara Hensel too comments on the high literary death rate amongst German children of the early twentieth century and refers to the concentration on these exceptional children who are unfit for adulthood as 'Neuromantik'.[79] We could cite numerous texts in

---

[75] *Pictures of Innocence: The History and Crisis of Ideal Childhood* (London, 1998), 8 and 193.

[76] *Corruption in Paradise*, 132.

[77] See Hagen, *Kinder*, 28–9 on Thomas Mann's Echo and 32 on Keller's Meretlein.

[78] Ibid. 26.

[79] *Das Kind und der Jugendliche in der deutschen Roman- und Erzählliteratur nach dem 2. Weltkrieg: Eine pädagogische Untersuchung* (Diss. Munich; Munich, 1962), 3. For a more recent study of the way adolescents withdraw from adult life in the literature of this period, see Joachim Noob, *Der Schülerselbstmord in der deutschen Literatur um die Jahrhundertwende: Non Vitae sed Scholae discimus* (Heidelberg, 1998).

this connection: Rainer Maria Rilke's *Die Turnstunde* (1899/1902), the school chapter of Thomas Mann's *Buddenbrooks* (1901), Emil Strauß's *Freund Hein* (1902), and Hermann Hesse's *Unterm Rad* (1906) amongst others.[80] Like their Romantic counterparts, these child figures can be seen as 'verstoßen in ein fremdes Land'[81] and their alien nature makes them another good medium for social critique. On the one hand such texts apparently mark a positive development in the history of the way the child is presented in German literature; these children are presented much more as psychological constructs than their predecessors and, while we may not yet hear their voice, we certainly see things from their perspective. For the first time the child's view of adult reality, as in the *Buddenbrooks* school chapter, is treated as worth considering in its own right.[82] But the idea of preserving the image of the child's innocence at the expense of its life seems to be not so much a resurgence of a Romantic image of childhood as a perversion of it. Whereas the Romantics, following in the footsteps of Schiller, had expressed a desire to attain a new and higher form of childhood, an essentially forward-looking impulse, in the stories from the early twentieth century quoted above there is a more regressive tendency, since any positive potential embodied in the child and its separate dimension is negated by its death. The birth of the child as an individual construct thus stands under a dark star, for as Coveney writes when he comments on the trivialization of the dying child in Victorian literature: 'It is a remarkable phenomenon, surely, when a society takes the child (with all its potential significance as a symbol of fertility and growth) and creates of it a literary image, not only of frailty, but of life extinguished, of life that is better extinguished, of life, so to say, rejected, negated at its very root.'[83] Hanno Buddenbrook seems to offer a particularly clear example of this regressive tendency. He himself recognizes his unfitness for adulthood when he tells his friend Kai 'Ich werde so müde davon. Ich möchte schlafen und nichts mehr wissen. Ich möchte sterben, Kai!' (Mann, *Buddenbrooks*, 743). He is a close

---

[80] The literary presentation of the individual and his relationship to school will be discussed in more detail in Ch. 1, below.

[81] Novalis, 'An Tieck'.

[82] Jens suggests that it would have been inconceivable for an author to adopt the child's perspective before the 20th cent. ('Erwachsene Kinder', 136).

[83] *Image of Childhood*, 193.

literary relative of the nineteenth-century child figures who were 'too good for this world' and whose death is an implied criticism of adult society. Like the saintly Helen Burns in Charlotte Brontë's *Jane Eyre* (1847) Hanno might say 'By dying young, I shall escape great sufferings. I had not qualities or talent to make my way very well in the world: I should have been continually at fault'.[84] His death from typhus is an implicit recognition of this state.[85]

Hanno is of interest to me for two reasons. First, the way he is depicted represents a turning point in the perception of the child, and secondly in the school chapter he prefigures the way children will be presented in the Third Reich. It is already clear from Mann's original plans to write a *Novelle* about a 'sensitiven Spätling' (*Gesammelte Werke*, xi. 554) that Hanno is central to *Buddenbrooks*. He is the only character in the book that we know from his much-trumpeted birth to his death; and no matter how short that time span actually is, it occupies over half of the novel. He is not merely a symbol, the living (and dying) proof that the complacent bourgeois society cannot in fact offer everything needed for individual fulfilment; Mann has invested too much psychological interest in him for this to be his sole function. Yet initially this interest in the child's inner life is not something we would have expected, since the childhood of the previous generation is treated in a brief, even casual manner. Tom, Tony, and Christian are presented mainly in cameos with only the briefest movements into their consciousness, and Tom and Christian develop perfectly in accordance with Hoffstede's predictions for them in chapter 2: Tom, the 'solider und ernster Kopf' does indeed become a businessman, while Christian, who is 'ein wenig Tausendsassa . . . ein wenig Incroyable' is unable to settle to any useful occupation (*Buddenbrooks*, 17). Any depiction of their childhood appears to be quite irrelevant; it is dismissed in the phrase 'Toms und Christians Jugendzeit . . . es ist nichts Bedeutendes davon zu melden' (p. 68). This suggests that at least initially this novel follows the *Bildungsroman* formula that the child is father of the man. But this dismissive presentation of Tom and Christian's childhood only emphasizes the sheer extravagance of devoting a

---

[84] *Jane Eyre* (London, 1985), 93.
[85] See Müller, 'Gestalt des Kindes', 32, where he refers to the typhus chapter as the 'äußere Ausdruck für eine innere Katastrophe'.

whole chapter (the longest in the novel at that) to one day in Hanno's school life.

This early use of the child's perspective bears on my main subject matter in a number of ways. First, given that Hanno's repressive school is experienced as a 'Staat im Staate' (p. 722), it is clear that this social misfit follows in the Romantic tradition of the child as representing an alternative sphere from that of a fallen society. This point is ironically underlined by the reference to the 'Goldenes Zeitalter' (p. 726) in the classical poetry the lads are studying. Secondly Hanno is the artist's representative; we know that he is a musician, but his artistic and critical faculties extend much further than this, as we see from the fact that he can both 'durchschauen' (p. 738) and empathize with the pathetic Kandidat Modersohn, an attitude that forcibly suggests the writer.[86] But Hanno occupies an ambiguous position. On the one hand he is able to see his society in a clear-sighted way that recalls Wordsworth's 'Eye among the blind' and is alienated by the values that operate in the schoolroom and, by extension, in the wider social environment. However, it is also clear that he has been socialized so as to unconsciously accept and indeed internalize the values of this society. This tension is evident when he accepts the classroom convention of cheating or is involuntarily impressed by a boy who has received what he knows to be undeserved praise from his teacher, for 'Auch Hanno Buddenbrook war außerstande, sich diesem Eindruck zu entziehen, obgleich er fühlte, wie etwas in ihm sich mit Widerwillen dagegen wehrte...' (p. 728). It is therefore not only in his death that we see that the values Hanno represents are doomed; they are already under threat from the pressure of the school environment.

THE CHILD'S VIEW OF THE THIRD REICH

Some Preliminary Considerations

Both the way that Hanno is socialized to regard his society's values as self-evident and his instinctive revolt against them look forward to accounts of the Third Reich written from the child's

---

[86] On Hanno's relationship with his school and how far this reflects Mann's own experiences and his later attitude to education, see now Ludwig Fertig, *Vor-leben: Bekenntnis und Erziehung bei Thomas Mann* (Darmstadt, 1993), esp. 25–34.

perspective. Recent autobiographical accounts have tended to emphasize the sheer ordinariness of a childhood under the Third Reich; in *True to Both My Selves* (1997) for example, Katrin Fitzherbert, who was born into a Nazi family in Berlin in 1936, writes:

Unlike most of my fellow Nazis, I had been too young at the time to feel any responsibility, shame or guilt for the evils of the regime that were subsequently revealed. While all their instincts were to deny, repress and dissociate themselves from their Nazi past, mine were the opposite. My memories of Nazism were an integral part of my childhood and most of them were happy. I had no desire to eradicate them. I also knew that, for the sake of my sanity, I must keep them alive in order to make sense of them one day, to understand what on earth had been going on. Could all the Nazis I had known—just about everyone I loved—really have been the loathsome brutes subsequently portrayed? Could all the Nazi ideals I had been taught to revere, notions like self-sacrifice and dedication to duty, really have been utterly vile? I couldn't accept that. Yet, if they weren't, how was it possible that the worst evil in the history of mankind had been going on in our society, all around me?[87]

This kind of statement makes it extremely problematic to assume that even a presentation of childhood innocence in the Third Reich context will provide us with a (morally) reliable narrator. Whilst an account that confines itself to the child's perspective will often offer a wealth of the kind of details we would not find in either a history textbook or an adult's account of the same period, and so present the period with an immediacy that preserves many of these books from having 'mere' historical interest, we can neither trust too much to the child's factual accuracy nor take at face value any moral judgements it may make.

And yet, as we shall see later, it is sometimes precisely the fact that a child narrator may present events and values of the Third Reich as though they were self-evident that has the most powerful of defamiliarizing effects upon us. Those who have read countless books, watched films, and learnt about the period in history classes run the risk of Shklovsky's habitualization; they 'know' about the Third Reich and it thus risks losing any kind of impact on them. But the child's unknowing gaze shows us that this (for us, exceptional) period of history was once someone's humdrum

---

[87] *True to Both My Selves: A Family Memoir of Germany and England in Two World Wars* (London, 1997), 4–5.

normality, and this in itself is defamiliarizing. Moreover, encountering a viewpoint that appears to take the values of this society for granted forces the active, responsible adult reader to fill in the moral gaps left by that perspective. The process by which we actively reject that narrative perspective can have a moral effect more than equal to that achieved by the traditional outsider view represented by a Parzival or a Simplicissimus.

It should be clear from the above that there is a considerable gulf between the positive myth of the child inherited from the Romantics as a being from a separate dimension, a symbol of innocence and spontaneity who has both artistic and redemptive potential, and the perception of the child as created by educationalists, psychologists, and Freud, and by our knowledge of the historical conditions of the Third Reich. This has made literary critics somewhat sceptical when children are used as a means of discussing the Nazi period. A depiction of children runs the risk of sentimentalizing at the best of times; when presenting them as victims of war or juxtaposing their assumed innocence with a pernicious political era it is particularly difficult to avoid the trap. Certainly this seems to be what Reich-Ranicki had in mind when he accused Heinrich Böll of evading the real problems of the post-war period by writing about the victims of war, especially women and children. Of the central figures of *Haus ohne Hüter* (1954), *Das Brot der frühen Jahre* (1955), and *Im Tal der donnernden Hufe* (1957) he noted: 'Mit diesen Gestalten hatte Böll allerdings das Problem des zeitgerechten Helden keineswegs gelöst—er war ihm eher ausgewichen'.[88]

Nor is unconscious evasion the most serious charge to be levelled against authors who have chosen to present the Third Reich from a child's viewpoint. Mecklenburg suggested that this perspective implied the risk of 'Verklärung', 'Idyllisierung', and 'Verharmlosung'.[89] More recently, Frank Schirrmacher took this idea a stage further when he suggested that the child's perspective in novels like Grass's *Die Blechtrommel* and Lenz's *Deutschstunde* was gratefully received by West German readers because it made

[88] *Deutsche Literatur in West und Ost: Prosa seit 1945* (Munich, 1963), 133.
[89] 'Faschismus und Alltag in deutscher Gegenwartsprosa: Kempowski und andere', in Hans Wagener (ed.), *Gegenwartsliteratur und Drittes Reich: Deutsche Autoren in der Auseinandersetzung mit der Vergangenheit* (Stuttgart, 1977), 25.

the Third Reich appear as 'eine böse, aber märchenhaft verzerrte Kindheitserinnerung, in mythischen Vorzeiten angesiedelt und aus aller Geschichte herausgefallen'.[90] Of course, given the long-standing association of the child and the artist it might be seen as particularly dubious practice for German writers to write about this time from the child's perspective, since this could be inter-preted as a desire to exculpate themselves from any knowledge of or responsibility for the crimes perpetrated by the Nazis. Such authors might be seen as exploiting the myth of the child's innocence very much for their own ends. However, I am more inclined to follow Bance, who suggests that the childhood theme became popular after the war because writers felt unable to deal with the past or adjust to the trauma of the present, and so adopted the child's point of view as an expression of powerlessness and withdrawal into fantasy. This might suggest the kind of evasion of which Reich-Ranicki accuses Böll, but Bance goes on to point out that this withdrawal from the problems of the immediate past was the only way to deal with it, writing of Grass that he 'exposed art as *play*, an impotent exercise which rests in fantasy, but was, nonetheless, the only possible way to a full expression of reality, both past and present'.[91]

While the myth of the child's innocence has certainly survived up to our own era, it is rare for authors writing about the Third Reich to attempt a simple juxtaposition between an ideal of child-hood and less than ideal historical conditions. Most attempt to do justice to the psychological reality of the time yet still want to ex-ploit the child's natural potential as a symbol of hope for the fu-ture. There is thus usually a tension between the myth of childhood innocence and historical conditions. We find a partic-ularly powerful instance of this in the concluding volume of Dieter Forte's family saga *In der Erinnerung* (1998), where the child is determined to write about his experiences of the war, despite the practical and emotional difficulties involved. Not the least of these is the 'innere Kampf zwischen links und rechts'[92] for, while

---

[90] 'Abschied von der Literatur der Bundesrepublik: Neue Pässe, neue Identitäten, neue Lebensläufe: Über die Kündigung einiger Mythen des westdeutschen Bewußt-seins', *Frankfurter Allgemeine Zeitung* (2 Oct. 1990).

[91] *The German Novel 1945–1960* (Stuttgart, 1980), 40.

[92] *In der Erinnerung: Roman* (Frankfurt, 1998), 148.

he is naturally left-handed, his teachers have forced him to write with his right hand:

Die Lehrer der Dorf- und Kleinstadtschulen, durch die er während seiner Evakuierungen geschleift wurde, hatten sich darauf konzentriert, ihm jedesmal, wenn er einen Griffel, Bleistift oder Federhalter in die linke Hand nahm, mit der scharfen Kante des Lineals auf die Hand zu schlagen. Die Hand war oft blutig, schmerzte, trotzdem nahm er immer wieder das Schreibzeug ohne Absicht in die linke Hand, die Schläge wiederholten sich ebenso automatisch, das Schreibzeug wanderte in die rechte Hand und war dann doch wieder unversehens in der linken, und wieder sauste das Lineal auf die linke Hand, hinterließ rote Striemen, hinterließ das Schreibverbot der linken Hand. Und so schrieb er nun als Linkshänder mit der rechten Hand, schrieb mit einer nach links gedrehten rechten Hand, in einer unnatürlichen Haltung, die oft Schmerzen bereitete, dazu noch in einer Mischung aus alter deutscher Schrift, die er noch gelernt hatte, und der jetzigen lateinischen Schrift ...[93]

This is a powerful image for the kind of conditioning to which the child has been subjected during the war years and in the light of this bleak picture the idea of the child representing any kind of fresh insight into the era he has lived through or hope for the future seems unlikely to say the least. And yet there is hope here, for the child's natural instinct to write with his left hand has taken an enormous amount of time and misguided adult energy to break. Moreover, his compulsion to write about what he has experienced is in itself a hopeful sign, both on a personal level and in a wider context, since it represents the possibility of others finding out more about the period and so engenders hope for them too. The child figure has come a long way from Wordsworth's tranquil image of the child communing with nature but, as will become clear, it has retained much of its earlier heritage and much of its significance; indeed, if anything, the desire of writers and readers alike to believe in the positive potential of childhood has been strengthened in our own era and thus the child continues to meet the deepest needs of writers and readers alike.

PRACTICAL CONSIDERATIONS

The child is a prominent figure in German literature and in German literary criticism alike: there are a number of studies of

[93] Ibid. 148–9.

the child's role in late eighteenth- and early nineteenth-century literature, reflecting the Romantics' intense interest in this figure, and some general studies of the child in twentieth-century literature. There are also many historical studies that discuss the way children were brought up under the Third Reich and how they experienced this era.[94] However, this study still has a gap to fill for, apart from Gillian Lathey's recent book *The Impossible Legacy*, which focuses specifically on children's literature about the Third Reich and World War II, I do not know of any study of literary accounts of childhood under the Third Reich.[95] This is a significant omission because, although we have plenty of historical data about childhood at this time, writers have very different agendas from historians, especially when dealing with such a potentially powerful symbol as the child. It is true that most of the authors I consider grew up in the Third Reich, but their perceptions of childhood are shaped not only by experience but also by various myths, whether biblical, Freudian, or literary.

Earlier general studies on the image of childhood in German literature have suggested a continuous tradition in the way children are represented.[96] This study will consider that tradition with specific reference to literary presentations of the Third Reich. I shall examine a number of texts ranging from the 1930s to the 1980s to demonstrate the different ideas about childhood that inform various authors' attempts to use this perspective, and consider the technical problems of using the child's perspective and language. I will conclude by considering to what extent this preoccupation with the child is embedded in the deeper artistic and moral concerns of post-war German literature.

The study could not be exhaustive: there is a wealth of texts about the Third Reich written from the child's perspective, ranging from the overtly autobiographical to the self-consciously literary. I have therefore limited the main discussion to a core of texts that demonstrate the tension between historical reality and the literary myth inherited from the Romantics: Grass's *Die Blechtrommel*, Lenz's *Deutschstunde*, Wolf's *Kindheitsmuster*, and Gert

---

[94] A range of these works is cited in the Select Bibliography.

[95] *The Impossible Legacy: Identity and Purpose in Autobiographical Children's Literature set in the Third Reich and the Second World War* (Berne, 1999).

[96] e.g. Hagen, *Kinder*, and Ueding, 'Verstoßen in ein fremdes Land'.

Hofmann's *Unsere Eroberung* (1984) and *Veilchenfeld* (1986). Some of these texts have of course been given extensive critical treatment over many years. Nonetheless I hope that this study, whilst drawing on earlier criticism, will also open up new ways of seeing these texts, by focusing on the childhood theme and by looking at them in relation to a range of lesser-known works. It should go without saying that this approach is only one of a myriad of ways of interpreting the works in question; focusing on a single theme is unlikely to reveal all their different aspects. The theme of childhood itself, however, encompasses a wide scope; the texts considered range from realistic, quasi-autobiographical attempts to come to terms with the Nazi past, as in *Kindheitsmuster* and *Veilchenfeld*, to much more self-conscious uses of the child figure, its perspective and language, as in *Die Blechtrommel* and *Unsere Eroberung*. This chronological and stylistic range alone suggests that the child figure fulfils a definite and ongoing need where the German desire for *Vergangenheitsbewältigung* is concerned.[97]

The texts cited above already suggest that my definition of childhood is fairly broad and to an extent this is a natural consequence of my chronological range. The early twentieth century was not an era that embraced the idea of adolesence as a separate stage of existence, and therefore Thomas Mann's 15-year-old Hanno Buddenbrook, like the adolescents of *Frühlings Erwachen*, can be considered as a child; indeed, given the insistence of Mann's narrator on referring to the adolescent only by a diminutive form of his name or as 'der kleine Johann' (*Buddenbrooks*, 710), we could see Mann as determined to present the image of a child even when describing an adolescent.[98] Equally, while Ellen in Ilse Aichinger's *Die größere Hoffnung* (1948) and the eponymous heroine of Anna Gmeyner's *Manja. Ein Roman um fünf Kinder* (1938) are teenagers by the end of their respective novels, they too are explicitly described by their authors as 'Kind'. Thus even as

---

[97] This is borne out by the fact that both autobiographical and fictional accounts of childhood under the Third Reich have continued to be published throughout the 1990s. See Select Bibliography, below, for details.

[98] Although there is one occasion when the narrator highlights the incongruity of this appellation ('Ja, er war nun schon ziemlich lang, der kleine Johann', *Buddenbrooks* 704), there are several later examples of this usage that are not tinged with such irony (pp. 710, 733, 747, and 751).

adolescents these figures contribute to their creators' understanding of what it is to be a child and to have a childlike point of view.

Nor is the age of the child presented the only problem in defining what we might call a 'child narrative', for the technical problems of rendering this viewpoint and voice mean that very few authors use a child narrator throughout their texts; Lenz and Wolf, for example, both use adult narrators to convey the child's perspective. And the case of Oskar Matzerath complicates this still further, for his childlike point of view is part of the assumed insanity of the adult narrator; nevertheless, the adult is describing events that took place during his childhood and it is not always clear whether the childlike ignorance of the narrative voice is assumed simply to give us an impression of what it was like to be a child during the Third Reich or adopted by a knowing adult in a spirit of amoral perversity. To subsume these very different narrators and narrative perspectives under the broad title of 'child' and 'childlike' may look like an attempt to cover a multitude of sins. But the breadth of my definition is justified by the fact that ultimately the authors under consideration are less concerned with children than with what it means to have a childlike perspective. In this sense the child is central to our aesthetic and moral concerns and in writing about children, even—or indeed especially—to describe such an extreme situation as the Third Reich, our authors are writing about themselves: what it is to be an artist and, moreover, what it is to be human.

'SCHULDIG, KEINER SCHULD BEWUßT?':[1] THE FALLEN CHILD

Da aber geschah das Gräßliche, daß Anton Klöterjahn zu lachen und zu jubeln begann, er kreischte vor unerklärlicher Lust, es konnte einem unheimlich zu Sinne werden.

Gott weiß, was ihn anfocht, ob die schwarze Gestalt ihm gegenüber ihn in diese wilde Heiterkeit versetzte oder was für ein Anfall von animalischem Wohlbefinden ihn packte. Er hielt in der einen Hand einen knöchernen Beißring und in der anderen eine blecherne Klapperbüchse. Diese beiden Gegenstände reckte er jauchzend in den Sonnenschein empor, schüttelte sie und schlug sie zusammen, als wollte er jemanden spottend verscheuchen. Seine Augen waren beinahe geschlossen vor Vergnügen, und sein Mund war so klaffend aufgerissen, daß man seinen ganzen rosigen Gaumen sah. Er warf sogar seinen Kopf hin und her, indes er jauchzte. (Mann, *Gesammelte Werke*, viii. 262)[2]

This passage from Thomas Mann's *Tristan* (1903) does not offer us what we might consider a normal presentation of babyhood. We are repelled by the negatively connoted words 'kreischte', 'wilde', and perhaps most powerfully by 'animalischem'. As T. J. Reed points out, we have already heard about Anton Klöterjahn's voracious appetite for 'Milch und gehacktem Fleisch' (viii. 249), and this, together with the 'knöchernen Beißring' which evokes a wild beast gnawing at a bone, the child's wide-open mouth, the violent way he tosses his head, and the tawny glow the setting sun casts over this final scene, suggests a lion rather than an infant.[3]

If we are to associate a child with an animal, then we tend to be more comfortable with Blake's lamb than with Mann's lion cub.[4] It is true that the twentieth century has seen children portrayed as

---

[1] 'Legende', in Johann Wolfgang von Goethe, *Werke: Hamburger Ausgabe*, 14 vols, ed. Erich Trunz (rev. edn., Munich, 1981), i. 363.

[2] This episode is discussed in Kuhn, *Corruption in Paradise*, 57.

[3] Reed, 'Nietzsche's Animals: Idea, Image and Influence', in Malcolm Pasley (ed.), *Nietzsche: Imagery and Thought* (London, 1978), 182–4.

[4] William Blake, 'The Lamb', in *Songs of Innocence* (1789).

wild animals, notably in Richard Hughes's *A High Wind in Jamaica* (1929) and in William Golding's classic rebuttal of Rousseauian innocence, *Lord of the Flies* (1954).[5] But, while the degeneration of these children is shocking to our culturally conditioned belief in childhood innocence, the fact that it is portrayed as a relatively long process at least makes it more comprehensible. Moreover, even if Golding is implying that the boys' true nature has been revealed by the circumstances in which they find themselves, then there is some slight comfort in the reflection that those circumstances are exceptional. But in Mann's *Tristan* we are confronted specifically with an unsocialized infant; the implication is not that he has been reduced to an animal state by circumstances but rather that he is inherently animalistic.

There are various explanations for the disturbing quality of this image. First, this child is in a sanatorium and therefore his very obvious 'exzessive Gesundheit' (*Gesammelte Werke*, viii. 249) becomes almost offensive by force of contrast with the other inhabitants. Moreover, while his behaviour appears instinctual and animalistic to the point of terrifying, this is partly explained by the fact that he is seen through Spinell's eyes. To Spinell the child is unambiguously hostile, but this is not surprising: the weak pseudo-artist cannot cope with life in the raw as represented by this baby. However, while we might not wish to identify ourselves with Spinell's point of view, our own cultural conditioning on the subject of childhood makes this image shocking for us too; Anton's vitality stands in bold contrast to the ethereal Romantic conception of childhood which influences the presentation of Mann's other major child figures (Hanno Buddenbrook, Tadzio, Echo). This infant is an exception, 'ein Prachtstück von einem Baby, mit ungeheurer Energie und Rücksichtslosigkeit' (viii. 221).

But, while Anton is portrayed in negative terms, he cannot be described as evil: he embodies the amorality which is much closer to Freud's view of childhood than the moral poles of guilt and innocence. *Tristan* pre-dates Freud's influential essays by two years, but it is a nice irony that Anton's surname should have sexual connotations. And although there is no direct debt to Freud here, this final leonine description of Anton does have faint echoes of

---

[5] See Kuhn, *Corruption in Paradise*, 150–61.

Nietzsche's *Also Sprach Zarathustra* (1892) where Zarathustra pro-
claims that 'der raubende Löwe' of the mind must give way to the
'Kind', for 'Unschuld ist das Kind und Vergessen, ein Neubegin-
nen, ein Spiel, ein aus sich rollendes Rad, eine erste Bewegung,
ein heiliges Ja-sagen'.[6] This is not the conventional description of
innocence that underlies the Romantic conception of childhood:
it is not conventional goodness but an amoral dynamism, a physical, instinctive force. In a sense Anton embodies the negative
pole of archetypal childlike qualities: the animal, instinctual, and
unsocialized aspects which represent a new philistine age to
come, one where the real artist has little chance of survival and the
pseudo-artists, those of Spinell's ilk, will be left fleeing from the
challenge.[7] Like the positive Romantic conception of childhood,
this one too had revolutionary potential for German cultural and
spiritual values, but the Nietzschean idea of childhood is clearly
much more threatening.

Söntgerath suggests that one twentieth-century tendency when
writers have addressed the subject of children has been to destroy
the myth of the innocent child, so clearing the way 'für ein neues
Bild vom Kind, nämlich für das böse Kind'.[8] But this is by no
means a new idea, for it goes back to biblical sources. And perhaps more importantly, the term 'böse' is to some extent subjective. Anton Klöterjahn appears threatening because we see him
through Spinell's eyes; considered objectively, the idea of being
terrified by a baby shaking his toys in the air seems absurd. While
the work of Freud and other insights from child psychologists
have made the conception of the ethereal, other-worldly beings of
the Romantic era untenable, new complexity of presentation
does not necessarily imply guilt. We cannot draw any crude dividing line between the twentieth century and those which preceded it, claiming that the child is innocent in the earlier era only
to become universally guilty in our own age. Certainly we cannot

---

[6] In *Werke: Kritische Gesamtausgabe*, ed. Giorgio Colli and Mazzino Montinari
(Berlin, 1967––), vi /1. 27. For a discussion of the influence of Nietzsche on *Tristan* and
specifically the figure of Anton, see Reed, 'Nietzsche's Animals', 180–5.

[7] Kuhn, *Corruption in Paradise*, 189.

[8] *Pädagogik und Dichtung: Das Kind in der Literatur des 20. Jahrhunderts* (Stuttgart, 1967),
145. This pessimistic view is shared by Ueding, who sees the modern image of the child
as the complete antithesis of Rousseau's, i.e. 'Von Natur aus . . . böse und verdorben'
('Verstoßen in ein fremdes Land', 356).

draw that line at 1905 with Freud, simply because he was a physician, not a moralist. The conception of the fallen child embraces a much broader spectrum than this; namely, how a child can be corrupted without necessarily incurring guilt and how far a child's 'guilt' is determined by subjective adult attitudes.

DANGEROUS LIAISONS?: THE SEXUAL CORRUPTION OF THE CHILD

In the eighteenth and nineteenth centuries the child's innocence was defined by its lack of sexual potential; its initiation into sex was perceived as putting an end to innocence and childhood itself. This sexual innocence is frequently manipulated by adult characters who want to veil their own sexual impropriety with an air of respectability. In Gustave Flaubert's *L'Éducation sentimentale* (1869) Mme Arnoux's Madonna-like nature is emphasized by the constant presence of her children, who flit in the background like a pair of guardian angels. Frédéric rarely sees her without them and her motherhood puts her sexually out of bounds and inhibits his response to her. The children's presence keeps this relationship within the limits of decency: on the one occasion when a night-time rendezvous is planned at the rue du Tronchet, Mme Arnoux's son providentially falls ill. She interprets this as a divine intervention to prevent her meeting Frédéric. But while this relationship is kept within certain bounds, there are other instances of sexual impropriety being disguised by the presence of children. In André Gide's *La Porte étroite* (1909) the narrator Jérome is scandalized in retrospect by the fact that his two younger cousins were with his aunt Lucile while she was flirting with a young army officer, and yet at the time this attempt to lend the scene an air of respectability was clearly successful: 'La présence de ces deux enfants m'apparaît aujourd'hui monstrueuse; dans mon innocence d'alors, elle me rassura plutôt'.[9] This motif still has common currency: in Karla Schneider's *Kor, der Engel* (1992) the little girl's mother tries to make her meetings with the French prisoner of war Yves less suspect by taking her daughter along, but her neighbour easily sees through this ruse: 'Sie soll zwar die Kleine als Tarnung

---

[9] In Gide, *Romans; Récits et Soties; Œvres lyriques* (Paris, 1958), 503.

dabei gehabt haben, aber der Umgang mit dem Feind ist in jedem Falle strafbar'.[10]

In the French texts cited above, the children's feelings are not discussed. They belong to the tradition of children who are 'seen and not heard', objects to be manipulated at the adult's will. That adult can be either a character in the text or indeed the author, who simply needs an innocent presence to juxtapose with the adults' more dubious behaviour, as in Tolstoy's *Anna Karenin* (1878) where Seriozha is described as 'the compass which showed them [Anna and Vronsky] the degree to which they had departed from what they knew but did not want to know'.[11] Authors and characters alike generally seem indifferent to the feelings of the manipulated child. This only changes in the late nineteenth and early twentieth centuries when writers become more interested in the effects of this involvement on children and their innocence.

We find particularly good examples of this kind of involvement in the sexual impropriety of the adult world in Henry James's *What Maisie Knew* (1897) and Stefan Zweig's *Brennendes Geheimnis* (1911), where adulterous liaisons are thrown into sharper relief by the presence of children, but where there is a greater sense of how children perceive this exploitation. The child focalizers Maisie and Edgar do not understand the game being played around them and so become unwittingly involved in adult machinations. James writes of Maisie:

She was taken into the confidence of passions on which she fixed just the stare she might have had for images bounding across the wall in the slide of a magic lantern. Her little world was phantasmagoric—strange shadows dancing on a sheet. It was as if the whole performance had been given for her—a mite of a half-scared infant in a great dim theatre.[12]

Coveney quotes two images that suggest she is an 'excluded witness', for she is 'present at her history in as separate a manner as if she could only get at experience by flattening her nose against a pane of glass', 'the hard window-pane of the sweet-shop of

[10] *Kor, der Engel: Ein Roman in 22 Geschichten* (Zurich, 1992), 43.
[11] *Anna Karenin*, trans. and introd. Rosemary Edmonds (Harmondsworth, 1978), 204.
[12] *What Maisie Knew*, ed. and introd. Paul Theroux (repr. Harmondsworth, 1985), 39.

knowledge'.[13] He comments that if these images were a true description of Maisie's experience then 'it is scarcely irrelevant to suggest that she could never have "known" anything'.[14] Kuhn's distinction between knowing and understanding is helpful here, for he suggests that, while Maisie may know everything, 'the reader is left wondering whether she understands anything'; he describes her consciousness as like an objective camera lens, and we may extend the simile to say that, while she takes in the whole panorama around her, she does not intellectually process or develop it.[15] She knows everything because, like the 'guardian angels' mentioned earlier, she is omnipresent, and indeed much more explicitly exploited than the young Arnoux and Bucolin. Miss Overmore, officially her governess but also her father's lover and future wife, actually tells her that she makes 'just the difference . . . of keeping us perfectly proper'.[16] Maisie's naivety is evident in her suggestion that in that case 'the gentleman' (her mother's lover) should become her tutor, asking 'Mightn't that make it right—as right as your being my governess makes it for you to be with papa?'[17] She is initially an unwitting accomplice to her parents' behaviour, a guarantor of their very tenuous respectability, but this situation cannot go on indefinitely. As Pattison points out, Maisie eventually joins in the adult game of bargaining and emotional blackmail when she concedes to Sir Claude that she will give up Mrs Wix, if he will give up Mrs Beale.[18] Even before she hears of this Mrs Wix is convinced that Maisie has lost her 'moral sense',[19] but in fact the child who has been exploited for her innocence and yet treated as an adult is simply turning exploiter in her turn, albeit one who is less conscious of the implications of her actions than the adults. How can she react any differently when such relationships form the standard by which she measures normality? By this late stage in the novel her innocence

---

[13] Ibid. 101 and 120. Coveney, *Image of Childhood,* 205–6.
[14] Coveney, *Image of Childhood,* 206.   [15] *Corruption in Paradise,* 21.
[16] *What Maisie Knew,* 58.   [17] Ibid. 59.
[18] *Child Figure,* 132. Pattison regards Maisie's 'innocence' as a 'purely negative state, a void into which all manner of evil intentions will rush' (ibid. 133), but while I agree with this, I do not accept his contention that 'what goodness she has is inseparable from her growing awareness of the depravity surrounding her', for that very knowledge leads her to make the offer that most clearly compromises her innocence.
[19] *What Maisie Knew,* 260.

is based on an ignorance of any other moral standard: the adult world into which she has been initiated is totally corrupt, and once fallen there is no way back to the paradise of childhood.

A similar discovery is made by Edgar in Zweig's *Brennendes Geheimnis*. Initially he is as uncomprehending as Maisie, and his innocence/ignorance is exploited by the baron, a guest at the hotel where Edgar and his mother are staying, when he befriends the boy in order to gain access to his mother. The boy's presence is the perfect cover for the baron's seduction attempts; even the mother does not seem to realize quite what the baron's intentions are until her son confronts her directly, when she sees him as 'eine innere Stimme, ihr Gewissen, abgelöst von sich selber, als Kind verkleidet'.[20] However, she refuses to heed her son or her inner voice until the baron attempts to force his attentions on her. Edgar reacts violently, causing a scene which has all the seeds of a real scandal, as does his subsequent flight from the hotel. Like Maisie, Edgar has been made the unwitting accomplice of adult behaviour for, while he is instinctively aware that there is something not quite right about the relationship between his mother and the baron, he is clearly not aware of the sexual motivation behind it, as we see when he tells his mother: 'Ich weiß nicht, was er dir versprochen hat und warum er zu dir freundlich ist, aber auch von dir will er etwas, Mama, ganz bestimmt'.[21] His mother may see him as the voice of conscience, but in fact his rebellion against the adults results not so much from moral indignation as from a fit of jealous pique at the way they have treated him. At the same time, however, his feelings at this betrayal are those of an adult rather than a child; once he is convinced of it, he indulges in 'ein reines, klares Gefühl: Haß und offene Feindschaft' and relishes disturbing their flirtation: 'Jetzt, da er gewiß war, ihnen im Weg zu sein, wurde das Zusammensein für ihn zu einer grausam komplizierten Wollust'.[22] When his mother tries to force him back into the role of the innocent, unknowing child by flatly denying any liaison between her and the baron, the boy seems to have become a man: he openly defies her by denying his childhood vulnerability and intellectual inferiority, saying 'Glaubst du, ich lasse mich einsperren im Zimmer wie ein kleines Kind! Nein, ich bin nicht so

---

[20] *Brennendes Geheimnis: Erzählung* (repr. Frankfurt, 1993), 80. [21] Ibid. 77.
[22] Ibid. 62.

dumm, wie ihr glaubt. Ich weiß, was ich weiß'.[23] His mother
makes a final desperate attempt to maintain her authority over
him, with the threat 'Oder ich prügle dich wie ein kleines Kind'.[24]
Yet even as she says it she realizes that it is no longer possible to
treat the boy in this way, and the blow she strikes is that of an adult
to an equal, just like those Edgar returns. The discovery of sex,
which has reduced his mother's authority in his eyes, has apparently put an end to his childhood. Ironically though, in the final
stages of the story he readopts the role of childhood ignorance
and *Ungezogenheit* in order to spare his mother. When his father
asks him why he ran away from the hotel he says: 'Nein, nein ... es
war kein Anlaß. Mama war sehr gut zu mir, aber ich war ungezo-
gen, ich habe mich schlecht benommen...und da...da bin ich
davongelaufen, weil ich mich gefürchtet habe.[25] Paradoxically,
this ability to adopt the mask of childhood is the greatest proof
(in Edgar's eyes at least) of his manhood: a moment before his
mother had signalled to him her 'flehende Bitte' that he should be
silent:

Da brach, das Kind fühlte es, plötzlich etwas Warmes, eine ungeheure
wilde Beglückung durch seinen ganzen Körper. Er verstand, daß sie ihm
das Geheimnis zu hüten gab, daß auf seinen kleinen Kinderlippen ein
Schicksal lag. Und wilder, jauchzender Stolz erfüllte ihn, daß sie ihm vertraute, jäh überkam ihn ein Opfermut, ein Wille, seine eigene Schuld
noch zu vergrößern, um zu zeigen, wie sehr er schon Mann war.[26]

Adults have now manipulated him twice; the baron by playing on
his innocence/ignorance, his mother by exploiting his natural
desire to become an adult. Edgar too has been drawn into the
world of adults as an unwitting accomplice, to the extent that he is
actually proud of his own 'guilt'. But while he feels he has become
a man and been accepted on adult terms, his mother wins this
game: by making her child feel important and trusted she has kept
him within the (for her) safe bounds of childhood silence and
unknowing. The end of the story apparently confirms Edgar's
unconsciousness and lack of real understanding of the events he
has been involved in. He has been sent to bed, segregated once
more from the adult world and, while he believes he has now seen

[23] Ibid. 104.   [24] Ibid.
[25] Ibid. 122.   [26] Ibid.

life as it really is, 'zum erstenmal . . . nicht mehr verhüllt von tausend Lügen der Kindheit',[27] Zweig's vocabulary suggests the child's still unknowing state. For example, he writes 'zum ersten Male *glaubte er* das Wesen der Menschen verstanden zu haben', 'Das war alles sehr süß und schmeichlerisch nun im Dunkel zu denken', the 'schmeichlerisch' suggesting Edgar's exaggerated idea of his own importance, while the 'im Dunkel' hints at a still unawakened state.[28] The word 'schmeichlerisch' is repeated shortly afterwards when his mother visits him, and this emphasizes the link between Edgar's sense of his own importance and the adult strategy which has produced it. There are also various hints at Edgar's lack of understanding: 'und nahm es nur als Versöhnung', 'er wußte nicht', 'All dies verstand das Kind von damals nicht'.[29] When we last see the boy he is asleep: the secret he thinks he has understood is 'schon umwölkt vom Schatten des Schlafes' and the author refers to him as 'das Kind', a clear indication that, whatever Edgar may think, he is still a child, the plaything of adults who have allowed him into their world as far as is convenient to them but no further.[30] Edgar, like Maisie, has been fully enough initiated never to regard adults in quite the same way again, never to see them as an absolute authority, and in this sense neither child can return to the full innocence or ignorance of childhood. But whether Edgar realizes it or not, for the moment at least he is still dependent on adults and their whims. These texts are examples of just how unconsciously a child can become involved in the designs of the adult world, becoming implicated in (indeed in Edgar's case consciously adopting) its guilt, while at the same time remaining essentially ignorant, an object to be manipulated at will.

These texts deal with an important twentieth-century theme, namely how far the child is involved in the adult world and how much guilt this implies. Paradoxically both Maisie and Edgar are corrupted without necessarily becoming guilty. The term 'guilt' describes a state brought about by our own conscious thoughts and actions, whereas corruption is a more insidious process, implying an infiltration of its object's thought without the object necessarily being aware of it. This paradox is particularly clear in

---

[27] Ibid. 124. [28] Ibid. emphasis mine.
[29] Ibid. 125. [30] Ibid. 126.

Maisie's case, for she knows of no emotional value system other
than that of her parents and their multiple lovers. She thus has a
perverted conception of normality for she has no other yardstick
by which to assess her existence and this explains her apparently
total acceptance of the situation. Edgar's case is slightly different:
the scandal he witnesses takes place outside his usual frame of reference, away from home and the security of his normal family life.
It is an exceptional circumstance, hence his violent reaction
against it. He has more of a chance to perceive the moral wrong of
the situation, but chooses to compromise with adult immorality
by protecting his mother on their return to 'normality'. However,
while this could be interpreted as Edgar taking on adult guilt, the
'brennendes Geheimnis' of sexuality is still a 'Geheimnis' to him
at the end of the story: he cannot yet fully understand the implications of what he has witnessed. His mother has manipulated
him into seeing guilt as an integral part of the adult condition, and
by so doing she has warped his perceptions, as the adults in
Maisie's life have warped hers. These children have been corrupted but they are not guilty: the blame for their corruption lies
at the adults' door.

CORRUPTION BY LEARNING

In the previous section I dwelt on the sexual aspect of 'the Fall'
because since Freud there has been so much emphasis on the potentially sexual nature of children. But the idea of the Fall goes
back well beyond Freud: it has its roots in the Garden of Eden
where it is not necessarily a matter of sexuality or even good and
evil, although it comprises these things. The Fall is a product of
knowledge.

As we saw in the Introduction, for Romantic writers the purity
and intuitive knowledge represented by the child was far superior to the acquired learning of adults, and this explains the gen-
eral aversion to what Wordsworth calls 'the monster birth |
Engendered by these too industrious times', the precociously
book-learned child who 'can read lectures upon innocence'.[31]

---

[31] *The Prelude 1799, 1805, 1850: Authoritative Texts, Contexts and Reception; Recent Critical Essays*, ed. Jonathan Wordsworth, M. H. Abrams, and Stephen Gill (New York and
London, 1979), (1805 version), ll. 292–3 and 313.

Writers of this period tended to see the imposition of mere academic learning as injurious; they felt that it inhibited the child's natural spontaneity and imagination. This is clear in *Das fremde Kind* where Hoffmann uses Magister Tinte to make a satirical comment on contemporary educational practice.[32] The mysterious tutor's less charming habits include pricking the children with a pin when shaking hands and Felix and Christlieb are judged to be so lacking in elementary 'Wissenschaften' that they have to 'beinahe den ganzen Tag zwischen den vier Wänden sitzen und dem Magister Tinte Dinge nachplappern, die sie nicht verstanden'.[33] Given that these are 'Naturkinder' par excellence, this is a grim fate indeed, from which they are mercifully rescued by the 'fremdes Kind'.

As Coveney points out in his discussion of Wordsworth's *Prelude*, we do not have to look far for the common root of this antipathy towards book learning.[34] In *Émile* Rousseau writes: 'En ôtant ainsi tous les devoirs des enfants, j'ôte les instruments de leur plus grande misère, savoir les livres. La lecture est le fléau de l'enfance, et presque la seule occupation qu'on sait lui donner.[35] It is not merely that book learning is irksome: knowledge represses and corrupts those aspects of childhood the Romantics found most appealing, namely its spontaneity, its affinity with nature, and its imagination—the qualities of the artist. Hostility towards academic learning became a veritable institution in Germany following Rousseau's pronouncements; in *Levana* Jean Paul advised against 'Lernzwang' in the early years of childhood[36] and Pestalozzi proposed a child-centred education based not on reading but on 'Anschauung', 'Sprache', and an exploitation of the natural environment which for him is in harmony with the child's true nature.[37]

This attitude may derive partly from the lack of real children's literature before this period. As Gillian Avery points out, children's literature as a separate category only made its first appearance in the seventeenth century and even then, in England and

---

[32] This is discussed in Richter, *Fremde Kind*, 274–5.

[33] E. T. A. Hoffmann, *Dichtungen und Schriften, so wie Briefe und Tagebücher. Gesamtausgabe*, ed. Walther Harich, 15 vols. (Weimar, 1924), vii. 123.

[34] *Image of Childhood*, 82.   [35] *Émile*, 115.

[36] *Werke*, v. 867.

[37] *Wie Gertrud ihre Kinder lehrt*, in *Ausgewählte Werke*, ed. Otto Boldemann, 2 vols. (Berlin, 1962–3), ii. 272–4.

America at least, these 'recreational books' were still intended to further the child's religious and moral education.[38] The German trend was similar: early children's literature was made up mainly of didactic stories where the basic pattern was that of 'Kinder-leben mit tödlichem Ausgang', 'Warngeschichten' designed to repress the child's natural spontaneity.[39] Hostility towards this kind of literature may explain the apparent contradiction between Wordsworth's aversion to book learning in *The Prelude* and this passionate appeal:

> Oh, give us once again the wishing-cap
> Of Fortunatus, and the invisible coat
> Of Jack the Giant-Killer, Robin Hood
> And Sabra in the forest with St. George!
> The child whose love is here, at least doth reap
> One precious gain—that he forgets himself.[40]

Levana follows the same pattern, for Jean Paul gives only a luke-warm response to book learning, yet greets works which will stim-ulate the imagination with enthusiasm:

Wir sind hier der Frage über die Inhalt-Wahl der Kinder-Erzählungen so nahe, daß eine Antwort verstattet sein mag. Orientalische, romantische scheinen die angemessensten zu sein; viele Märchen aus 1001 Nacht, Geschichten aus Herders Palmblättern und Krummachers Parabeln. Kinder sind kleine Morgenländler. Blendet sie mit einem weiten Mor-genlande, mit Taublitzen und Blumen-Farben. Setzt ihnen wenigstens im Erzählen die Schwingen an, die sie über unsere Nord-Klippen und Nord-Kaps wegführen in warme Gärten hinein.[41]

Even Rousseau would allow Émile one book, *Robinson Crusoe*, for by empathizing with the protagonist, Émile will realize the possi-bility of man's self-sufficiency in the natural environment. None of these educationalists actually opposes the child becoming literate: they are merely against the adult determining when and how this should happen. Rousseau predicts that Émile will know how to read by the age of 10, simply because he will discover that it is to his advantage to be able to do so: 'le désir d'apprendre'[42]

---

[38] 'The Puritans and their Heirs', in Gillian Avery and Julia Briggs (eds.), *Children and their Books: A Celebration of the Work of Iona and Peter Opie* (repr. Oxford, 1990), 95.
[39] Richter, *Fremde Kind*, 43.
[40] *The Prelude* (1805 version), v, ll. 364–9.   [41] *Werke*, v. 815.
[42] *Émile*, 116.

will be his strongest motivating force; Pestalozzi's basic premiss is that by following the child's own inclinations the educator will give the pupil what is best for him and develop an individual, in Rousseau's terms an 'homme' rather than a 'citoyen'. Rousseau regards these terms as mutually exclusive, noting: 'il faut opter entre faire un homme ou un citoyen'. His own ideal is to create 'l'homme naturel . . . tout pour lui', which he qualifies thus: 'Les bonnes institutions sociales sont celles qui savent le mieux déna-turer l'homme, lui ôter son existence absolue pour lui en donner une relative, et transporter le *moi* dans l'unité commune; en sorte que chaque particulier ne se croie plus un, mais partie de l'unité, et ne soit plus sensible que dans le tout.'[43]

But the great advantage of Rousseau's method is that Émile is brought up alone rather than in a school. As the personal tutor gave way to school as the educational norm for all social classes, a new genre was born: the *Schulroman*.

CORRUPTION BY SCHOOL

If the nineteenth century was broadly speaking the time of the *Bil-dungsroman*, then the early twentieth century was apparently that of the *Schulroman*. Both seem to be particularly German forms, stemming from a strong interest in the artist and the belief that for-mal academic training can only inhibit artistry. In the *Bildungsro-man* the emphasis was definitely on *Bildung* rather than *Ausbildung*, and characters like Keller's Heinrich learn much more from other people and their natural environment than they do in the class-room; this was the ideal education for the artist. The emergence of the *Schulroman* was not merely a matter of literature reflecting social reality; the institution of school also gave writers a legiti-mate target for their hostility towards a society they found oppressive. Hence the widely acknowledged bad press schools get in German literature.[44]

---

[43] Ibid. 9.
[44] Jens, 'Erwachsene Kinder', 139. The importance of the school theme in German literature is pointed out by Söntgerath, *Pädagogik und Dichtung*, 16–18. See also Peter Grotzer, *Die zweite Geburt: Figuren des Jugendlichen in der Literatur des 20. Jahrhunderts*, 2 vols. (Zurich, 1991), i. 75–7. Grotzer emphasizes the negative perception of both schools and teachers in German literature. For a discussion of the theme as it appears in the late 19th and early 20th centuries, see Fertig, *Vor-leben*, 51–64.

It is illuminating to compare the German *Schulroman* with its
English counterpart since this highlights the distinctive features of
the German form. There is a long tradition of English school stories dating from Thomas Hughes's *Tom Brown's Schooldays* (1857)
and these generally emphasize the individual learning to conform
to the schoolboy honour code and becoming an upstanding
member of the Christian community. In addition there are less
typical examples like Rudyard Kipling's *Stalky & Co.* (1899),
apparently conceived as a parody of the attitudes set out in
Hughes's novel, for here the 'right-minded' schoolboy is at odds
with dull-witted authority, and the boys usually triumph due to
their sheer native cunning and survival instinct. But, however different these types of story appear, one thing they have in common
is that in neither does the boy appear as victim.[45]

Unlike English school stories German *Schulromane* appear to be
written for an adult rather than a schoolboy audience and their
emphasis is very different. Here the individual is no longer triumphant; as Jens points out, the standard *Schulroman* portrays
school life through the eyes of a sensitive, artistic individual who
is eventually crushed by the system.[46] As we saw in the discussion
of the school chapter of *Buddenbrooks* in the Introduction, what
comes over in such works is school's importance as a socializing
agent. The description of the school as a microcosm of Prussian
society recalls W. H. Auden's statement: 'The best reason I have
for opposing Fascism is that at school I lived in a Fascist state'.[47]

Hanno's instinctive revolt against the values of this school is
typical of the German literary interest in education, a dominant
theme since the *Bildungsroman*. There is a constant tension
between the demands of institutions and the claims of the individual, and this prefigures the odd combination of conformity
with instinctive revolt found in so many child narratives set in the
Third Reich. Even when apparently utopian pedagogical institutions are portrayed, as in Goethe's *Wilhelm Meisters Wanderjahre*
(1829) and Hesse's *Das Glasperlenspiel* (1943), authors still focus on
the needs of the individual.

---

[45] For a discussion of the English school story, see Isabel Quigly, *The Heirs of Tom
Brown: The English School Story* (London, 1982).

[46] 'Erwachsene Kinder', 139.

[47] 'Honour' (Gresham's School), in Patricia Craig (ed.), *The Oxford Book of Schooldays*
(Oxford, 1994), 317.

Wilhelm Meisters Wanderjahre presents an apparently very Rousseauian conception of education. When Wilhelm and Felix arrive in the 'pädagogische Provinz' the children are preparing for the harvest, and this not only reflects the need for useful manual work rather than sterile academic knowledge, but also allows the children to be presented in a pastoral setting suggesting spontaneity and innocence just as it has since *Émile*. This setting is described in terms appropriate to a *locus amoenus*:

beim ersten Eintritt gewahrten sie sogleich der fruchtbarsten Gegend, welche an sanften Hügeln den Feldbau, auf höhern Bergen die Schafzucht, in weiten Talflächen die Viehzucht begünstigte. Es war kurz vor der Ernte und alles in größter Fülle; das, was sie jedoch gleich in Verwunderung setzte, war, daß sie weder Frauen noch Männer, wohl aber durchaus Knaben und Jünglinge beschäftigt sahen, auf eine glückliche Ernte sich vorzubereiten, ja auch schon auf ein fröhliches Erntefest freund-liche Anstalt zu treffen.[48]

The principles of the province are apparently intended to create a sense of individuality within a harmonious whole, as suggested by the 'Mannigfaltigkeit' of the children's clothing and the singing which accompanies their corporate labours.[49] This ideal is consistent with Goethe's conception of the natural world, whose individual parts form a perfect whole, witnessing to a benign innate order. Here, as in the educationalists cited earlier, the emphasis is apparently on allowing the children's natural potential to develop with minimal adult interference. As one of the superiors notes: 'die Natur hat jedem alles gegeben, was er für Zeit und Dauer nötig hätte; dieses zu entwickeln, ist unsere Pflicht, öfters entwickelt sich's besser von selbst'.[50] The final stage of this *Bildung* consists in learning 'die Ehrfurcht vor sich selbst' and this can be compared with the self-confidence and self-respect cultivated by Rousseau, Jean Paul, and Pestalozzi.[51]

But while this form of education may appear idyllic, Adolf Muschg points out that it is in fact a 'forciertes Idyll' which is highly ambivalent and vulnerable to perversion, especially when examined from a modern standpoint.[52] The various 'Grüße'

---

[48] *Werke*, viii. 149.   [49] Ibid. 149.
[50] Ibid. 154.   [51] Ibid. 157.
[52] Afterword to Goethe's *Wilhelm Meisters Wanderjahre oder Die Entsagenden* (Frankfurt, 1982), 502 and 516.

imposed on the children may seem joyous: the youngest 'blickten fröhlich gen Himmel' and the middle children 'schauten lächelnd zur Erde'.[53] However, these gestures are not spontaneous but prescribed: the adults have created an image of childhood to suit themselves. And, although the superior states 'der Uniform sind wir durchaus abgeneigt', this principle is not the plea for individualism it may seem, for he goes on to say that uniform 'entzieht die Eigenheiten der Kinder, mehr als jede andere Verstellung, dem Blicke der Vorgesetzten'.[54] This supposed freedom in the children's choice of clothing simply gives the authorities better opportunities to observe and so control the youngsters. Not only that; the superior goes on to describe strategies for keeping children from their own tendency to follow a particular fashion, a form of manipulation that is hardly consistent with the idea of allowing children the freedom to develop according to their own inclinations: from a modern pedagogical standpoint it might be regarded as less honest than a straightforward prohibition from the parent or instructor. This point is made by von Braunmühl when he criticizes the following passage from *Émile*:

Prenez une route opposée avec votre élève; qu'il croie toujours être le maître, et que ce soit toujours vous qui le soyez. Il n'y a pas d'assujettissement si parfait que celui qui garde l'apparence de la liberté; on captive ainsi la volonté même. Le pauvre enfant qui ne sait rien, qui ne peut rien, qui ne connaît rien, n'est-il-pas à votre merci? Ne disposez-vous pas, par rapport à lui, de tout ce qui l'environne? N'êtes-vous pas le maître de l'affecter comme il vous plaît? Ses travaux, ses jeux, ses plaisirs, ses peines, tout n'est-il pas dans vos mains sans qu'il le sache? Sans doute il ne doit faire que ce qu'il veut; mais il ne doit vouloir que ce que vous voulez qu'il fasse; il ne doit pas faire un pas que vous ne l'ayez prévu; il ne doit pas ouvrir la bouche que vous ne sachiez ce qu'il va dire.[55]

Von Braunmühl comments: 'Eines muß man zugeben: ROUSSEAU ist ehrlich. Zwar nicht zu Kindern, aber zu sich selbst und zu seinen Lesern', and he goes on to question whether 'Freiheit' and 'Erziehung' are mutually compatible concepts.[56] On the evidence

---

[53] Goethe, *Werke*, viii. 149.   [54] Ibid. 166.   [55] *Émile*, 121.

[56] *Zeit für Kinder; Theorie und Praxis von Kinderfeindlichkeit, Kinderfreundlichkeit, Kinderschutz; Zur Beseitigung der Unsicherheit im Umgang mit Kindern; Ein Lernbuch* (Frankfurt, 1993), 35–6. Kuhn also points out the 'basic hypocrisy' underlying Rousseau's pedagogy (*Corruption in Paradise*, 113).

of *Émile* and *Wilhelm Meisters Wanderjahre* it would seem that they are not. Indeed, any form of *Erziehung* presupposes a higher adult will which, whatever the attempts to create an aura of freedom, will always direct developments to some extent. The 'pädagogische Provinz' comes dangerously close to the idea of the state moulding children for its own (albeit benign) ends: while Rousseau emphasizes the idea of bringing up Émile alone in order to create an individual, Goethe's novel has a broader social focus. And, as Muschg suggests, for all their aura of freedom the new colonies will be characterized by the 'Unterdrückung jeder spontanen Bewegung' learned in the 'pädagogische Provinz'.[57] There is a tension between the vision of a utopian society and the right of the individual to spontaneous development, prefigured in Wilhelm's relationship to the 'Turmgesellschaft' in the *Lehrjahre*. As Muschg points out, Goethe does not completely endorse the province: the fact that there is scope for individual freedom and spontaneity beyond the institution is suggested by Felix, who emerges from it with all his independence and high spirits intact.[58] The fact that he is evidently approved by both his father and the narrator undermines the corporate aims of the province, just as Josef Knecht's defection from Kastalien and his subsequent decision to teach Tito along Rousseauian lines undermine the corporate ideals of that pedagogical province.

Muschg's critique of the 'pädagogische Provinz' goes further than the idea that it attempts to repress individuality. He regards some aspects of it as particularly sinister when seen from a modern-day perspective, as they prefigure the abuses of Nazism. The province is characterized by what looks worrying like unquestioning obedience to superiors (the youngest children's 'Gruß' is in recognition 'daß ein Gott da droben sei, der sich in Eltern, Lehrern, Vorgesetzten abbildet und offenbart',[59] and even the fact that the Jewish nation has been chosen as a 'Musterbild'[60] for the province because of its powers of endurance cannot erase the latent anti-Semitism Muschg observes in the superior's comments.[61] Hitler's *Reichsjugendführer* Baldur von Schirach claimed Goethe as an intellectual forerunner of the Nazi movement, and

---

[57] Afterword to Goethe's *Wilhelm Meisters Wanderjahre*, 502.
[58] Ibid. 507, 516. [59] Goethe, *Werke*, viii. 155.
[60] Ibid. 160. [61] Afterword to Goethe's *Wilhelm Meisters Wanderjahre*, 516.

in his 1937 speech 'Goethe in unserer Zeit' he quoted (selectively!) from *Die Wahlverwandtschaften* and *Wilhlem Meisters Wanderjahre* in support of this claim. He specifically quoted the idea that the highest form of 'Ehrfurcht' is 'die Ehrfurcht vor sich selbst'–a prime example of the way Nazi leaders exploited the German cultural heritage and any ambiguities in it for their own ends.[62]

'UND SIE WERDEN NICHT MEHR FREI, IHR
GANZES LEBEN':[63] NAZI EDUCATION AND THE PERVERSION
OF ROMANTICISM

As we saw in the previous section, authors and educators alike display a highly ambivalent attitude to schools as imparters of knowledge and as socializing instruments, and this forms an important socio-historical background to what went on in German schools between 1933 and 1945. In what follows I will give an overview of the role of schools and youth organizations in the Third Reich so as to show the extent of children's practical, intellectual, and emotional involvement in the regime and thus facilitate an understanding of the fictional perspectives of those subjected to Nazi indoctrination. This account is intended only to shed light on my literary texts rather than to provide detailed information on historical circumstances.[64]

Writers' aversion to the rote-learning and regimentation inflicted on children in the early twentieth century was due to a belief that these activities stunted the child's individuality and spontaneity. But this was as nothing compared with the abuses committed in the name of education under the Nazis. There are no indications that Hitler was a closet intellectual, versed in pedagogical theories; his educational programme, contained in *Mein Kampf*, is informed mainly by personal resentment at his own academic failure.[65] And, while he is said to have been a voracious

---

[62] 'Goethe in unserer Zeit', in *Revolution der Erziehung: Reden aus den Jahren des Aufbaus* (Munich, 1938), 173.

[63] Hilter's speech of 2 Dec. 1938 at Reichenberg, quoted in Max von der Grün, *Wie war das eigentlich? Kindheit und Jugend im Dritten Reich* (1979; repr. Hamburg and Zurich, 1988), 100.

[64] For further information, see sources, cited in the Select Bibliography.

[65] Kurt-Ingo Flessau, *Schule der Diktatur: Lehrpläne und Schulbücher des Nationalsozialismus* (Munich, 1977), 23. For Hitler's academic achievements–or the lack of them–see Klaus P. Fischer, *Nazi Germany: A New History* (London, 1995), 80.

reader in later life, this did not enable him to achieve any coherent or objective world-view.[66] His intellectual pretensions are aptly summed up by one of Ernst Toller's fellow inmates in Niederschönfeld, who described the future Führer as 'einer, der viel Bücher liest und sie nicht verdaut'.[67] Nevertheless, Hitler had something of a genius for assimilating ideas that were in the air and using them for his own ends, and this ability to exploit accepted cultural assumptions made his task of universal corruption considerably easier.[68] It is of course commonly held that he corrupted a generation of children. What is less commonly realized is that to do so he first perverted the long-cherished Romantic myth of childhood. Compare, for example, these two passages from *Levana* and *Mein Kampf* respectively:

Körperliche Abhärtung ist, da der Körper der Ankerplatz des Mutes ist, schon geistig nötig. Ihr Zweck und Erfolg ist nicht sowohl *Gesundheit-Anstalt* und *Verlängerung* des Lebens–denn Weichlinge und Wollüstlinge wurden öfters alt, so wie Nonnen und Hofdamen noch öfter–als die *Aus-* und *Zurüstung* desselben wider das Ungemach und für Heiterkeit und Tätigkeit . . . Die meisten [Erziehschreiber] (vor Pestalozzi) schlugen vor, nur recht viele Kenntnisse aller Art einzuschütten: so bilde sich ein tüchtiger Mensch, denn Geist komme (nach Klopstock) von Gießen. Gelähmte Allwisser, ohne Gegenwart des Geistes und ohne Zukunft desselben[69]

in der Masse genommen wird sich ein gesunder, kraftvoller Geist auch nur in einem gesunden und kraftvollen Körper finden. . . .

Der völkische Staat hat in dieser Erkenntnis seine gesamte Erziehungsarbeit in erster Linie nicht auf das Einpumpen bloßen Wissens einzustellen, sondern auf das Heranzüchten kerngesunder Körper. Erst in zweiter Linie kommt dann die Ausbildung der geistigen Fähigkeiten.[70]

Obviously the emphasis in these two extracts is entirely different, for while the former focuses on the child as an individual, the

---

[66] Fischer, *Nazi Germany*, 81. Flessau comments on Hitler's reading in the educational context in *Schule der Diktatur*, 27–31.

[67] Ernst Toller, *Eine Jugend in Deutschland*, in id., *Prosa, Briefe, Dramen, Gedichte*, with foreword by Kurt Hiller (Reinbek, 1961), 165.

[68] See Peter Malina's introd. to Alois Kaufmann, *Spiegelgrund, Pavillon 18: Ein Kind im NS-Erziehungsheim* (Vienna, 1993), 20–1. Malina points to continuities between the Weimar Republic and the Hitler years, as well as to the continuation of 'Nazi' thought in Austrian education well after the Third Reich. Hitler's views on education are discussed in Flessau, *Schule der Diktatur*, 22–31.

[69] Jean Paul, *Werke*, v. 652–3 and 825.

[70] Hitler, *Mein Kampf*, 2 vols. (repr. Munich, 1936), ii. 452.

latter emphasizes its importance to the state. Nevertheless, many of the educational ideals expounded in *Mein Kampf* have their roots in the anti-intellectualism of the Romantic era. There is a preference for 'körperliche Ertüchtigung' over the much-scorned 'rein wissenschaftliche Ausbildung'; boys are to be taught boxing in order to 'Schläge ertragen lernen' and the '*Ziel* der weiblichen Erziehung hat unverrückbar die kommende Mutter zu sein'.[71] In *Levana* Jean Paul too advocates 'Übungen im Ertragen des Schmerzes, Kreuzschulen im stoischen Sinne' for boys and he also notes 'Die Natur hat das Weib unmittelbar zur Mutter bestimmt', adding that maternal love is 'das Höchste und Schönste, womit die Natur das Weib ausstatten konnte'.[72] And, if Hitler was able to exploit such cultural assumptions, how much more did he manage to exploit the ambiguities inherent in them. The tension between the child's freedom to develop according to its own inclinations and the all-pervasive adult will which controls this 'free development' certainly informs his rhetoric. He apparently makes concessions to Romantic anti-intellectualism and, indeed, cites Nietzsche's vitalism when he says 'Das freie, herrliche Raubtier muß erst wieder aus ihren Augen blitzen. Stark und schön will ich meine Jugend. . . . So habe ich das reine, edle Material der Natur vor mir' and 'Ich will keine intellektuelle Erziehung. Mit Wissen verderbe ich mir die Jugend. Am liebsten ließe ich sie nur das lernen, was sie ihrem Spieltriebe folgend sich freiwillig aneignen'.[73] However, there is little sense of that freedom to become an individual in the following notorious speech, made on 2 December 1938 in Reichenberg:

Diese Jugend, die lernt ja nichts anderes als deutsch denken, deutsch handeln. Und wenn nun dieser Knabe und dieses Mädchen mit ihren zehn Jahren in unsere Organisationen hineinkommen und dort nun so oft zum erstenmal überhaupt eine frische Luft bekommen und fühlen, dann kommen sie vier Jahre später vom Jungvolk in die Hitlerjugend, und dort behalten wir sie wieder vier Jahre, und dann geben wir sie erst recht nicht zurück in die Hände unserer alten Klassen- und Standeserzeuger, sondern dann nehmen wir sie sofort in die Partei oder in die Arbeitsfront, in die SA oder in die SS, in das NSKK und so weiter . . . Und sie werden nicht mehr frei, ihr ganzes Leben.[74]

---

[71] Ibid. 453, 455, 460.   [72] *Werke*, v. 773, 688, 690.
[73] Quoted in: Grün, *Wie war das eigentlich?*, 100.   [74] Ibid. 101.

Hitler's vehement anti-intellectualism, like that of the Romantic era, apparently equates innocence with ignorance, but while Romantic educationalists regard children as spontaneous and untrained like young animals, Hitler's anti-intellectualism appeals not merely to the 'Tier' but to the 'Raubtier', Nietzsche's 'blonde Bestie'. That is, it plays on the amoral, instinctual elements of childhood observed in Anton Klöterjahn.

This less than conventionally innocent aspect of childhood is emphasized in Ludwig Harig's account of a youth in the Third Reich, *Weh dem, der aus der Reihe tanzt* (1990), which begins with the narrator's first day at school in spring 1933. The date is significant: the children have not yet been subjected to Nazi indoctrination, partly because they have not yet come under the systematic socializing influence of school, but mainly because the regime is still in its infancy. Consequently there is nothing specifically National Socialist about Harig's recollections of his early schooldays; the 'preußische Obrigkeitsgeist' (*Weh dem, der aus der Reihe tarzt*, 8) that breathes through the school is much the same spirit as Hanno Buddenbrook encountered. As far as the boy is concerned, the school derives its authority mainly from family tradition, for 'Hier ist der Vater schon zur Schule gegangen' and this, together with the imposing symmetry of the façade, is enough to fill the child with 'ein gebührender Respekt vor diesem Schulhaus' (p. 9). While the adult narrator's troubled dreams present his former teacher to him complete with 'Adolf-Hitler-Bärtchen' (p. 18), the teacher's authority over the child is not specifically Nazi in origin; his pet phrase that 'keiner habe das Recht, aus der Reihe zu tanzen' (p. 13) simply echoes 'die unbarmherzige Lehre der Steine: Weh dem, der aus der Reihe tanzt!' (p. 9).

And yet Harig's account of this first day at school presents us with what at a first glance appear to be Nazi patterns of behaviour as the children close ranks against one of their new classmates, René. Even before the children go into school for the first time the narrator notes:

Wir waren vierzig, jeder hätte einen Nachbarn an seiner Seite haben können, doch schon am ersten Schultag und alle die Tage danach bis ins nächste, ins übernächste Jahr, fand der kleine Junge niemanden, der ihn an seine Seite genommen hätte. Immer blieb er übrig. Und hatten wir uns in langer Reihe zu zweien hintereinander aufgestellt und es fehlte niemand, so daß für ihn ein Nachbar hätte da sein müssen: Es war niemals jemand zu finden, der sich neben ihn in die Reihe gestellt hätte. . . . Er war überzählig, er war überflüssig. (p. 11)

There are obvious reasons (or pretexts) for René's outsider status: the narrator remembers him being of higher social standing than the other children and his French name 'verursachte . . . einen Mißklang in unseren Ohren'. But the irrationality of the children's instant dislike for him is brought out by the blanket statement 'Er war anders *und* hieß René' (p. 13, my emphasis). Effectively the group needs an outsider figure and René draws the short straw:

War der Kleine etwa doch nicht überzählig, nicht überflüssig? Wir brauchten ihn. Er war unentbehrlich. Hätte es ihn nicht gegeben, wir anderen wären viel länger im Dunkeln getappt und hätten an Herrn Peiters Lebensregel herumgerätselt. Wir lernten es im Handumdrehen. Jedesmal, wenn der Junge in den Kreis trat, spürten wir, daß wir nicht so waren wie er und er nicht war wie wir und außerhalb stand, weil er anders war. (pp. 12–13)

The passing reference to the teacher suggests his authority merely reinforces an already existent group mentality. The results of these instincts, especially when confirmed by an authority figure, are made explicit when the narrator notes: 'Und wir brauchten ihn [René], er war so nützlich in unserem deutschen Charakterstück, in dem es ja nie an einem Außenseiter fehlen darf, sei es, daß er Jude, Zigeuner oder Franzose ist' (p. 21). The specifically National Socialist undertones of this analysis and the behaviour of Herr Peiter suggest a point that historians have made explicit; namely, that the pre-1933 German school system, with its traditionally authoritarian structures and teachers, was not difficult to adapt to the needs of the National Socialist regime.[75] Harig's reference to the 'gebührender Respekt' the narrator feels for the school building reflects the experience of most children when they first start school; they tend to regard the new institution with a certain awe and unquestioning belief in its authority. It was

[75] See Fischer, *Nazi Germany*, 347; also Detlev J. K. Peukert, *Inside Nazi Germany: Conformity, Opposition and Racism in Everyday Life*, trans. Richard Deveson (repr. Harmondsworth, 1993), 175 and Richard Grunberger, *A Social History of the Third Reich* (London, 1971), 285. The ideological continuity of lessons can be assessed from Joachim S. Hohmann and Hermann Langer (eds.), *'Stolz, ein Deutscher zu sein...': Nationales Selbstverständnis in Schulaufsätzen 1914–1945* (Frankfurt, 1995).

therefore imperative for the National Socialist regime to harness this traditional respect for its own ends as rapidly as possible.

The first official steps in the *Gleichschaltung* of schools were taken in 1933, but even before the 'Gesetz zur Wiederherstellung des Berufsbeamtentums' was announced on 7 April 1933 the process of voluntary self-regulation had begun amongst teachers; according to van Dick, they began to flood into the National-sozialistischer Lehrerbund (NSLB) directly after Hitler's 'Machtergreifung', so that by April–May 1933 80 per cent of teachers were incorporated in this association, and by the end of 1933 this figure had reached 95 per cent.[76] By 1936 Nazi pedagogues were claiming that 32 per cent of teachers belonged to the NSDAP itself, the highest figure amongst civil servants.[77] Van Dick argues that there was little external compulsion for teachers to comply with the new regime with such alacrity. Moreover, he points to evidence that, after the initial flurry of 1933 when one might have expected a lull, many teachers were overzealous, not merely in their passive cooperation with the regime, but even in their active denunciation and victimization of less compliant colleagues and pupils who were undesirable according to Nazi lights.[78] If we wanted to plead mitigating circumstances for teachers' swift self-regulation we might cite Grunberger, who points out that teachers, like civil servants, were employed directly by the state and so were subject to more direct political pressure than other groups.[79] Grunberger also refers to the 'ever-present occupational hazard' of being denounced by a pupil, which might have been expected to make teachers toe the line.[80] There is some disagreement about how great a danger this was; Koch states that it was rare for pupils to denounce a nonconformist teacher, but concedes the possibility that a pupil would challenge a teacher's authority in the classroom if he appeared insufficiently enthusiastic about the National Socialist regime.[81] The feelings of insecurity generated by this threat may have led teachers to submit to the

---

[76] *Lehreropposition im NS-Staat: Biographische Berichte über den 'aufrechten Gang'* (rev. edn., Frankfurt, 1990), 14–15.

[77] Ibid. 14. Erika Mann states that by 1937 97 per cent of teachers were in the NSLB, and of them 32.2 per cent were in the NSDAP (*Zehn Millionen Kinder*, 61).

[78] *Lehreropposition*, 15.   [79] *Social History of the Third Reich*, 128.

[80] Ibid. 286.

[81] *The Hitler Youth: Origins and Development 1922–1945* (London, 1975), 174.

new regime more readily and completely than was strictly necessary for self-preservation. But it is perhaps unfair to say now that there were not many cases of pupils denouncing their teachers and to judge teachers on this basis; while they may have acted in accordance with an exaggerated perception of the threat to them, it is all too easy to condemn them in retrospect.

Certainly not all teachers who complied with the regime were committed to National Socialist ideology. The fundamental structures and tone of school life remained much the same as under the Weimar Republic, and thus many teachers were able to go on with their work much as they had in the past, adapting their classroom practice to the changed political climate by using what Koch calls 'double talk'.[82] Barbara König provides an example of this when she writes of her biology teacher: 'Und ich könnte schwören, daß ihr Ton anders wurde, trocken, distanziert, wenn sie von den biologischen Theorien der Nazis sprach: man brauchte da nicht mitzudenken'.[83] But not all pupils were as perceptive as the young König; it is likely that most did not notice their teachers' indifference to the Nazi ideals they dutifully if unenthusiastically preached. Indeed, even teachers who acted on their anti-Nazi convictions were not always appreciated by their pupils: witness Elisabeth Flügge, whose concern for the Jewish children in her class caused her to be honoured as 'righteous amongst the nations' in Yad Vashem in 1976.[84] Her daughter reports that after the war her mother was reproached by one of her brightest former pupils for not telling the younger generation the truth about the National Socialist state: the girl had not noticed her teacher's nonconformist attitude, 'Denn meine Mutter war als Lehrerin natürlich auch eine Repräsentantin jener Zeit'.[85] Those in authority were naturally associated with the state whatever their personal convictions; no wonder then that the Nazi regime was so keen to exploit the time-honoured respect that schools had in the eyes of children and parents alike.

But the Nazi regime could not be satisfied with teachers belonging to the NSLB or even the NSDAP, for the teachers were merely a means to an end; namely, gaining the hearts and minds

---

[82] Ibid. 167. [83] *Die verpaßte Chance*, in Reich-Ranicki (ed.), *Meine Schulzeit*, 137.
[84] Van Dick, *Lehreropposition*, 85. Elisabeth Flügge's biography is given ibid. 84–94.
[85] Ibid. 92.

of their pupils. For this purpose the school curriculum was substantially revised. The new subject 'Rassenkunde' was made compulsory for all pupils from 1 October 1933 and Hitler's belief in the importance of physical fitness was reflected in a significant increase in the amount of time devoted to PE as well as greater status for the subject.[86] And in a move that affected both 'Rassenkunde' and sport, on 7 June 1934 Baldur von Schirach announced that he was introducing a 'Staatsjugendtag' in place of traditional Saturday schooling. Those in the Hitler Youth spent this day (as well as Wednesday afternoons) in their 'Dienst' for the organization (mainly sport and ideological training), while those who were not members received similar fare in school.[87]

There were also other less explicit changes in the curriculum. Traditional school subjects were insidiously infused with Nazi doctrine, although initially the extent to which this happened depended on the strength or otherwise of individual teachers' political convictions. But, as time went on, the Nazis' grip on schools tightened considerably; even before National Socialist textbooks were available, teachers could supplement their traditional teaching aids with specifically National Socialist 'Ergänzungshefte'.[88] And while the incompetence of the education minister Bernhard Rust made him something of a figure of fun,[89] nonetheless, the state apparatus that backed him was no joke; one suspects that most teachers reacted to his inconsistencies and U-turns in the spirit of Brecht's harrassed teacher in *Furcht und Elend des Dritten Reiches* (1938): 'Ich bin ja bereit, alles zu lehren, was sie gelehrt haben wollen, aber was wollen sie gelehrt haben?'[90]

---

[86] For the decree of 13 Sept. 1933 introducing 'Vererbungslehre' and 'Rassenkunde', see Renate Fricke-Finkelnburg (ed.), *Nationalsozialismus und Schule: Amtliche Erlasse und Richtlinien 1933–1945* (Opladen, 1989), 214. For a discussion of the importance of PE, see ibid. 158–61.

[87] For the documents relating to this change, see Fricke-Finkelnburg, *Nationalsozialismus und Schule*, 243–5.

[88] The propaganda role of these pamphlets is highlighted by Mann, *Zehn Millionen Kinder*, 66–8.

[89] According to popular wisdom, a 'Rust' denoted 'diejenige Spanne Zeit, die von der Erlassung eines Gesetzes durch den Unterrichtsminister, bis zur Zurückziehung eben dieses Gesetzes durch den Unterrichtsminister vergeht' (ibid. 59).

[90] *Werke*, 30 vols., ed. Werner Hecht et al. (Berlin and Frankfurt, 1988), iv. 399.

Of the traditional school subjects biology and history were the most obvious candidates for corruption by Nazi ideology. Biology was the official vehicle for 'Rassenkunde';[91] history allowed for a glorification of Germany's past, and indeed present, given that Hitler had referred to politics as 'werdende Geschichte' in *Mein Kampf*.[92] Gradually, though, even more abstract subjects such as mathematics were perverted, with questions worded so as to exemplify points of National Socialist ideology.[93] Hans Bender's account of his schooling between 1935 and 1939 indicates that it became the norm for all school subjects to be infused with Nazi doctrine:

Der Lateinlehrer spickte die Texte, die ins klassische Latein zu übersetzen waren, mit aktuellen Vorgängen; immer wieder mit den Siegen, die der Duce und seine Generäle eben auf den Schlachtfeldern von Abessinien errangen. Der Erdkundelehrer brachte uns bei, das ganze Mittelmeer gehöre rechtens den Italienern—so wie uns Deutschen der Osten gehöre. Der Biologielehrer zeigte Lichtbilder, die uns den Unterschied der Rassen beweisen sollten, und selbstverständlich war die semitische die verachtenswerteste. Der gleiche Biologielehrer führte uns in die Anstalt für Unheilbare, die 'Hub', wo die irre-redenden, geifernden, triefenden Kranken—arme, zum Tod bestimmte Geschöpfe—uns Schüler überzeugen sollten, wie berechtigt es war, die 'Euthanasie' zu vollziehen.[94]

Even the most strong-minded individual found it difficult to stand out against this prevailing atmosphere: 'Auch wir, Heinz und ich, die sich gern absonderten, die nicht für die HJ sich gewinnen ließen, waren infiziert von den Bazillen, die umherflogen. Wir bockten auf, wir witzelten über Goebbels-Reden und verachteten die Nazi-Barden und waren doch fast der gleichen Meinung wie die Mehrheit.'[95] This education reached its climax with Bender's

---

[91] See the document of 13 Sept. 1933 in Fricke-Finkelnburg, *Nationalsozialismus und Schule*, 214. 'Rassenkunde' was intended to inform all school subjects, but biology was to carry the main burden.

[92] *Mein Kampf*, ii. 467. For a detailed account of history teaching under the Third Reich, see Flessau, *Schule der Diktatur*, 59–62 and 76–82; the ideological function of biology teaching is discussed ibid. 155–61.

[93] For a discussion of maths teaching and some chilling examples, ibid. 143–154, esp. 147.   [94] *Willst du nicht beitreten?*, in Reich-Ranicki (ed.), *Meine Schulzeit*, 37–8.

[95] Ibid. 38.

Abitur in 1939. He emphasizes that the 'blasphemische Konstella-
tion' of the 'Abiturthemen', 'Die Humanität in Goethes *Iphigenie*',
'Ist die Euthanasie berechtigt?', and 'Österreichs Heimkehr ins
Reich' was set, not by the 'übergeordnete Schulbehörde–von ihr
hätte man es erwarten können–sondern die Lehrer unserer
Schule'.[96] This is a clear case of fear leading to self-regulation, for
Bender's school was the last private school allowed to award its
students the state *Abitur*.[97] This fear and compliance at teacher
level obviously affected the pupils, for Bender states: 'Keiner
jedoch hätte die Fragen, die im zweiten und dritten Thema zu
beantworten waren, zu verneinen gewagt'.[98]

Even the youngest children could not escape this all-pervasive
indoctrination: von der Grün cites texts from a first reading book
using the *Buchstabenmethode*. Under 'R' the word *Reichswehr* is considered the most useful and familiar for children to recognize, and
the little story which follows concludes with the paragraph:
'Robert sagt: Am liebsten ginge ich schon heute zur Reichswehr.
Rudi und Reinhold möchten das auch. Rudi aber möchte gleich
Hauptmann sein'.[99] Learning to read is clearly not the only item
on the agenda here.

Gradually the whole atmosphere of schools changed, both inside and outside the classroom. It may be dangerous to attach too
much importance to the contemporary documents that emanated
from schools, since they were certain to be scrutinized by higher
authorities, but the tone of this yearly report of 1941 by the
headmaster of an Erlangen grammar school is not particularly
ambiguous:

Daß wir Erzieher jeden Anlaß benutzen, sowohl im Rahmen des Unter-
richts wie auch in besonderen Stunden und bei Feiern der uns anver-
trauten Jugend ein klares Verständnis für die Größe unseres Führers und
der von ihm geprägten Zeit und ebenso klare Einsicht in den brutalen
Vernichtungswillen des Judentums und seiner angelsächsischen Miet-
linge zu vermitteln, in unserer Jugend das Feuer des Glaubens an den
Führer, an Deutschland und an den Endsieg unserer gerechten Sache
stets hellbrennend zu erhalten, das ist selbstverständlich.[100]

[96] Ibid. 39.   [97] Ibid. 37.   [98] Ibid. 39.   [99] *Wie war das eigentlich?*, 69.
[100] Wolfgang Benz, 'Kinder und Jugendliche unter der Herrschaft des Nationalsozialismus', in Ute Benz and Wolfgang Benz (eds.), *Sozialisation und Traumatisierung:
Kinder in der Zeit des Nationalsozialismus* (Frankfurt, 1992), 17.

It is perhaps the 'Selbstverständlichkeit' that we find most unnerving.

The foregoing suggests that the Nazi government gained a strong grip on the education system from an early stage in the regime, even if only through self-regulation by teachers and schools. Of the teachers who survived the initial *Gleichschaltung* some felt no need to take an active stance either for or against the regime; they could continue to do their job much as they had done under the Weimar Republic. Others were opposed to the regime and yet frequently not perceived as such by their pupils. And then there were teachers who were committed Nazis and consciously used their position to inculcate the new ideology in their pupils. The prevailing atmosphere seems to be accurately summarized by Erika Mann when she says of the school environment 'gewiß findet sich nichts innerhalb seiner, was dem Nazi-Geist widerspräche'.[101]

According to Mann, the child was surrounded by three concentric circles during the Nazi era: family, school, and the Hitler Youth organization. The prestige of these circles increased with their width, with school having greater standing in the child's eyes than the family: 'Hier [in school] herrscht mehr staatlicher Ernst, dies fühlt das Kind'.[102] Even the most vehemently anti-Nazi parent would have had little chance of countering the prevailing atmosphere of Nazi-controlled schools, let alone the systematic indoctrination to which many children were subjected. At best, children who grew up in fervently anti-Nazi homes might have grown up in a rather schizophrenic manner, as described in Peter Abraham's *Die Schüsse aus der Arche Noah* (1970) where Klaus Wensloff has some difficulty resolving the contradiction between his Communist home and his school life:

Und während dieses Fräulein Schulze [his teacher] mit ihrer klaren Stimme jemanden 'unser Führer' nannte, bezeichnete der Vater denselben als 'Lumpen' oder 'Verbrecher'. . . .

Die Welt war für Klaus in zwei Teile gespalten, und er wanderte zwischen diesen Welten hin und her.[103]

---

[101] *Zehn Millionen Kinder*, 145.   [102] Ibid. 144.
[103] *Die Schüsse der Arche Noah oder Die Irrtümer und Irrfahrten meines Freundes Wensloff* (Berlin, 1971), 35.

While Klaus grows up to be an ardent Communist, it is clear that as a child he suffers enormous confusion as a result of the contradictions between home and school; initially the best he can do is act appropriately for the context he is in at the time.

In the case of Klaus Wensloff parental influence ends up winning through, but in most cases the influence of home was not as concentrated and systematic as the indoctrination children received in school and therefore the family lost out to the state. In any case, parents might well have been wary of expressing anti-Nazi sentiments in front of children who could inadvertently have betrayed them to the authorities.[104] But it is difficult to generalize about the atmosphere in different families or, indeed, schools. Both institutions pre-dated the Hitler regime and so allowed for the spirit, if not of active resistance, then at least of indifference. Home still had room for anti-Hitler opinion, albeit often expressed in a very guarded way; school still had traditions of academic integrity that pre-dated Hitler: hence the government's need for the purpose-built 'Staatsjugend' which Mann designates the 'Nazi-Kreis ohne Lücke'.[105] This organization represented Hitler's best chance of attaining his dream of a closed system as described in the 1938 Reichenberg speech.

The Hitler Jugend was established in 1926 and so by the time of the *Machtergreifung* there was already a considerable mythology surrounding the youth organization and its martyrs—a mythology readily exploited by von Schirach when addressing his youth.[106] The *Reichsjugendführer* drew a sharp distinction between the different functions and competences of family, school, and youth movement, and, while he paid lip-service to the idea that teachers had absolute authority within their own sphere, he was keen to emphasize 'daß die Autorität des HJ.-Führers die höchste Autorität außerhalb der Schule ist'.[107] In practice these authorities were bound to clash, given the government's preference for 'körperliche Ertüchtigung' and ideological training over 'rein wissenschaftliche Ausbildung' and so it is not surprising that relations between schools and the Hitler Youth were often fraught with

---

[104] This possibility is highlighted in Mann, *Zehn Millionen Kinder*, 32–3.

[105] Ibid. 145.

[106] See his radio broadcast 'Neujahrsbotschaft vom Grabe Herbert Norkus'' (1 Jan. 1935), in von Schirach, *Revolution der Erziehung*, 18–25.

[107] von Schirach, *Die Hitler-Jugend: Idee und Gestalt* (Berlin, 1934), 169–75: at 169.

difficulties. The documents collated by Fricke-Finkelnburg suggest uneasy compromises between schools' desire to maintain academic standards and von Schirach's insistence on more time for ideological training and sport; there is documentary evidence of concern about the amount of time youngsters were spending on extramural activities as early as 1933.[108]

However, as Mann points out, Hitler attached the greatest importance to his youth movement.[109] The motto he gave it, 'Jugend muß von Jugend geführt werden', already points to its self-contained nature, for it meant that youngsters were given their ideological training by people not much older than themselves.[110] The enthusiasm of these younger *Führer* often contrasted starkly with schoolteachers' dutiful but unenthusiastic mouthing of Nazi doctrine and in practice this meant that the younger generation was increasingly cut off from influences beyond its own circle.[111] Hitler himself stated: '*Die Jugend hat ihren Staat für sich*; sie steht dem Erwachsenen in einer gewissen geschlossenen Solidarität gegenüber, und dies ist selbstverständlich'.[112] Von Schirach, too, commented on the particularly fortunate position of those who had never known any political regime but Nazism when he described the 10-year-olds in the Jungvolk:

Er [der Jungvolkjunge] wuchs als Nationalsozialist auf. Er mußte sich nicht mit anderen Ideen abplagen und die inneren Kämpfe des Zweifelns durchmachen, die der Hitlerjunge ertragen mußte, bis er seinen Weg zu unserer Fahne fand. Er ist gleichsam als Nationalsozialist geboren, denn als er in das Jungvolkalter trat und zum Jungenleben erwachte, gab es in Deutschland nichts anderes mehr als Adolf Hitler und Nationalsozialismus.[113]

Ironically, von Schirach looks at these 'Jungvolkjungen' and exclaims 'So marschiert ein freier Mensch'.[114] This is the ultimate freedom envisaged by the Nazi state; the freedom of knowing no alternative. It is the closed system evoked by Hitler's

---

[108] See document of 23 Dec. 1933 in Fricke-Finkelnburg, *Nationalsozialismus und Schule*, 242–3.

[109] *Zehn Millionen Kinder*, 145.

[110] Von Schirach clearly attributed great importance to the 'Prinzip der Selbstführung': see *Hitler-Jugend*, 57–65.

[111] Mann, *Zehn Millionen Kinder*, 147.

[112] Quoted in von Schirach, *Hitler-Jugend*, 55.   [113] Ibid. 83.   [114] Ibid. 84.

(unconsciously?) more honest Reichenberg speech quoted above: 'Und sie werden nicht mehr frei, ihr ganzes Leben'.

Once the school system had been redesigned along Nazi lines it already formed a substantial step in this direction. But adapting this pre-existing model took time and, even when it was running at its smoothest, it still allowed room for indifference, even muted dissent from traditional teachers. The Hitler Youth on the other hand was a purpose-designed organization and von Schirach was quick to see to it that it was the only viable 'option' for youngsters of the day. Peukert notes that by the end of 1933 all youth organizations other than Catholic ones had either been banned or *gleichgeschaltet*.[115] The 'Gesetz über die Hitlerjugend vom 1. Dezember 1936' already appeared to make membership of the organization compulsory and, as Mann points out, even if this decree was not legally binding, its wording was forceful enough to have the desired effect; meanwhile, whilst maintaining the aura of voluntary service around the Hitler Youth, the Nazi regime did all it could to undermine the status of alternative associations.[116] This strategy seems to have been effective, since from 1937 onwards von Schirach was claiming that over 90 per cent of German youth was incorporated in the Hitler Youth.[117] Nor was this more underhand form of law enforcement necessary for long; on 25 March 1939 two ancillary orders to the Hitler Youth Law made membership a legal requirement.[118]

From its very inception the Hitler Youth invested youngsters with a sense of importance such as they had never had before. They were constantly being reminded of their role in the future of Germany;[119] the uniform, songs, rituals, and mottoes of the movement gave them a welcome sense of belonging to a greater and more powerful whole;[120] and the sense of invincibility this engendered was reinforced by von Schirach's official 'Marsch der Hitler-Jugend' whose chorus ran 'Vorwärts! Vorwärts! schmettern die hellen Fanfaren | Vorwärts! Vorwärts! Jugend kennt keine

[115] *Inside Nazi Germany*, 150.   [116] Mann, *Zehn Millionen Kinder*, 148–9.
[117] Grunberger, *Social History of the Third Reich*, 275.
[118] Peukert, *Inside Nazi Germany*, 150–1.
[119] Hermann Graml, 'Integration und Entfremdung: Inanspruchnahme durch Staatsjugend und Dienstpflicht', in Benz and Benz (eds.), *Sozialisation und Traumatisierung*, 75–6.   [120] Grunberger, *Social History of the Third Reich*, 277.

Gefahren!' The steady progression through the ranks of the organization, with *rites de passage* marked by impressive pagan ceremonies, also gave the youngsters a sense of purpose and importance. Especially in the period before membership became compulsory, the organization seems to have exercised the attraction of a privileged elite. König notes of September 1938: 'Noch war es nicht Zwang, sondern eine Ehre, in diesen Bund [Bund deutscher Mädel] aufgenommen zu werden, die Mädchen rissen sich darum, man sprach von Rangabzeichen, Knoten und Schnürchen.'[121]

The activities of the Hitler Youth organization varied throughout the course of the Third Reich. Initially 'Dienst' consisted mainly of the ideological training and 'körperliche Ertüchtigung' that filled the 'Staatsjugendtag' and the Wednesday 'Heimabend'.[122] The latter in particular has an innocuous, cosy ring emphasized by von Schirach's own description of its function: 'Der Heimabend soll die Bindung des Kameraden zum Kameraden herstellen und darf deshalb kein Massenabend sein . . . Es wird gesungen, gelesen und gesprochen, und an das Gelesene und Gesprochene schließt sich eine Aussprache an, an der jeder beteiligt werden soll.'[123] This sounds like a case of Hitler's youth learning by following its own 'Spieltriebe' but, as with most statements by the Nazi leadership, the underlying compulsion is not long in making itself felt; von Schirach continues: 'Der Heimabend ist ein Teil des Dienstes der HJ., darum darf seine Form nie so gelockert werden, daß der Gedanke des Dienstes dabei verloren geht.'[124]

Increasingly however, 'Dienst' embraced a wider spectrum and took on less congenial forms. Youngsters were used to collect money for the 'Winterhilfswerk' and recyclable waste for the war effort;[125] the 'körperliche Ertüchtigung' became more overtly militaristic, with the Hitler Youth being sent off to

[121] *Die verpaßte Chance*, 136.
[122] See Fricke-Finkelnburg, *Nationalsozialismus und Schule*, 238–9 for a discussion of the reasons behind the 'Staatsjugendtag'. For documents relating to the inception and demise of the day, ibid. 243–5 and 251. For a description of the farcical effects it had on the school timetable see Mann, *Zehn Millionen Kinder*, 58–9.
[123] *Hitler-Jugend*, 106.   [124] Ibid. 106.
[125] Rust's decree of 16 Feb. 1940 stressed the importance of youngsters participating in the collections of 'Altmaterialien'. See Fricke-Finkelnburg, *Nationalsozialismus und Schule*, 235–6.

'Wehrertüchtigungslager' rather than the camps von Schirach had once described as 'der schönste Traum einer Jugend'.[126] With the outbreak of war and extensive bombing raids on German cities, 'Dienst' took two main forms; grammar school pupils were intended to spend the duration of the war in 'Kinderlandverschickung' (KLV) camps, well away from the most vulnerable areas of Germany, while those who were not evacuated were left to contribute what they could to the home front. But the KLV programme was not intended simply to ensure youngsters' physical safety; once removed from the influence of home it was thought that they could be subjected ever more intensely to Nazi ideology.[127] Koch suggests that this was something of a forlorn hope since the ideological content of the Nazi era was not intellectually rich enough to impress itself very deeply on the children.[128] But there are accounts that suggest otherwise; Jost Hermand points to the decline of his teacher's influence over the boys in his charge during the KLV programme and the boys' progressive convergence with Hitler's ideals:

Den meisten Jungen machte der Sport einen Heidenspaß. Viele warteten den ganzen Vormittag ungeduldig darauf, nachmittags auf den Hof hinter der Schule zu laufen und mit dem Völkerball zu beginnen, bei dem die schwächeren Jungen von den wurfgewaltigen Sportassen wie die Hasen übers Feld gejagt wurden. Dieses Herumtoben–verbunden mit der ewigen Marschiererei–trug im Laufe der Zeit zu einer merklichen Verrohung vieler Jungen bei. Selbst Dr. Fette konnte dem, obwohl er es durch vermehrte Hausaufgaben, naturkundliche Exkursionen und Lektüreempfehlungen zu unterbinden suchte, keinen effektiven Widerstand entgegensetzen. Angesehen war unter den meisten Jungen nur derjenige, der ein großes Maul hatte, über die ersten Ansätze zu einem Bizeps verfügte, sich mit Brachialgewalt durchsetzen konnte und die schwächeren Jungen unbarmherzig tyrannisierte, kurz: der 'flink wie ein Windhund, zäh wie Leder und hart wie Kruppstahl' war, wie es in der Sprache der Hitler-Jugend hieß.[129]

This passage certainly does not suggest any deep intellectual engagement with Nazi philosophy, but that is the whole point; the boys are not engaging with an ideology, they are living it in

---

[126] *Hitler-Jugend*, 107.   [127] Koch, *Hitler Youth*, 241.   [128] Ibid. 242.
[129] *Als Pimpf in Polen: Erweiterte Kinderlandverschickung 1940–1945* (Frankfurt, 1993), 37–8.

the unconscious manner of young animals. Once alienated from the values of home and school they become increasingly mindless, imbued with an ideology that they are not expected to understand but simply to absorb.

Those members of the Hitler Youth who were not evacuated to KLV camps were left to contribute what they could to the home front, and even to the armed combat itself, where they sometimes distinguished themselves by far greater fanaticism than that of their adult comrades.[130] By this time, as Koch points out, Hitler Youth activities had been given a new sense of purpose, with activity taking the place of mere ideological training and confirming the youth of Hitler's Germany in its belief that it had a historic mission to fulfil.[131] For all von Schirach's comments in 1934 that 'Die HJ. will die deutsche Jugend nicht für den Krieg, sondern für den Frieden mobilisieren',[132] the youngsters' training in self-sacrifice seems really to have been building towards this ultimate end of war; it is therefore hardly surprising that, to quote Koch's chilling phrase, the Hitler Youth 'frequently fought to the last child'.[133]

In the Hitler Youth the Nazis created the nearest thing possible to a closed system. It played with deadly psychological accuracy on the group instincts of youth: its desire to test its strength and powers of endurance, and its capacity for idealism and self-sacrifice. It also created a generational conflict of a kind not seen before: a conflict based on the widespread assumption, articulated by von Schirach, '*daß die Jugend in einem höheren Sinne immer recht hat, weil sie das neue Leben trägt*'.[134] This was a reversal of the traditional generation conflict, for the youngsters were more fanatical about the new ideology than the older generation and thus looked down on their elders.[135] To some extent, then, the youth of the time was cut off from the alternative political and social experiences of the older generation. Given the situation at school and in the Hitler Youth as sketched above, there was little chance of youngsters questioning the ideals imposed upon them; Georg Hensel refers to his youth in the Third Reich as growing up with a 'Sack überm Kopf', noting astutely with hindsight: 'Die Schule war weniger nationalsozialistisch durch das, was sie lehrte, als

---

[130] Koch, *Hitler Youth*, 233–50.   [131] Ibid. 233.   [132] *Hitler-Jugend*, 139.
[133] *Hitler Youth*, 249.   [134] *Hitler-Jugend*, 174.
[135] Koch, *Hitler Youth*, 131; Grunberger, *Social History of the Third Reich*, 290.

durch das, was sie nicht lehrte. Was uns aus politischen Gründen vorenthalten wurde, das konnten wir nicht wissen'.[136] He adds, significantly: 'Wir kannten nur die Welt, in der wir lebten, und wir hielten sie für normal'.[137] Like Maisie in the sexual sphere, children brought up in this way, with only the most minimal chances of acquiring an alternative value system, had a perverted conception of political normality. The main aim of upbringing under the Third Reich was to keep the children in ignorance of any kind of political, social, or moral alternative to the ideals with which they were being confronted. It is no accident that a document of 1935 describes the task of senior schools as educating 'den körperlich, *charakterlich* und geistig besonders gut veranlagten Teil der deutschen Jugend', for the order in which the adjectives appear clearly suggest the qualities that were most important to the Nazi state.[138] Youngsters were not to be encouraged to gain the critical faculties required to see through the regime.

This tacit emphasis on ignorance contains a fascinating paradox when Nazi education is seen as a perversion of the Romantic myth of childhood. In the Romantic era academic ignorance was seen as virtually tantamount to innocence because the untrained child was apparently a free spirit. However, Hitler needed to keep children in ignorance because he feared that they might grow up with the critical intelligence required to see through his manipulations and barbarous policies. By appealing to their idealism in the service of their amoral instincts, he was apparently able to hypnotize a generation, moulding them into unthinking beings, like the concentration camp guard in Peter Weiss's *Die Ermittlung* who says: 'Jedes dritte Wort in unserer Schulzeit | handelte doch von denen | die an allem schuld waren | und die ausgemerzt werden mußten . . . Uns wurde das Denken abgenommen | Das taten ja andere für uns'.[139] Like Maisie, they are corrupted rather than guilty because their whole conception of normality has been perverted. Hildegard Adler suggests this when she says that those who were children during the Nazi era tend to feel 'mitschuldig' because of their identification with the events of the time, for 'niemand kann sich einer allgemeinen Luftverpestung

[136] *Sack überm Kopf*, 115.   [137] Ibid. 117.
[138] Fricke-Finkelnburg, *Nationalsozialismus und Schule*, 93.
[139] *Die Ermittlung*, in *Werke*, 6 vols. (Frankfurt, 1991), v. 119–20.

entziehen'.[140] But while we might agree that children's perceptions are inevitably affected by their environment, it seems
impossible to talk in absolute terms like guilt and innocence when
children have been forced to measure themselves against a perverted normality. All we can say is that ignorance, rather than
knowledge, is the cause of these children's fall, but as ever the fall
is prepared for them by adults.

'DIE BANALITÄT DES BÖSEN'?: CHRISTA WOLF'S
KINDHEITSMUSTER

With the benefit of hindsight we may find it difficult to imagine
how imperceptibly children were corrupted under the Nazi
regime; *Kindheitsmuster* is one of the clearest demonstrations of
this insidious process. Although Wolf credits especially the younger
Nelly with a kind of intuitive moral sense, she does not shy from
showing the girl's progressive and eventually complete acceptance of Nazi ideals as they are transmitted to her by school and the
youth movement. Her home environment offers some possibility
of cutting through the 'Sack überm Kopf', for while her parents
acquiesce in the Nazi regime, they are by no means fervent sup-
porters of it; indeed, by the standards we considered in the previous section, her mother is occasionally quite outspoken in her
opposition, and it is only against her 'erklärten Widerstand' that
Nelly becomes a 'Führerinanwärterin' (*Kindheitsmuster*, 285) in the
youth movement.[141] But even before this point there is a stark example of Charlotte's nonconformism when she greets the post-
man bringing her husband's call-up papers with the exclamation:
'Ich scheiß auf euren Führer!' (p. 244). This is a particularly violent
expression given that on the whole the Führer myth survived
even the darkest days in Germany intact;[142] failures of the regime
were generally attributed to his underlings who were assumed to
be acting without his knowledge or consent.[143] The fact that Nelly

[140] 'Scham und Schuld: Barrieren des Erinnerns in Christa Wolfs und Peter
Härtlings Kindheitsmustern und im psychoanalytischen Prozeß', *Deutschunterricht*,
35/5 (1983), 12.
[141] For a discussion of the Jordans' passive compromises with the Nazi regime, see
Robert K. Shirer, *Difficulties of Saying 'I': The Narrator as Protagonist in Christa Wolf's
'Kindheitsmuster' and Uwe Johnson's Jahrestage'* (New York, 1988), 148–53.
[142] Grunberger, *Social History of the Third Reich*, 39–40 and 88–9.
[143] Peukert, *Inside the Third Reich*, 72–3.

questions her mother's use of the possessive ('Warum sagt sie euern? dachte Nelly. Euern Führer?', p. 244) suggests that she has suddenly realized there are two possible responses to Hitler, one represented by her mother, one by forces outside her family, but her condemnatory thought 'Die Mutter läßt also den Führer im Stich' (p. 247) shows that in any conflict between family and the Nazi regime the 10-year-old's allegiance is already established.[144] For, while Nelly's attempt at self-reassurance sound suspiciously as though she is simply parroting all-too-familiar propaganda ('Der Führer weiß, was er tut. Jetzt muß jeder Deutsche tapfer sein', p. 247), the child is not merely dutifully mouthing propaganda. As Shirer suggests, she is also expressing inner conviction.[145] Even before she starts school or sees the Führer in the flesh, Nelly feels an allegiance to him that is described in almost erotic terms: 'Der Führer war ein süßer Druck in der Magengegend und ein süßer Klumpen in der Kehle, die sie freiräuspern mußte, um mit allen laut nach ihm, dem Führer, zu rufen, wie es ein patrouillierender Lautsprecherwagen dringlich forderte' (p. 73). This passage contains an interesting mixture of personal passion ('süßer Druck', 'süßer Klumpen') and external compulsion ('ein patrouillierender Lautsprecherwagen'). Nelly's allegiance to Hitler suggests that she is simply transferring the values she has learnt from her home to her political world; she has learned to equate 'Gehorchen und Geliebtwerden' (p. 30) in her family and so feels compelled to stay in the crowd which gives her the security of belonging to a larger and more significant whole. She does not even resent it when Hitler does not finally appear, for 'Um wie vieles schöner und besser war es doch, mit allen zusammen erregt an der Straße zu stehn, als allein im Laden Mehl und Zucker abzuwiegen' (p. 74).

Nelly's need for approval and security at a level beyond the domestic thus overrides her family loyalties, and this is consistent with what was said in the previous section about the public domain having a higher status in the child's eyes than the family. But Nelly's allegiance to Hitler is not simply a matter of seduction by a greater whole; there is also an underlying element of

---

[144] Shirer instances this episode as proof of the Jordan family's doubts about the Nazi regime but points out that the Jordan parents are too fearful and concerned with their own social integration to give Nelly any indication that her own doubts are justified (*Difficulties of Saying 'I'*, 173 and 157–8).

[145] Ibid. 173.

compulsion engendered by vague fears about the consequences of not belonging. Nelly can see from her father's reaction that her mother's outspokenness could be dangerous ('Mädel! Du redest uns um Kopf und Kragen!', p. 244) and, while the child does not apparently draw any very clear inferences from this, the fact that the statement has remained in the narrator's memory suggests that subconsciously it made an indelible impression on her.

Nelly's need to please those in authority over her as created by her family is easily directed into the paths of Nazi ideology by her teacher Herr Warsinski, who is a committed Nazi. This doctrine is conveyed not only in formal lessons but even in the most trivial incidents:

Herr Warsinski merkt alles. Einmal will er wissen, wer sich morgens den Oberkörper eiskalt wäscht, um sich abzuhärten, wie es sich für ein deutsches Mädel gehört. Nelly ist nicht unter denen, die stolz die Hand heben können, und wird einzeln getadelt: Was, auch du nicht? Das enttäuscht mich aber, und zwar besonders von dir. Der sportlich erzogene Mensch beider Geschlechter ist der Staatsbürger der Zukunft. Adolf Hitler. (p. 152)

Nelly's mother shows scant concern for her daughter's distress over this incident: she is indifferent to the ideals propagated by Herr Warsinski, and 'muß sich Gedanken machen über den Wahrheitsfimmel ihrer Tochter' (p. 152). As Nelly grows up and joins the BdM, this generational conflict is heightened, for the BdM comes to complement or even replace an inadequate home atmosphere, just as the 'Jungvolk' does in Peter Härtling's *Nachgetragene Liebe* (1980). Härtling notes that he rejected his mother's reproaches about the company he was keeping thus: 'Sie und Vater waren nicht unschuldig, daß ich mich "solchen" Kerlen anschloß, denn bei denen wußte ich, woran ich war. Die trugen stolz die Uniformen des Jungvolks, bereiteten sich auf ein Heldenleben vor und hofften, noch als Freiwillige "ins Feld ziehen" zu können.'[146]

For Nelly, as for the young Härtling, the youth organization guarantees 'Kameradschaft' and a 'gehobenes Dasein' (p. 278) which are far removed from her mundane life as a grocer's daughter. The BdM's appeal for her is evident: it is not so much a

---

[146] *Nachgetragene Liebe* (Frankfurt, 1988), 29.

question of finding acceptance amongst her peer group, for she never ceases 'sich unter den anderen fremd zu fühlen' rather, it is the joy of being able to strive for a set of higher ideals, even (indeed particularly) when the effort to do so is painful or unpleasant. She desperately wants to be the 'Mensch . . . den Micky [her group leader] aus ihr machen wollte', even when this means taking part in a detested 'Geländemarsch' on the day her mother is discharged from hospital after a serious operation. The child regards it as self-evident that she should go on the march 'ungeachtet der Verstimmung, die sie dadurch verschuldete' (p. 279) because only thus can she overcome the weaker aspect of her own self: by raising self-denial to the level of a virtue, as suggested by the Annacker poem 'Vom Ich zum Wir' cited later (p. 281), the youth organizations appealed to the child's natural idealism. Nelly's increasing commitment to the regime and her mother's opposition to it provide us with a number of examples of the kind of reversed generational conflict we saw in the previous section:

Wochenlang tragen sie alle in der Schule die Hitler-Jugend-Uniform, und das, wie Charlotte nörgelt, in Zeiten, da es keine Bezugsscheine für BDM-Blusen gibt und es schier unmöglich ist, eine der zwei weißen Blusen, die Nelly besitzt, immer einsatzbereit zu haben. Nelly findet es nicht übertrieben, daß man die Treue zum Führer auch äußerlich zeigt. Charlotte meint, man solle Treue nicht durch Blusen zeigen müssen. Nelly schmerzt es, wenn die Mutter über heilige Gegenstände vom Standpunkt ihrer Waschküche aus urteilt. (p. 405)

It is natural that children brought up at this time should feel a more passionate attachment to the ideals of the Nazi era than their parents, for this is their normality and they know no other. Their parents on the other hand have other social and political experiences and therefore different yardsticks against which to measure events. Nelly too belongs to the generation with a 'Sack überm Kopf': this is evident both from her passionate commitment to Nazi ideals and from her numbed response to the German capitulation. She hears of Hitler's death with a sense of incredulity at her own survival: 'Ein neuer Gedanke: Das Ende der Welt mußte nicht den eigenen Tod bedeuten' (p. 468), and considers a former concentration camp inmate 'der sich offen selbst bezichtigte, Kommunist zu sein' (p. 482) with a kind of fascinated horror. By this point she has been so thoroughly indoctrinated that any form of alternative value system comes as an immense shock, notwithstanding the occasional uneasy murmurs in her family; it is no wonder that the adult narrator comments of her 'Je näher sie dir in der Zeit rückt, um so fremder wird sie dir' (p. 309), for the more the child is subjected to the influence of the school and youth organizations, the fewer her chances of escaping with her moral sense intact. Nelly's realization 'sie habe zwölf Jahre lang, anscheinend ohne es zu merken, in einer "Diktatur" gelebt' (p. 574) comes very late and points to the difficulty these children have in establishing a critical distance towards this era. The dissent Nelly hears in her family—usually muted or stifled for fear of reprisals—is not enough seriously to undermine the lessons learned in school and the BdM; her wider environment is such that the child cannot help but be corrupted for it is virtually impossible for her to gain a superior perspective on her situation.

LOST IDENTITIES?: GERT HOFMANN'S *UNSERE EROBERUNG*

Turning now to Gert Hofmann's *Unsere Eroberung*, we are confronted by a narrator who has even less chance than Nelly of gaining this superior perspective on the era into which it has been 'hineingeboren', since the family depicted here has obviously been committed to the National Socialist government.[147] The father owns a 'Peitschenfabrik' and appears to have prospered under the regime before being called up; the mother's bonfires of paperwork and Nazi artefacts after the conquest suggest that there is plenty of incriminating evidence against the family. The narrator's speech reflects his home environment, for he is constantly parroting his parents, whether consciously, as introduced by formulas of the 'wie der Vater sagt' and 'wie die Mutter sagt' variety, or more often unconsciously. Grünzweig suggests that the narrator is caught up in the ideological discourse of his parents to such

---

[147] Some of the narrative implications of Hofmann's use of the child's perspective are discussed in Birgit Krebhenne, 'Kindnahe Erzählperspektive bei Gert Hofmann: Untersuchungen zu "Unsere Eroberung", "Veilchenfeld", "Der Kinoerzähler"' (unpublished MA thesis Göttingen, 1992). The Third Reich context is discussed ibid. 99–118. A further work which appeared too recently to be considered in detail here is Hans-Georg Schede, *Gert Hofmann: Werkmonografie* (Würzburg, 1999). Hofmann's narrative techniques are discussed ibid. 206–74; for *Unsere Eroberung* see ibid. esp. 214–20 and for *Veilchenfeld* ibid. 231–9. Hofmann's treatment of National Socialism is discussed ibid. 275–335.

an extent that it is impossible for him to gain any new 'Erkennt-nisse' into the Nazi regime.[148] He too belongs to the generation with the 'Sack überm Kopf', but he has had even less chance than Hensel or even Nelly of beginning to cut himself out.

This total ignorance of any alternative value system makes the narrator an amoral creature, whose inability to detach itself from the era it has grown up in and its subsequent loss of individual identity is expressed in Hofmann's idiosyncratic use of the pro-noun *wir*.[149] The narrator constantly refers to 'wir' and 'uns', even when the context suggests that only one child is speaking, as in the references to 'unsere Mütze' and 'unser Anzug'. We might ini-tially imagine that this can be explained by the fact that he spends all his time with another boy, 'unser Edgar', but that does not explain the 'unser' in this phrase. It cannot refer to the narrator's mother, who distances herself as much as possible from Edgar. And when the child notes that Edgar lies 'zwischen uns' in bed, to whom does the 'uns' refer here? Since the child is in the 'Ehebett' we could assume that Edgar is between the boy and his mother (though this seems improbable) but even this does not explain the 'wir' of the preceding phrase, 'und in dem grenzenlosen Ehebett unserer Eltern, in das wir uns in dieser Nacht hineinlegen dürfen, schlafen wir, mit unserem Edgar erst zwischen uns' (*Unsere Eroberung*, p. 14). The ambiguities created make it impossible to ascribe much more than a very shadowy presence to this child figure: all we really know is that he is male, since he is sent out to cadge an 'Anzug' and is very embarrassed at the thought of chang-ing into it in front of Frau Henne. The children may be socially integrated as 'die kleinen Imbachs' but nonetheless the sense of a presence rather than a psychologized character may refer us back to the more allegorical/symbolic children of the Romantic era.

The 'wir' narrator and the ambiguities and confusion it implies suggest a tension between an individual and a collective narrative

---

[148] See Walter Grünzweig, 'Die vergebliche Enttrümmerung beschädigter Kinderköpfe: Nationalsozialismus in den Werken Gert Hofmanns', *GSR* 1 (1989), 62.

[149] This problematic pronoun is discussed in Lily Maria von Hartmann, 'Auf der Suche nach dem Autor: Erzählstrukturen im Werk Gert Hofmanns', 108–9 and 119–20; Jochen Hieber, 'Die Schrecken der Welt am Tage Null', 152–3 and Hanno Helbling, '"Unsere" Identität', 154–5: all in Hans Christian Kosler (ed.), *Gert Hofmann: Auskunft für Leser* (Darmstadt and Neuwied, 1987). See also Grünzweig, 'Vergebliche Enttrüm-merung', 58–9.

presence. It is never quite clear how many children we are dealing with and Hofmann's explanatory comment is little help, for his statement 'Hier erzählt ein ganz individuelles Kind, das zwar seine kollektive Vergangenheit hat, seine ganz individuelle Geschichte' does not resolve the linguistic illogicalities noted above.[150] If anything, in this interview Hofmann emphasized the fictitious, *Märchen*-like aspect of the novel, the imaginative element that makes the narrator's story individual. However, while the opening sentence may well recall the *Märchen* style as Hofmann pointed out, it also clearly offers us a group perspective: 'Eines Tages ist unsere kleine Stadt von Norden nach Süden erobert, oder, wie die Mutter sagt, *aufgerollt* und von allen darum herumliegenden Dörfern und Städten abgeschnitten gewesen' (p. 7).[151] Walter Grünzweig suggests that this group can be identified quite precisely since phrases like 'unsere Peitschenfabrik' and 'unser Schlachthof' have a bourgeois, proprietorial ring.[152] Certainly this would tally with the fact that Hitler found his greatest support amongst the middle classes.[153]

This novel is thus informed from the very beginning by a tension between the child's narrative style and a social perspective and it demonstrates that in fact the child experiences history in a similar way to the adult: one of the elements which we might classify as belonging to the child's style, namely the lack of a sense of objective time, is also common to any account of historical events as narrated by those who are directly involved in them without being aware of their later implications. There is no date given for 'unsere Eroberung' (it simply happens 'eines Tages', p. 7): time is measured by the events within the war, the only 'normality' the boy knows.

The fact that war is the child's normality is expressed by a singularly pregnant symbol, his 'Mütze'. This is described with the loathing only a child can evince, but even on those terms the boy's protest seems unusually vehement:

Ein häßliches Ding, schwarz, mit Ohrenklappen, an das wir gar nicht gerne denken und das wir auch immerzu verlieren, aber was nützt uns

---

[150] Hans Christian Kosler, 'Aus den Fenstern noch einmal das Abendland begrüßen: Ein Gespräch mit Gert Hofmann', in id. (ed.), *Gert Hofmann*, 48.

[151] Ibid. 47–8.

[152] 'Gert Hofmann', in *Kritisches Lexikon zur deutschsprachigen Gegenwartsliteratur* (Munich, 1995), 7.

[153] For an account of the development of relations between the NSDAP and the middle classes, see Peukert, *Inside Nazi Germany*, 86–100.

das? Jedes Mal ist sie noch gefunden und uns zurückgegeben worden, weil keiner sie haben will. Als ob wir die Mütze wollten! Wir leiden ja an dieser Mütze, merkt das denn die Mutter nicht? Wir lehnen, aufrichtig angeekelt, die Mütze ja von Herzen ab. (p. 22)

This vehemence can only be explained by the increasing symbolic importance of the cap. It is closely associated with the father who gave it to him a year before 'und sie uns eisern, wie für alle Zeiten, über den Kopf gezogen hat'. The 'eisern' and the all-embracing quality of the 'über den Kopf gezogen' suggest a military helmet rather than a piece of civilian clothing. Moreover, the narrator is expected to wear the cap at all times, for 'ohne Mütze sind wir nicht mehr zu denken' (p. 22). This emphasis seems disproportionate at this early stage, but it is explained later when the cap becomes a symbol of the indoctrination to which the children of this era have been subjected: 'Und wir mit der Mütze auf dem Schädel, sehen ja wie alle Jungen aus. Weil die Mütze mit den dicken Ohrenklappen, die wir am liebsten abreißen möchten, ja von *allen* getragen wird und sie auch unseren Gesichtern den von unserem Vater gewünschten Ausdruck von Stumpfsinn und Beschränktheit gibt' (p. 117).

It is significant that this much-loathed article of clothing should be for the head, the site of sense perception and independent thought. It fits into a pattern of images of the head, both in *Unsere Eroberung* and Hofmann's other works, indicating the extent to which characters have been affected by the war. Frau Imbach's headaches allow her to present herself as a victim, but are actually the perfect excuse for her to avoid seeing the townspeople who appear hostile to her now the war is over, whereas Edgar's 'Geschwür' (p. 97), which the narrator thinks is 'unheilbar' (p. 134), is the mark of his real and irremediable victim status. The narrator does not suffer from headaches: when describing his mother's illness to the 'Schlachthofdirektor' he holds 'unseren eigenen, vorläufig noch gesunden Kopf' (p. 90), but the 'vorläufig' is disturbing. He may not suffer from headaches but he is still expected to wear the cap which symbolizes Nazi indoctrination and, although he keeps taking it off, he finds himself forced to put it on again when he meets up with the townspeople. In the same way he will not be able to cast off the effects of the Third Reich as easily as he may imagine. Grünzweig suggests that he has an adult counterpart in the obsessive Reißer in Hofmann's *Unsere*

Vergeßlichkeit (1987), for Reißer's experiences correspond with those of the 'wir' and he claims 'Daß sein Kopf nach Kriegsende nicht *enttrümmert* worden sei'.[154] Grünzweig points out that in both *Unsere Eroberung* and *Veilchenfeld* Hofmann is exposing the fallacy of Helmut Kohl's idea of the 'Gnade der späten Geburt', for these children have been irrevocably conditioned by their Third Reich upbringing. This also points to the impossibility of any kind of 'Stunde Null', for it is the generation that had unconsciously inherited Hitler's legacy that determines present society.[155]

Like Beckmann's 'Gasmaskenbrille' in Wolfgang Borchert's *Draußen vor der Tür* (1947), the cap, another remnant of the war carried over into peacetime, has a distorting function. But whereas at the beginning of Borchert's play Beckmann seems to have internalized the perception imposed upon him, the 'Mädchen' telling him 'Ich glaube, Sie tragen innerlich auch so eine Gasmaskenbrille',[156] the narrator of *Unsere Eroberung* is still apparently trying to resist the distorted perception imposed on him by the adult world. The child constantly states that he simply wants to 'uns nun ein bißchen *umschauen*' (p. 23) and 'uns alles anschauen' (p. 24), an emphasis on the visual which suggests his unprejudiced, all-encompassing vision; however, his mother's response ('Ohne Mütze, ruft die Mutter und runzelt die Stirn' (p. 23)) indicates that the adults fear these qualities.

Despite the fact that the narrator stuffs his cap into his shopping bag at the earliest opportunity, there is something horribly distorted about the things he witnesses on this day after the conquest and this suggests that to some extent he has in fact internalized the perspective imposed upon him. Hofmann's highly allusive style suggests some of the worst horrors of the Nazi regime but, because everything is filtered through the child's ignorant perspective without any external frame of reference, it is difficult to decide whether we are guilty of over-interpretation or whether the citizens of this provincial town with its 'Peitschenfabrik' and 'Schlachthof' have been guilty of far worse. Both these institutions have obvious connotations of violence and death, but the child's

---

[154] Gert Hofmann, *Unsere Vergeßlichkeit* (Darmstadt and Neuwied, 1987), 116.
[155] 'Vergebliche Enttrümmerung', 65–6.
[156] Wolfgang Borchert, *Das Gesamtwerk* (Hamburg, 1949), 145.

naive and uncomprehending view of them allows us to infer even more sinister implications.

The 'Peitschenfabrik' is no less an object of the child's loathing than the cap. It is referred to as 'unsere uns beschämende Fabrik' (p. 15), whose vile smell of animal corpses had hung over the town every delivery day. The child has never been in the vat room where the corpses are boiled, but nonetheless knows the stench all too well:

Die Gerüche an diesem Tag sind natürlich fürchterlich. Sie sind wahrscheinlich auch der Grund, weshalb sich der Vater immer so stark parfümiert. Als ob das viel helfen würde! Und nicht nur auf ihn, auch auf uns legen sich die Gerüche, und auf die Mutter, die am Dienstag immer ganz weite Kleider trägt. Sogar auf unseren Edgar legen sie sich, der mit unserer Fabrik gar nichts zu tun hat, sowie auf unseren Nachbarn, die an diesem Tag alle Fenster und Türen schließen und fluchend, mit zugehaltenen Nasen, hinter ihren Gardinen verschwinden. (pp. 17–18)

This universal revulsion at the 'Peitschenfabrik' is expanded on later when the boy says:

So daß wir, wenn wir zufällig an der kleinen Peitschenfabrik unseres Vaters vorbeikommen, uns oft nicht nur, wie jedermann, die Nase zuhalten, sondern, weil wir auch nichts sehen wollen, auch die Augen schließen, was unserem Edgar, der zwischen uns geht, natürlich immer auffällt. . . . Jetzt, sagt unser Edgar, wenn wir dann vorüber sind, sind wir vorüber. Danke, Edgar, sagen wir und öffnen unsere Augen (Ohren, Mund, Nase, Kopf) wieder. Unser Edgar, der weiß, daß wir den Anblick, Lärm, Geruch, ja *den Gedanken des Bottichraums* nicht ertragen. (p. 147)

'Unser Edgar' is a little older than the 'wir' and is the son of one of their father's workers. Edgar's father appears to have opposed the Nazi regime: his 'verbotene Witze' have resulted in his being posted to a 'Strafkompanie' and he is missing, presumed dead (p. 64). Edgar therefore represents the narrator's only means of gaining an alternative world-view from that of its family. They know that Edgar is not liked by their own father because of his dark allusions to sinister events during the Nazi era and his ominous comments about the Imbach family's own future fate (pp. 111–14) and, while Edgar's role is not necessarily to enlighten the narrator (let alone the reader), he does ask uncomfortable questions that force the narrator to reflect on his family's past. He prompts the narrator's imaginings about the 'Vaterverbrechen' and the 'Tschechengrab' (pp. 146–51) which are so vivid that it makes it difficult to decide what he actually knows about the factory and what he has made up. However, the fact that the narrator represses the very 'Gedanken des Bottichraums' makes it clear that there is a grim mystery attached to the place and that the child is practising a strategy common to many German adults under the Third Reich: a refusal to see, hear, or even think about anything unpleasant. This means either that the child is implicated unwittingly in adult guilt or that the adults are being exculpated because they are as ignorant as the children, an ambiguity which Hofmann exploits to the full in the 'Schlachthof' episode.

The 'Schlachthof' is perhaps the most sinister feature of the grim landscape the narrator tours. It is described so as to recall a concentration camp, for it is 'zwischen unserem Gaswerk und Wundenplan', and 'viel größer, als man denkt', a lonely spot far away from the town, 'von Wäldern umgeben' (p. 48) with 'zwei, allerdings sehr breite Tore' (p. 49) and 'die beiden, wie Wahrzeichen emporgereckten Schornsteine' (p. 50). However, although it seems well hidden, the narrator notes 'Dabei ist unser Schlachthof, weiß man, daß er hier ist, gar nicht zu übersehen' (p. 48), and this again points to denial strategies. Further, there are sinister implications to his repetition of local gossip:

Doch hat unser Schlachthof, Gott weiß warum, eben immer wieder Leute in sich hineingezogen, er ist dafür bekannt. Ist bei uns jemand vermißt oder verschwunden, wird zuerst auf dem Schlachthof gesucht. Meist sind es fremde Arbeitskräfte, also Tschechen, die sich hier verkriechen. Aber auch Scheckfälscher, Selbstmörder, uneheliche Väter, Fahnenflüchtige und aussichtslos Verliebte sind, wie uns die Mutter sagt, hier schon gefunden worden. Wenn man ihn einmal gründlich durchkämmen würde, würde man seine Wunder erleben. (pp. 50–1)

Hofmann's skill lies in his refusal to move beyond the literal landscape familiar to the child, whilst yet imbuing it with these sinister implications. The agitation of the 'Schlachthofdirektor' when he first finds the children on his property could be explained on a very literal level: he is annoyed that they are trespassing, and the way he bullies his subordinate might simply reflect how angry he is that the place has not been cleaned up properly. And yet when he asks 'Und was habt ihr gesehen' (p. 67) and quickly shuts the door we suspect that he has something to hide. He overreacts badly when he sees the pool of unidentified 'dunkle Flüssigkeit' (p. 71) his subordinate had promised to clean up, and this makes him look guilty and furtive: not only does he tell Müller 'So etwas, wenn es jemand sieht, macht den denkbar schlechtesten Eindruck' (p. 74) but even the child perceives how important this is to him: 'Und gesehen haben wir, bis auf die Lache, viel weniger als Sie wahrscheinlich glauben' (p. 76). In fact, the only other thing they have seen is a few 'schemenhaft herumliegende Gegenstände, die wir für vergessene oder übersehene Körper (Tierkörper) halten' (p. 67). The sly parenthesis suggests that at this moment the narrative 'wir' is made up of the child narrator and his creator,[157] who is playing with and indeed frustrating his reader's attempts at a symbolic reading. Hofmann's grim joke at his reader's expense certainly allows for the idea of the abattoir symbolizing a concentration camp, but it is not clear whether it has actually been used as such.

The 'Schlachthof' achieves its greatest symbolic significance in an episode related in flashback, when the narrator describes how he had taken his piano lessons there whilst his music school was being used as a hospital. The narrator comments on this almost blasphemous juxtaposition of death and culture as follows:

Gewiß, die Leute waren damals verwirrt, und das Chaos war allgemein, aber trotzdem, trotzdem! Uns mit unserem Klavier in den Schlachthof zu schicken, ob das richtig gewesen ist? Wenn man bedenkt—wieder wird an den Kopf gegriffen, wieder wird daran geklopft–, daß es kunstliebende und gutherzige und kluge und angeblich *menschliche* Menschen waren, die auf den Gedanken kamen, unsere Stunden hierher zu verlegen! Natürlich haben wir uns oft gefragt, was haben sie sich dabei gedacht, und lange keine Antwort gefunden. Bis wir kürzlich darauf gekommen sind, daß sie sich wahrscheinlich gar nichts dabei gedacht haben, sondern daß sie auf ihren Einfall, uns den Schlachthof zu erschließen, auch noch stolz gewesen sind. Und wir? Ach, wir waren ja Kinder! (p. 55)

The school's attempts to make this situation seem normal could refer to the way Nazi indoctrination was passed off as part of the normal curriculum. Moreover, given that the Holocaust was at least partly motivated by a perverted belief in the supremacy of

---

[157] This possibility is highlighted by von Hartmann 'Auf der Suche', 108–9 and 119–20, and Hieber, 'Schrecken', 152–3.

German culture and a desire to eliminate its non-Aryan influences, there is a dreadful appropriateness to this conflation of culture and death. Again, the child is a victim of adult actions but, although he emphasizes his childhood in the spirit of 'ours not to reason why', his obedience does not preclude an *awareness* of the abattoir's true purpose: the evidence of these activities may be curtained off, but the child comments '(Als ob wir nicht wüßten, *was* von dem Vorhang verdeckt wird, und beim Musizieren nun nicht immerzu an *das darunter* dächten!)' (p. 56). He even claims he can smell the 'Todesgeruch', scornfully rejecting his music teacher's suggestion that someone has told him what it smells of with the words 'Niemand, wir riechen es von alleine' (p. 58).

But the flashback structure of this episode makes it problematic, for the reader does not witness it directly: it is presented in an extended internal monologue and this has led more than one critic to doubt that it actually happened. Kosler highlights the narrator's own suggestion that he may have imagined the scene between the slaughterer and the piano teacher (p. 63) and suggests that the reader might take this as a warning as to the plausibility of the interrogation scene at the 'Schlachthof'.[158] This reading would be consistent with Hofmann's own commentary on the opening sentence of *Unsere Eroberung*: 'Hier habt ihr es mit einem Werk der Phantasie zu tun, mit etwas, wie man im Märchen sagt, "hinter den Bergen bei den sieben Zwergen" '.[159] But in a sense it is irrelevant to ask whether the episode really happened: its symbolic truth remains. The narrator communicates the truth about the Nazi era in two very different ways: first through his sense perceptions and secondly through his vivid imagination. The first can to some extent be repressed, whether by the adults (suggested by the 'Mütze') or by his own volition, as when he walks past the factory. Thus while his ignorance is partly enforced by adults, it is also a result of his own determination and this denial implies some form of guilt rather than mere corruption. However, his imagination is less easy to control and in the case of the piano lessons can present us with images which seem surreal only because they

---

[158] 'Das fremde Kunstwerk: Anmerkungen zu einem Artisten', in Kosler (ed.), *Gert Hofmann*, 87–8. See also Krebhenne, 'Kindnahe Erzählperspektive', 60–1. Krebhenne contends that Hofmann is thematizing the possibility that everything the children claim to have witnessed could simply be 'vorgestellt'.

[159] Kosler, 'Aus den Fenstern noch einmal das Abendland begrüßen', 47–8.

encapsulate the essence of a shocking truth in such a starkly symbolic form.

The child's imagination can thus compensate for his ignorance[160] and so fulfils a moral function. This becomes obvious when Edgar insists that the narrator should atone for his father's crimes, for at this point the narrator's imaginings result not from the spontaneous fancy of the piano lessons but from a conscious effort leading to moral awareness:

Kurz und gut: Es ist des Vaters wegen, der niemals bestraft worden ist, während Edgars Vater und Edgars Mutter verschüttet und verschollen sind. . . . Obwohl wir uns an nichts erinnern, auch gar nicht erinnern können, weil wir die Drohung ja nicht gehört, den Bottichraum nie betreten haben. Trotzdem wissen wir, daß unser Edgar recht hat und Schmerzen nötig sind, und versuchen, uns das Vaterverbrechen genau vorzustellen. (p. 150)

These glimmerings of moral awareness suggest that Grünzweig is unduly pessimistic to think that the narrator is unable to gain any new 'Erkenntnisse'.[161] This interpretation ignores moments of independent moral thought which occur before the 'Blutritual', for example:

Wie oft haben wir uns nicht gefragt, wie der Vater in so einen Raum Menschen schicken und rühren lassen kann, die natürlich, weil sie noch jung, zum Teil kaum aus der Schule sind, viel gähnen und immer schläfrig sind und vom Vater nie genug Essen, Auslauf, frische Luft bekommen, . . . während wir gut ausgeschlafen in die Schule gehen. (p. 147)

While it is true that the narrator tries to suppress such concerns, this passage nonetheless shows the spark of positive moral potential Hofmann sees even in apparently amoral children.

However, *Unsere Eroberung* presents a rather pessimistic view of the narrator's future prospects. The idea that the sins of the father have been visited on the son(s) is developed when old Frau Henne enquires about the wound with the ambiguous 'Da seid ihr wohl gefallen' (p. 183) and when Edgar tells the actor 'Sie sind gefallen' (p. 237), a biblical resonance which is not lost on the reader: even

[160] See Peter Urban-Halle, 'Schauplatz Menschenkopf: Wahrheit und Wirklichkeit bei Gert Hofmann', in Kosler (ed.), *Gert Hofmann*, 96. Also Grünzweig, 'Vergebliche Enttrümmerung', 62.   [161] 'Vergebliche Enttrümmerung', 62.

if the child narrator has not committed any evil action, his whole life will be conditioned by what he has experienced during the Third Reich. That there cannot be any 'Stunde Null' is clear from the opening of chapter 2:

Dieses Zischen, wie man es in der nun stillgelegten kleinen Peitschen-fabrik unseres Vaters bis vor kurzem noch ab und zu gehört hat, folgt uns in den Morgen hinein. Ab und zu zucken wir also zusammen, ducken uns wahrscheinlich auch. Eigenartig, denn *wir* haben eine Peitsche im Ernst nie zischen hören, jedenfalls nicht gegen uns. Langsam, zwischen Dämmerung und Tag, schälen wir uns aus den Betten der Eltern und gehen in unser Zimmer zurück. . . . Und sehen: Ein neuer Tag. Und von diesem Tag soll hier die Rede sein, bis in seine Nacht hinein. Wir sehen: Ein paar Wolken, frischgetüncht, stehen in unserem Himmel, der gleich hinter dem Apfelbaum beginnt, ein paar Vögel sind wieder im Garten und zirpen aus den Büschen dünn hervor, und auch die Luft in unseren Gassen wird über Nacht erneuert worden sein. (p. 21)

There are apparent signs of renewal here; indeed, some of the elements in this description echo the Garden of Eden. But as ever Hofmann's suggestive details are ambiguous, for they include principally the 'Apfelbaum' and a 'Zischen' which evokes the ser-pent. And other details which suggest new beginnings are also undermined: the new 'Morgen' is still haunted by the 'Zischen'; the image of the child peeling himself out of bed suggests new life, but he is emerging from his *parents'* bed; the birdsong is 'dünn'. The narrator constantly tries to emphasize the sense of a new beginning after the war, but he realizes later that his efforts are in vain: 'Und möchten die Einmaligkeit des ersten Tages nach unserer Eroberung mit Worten oder Gedanken, die ja auch bloß Worte sind, gern beweisen, können es aber nicht' (p. 156).

The cap is not the only legacy of war that the child is forced to wear: Herr Henne's suit also has symbolic importance for, although the narrator refers to it as his 'neuer Anzug' (p. 188), it is no such thing: the secondhand suit does not even fit him properly, and worse, 'Kaum daß wir bei den Arkaden sind, fangen wir an, Herrn Henne in dem Anzug auch zu riechen' (p. 191). Given the child's anxiety about smells earlier in the novel when the all-pervasive stench from the 'Peitschenfabrik' apparently sym-bolizes collective guilt (p. 21), this reference to smell is clearly sig-nificant. Again the child symbolizes a potential new beginning but any fresh start or 'Stunde Null' is problematic because it is the responsibility of the young–who, as *Unsere Eroberung* makes clear, have been made in the Nazi image.

Superficial changes like the 'new' suit apparently satirize the post-war *Entnazifizierung* programme, which, as in the mother's activities in *Unsere Eroberung,* is often presented as simply disposing of the external emblems of Nazism and resuming 'normal' life as rapidly as possible. In Margarete Jehn's short story *Niemands Land,* two girls watch as the adults dispose of the evidence of the Nazi era:

> Damit treten sie an den Brunnenrand und werfen alles hinunter, Hitlerbilder und Fotografien von Stukas und Reichsparteitagen, und Fotos von ihren Kindern in HJ- und BDM-Uniformen, Parteiabzeichen und Ritterkreuze. Sie werfen das einfach in den tiefen Brunnen, und nun können sie so tun, als wäre nichts gewesen.[162]

In this episode the adults are symbolically poisoning the very source of life, and this casts doubt on any possibility of new beginnings. Similarly, in *Unsere Eroberung* the apparently epoch-making day does not see much real change. Still wearing the ill-fitting suit, the narrator sets off,

> statt in Richtung Hindenburgallee in Richtung Adolf-Hitler-Straße, welche, wie die Mutter sagt, nun sicher bald einen neuen Namen bekommt. . . . Tatsache ist, wir wissen nicht, wie wir uns in dem neuen Anzug fühlen, ehe wir uns darin gesehen haben. So daß wir uns in dem Anzug, ehe wir zur Kirche gehen, in den großen Schaufenstern in der Adolf-Hitler-Straße, die den Krieg wunderbarerweise heil überstanden haben, erst ein wenig studieren müssen. (p. 189)

This clearly suggests that the boy's perceptions, both of himself and external reality, have been shaped by the Hitler era. He is the innocent (in the sense of ignorant) accomplice of a pernicious era and, as Hofmann indicates, the real tragedy is that the disturbed generation the 'wir' represents will eventually come to adulthood, possibly still not knowing any better. The closing words of the book recall a number of the novel's motifs and offer a bleak picture of Germany's future:

> So daß wir, . . . als Verletzte gut erkennbar, in Herrn Hennes frischgewaschenem Anzug, den wir immer noch nicht mögen, unser

---

[162] *Niemands Land,* in Böll (ed.), *Niemands Land,* 30.

Schatten zitternd neben uns, von nun an einen Bogen machen um das Schellenbaumhaus. Auch wenn der Gestank, der daraus hervorkommt, von uns wahrscheinlich nur vorgestellt ist. (p. 312)

'KINDER—ZU ALLEM FÄHIG'?: GERT HOFMANN'S *VEILCHENFELD*

Hofmann takes up the childhood theme again in *Veilchenfeld.* This is a more conventional *Ich-Erzählung* by a 9-year-old boy, but while Grünzweig suggests that whereas the 'wir' of *Unsere Eroberung* was the 'Sprachrrohr einer nicht verstandenen Volksgemeinschaft', the occasional use of 'wir' in *Veilchenfeld* refers exclusively to Hans and his sister, this is to ignore a number of instances where Hans's 'wir' identifies him with a social perspective.[163] The opening sentences exemplify this: 'Unser Philosoph ist plötzlich gestorben, unser Leichenwagen hat ihn abgeholt . . . Wir lehnen an Höhlers Gartenzaun und machen uns nicht schmutzig' (*Veilchenfeld,* p. 7). While the second sentence clearly refers to the narrator and his younger sister, the mention of 'our' hearse in the first implies the children in a social context. The first 'unser' is less clear: it might refer just to the children (given the sympathy they alone seem to feel for Veilchenfeld by the end of the story); to their family, which had initially been sympathetic towards the older man; or to the town population as a whole. The identification of the child with the local populace is particularly significant in view of his final encounter with Veilchenfeld, who asks the boy to buy the insecticide he uses to commit suicide. The child has no inkling that he is responsible for Veilchenfeld's death: while his father gives his mother a detailed account of his visit to Veilchenfeld's home (pp. 170–4), it is not clear exactly how much of this account Hans hears; moreover, his lack of comprehension is evident when Hofmann uses italics for the word 'Dardanellendurst' (p. 173). There is no sense of guilt or self-accusation but nevertheless the child has unwittingly carried out the death sentence that the Nazi regime would have inflicted on the Jewish intellectual sooner or later.

It may seem harsh to blame the child for Veilchenfeld's death, but although Hofmann is not so explicitly concerned with indoctrination as Wolf in *Kindheitsmuster,* the symbol of the cap in

---

[163] Grünzweig, 'Vergebliche Enttrümmerung', 63.

Unsere Eroberung and the use of 'wir' in *Veilchenfeld* both show how far the child can be unwittingly corrupted by adult society. Hans's perspective is initially quite distinct from that of the adults, as is suggested by the 'und machen uns nicht schmutzig' (p. 7). This opening position suggests his function as an observer, and also that he is able to observe events without becoming morally tainted ('schmutzig') by them. But while it is true that the children maintain a naively independent attitude in the earlier stages of the narrative, where their persistent questions clearly exasperate their parents, that opening symbolism is undermined in two respects. First, the concern with not getting dirty may seem childlike, but in fact it is generally imposed by adults: the narrator is thus unconsciously parroting an adult expectation.[164] And secondly, the narrative is circular: when it opens, Veilchenfeld is already dead and Hans, however unwittingly, has caused that death.

Hans's family, like Nelly's, is not fervently pro-Nazi; his father, the local doctor, begins by sympathizing with Veilchenfeld and inviting him to dinner, but gradually the parents succumb to social pressure to ostracize the old philosopher and the children are discouraged from acknowledging him in the street or mentioning his name. As in *Kindheitsmuster*, the child's initially independent position comes under attack from relentless social conditioning, and he becomes increasingly implicated in the social milieu he is describing. The stark title *Veilchenfeld* itself implies a social perspective, for it supposes we know who and what the protagonist is: it suggests an initiated audience and thus implicates us in the society being described. Veilchenfeld's case has representative value, for his was the lot of many Jewish intellectuals under the Nazi regime. But he is not the only representative figure: the children's wider significance is suggested by the names Hans and Gretel.[165] The fairy-tale echo is ambiguous: their namesakes in the Grimms' *Märchen* are the archetypal innocent

---

[164] Rüdiger Steinlein, 'Gert Hofmanns Erzählung "Veilchenfeld" (1986) und der Nationalsozialismus im fiktionalen Jugendbuch: Überlegungen zu einer erzählstrukturellen und rezeptionsästhetischen Herausforderung', in Malte Dahrendorf and Zohar Shavit (eds.), *Die Darstellung des Dritten Reiches im Kinder- und Jugendbuch* (Frankfurt, 1988), 101.

[165] The fairy-tale context is highlighted by Thomas Schmid, 'Hänsel und Gretel, 1938' and Paul Michael Lützeler, 'Gert Hofmann: Der verstoßene Sohn, Ein Werk-Porträt': in Kosler (ed.), *Gert Hofmann*, 170 and 53 respectively.

victims of weak and evil adults. However, the *Märchen*, like so many of the cultural artefacts of the Romantic era and indeed the Romantic conception of childhood itself, was perverted by the Nazi party in the interests of promoting pride in the supreme German culture rooted in the *Volk*. The children's names are thus ambiguous: they represent both innocence and the possibility of exploitation and corruption. This point is vividly illustrated when Hans plays a 'Holzfäller' in the town carnival, for this echo of the *Märchen* is perverted by the 'geschwungenen und phantastischen Stiel' (p. 153) which recalls the Grim Reaper rather than a woodcutter. Significantly this is the day that Hans buys the insecticide for Veilchenfeld.

The child's view is made socially representative in a number of ways in *Veilchenfeld*. First there is the ambiguous 'wir' which culminates in a very obvious identification with the social perspective when Veilchenfeld advertises for a cleaner and Hans comments 'Die meisten *von uns* dachten, es meldet sich keine, weil sie sich keine vorstellen konnten, die *so einem* den Dreck nachräumt' (p. 94, first emphasis mine). The child seems gradually to adopt a more social perspective: he certainly asks fewer questions of the adults' behaviour. Moreover, in many instances he acts as a mere uncomprehending mouthpiece who either relays conversations where several people with different opinions take part, or reports incidents at which he was not himself present, simply giving the account of someone who was.[166] As the work progresses he sees less and less of Veilchenfeld and yet the town gossip is such that he hears ever more about the man and his fate. He is thus cut off from the direct experience also favoured by the narrator of *Unsere Eroberung* and is subjected to social influences and indoctrination instead. This affects his narrative stance, to the extent that, while he does not entirely accept what is happening to Veilchenfeld, he realizes he cannot do much about it. This is understandable in a child accustomed to obeying adult authority: it would be extremely difficult for him to defy his parents' direct

---

[166] See *Veilchenfeld*, esp. 55–68, where the children's parents discuss the attack on Veilchenfeld with their neighbours. This conversation is discussed by Heinz Schumacher, 'Gert Hofmann, *Veilchenfeld*', in Herbert Kaiser and Gerhard Köpf (eds.), *Erzählen, Erinnern: Deutsche Prosa der Gegenwart, Interpretationen* (Frankfurt, 1992), 293–4. The best example of the child describing a scene where he is not present occurs after Veilchenfeld's suicide when Hans cites his father's account of his visit to Veilchenfeld's home (170–4).

orders regarding Veilchenfeld. On the other hand, this passive cooperation with adult evil is paralleled by the adult 'Mitläufer' who, although they do not take part in the attack on Veilchenfeld in the police station (p. 70), nevertheless feel a ghoulish desire to visit the places where he was seen during his ritual humiliation at police hands. Hans's father actually says 'Wenn wir die Schand-taten schon nicht sehen, wollen wir wenigstens die Schandorte sehen' (p. 71). Both children and adults treat this event almost as a theatrical spectacle: there is a sense of shared anticipation in the phrase 'Und fragen uns, ob heut wieder was geschieht, und warten lange drauf' (p. 72). This recalls the specifically theatrical imagery used in a similar context in Hofmann's *Die Denunziation* (1979); such images seem particularly appropriate to the child's perspective in Hofmann's work since they imply not only a social perspective but also a sense of passivity and even powerlessness, as no audience can affect events on stage.[167]

The townspeople's passive cooperation with evil when Veilchen-feld is humiliated by the police is thrown into sharper relief by the later attack on the philosopher where the adolescent assailants are described specifically as 'Kinder'.[168] Hofmann's ambivalent atti-tude to children is nowhere clearer than in his description of one of these 17-year-olds, which might almost (apart from its hints at a later development) form part of a Romantic depiction of child-hood: 'Das Kind ist schlank und hat gerade Zähne und bleibt auch noch etwas so, bis es gröber und kantiger wird. Sein Haar ist blondgelockt, eine lange Strähne fällt ihm in die Stirn'. The fact that this physical perfection conforms precisely to the Nazi ideal of childhood is neatly expressed here: 'Es hat, wie alle anderen auch, sein ganzes Leben in unserer Stadt verbracht und stößt in dieser Nacht überraschend auf Herrn Veilchenfeld, es wundert

---

[167] In *Die Denunziation* the anticipation of two young brothers and indeed the rest of the town populace as they await the arrest of the half-Jew Silberstein is described as them awaiting 'den Beginn des Stückes mit Ungeduld' (Gert Hofmann, *Die Denunzia-tion: Novelle* (Darmstadt and Neuwied, 1987), 44). This theatrical imagery can be com-pared with other narratives where the child is both solitary and excluded: in *What Maisie Knew*, Maisie is constantly putting her nose up against figurative window panes (see above), which become literal in Lenz's *Deutschstunde*. In both these works the child's perspective is quite different from the adult's, for even when theatrical imagery is used of Maisie, the whole point of it is that she is *alone* in the theatre: in Hofmann's work the child and the adult watch the same play from virtually the same position.

[168] Urban-Halle, 'Schauplatz Menschenkopf', in Kosler (ed.), *Gert Hofmann*, 102.

sich, daß es so etwas gibt. In *seinen hübschen glatten Kopf* paßt er nicht hinein' (my emphasis). The role of social conditioning in this refusal to accept Veilchenfeld is also evident, for 'Er hat nichts gegen Herrn Veilchenfeld, nur man hat ihm gesagt, daß er leichter atmen könnte, wenn er aus der Welt ist' (p. 128). The casual cruelty this lad inflicts on Veilchenfeld is merely an intensification of what is inflicted on him by adult 'Mitläufer', just as Hans's unwitting delivery of the insecticide parallels his father's statement following the incident at the police station: 'Aber vielleicht wäre es angesichts dessen, was auf Veilchenfeld zukommt, gar nicht das schlechteste, wenn er sich umbrächte' (p. 77). Hans's act is unwitting, but the violence of these adolescents who have been subjected to the same conditioning clearly demonstrates what could become even of this innocent child.

Hofmann's children are not naturally disposed to viciousness and cruelty. Like Hans, and indeed like Nelly in *Kindheitsmuster*, they are capable of sharp, unblinkered observation, open-minded questions that beat against adult taboos, and thus real clarity of vision. But the potential Hofmann sees in children is not all positive: when Herr Urmüller sees the lads outside Veilchenfeld's house, 'erschrickt Herr Urmüller bei dem Gedanken: Kinder, weil Kinder, wie er weiß, zu allem fähig sind' (p. 123). Given the right (or wrong) conditions, children can be moulded in any way; those in Hofmann's books, despite moments of essentially childlike vision and revealingly grim flights of fancy, tend to adopt a social perspective which blurs the distinction between child and adult, and in a sense it is because they lack knowledge (with which come taboos and inhibitions) that the children are capable of performing deeds which adults might merely consider or passively condone. Like the other children considered here, they have been corrupted without necessarily incurring conscious guilt, drawn unwittingly into an adult world where their positive potential is undermined by their ignorance.

'DAS BÖSE KIND'?

So far the children considered have all been corrupted by the adult world because of their ignorance: they fall unwittingly, and if they commit evil acts then they do so unconsciously. However, Söntgerath suggests that certain twentieth-century authors have gone beyond this in their negative portrayal of the child figure: not only do they destroy 'den Mythos vom guten Kind', but by presenting evil in the child they create a new myth, that of the 'Kind-Dämon' or 'Anti-Kind':

Solch ein Anti-Kind ist Oskar in Günter Grass' *Blechtrommel*, mit seiner lautlosen Allwissenheit, seiner mächtigen Zerstörungsfähigkeit, seiner impertinenten Präsenz in allen erdenklichen Situationen, seinen unbarmherzigen Reflexionen und seinen ekelerregenden Angewohnheiten. Ferner Lothar in den *Riesenzwergen*, mit seiner scheinbar naiven, aber auf eine beängstigende Weise präzisen Beobachtung, seiner höhnischen Kritik und seiner beklemmenden Augen- und Ohrenzeugenrolle, die er, in der Gestalt eines Vierjährigen, mit den Fähigkeiten eines Universitätsprofessors im Analysieren und Kombinieren ausübt.[169]

This is apparently a return to the idea of the Fall as a product of knowledge ('Allwissenheit'), an almost Romantic conception which explains our peculiarly pejorative use of the word 'knowing' with reference to children. But Söntgerath's choice of texts invites the question: *what* do these children know? It is true that they are unprepossessing because their observations on the adult world are so unequivocally hostile, and Oskar's precocious knowledge of sexual and political matters, albeit apparently concealed beneath a façade of childish language, is not merely unchildlike but extremely threatening. However, this fear of the 'Anti-Kind' takes us back to the point made at the beginning of this chapter regarding Spinell's fear of Anton Klöterjahn, for adult fear of the child is as dependent on adult attitudes as it is on anything the child does. If Oskar's and Lothar's view of the adult world is hostile, it is because there is much in the adult world that merits this hostility: the main reason for adults (whether characters in the texts or readers) to be afraid of such children is their terror of the children's ability to see through the adult world. This also explains why narrators like Oskar and Siggi Jepsen are officially labelled delinquents and separated from mainstream society: the apparently objective statement of their 'guilt' results partly from society's fear of them and partly from their own disgust at

---

[169] *Pädagogik und Dichtung*, 145. Ueding also refers to these texts and suggests that this negative image of childhood is created by 'die Ängste einer Gesellschaft, die vom Neuen nur noch die Enttäuschung, von der Zukunft nur Zerstörung erwartet' ('Verstoßen in ein fremdes Land', 356).

adult society, which makes each want to stay in his institution.
There are aspects of Oskar which may be described as evil, but to
denounce him for his 'Allwissenheit' is to put oneself on
the same level as Heinrich Mann's Professor Unrat, who feels
threatened by the knowledge of the youngsters around him and
inadequate in the face of it.

When dealing with the fallen child we must remember that it is
created in our own image. Oskar can be seen as evil precisely
because he is a pseudo-child with many adult attributes, one
whose very childish, self-centred attitudes parody those of contemporary adults. The adult world is the environment that corrupts the child, and adults classify children as evil whenever this is
preferable to having to admit adult inadequacies. It is all too easy
to discuss 'delinquent' characters like Oskar and Siggi as 'children
of their time' and 'representatives of a generation', but such discussion always invites the question as to how they became what
they are. Their delinquency is to some extent a product of the conditioning they have received but it is considerably more than that:
a form of violent revolt against prevailing social and political
conditions.

In this chapter I have examined mainly what can be called a
negative conception of childhood innocence as ignorance. This
appears in allegorical form in Thomas Mann's *Mario und der
Zauberer* (1930) where the children's joy at being present at the
adults' entertainment is by no means diminished by their lack of
understanding: 'Für die Kleinen gehörte es schon zum Vergnügen, sich daran zu beteiligen. Alle Kinder lieben es, Beifall zu
klatschen' (*Gesammelte Werke*, viii. 673). They are entirely innocent of any involvement in the evening's events, which are well
beyond their comprehension; nonetheless, they are swept along
by the crowd and the desire to participate. This innocence, like
that of Maisie and Edgar, is that of unawareness. But while children, in literature as in life, may seem vulnerable and malleable,
the child is also frequently presented as an elusive being with
untold reserves of strength and resilience. In Chapter 2 I shall
examine a more positive conception of childhood innocence: not
the passive ignorance that both involves them in events beyond
their control and absolves them from any guilt, but rather a
powerful force for good and an element of hope in a fallen world.

2

BEYOND THE FALL

In his study of childhood in English literature, Coveney states: 'It is not remarkable perhaps when major authors see the child as a symbol of growth, life, and fertility, as a means of establishing human values in an increasingly secular age'.[1] But in the light of Chapter 1, I would suggest that it is in fact remarkable for the child to represent positive values in post-war German literature. The historical situation of a generation which grew up with a 'Sack überm Kopf' was hardly conducive to building a new society based on human values, for the psychological damage caused to individuals had broader implications. This is made clear by Wolf's prefatory note to *Kindheitsmuster*, where the obligatory disclaimer about the fictional nature of the characters has a sting in the tail:

Wer Ähnlichkeiten zwischen einem Charakter der Erzählung und sich selbst oder ihm bekannten Menschen zu erkennen glaubt, sei auf den merkwürdigen Mangel an Eigentümlichkeit verwiesen, der dem Verhalten vieler Zeitgenossen anhaftet. Man müßte die Verhältnisse beschuldigen, weil sie Verhaltensweisen hervorbringen, die man wiedererkennt.

However, the historical situation of Wolf and her contemporaries clashes with the positive, even idealistic, conception of childhood inherited from the Romantics. The myth of the 'fremdes Kind' who represents an alternative dimension to that of society has persisted in works about the Third Reich and it is the clash between historical situation and the literary myth of childhood that I shall examine in this chapter. I shall consider two groups of fictional child figures : first, Jewish children under the Third Reich, and secondly Gentile children of the same era. While the historical reality of these two groups is very different, I shall demonstrate that the potential writers see in them is very similar. And, to show the diverse treatment the myth of the 'fremdes Kind' has received,

---

[1] *Image of Childhood,* 340.

I will also consider some of Grass's child figures, demonstrating the tension between a Romantic and a Freudian view of child-hood. This chapter culminates in a consideration of Oskar Matzerath and Siggi Jepsen as Romantic children for our own time.

JEWISH CHILDREN UNDER THE THIRD REICH

As writers have moved away from the ethereal Romantic concep-tion of childhood towards more flesh-and-blood characters, an apparently obvious point has been emphasized: the child's vul-nerability. This shift in perception was already apparent in our introductory discussion of *Bergkristall*, and this sense of vulnera-bility in a literary context appeared to reach a peak in the *Schulro-mane* of the early twentieth century. But historically there can have been few groups as vulnerable as Jewish children under the Third Reich. Consequently we may be surprised to find that idea of the child figure as an embodiment of hope and new life remains strong even in literary works dealing with this subject. One notable example is Bruno Apitz's novel *Nackt unter Wölfen* (1958) which describes the last days of Buchenwald concentration camp and the risks its inmates take to conceal and save a Jewish child. While the child is not often physically present, it is constantly in the background, symbolizing a principle of hope and bringing out the most humane impulses in the inmates, sometimes against all rational considerations for their own survival. As this example suggests, the positive presentation of Jewish children under the Third Reich is not simply a case of whitewash by authors plagued by guilt feelings; Apitz spent eight years in Buchenwald for his political activities and the authors I shall discuss in more detail, Jurek Becker, Anna Gmeyner, and Ilse Aichinger, were all vic-tims of the Nazi regime. All are at least part-Jewish, and Becker's and Aichinger's families suffered considerable persecution: Becker spent most of his childhood in a ghetto and concentration camps and several members of Aichinger's family were deported and murdered. Only Gmeyner had the relative good fortune to spend the Third Reich in exile.

It is obviously dangerous to build too much on the positive por-trayals of Jewish children: we are all too susceptible to the kind of myth that surrounds the most famous child victim of World War II,

Anne Frank. While it is clear from her diary that she was both sensitive and courageous, the sentimental myth that began to emerge shortly after the war seems a conscious distortion of the facts, or at least an edifice built on shaky foundations. It is not only that this myth makes it seem sacrilegious to think that Anne was a normal, often confused and rebellious teenager, for which there is equal evidence in the diary, especially if we consider the original version before Anne and subsequently her father edited it for publication,[2] it even ascribes to her a 'profound smile' of 'happiness and faith' which 'was not lost, even in Belsen'.[3] There is a powerful desire to see this girl's spirit transcending the brutality of the Nazis and to see her diary as an affirmation, art derived from human suffering.[4] Some versions of the myth come perilously close to implying that the beauty of her diary somehow makes her death worthwhile; we might think of the phenomenally successful stage version of 1954, where in the penultimate scene, with the Gestapo already in the house, Anne writes a postscript asking Miep and Kraler to keep the diary safe.[5] While Anne clearly intended to publish a version of her diary after the war, it seems profoundly unlikely that this would have been her only thought at this juncture. This sentimental attitude which all too clearly served a therapeutic purpose for Germans immediately after the war is the worst kind of betrayal of the victims of the Holocaust, for the treasured image of a smiling Anne sitting at a table with her notebook is as far from the reality of the death camps as we can get.

[2] See *The Diary of Anne Frank: The Critical Edition*, ed. David Barnouw and Gerrold van der Stroom, trans. Arnold J. Pomerans and B. M. Mooyaart-Doubleday (London, 1989) for alternative versions of the text. For a discussion of the different versions, the editing process, and the history of publication, see ibid. 59–77. There is now also an expanded version of the diary for general readers: Anne Frank, *The Diary of a Young Girl: The Definitive Edition*, ed. Otto H. Frank and Mirjam Pressler, trans. Susan Massotty (London, 1997), though its claims to definitiveness have been questioned in Laureen Nussbaum, 'Anne Frank, The Writer', in: Viktoria Hertling (ed.), *Mit den Augen eines Kindes: Children in the Holocaust, Children in Exile, Children under Fascism* (Amsterdam and Atlanta, Ga.1998), 113.

[3] Storm Jameson's foreword to *The Diary of Anne Frank*, trans. B. M. Mooyaart-Doubleday (London, 1981), 11.

[4] In *Art from the Ashes: A Holocaust Anthology* (New York and Oxford, 1995), 7, the editor Lawrence L. Langer cites *The Diary of Anne Frank* as typical of the kind of Holocaust literature that allows readers to come to such conclusions.

[5] Frances Goodrich and Albert Hackett, *The Play of the Diary of Anne Frank* (Oxford, 1991), 140.

In her memoir of her youth in a concentration camp Cordelia Edvardson comments:

Sie sollten nicht über sie weinen dürfen, so wie sie über Anne Franks Tagebuch schluchzten. Über dieses typische Jungmädchentagebuch, das gnädig endet, als die Henker die Tür zu Annes geschützter Welt und der ihrer Familie eintreten. Ja, der trotz allem geschützten Welt, selbst wenn sich die Geborgenheit als so verräterisch erwies wie dünnes Eis. Aber das Tagebuch endet, als das Eis bricht, und Annes altklugen und ach so versöhnlichen Grübeleien werden im Würgegriff der Angst erstickt und durch einen Schlag mit dem Gewehrkolben auf den Mund zum Schweigen gebracht.

Durch die rührenden Briefe an 'Kitty' erhielt die Welt ihre Katharsis zu einem allzubilligen Preis.[6]

The example of Anne Frank is useful in two almost contradictory ways. First the moral strength and spirit expressed in the diary may give us pause when we feel tempted to scoff at positive, even idealistic, portrayals of Jewish children in the Third Reich context. But equally the sentimental myth surrounding her stands as a warning. Anne fits the German Romantic conception of childhood to perfection, and thus forms a natural focus for myth-making: in her diary she comes across as a vital, spontaneous, and mercurial character who wants to be a writer, and it is a bitter irony that even her early death fits the pattern because her innocence stands no chance of being tainted. The obsessive interest in her story since the end of World War II and the various versions of it, most of which stop short of portraying her death in Bergen-Belsen, suggest, as Langer points out, that this girl's story has been taken over by people who are using it to meet needs of their own.[7] The Anne Frank myth is proof of the deep-seated human need to believe in the power of good to overcome evil, even if that supposed victory can only occur on a transcendent level, beyond death. This need is particularly evident in the works of Gmeyner and Aichinger.

---

[6] *Gebranntes Kind sucht das Feuer*, trans. Anna-Liese Kornitzky (repr. Munich, 1991), 110–11 (1st pub. in Swedish, 1984).

[7] *Art from the Ashes*, 7. For a discussion of different versions of the Anne Frank story and their impact, see Carol Ann Lee, *Roses from the Earth: The Biography of Anne Frank* (London, 1999), 226–9. For an account of how the play came to be written and the legal controversies surrounding it, see *Diary: Critical Edition*, 78–83.

But before turning to these two authors I shall consider two works by Jurek Becker to demonstrate the extent to which even a more sober-minded author emphasizes the positive potential of childhood in this grim context.

Speaking from Experience: Jurek Becker's Die Mauer *and* Jakob der Lügner

Becker's *Die Mauer* (1980) draws on his own childhood experience of the Lodz ghetto and illustrates the way a child can adapt to circumstances. Like the children cited in Chapter 1 the 5-year-old narrator has a perverted conception of normality. Although he experiences all the grim reality of ghetto life, he seems oblivious to its implications. This is partly because his parents protect him from this knowledge with stories of an invisible barrier beyond which children are caught and taken away. But the child is not entirely ignorant: 'Einmal sage ich: "Wer ist es überhaupt, der die Kinder wegfängt?" Er [his father] fragt: "Wozu mußt du das auch noch wissen?" Ich sage: "Es sind die deutschen Soldaten"' (*Die Mauer*, 62). Given that even the youngest children shared the same living conditions as adults, it would be surprising if an intelligent child were not party to the speculation of ghetto life: 'Ist es ein gutes Zeichen, hier zu sein, ist es ein schlechtes, darüber wird in den langen Steinbaracken Tag und Nacht gesprochen' (p. 68). But while the child is apparently aware of the rules of the game, he does not know the forfeits, and thus unwittingly betrays Kaufmann Tenzer. When the boy first sees Tenzer's cactus plant, which is forbidden by ghetto law, the two have the following conversation:

Er sagt: 'Du sprichst mit niemandem darüber.' Ich sage: 'Natürlich spreche ich mit keinem.' Er sagt: 'Du weißt, daß niemand eine Pflanze haben darf?' Ich sage: 'Natürlich weiß ich das.' Er sagt: 'Du weißt was jedem blüht, der ein Verbot mißachtet?' Ich sage: 'Natürlich.' Er fragt mich: 'Na, was machen sie mit dem?' Ich antworte nicht und schaue ihn nur an, weil er es mir gleich sagen wird. Wir sehen uns ein bißchen in die Augen, dann greift sich Tenzer ein Stück Wäsche aus der Schüssel und wringt es gewaltig aus. Er sagt: 'Das machen sie mit ihm.' Natürlich erzähle ich die Sache Millionen Leuten, den Eltern nicht, doch allen meinen Freunden. (p. 65)

The fourfold 'natürlich' makes the point. The rules of the ghetto are self-evident to the boy but, because adults try to protect him by hiding behind bogeymen and gestures, it is equally self-evident that he should tell his friends about the plant. Even when his father reports that Tenzer has been 'geholt' (another grim euphemism), the child apparently does not understand the full implications of the phrase: he merely comments 'oft schon haben sie einen geholt, der plötzlich nicht mehr da war' (p. 65). It is not even clear whether he feels any responsibility for the event: admittedly, at the beginning of the story he notes 'Am Ende habe ich den Kaufmann Tenzer umgebracht, nie werde ich es wissen' (p. 63), but this concern is retrospective, like his knowledge regarding the 'Lager' in the middle of the ghetto, whose function he can now explain 'obwohl es mir damals keiner erklärt hat' (p. 68). The basic narrative tone and frame of reference are set by the initial 'Mein Gott, ich bin fünf Jahre alt' (p. 62), and in this narrative present his concern is more for himself than for Tenzer: 'ich bin der eigentlich Betroffene hier, und keiner kümmert sich um mich' (p. 66). His relative ignorance forms a protective shell around him, allowing him to lead an essentially normal life with the usual concerns of the 5-year-old. These emerge in his pride at finally being allowed to say his own number at the daily 'Appell', but also in less day-to-day events. When a German soldier catches him and Julian outside the camp enclosure the boy's domestic concerns are still uppermost in his mind: 'Ich sehe mir meine Unterhose an und weiß, es wird nicht wenig Ärger mit meiner Mutter geben, falls ich das hier überstehe' (p. 97). Even in the ghetto he is allowed the blessing of a protected childhood and the occasional hints at retrospective knowledge imply that he survives the war; the story is open-ended in a way that *Jakob der Lügner* (1969) is not.

If *Die Mauer* presents us with the possibility of a near-normal childhood and physical survival, then other works dealing with Jewish children are even more positive about the child and the qualities it embodies. In *Jakob der Lügner* 8-year-old Lina demonstrates again the kind of potential Becker sees in children, and on this occasion it goes beyond mere physical survival.

Like the narrator of *Die Mauer* Lina regards the ghetto existence as normality. She is not noticeably disturbed by its dangers: in fact she owes her survival to disobeying parental rules intended to keep her safe, for when her parents are loaded onto a transport east Lina only avoids being sent with them because she is playing some distance from the house. But she does not represent mere physical survival, for at the end of the novel she is on the same transport as Jakob. She is closely associated with him and his fate; however, by the same token she is associated with the non-existent radio. She and the radio occupy parallel spaces in relation to Jakob, for his need to keep Lina hidden corresponds precisely to the danger of keeping a real radio: in both cases he has taken on a burden that entails danger and self-sacrifice, but fosters hope for the future. He is the only person in the ghetto who cannot derive hope for the future from the radio, but when with Lina he too is able to talk about what life will be like after the war: 'Wirst ihr . . . etwas über die Welt von morgen erzählen, die interessiert dich doch auch' (*Jakob der Lügner*, 118). Her natural optimism fosters hope in him: how could he supply the rest of the ghetto with this life-giving commodity if he had none himself?

But Lina is not just the human embodiment of the hope principle symbolized by the radio. Her significance is increased when Jakob allows her to listen to the 'radio', for unbeknown to him she sees through his imitation, and so becomes his sole accomplice. Her new knowledge makes surprisingly little difference, for 'Sie setzt sich still zurück auf ihren Platz, das Vergnügen am Zuhören ist nicht kleiner geworden, nur vermischt mit ein paar Gedanken, die niemanden etwas angehen' (p. 170). As Jakob tells the narrator, 'Alle anderen wären über die Wahrheit entsetzt gewesen, sie hat sich hinterher gefreut' (p. 162).

This makes Lina an embodiment of hope, but of a very particular kind, as becomes clear if we compare her with Siegfried and Rafael. They hatch courageous escape plots, including blowing up the soldiers' quarters (the problem is that they don't have any dynamite). Their youthful optimism in the face of insuperable odds is something we have all occasionally seen or experienced, but Lina is already able to dismiss such nonsense: when she overhears this plan she 'lacht und hält sich die Hände vor den Mund, der kreischen möchte, es ist wirklich kaum zu glauben, wie dämlich zwei Bengels von zehn noch sein können' (p. 96). This amusement where we might expect despair at the hopelessness of her friends' plans seems odd. True, at this point Lina does not know the truth about the radio and so may still be relying on the imminent arrival of the Russians, but this is unlikely, for if it were so she would hardly be so composed when she learns the truth about the radio. Lina is ignorant of many things: like the narrator of

Die Mauer, she does not realize the fate that awaits the ghetto inhabitants, for when their departure is announced she is simply excited at the prospect of a journey. But, although she is deceived in this, she is not deceived by the radio. So what kind of hope does she represent?

In fact Lina represents the same kind of hope as Jakob, that of the storyteller: he overhears her retelling the story that he, as the radio's 'Märchenonkel', had told her. But, just as the information he has given others in the ghetto has been embroidered and distorted, so the story he told her has undergone a kind of 'Chinese whispers' process. He had told a story about a princess who said that her illness could only be cured by the gift of a cloud. The doctors and wise men of the kingdom were baffled and only the lowly 'Gartenjunge' thought to ask her what clouds are made of. Her answer, namely that they are bits of cottonwool as big as her pillow, solved the problem and everyone lived happily ever after. Lina has obviously not grasped the point of the story, for in her version the princess simply asks for 'ein Stück Watte . . . das so groß sein muß wie ihr Kopfkissen' (p. 183), to Rafael's derision. But, as Kaiser points out, for Lina the cottonwool can stand for the cloud, just as Jakob can stand for the radio: like most children she exists on the boundary between reality and fantasy rather than in the zone between truth and lies inhabited by most adults, and thus the concept of hope, which is necessary even when it is illusory, is comprehensible to her.[8] It is possible to see both Jakob and Lina as symbols of the artist, for both are storytellers whose tales cannot save them from their fate but who can at least raise morale in the ghetto: just as the princess is cured by the cottonwool cloud, so the ghetto suicide rate falls to zero thanks to Jakob's radio. Even knowledge of the truth does not destroy Lina's hope, or her belief in Jakob: the child and the storyteller are thus the guarantors of life-affirming hope against the odds.

'And the light shineth in darkness'?[9] *Anna Gmeyner's* Manja
and Ilse Aichinger's Die größere Hoffnung

Becker's children are presented positively but not idealistically. They show the possibility of physical and mental survival without

---

[8] Herbert Kaiser, 'Jurek Becker, *Jakob der Lügner*', in id. and Köpf (eds.), *Erzählen, Erinnern*, 112–14.   [9] John 1: 5.

descending into sentimentality, mainly because neither child is particularly conscious of its vulnerability. Nor does Becker weigh them down with symbolic significance too great for their young shoulders: even Lina acquires her symbolic aspect mainly by association with the radio and this does not affect her credibility as a three-dimensional character. They are psychologically convincing and the hope they engender is for them as individuals. The novels I turn to now, Gmeyner's *Manja* and Ilse Aichinger's *Die größere Hoffnung,* are rather different: the central characters of these novels are Jewish girls who are much more aware of their vulnerability. And, while Becker's sympathy with his characters is not intrusive, Gmeyner especially runs the risk of becoming too involved in her heroine's fate. She is so aware of the girl's vulnerability that she apparently wants to compensate her, not just by implying some measure of hope in a grim situation, but also by making the girl herself conscious of it. The events of *Manja* and *Die größere Hoffnung* are not very hopeful: both girls are persecuted for being Jewish and while their deaths are not a direct result of the Holocaust, the sexual assault which breaks Manja's spirit and leads to her suicide occurs because her Nazi attacker regards her as legitimate prey[10] and Ellen is killed by an exploding shell. Any hope has to be implied on a symbolic level and both writers achieve this by exploiting different aspects of the Romantic conception of childhood: the child's affinity with nature, its artistic sensibility, and its redemptive qualities. Manja may only be the illegitimate offspring of the would-be singer Lea and the failed composer David, but her symbolic potential is clear from the novel's religious subtext. Just after the sickly baby has begun to feed for the first time Gmeyner describes the maternity ward: 'Alle Mütter haben die demütig anbetende Gebärde frommer Verkündigungsbilder, und sie warten auf die drei Könige und den Weihrauch, wollen die Krone und nicht die Dornen darin' (*Manja,* 86). This is only one of many religious references Gmeyner uses to draw parallels between Manja and Christ. They begin with the girl's mysterious conception: her father is called David, which recalls the genealogy of Christ, the 'Son of David'; moreover, despite the fact that he shoots himself on the morning

---

[10] This point is made by Heike Klapdor-Kops in her preface to Anna Gmeyner, *Manja: Ein Roman um fünf Kinder* (repr. Mannheim, 1987), 9.

after Manja's conception, his role in her existence is heavily emphasized:

Ihr [Lea's] Körper spürte, was ihrem Verstand nicht faßbar war, fühlte Angst und Glut und Tod, die aus ihm in sie strömten, erlebte zum ersten Mal, wie nahe die Lust der Vereinigung die Qual des Sterbens streift, und mitzitternd in der Not, die ihn zerriß, wurde sie mehr als das Mädchen Lea, wurde eine Frau ohne Namen, ein Gefäß grenzenloser Bereitschaft. (p. 46)

Lea is apparently just a vessel for the child David creates, just as Mary was a mere vessel for the Holy Spirit, and Lea too has to find a foster father for her child. The oddly preordained quality of Manja's birth also recalls Christ in that she apparently arrives already named:

Aber ehe der Mann David Goldstaub, dessen Tod zwanzig Jahre in ihm gewachsen war, endgültig aus dem Gefängnis der Kiste ausbrach, ließ er in dem fremden Mädchen, das ihm die letzte Güte erwiesen hatte, ein Stück seines Lebens zurück, ein Kind, eine Tochter, Manja. (p. 47)

This passage is very different from those which describe the conception of the four boys. First, in those accounts there is no mention of individual parents' names, and this puts even more emphasis on David. And, secondly, in the other accounts there is a conscious parental decision about the child's name, whereas the triumphant triad here recalls 'Denn uns ist ein Kind geboren, ein Sohn ist uns gegeben'.[11] Any claim that Gmeyner is writing a strict Christian allegory would be problematic because, although a number of incidents at the end of Manja's life recall Christ's death and resurrection, these episodes occur out of sequence, with Manja's 'arrest' preceding the Gethsemane scene. But given Gmeyner's background (a non-Orthodox Jew married to a philosopher of religion in whose work she was very interested) it seems clear that she was consciously developing a religious subtext.[12]

Manja has an electrifying effect on her four friends, who come from a wide range of family backgrounds. Despite her own victim status she holds this disparate band together in a way that

---

[11] Jesaja 9: 5. German biblical quotations are to the *Lutherbibel* (Stuttgart, 1985).
[12] For biographical information on Gmeyner see Heike Klapdor-Kops, '"Und was die Verfasserin betrifft, laßt uns weitersehen": Die Rekonstruktion der schriftstellerischen Laufbahn Anna Gmeyners', *Ef* 3 (1985), 313–38 and her preface to *Manja*.

transcends political differences.[13] This transcendence is specifically associated with Cassiopeia, the rather obvious leitmotif
which accompanies their meetings. This constellation consists of
five stars in the shape of a giant W, and Manja cites it as the seal on
their oath of eternal friendship:

'Es ist schon aufgeschrieben!' Ihr ausgestreckter Arm zeigte noch einmal
auf das Sternbild der Kassiopeia. . . .
    'Eins, zwei, drei, vier, fünf!' Ihre Stimme erkletterte eine Tonleiter von
Triumph. 'Mein Stern ist der in der Mitte. Heini, Karl, Manja, Harry,
Franz. Es ist im Himmel aufgeschrieben'. (p. 181)

None of these children is a tabula rasa: their different backgrounds range from Nazi to Communist and at times their home
circumstances threaten their friendship.[14] The detailed depiction
of their parents and the nights when the children were conceived
is intended to show from the outset what we may expect from
them. But their hideout 'an der Mauer' represents the protective
space of childhood and there, on many occasions, they are able to
transform 'ein bitterstes Stück Leben wieder in Spiel' (p. 274). The
fact that this space is associated with Cassiopeia emphasizes its
transcendent quality and also recalls the Romantic tradition of as-
sociating childhood with nature. Manja especially is associated
with the stars and so gains a different perspective on events:
'Manchmal abends, wenn ich im Bett lieg', mach' ich mich steif
und still wie eine Puppe, und dann fliegt etwas aus mir heraus.
Dann sitz' ich auf einem Stern, und es ist hell und alles ist ganz
weit weg, wie wenn man verkehrt durch ein Opernglas sieht'
(p. 330). But while this may seem to indicate her relationship with
the children of the Romantic era, the fact that she uses the star
symbol and by implication is conscious of her own significance
actually indicates a massive gulf between her and them. They
were unconscious of their effect and their significance was merely
suggested by their creators. Gmeyner on the other hand has

---

[13] Manja's charisma holds the boys together in much the same way that Christ did
his disciples, another disparate group including Matthew the taxcollector and therefore a collaborator with the Roman oppressors and Simon the Zealot, an arch-patriot.
[14] See Klapdor-Kops's preface to *Manja*, 7. She implies the contradiction inherent in
Manja when she emphasizes the role of family influence and then immediately refers
to the idealistic way the children's friendship and esp. Manja herself are presented. She
discusses Gmeyner's 'Philosophie der Kindheit' in more detail in 'Und was die Verfasserin betrifft', 327.

become so involved with her heroine that she feels compelled to
offer Manja herself consolation by making her aware of her effect
on others.

This effect is profound, for Manja embodies qualities which are
vital for survival. She is constantly associated with light and
warmth, which also have religious connotations since Christ
referred to himself as the light of the world.[15] Klapdor-Kops calls
her 'der emphatische Begriff des Humanen';[16] she represents not
just what is necessary for physical survival, but also the things that
make life worth living: love, imagination, and hope. Even
Manja's suicide is underpinned by a religious subtext which suggests a transcendent hope. Her fury with the mob that taunts her
little brother for being Jewish is paralleled with Christ's anger in
the temple:[17] 'Mit solcher Stimme und solcher Geste eine Menge
herauszufordern, ist ungestraft nur einem gestattet, mit dem sich
die Götter in Blitz und Donner gleichsetzen' (p. 371). From this
point her fate parallels Christ's: her walk home from the police
station accompanied by a jeering mob is a conflation of the triumphant entry into Jerusalem and the Via Dolorosa: 'Sie geht
inmitten der Gasse mit erhobenem Kopf. Sie könnte sich nicht anders halten, wenn sie in einer Equipage durch die grüßende
Menge führe und die Schmutzstücke und Steine, die an ihr vor-
beifliegen, Blumen und grüne Zweige wären, die man ihr zuwirft,
und die Schimpfworte jubelnde Grüße' (p. 374). Her subsequent
arrival and wait at the 'Mauer' are described so as to recall the
Garden of Gethsemane: 'Manja wartete regungslos. Nicht mehr
auf die Freunde. Nicht auf etwas Bestimmtes. Auf etwas Helles
und Entscheidendes, das ihr Geschick aufhalten und zum Stehen
bringen werde. Es kam nicht'. She is apparently communing with
the transcendent part of herself, her star, and her isolation at this
point is reflected in the comment 'Ein einziger Stern stand am
Himmel' (p. 376) when she arrives. This recalls Christ's final solitary communion with his father, as does the fact that she too has to
go through with death. But her death is presented so as to suggest
a new beginning as well as an end. For when the four boys next
meet at the 'Mauer' they suddenly have a powerful sense of
Manja's presence: 'Und dann geschah, was in den mehr als vier

---

[15] John 8: 12.   [16] 'Und was die Verfasserin betrifft', 328.
[17] See the accounts in Matt. 21: 12–13, Mark 11: 15–17, Luke 19: 45–6 and John 2: 13–17.

Jahren, seit sie herkamen, schon einige Male geschehen war, daß das Erlebte sich wandelte und aufhob und in einer besonderen Spiegelung von Traum und Spiel eine neue Wirklichkeit entstand. In ihr, lebend und nah, war Manja' (pp. 379–80). Nor are they left with just a vague sense of her presence: at this very moment the clouds part to reveal Cassiopeia producing 'eine ungeheure, alles erfüllende Freude'. Manja is present, albeit on a transcendent level, and the boys feel united with her, for 'der schützende Raum um sie war bis in den Himmel erhöht und ein Teil des Gewölbes von Stille, das den regungslosen Kristall des Augenblicks umschloß wie mit tausend sanft darübergelegten Händen' (p. 380). This too has biblical resonances, for it recalls Christ's post-Resurrection appearance to his joyful disciples in the locked room.[18]

Admittedly our feeling of muted optimism on this final page may be tempered by our recollection of the 'Ende als Vorspiel', when all seems dark and cold and the boys know they have to part. Yet, as Cassiopeia disappears behind the clouds and the boys are left feeling bereft, we are reminded of Christ's ascension, for he too disappeared into the clouds before his disciples' eyes.[19] And, although the boys have to part, there is no acrimony: 'Sie verstanden, jeder auf seine besondere Weise, daß sie einander nur halten konnten, wenn sie sich losließen, nur beisammen bleiben, wenn sie sich trennten' (p. 16). As they go off into their separate political realities, the boys can still hold on to the spirit of unity they enjoyed with Manja. Gmeyner leaves us with the hope that her effect on them will last.

However, in the cold light of day this hope seems fragile, for Gmeyner falls between the stools of a realistic narrative and the idealistic/mythologizing presentation of her heroine. The somewhat heavy-handed religious subtext and obvious poetic conceit of Cassiopeia sit uneasily alongside the more realistic depiction of Nazi persecution and Gmeyner has not found any way of resolving this tension. This is suggested by the fact that the scenes at the 'Mauer' where Cassiopeia appears all occur outside the main text in the 'iEnde als Vorspiel', the 'Zwischenspiel', and the 'Nachspiel'. While it could be argued that the 'Mauer' represents an

---

[18] John 20: 19–21.   [19] See Acts 1:9.

alternative dimension and that Gmeyner wished to stress this in the structure of the text, in fact this positioning simply emphasizes the division between the realist plot and the symbolic level. The attempt to introduce an unambiguously Romantic conception of the child into the context of Nazi persecution is flawed because the realistic genre cannot accommodate it.

But this does not mean that a positive symbolic conception of the child cannot convincingly exist in twentieth-century literature. Aichinger's *Die größere Hoffnung* has a similar theme to *Manja*, for it also suggests the moral triumph of an innocent child over Nazism. But stylistically the texts are very different: while *Manja* is a basically realist narrative with an anachronistic Romantic child, *Die größere Hoffnung* consists of loosely connected scenes where dream sequences and personifications (notably of 'die Nacht' and 'die Verfolgung' in the chapter 'Der Tod der Groß-mutter') are juxtaposed with more realist sequences as in Borchert's *Draußen vor der Tür*.[20] The action is focalized largely through Ellen's perspective and so has the same surreal, poetic quality of Beckmann's vision: like him, she lives in what Kaiser calls a 'Schwebezustand' between dream and a nightmare reality where she can be thrown out of a cake shop because she is wearing the 'Judenstern' and so 'war nicht sicher, auch wirklich wach zu sein' (p. 103).[21] This uncertainty anticipates the child figures of Gert Hofmann, whose dreams and flights of fancy often mirror their everyday reality to an alarming degree.

The tension between dream and reality results in an intensely symbolic text which demands a very different reading from *Manja*. To some extent the text resembles those from the Romantic era where the child figure appears in an essentially non-realistic setting; here, however, reality constantly threatens to break in. This is particularly evident in the chapter 'Das große Spiel', which critics have tended to see as the central chapter of

---

[20] This comparison is drawn by Hedi Kaiser who suggests that the style of *Die größere Hoffnung*, together with its early appearance after the war, led to its relative neglect by German critics who were unable to come to terms with the poetic form of the text and the fact that Ellen's fate was set in an existential context ('Ilse Aichinger, *Die größere Hoffnung*', in Herbert Kaiser and Köpf (eds.), *Erzählen, Erinnern*, 20).

[21] See ibid. 23–4 for a discussion of the tension between dream and reality, real and imaginary locations.

the book.[22] The children are rehearsing a nativity play and initially they are referred to only by their roles, which suggests that they inhabit a self-contained dimension characterized by religious mythology, play, and art. This recalls the dimension inhabited by Romantic children, but here the children are all too aware of the Nazi reality which intrudes and cuts the game short; indeed, as Purdie points out, by incorporating their awareness of that reality into their game they find new reserves of moral courage and compassion as they accept their fate.[23]

Ellen frequently appears in starkly realistic settings, and her uncompromising vision and demands make her seem an alien in this reality. This is clear from the very first chapter in her demands to the initially baffled consul, though he is influenced by her to such an extent that the two end up speaking the same symbolic language. Her alien nature is emphasized by the 'Flügeltraum' chapter when she is caught amongst the munitions trains. When she interrupts the stationmaster, who is reminding the engine driver of the importance of 'Vorschrift' and threatening him with 'Galgen' and 'Schafott' (*Die größere Hoffnung*, 188), Ellen introduces a metaphysical element and so changes the tone completely: ' "Es gibt eine Hölle", schrie Ellen drohend über das Dach des dritten Waggons, "und es gibt Lokomotivführer, die wissen nicht, wohin die Reise geht! . . . Fahr nicht, fahr nicht, solang du es nicht weißt!" Sie sprang ab' (pp. 188–9). Her sudden appearance above them and her imperative, prophetic tones make her resemble an avenging angel, and her rapid disappearance into the fog and the subsequent chase where she leaps across the tracks just in front of a moving train reinforce the impression of her elusive, other-worldly nature. At the interrogation which follows she baffles and exasperates the officer by refusing to answer his questions: effectively they are talking different languages, culminating in the exchange ' "Geboren?" "Ja", sagte Ellen', who is 'erstaunt' to receive a blow. She tells the officer 'Sie fragen falsch' (p. 201) and gradually even he becomes uneasy: his inkling that he is dealing with someone out of the ordinary is suggested by his 'Wie heißt du,

[22] See esp. Catherine Purdie, *'Wenn ihr nicht werdet wie die Kinder': The Significance of the Child in the World-View of Ilse Aichinger* (Frankfurt, 1998), 71–7 for a discussion of this chapter. Purdie discusses the concept of 'Spiel' as central to Aichinger's work.

[23] Ibid. 72–3.

zum letztenmal, wer bist du?' (p. 204), the second question implying doubts as to her nature rather than to her identity. Her speech
becomes ever more symbolic as she asks 'Warum habt ihr eure
Flügel zerbrochen und gegen Stiefel vertauscht? Barfuß muß
man über die Grenze gehen, man kann es nicht besetzen, dieses
Land. . . . Der Himmel ist unterwegs' (pp. 206–7), and the officer
becomes increasingly unsettled by this intrusion into his reality:
'Ein fiebernder Polizist schob ein fremdes Kind durch die Tür und
alles bisher Festgestellte erwies sich als falsche Angabe. Die
Wachstube drohte zu erwachen' (p. 210). The reference to the
'fremdes Kind', an echo of the Romantic tradition, becomes more
significant as we discover that it is St Nikolaus's eve (p. 211).[24] This
realization apparently causes Ellen's words quoted above to res-
onate within the two policemen guarding her: 'wo liegt die
Grenze? Ihr kommt nicht hinüber, barfuß müßt ihr gehen. Stellt
die Stiefel ins Fenster, denn morgen ist Nikolaus. Freut euch, freut
euch!' (p. 212). The 'Grenze' refers back to an earlier dream
sequence (pp. 73–80) when Ellen and Georg had discovered 'das
heilige Land' and thus the message, albeit encoded, is clear:
Christ's dictum 'Except ye be converted, and become as little children, ye shall not enter into the kingdom of heaven'.[25] The parallel between Ellen and Christ is thus evident.

The children fulfil a positive symbolic role, but this novel is more
ambiguous than *Manja*. This is evident in the novels' shared star
motif for, while Gmeyner's stars are those of Cassiopeia, Kaiser
notes that for Aichinger the star is, 'höchstes Paradox, Judenstern
und Stern Davids'.[26] It thus symbolizes both death and a hope beyond it. The 'große Hoffnung' of the first chapter, that of escape to
America, gradually changes into the 'größere Hoffnung' associated
with the star, a transcendent freedom which consists in freely
accepting one's fate whilst never giving up the ideas of hope and joy.

[24] The significance of this is discussed in some detail, ibid. 84–9.
[25] Matt. 18: 3. Purdie particularly emphasizes the importance of this biblical dictum,
quoting from Aichinger's *Aufzeichnungen 1951* in *Kleist, Moos, Fasane* (Frankfurt, 1987)
where the author refers to it as 'vielleicht das härteste Gebot der Bibel' (*'Wenn ihr nicht
werdet wie die Kinder'*, 17).
[26] 'Ilse Aichinger', 31. See also Purdie, *'Wenn ihr nicht werdet wie die Kinder'*, 67–9.
There is a simple reason why Gmeyner does not exploit the 'obvious' duality of the
star, namely that the 'Polizeiverordnung über die Kennzeichnung von Juden in
Deutschland' was passed on 1 Sept. 1941, whereas *Manja* was published in 1938.

Like the older girl Anna, who is on her way to near-certain death in Poland, Ellen accepts the dangers but also the hope offered by her star. Anna's 'tödliche Angst' (p. 119) is evident, even if only 'eine Sekunde lang', but both before and after this momentary lapse her belief in her star seems unshakeable, for she tells Ellen 'die Freiheit ist dort, wo dein Stern steht' (p. 118) and reassures the other children:

'Wenn es finster wird', sagte Anna, 'wenn es sehr finster wird, was geschieht dann?'
'Man hat Angst.'
'Und was tut man?'
'Man wehrt sich.'
'Man schlägt um sich, nicht wahr?' sagte Anna. 'Man merkt, daß es nichts nützt. Es wird noch finsterer. Was tut man jetzt?'
'Man sucht ein Licht', rief Ellen.
'Einen Stern', sagte Anna. 'Es ist sehr finster um die geheime Polizei'. (p. 121)

These comments could seem unconvincing: like Manja, Anna might seem overconscious of her symbolic significance. On the other hand, they are better psychologically motivated than in *Manja*, for they could read as Anna's attempt to reassure the other children despite her own fears. But in this essentially symbolic work psychology is not the principal consideration:[27] Anna is what Kaiser calls a 'Grenz-' or 'transitorische Figur' who, like Ellen and Romantic children I have discussed, straddles the space between reality and dream reality.[28] Certainly there is no indication that Aichinger intended to ironize her comments as if they were the mere childish bravado of Siegfried and Rafael in *Jakob der Lügner*. But if Anna hopes for 'alles' from her star and Ellen concurs, then what is the hope it represents?

When Ellen first decides to wear the 'Judenstern', despite the fact that as a half-Jew she does not have to, she is proud to wear the symbol of her religion: '"Laß' dir das nicht einfallen", hatte die Großmutter gesagt, "sei froh, daß er dir erspart bleibt, daß du ihn nicht tragen mußt wie die andern!" Aber Ellen wußte es besser. Dürfen, so hieß das Wort: Dürfen' (p. 100). She only realizes later what sacrifices this entails: 'Man hatte zu wählen zwischen seinem

---

[27] Kaiser makes this point with reference to the children's unrealistically adult speech in: 'Ilse Aichinger', 25–6.　　　　[28] Ibid. 24–5.

Stern und allen übrigen Dingen' (p. 104). But the star is not merely
a symbol of the Jewish religion: Anna refers to it in specifically
Christian terms and both she and Ellen ascribe to it the properties
of real stars ('leuchten', pp. 101 and 116). As in *Manja* the star represents a transcendent dimension, but there is no pretence that
this can compensate for the hardships: those have to be freely
adopted to attain the 'größere Hoffnung'. The children have access to this hope through their dreams ('Das heilige Land') and in
their nativity play ('Das große Spiel') and, although the threatening reality is always poised to break in, their moral resistance
holds firm. The hearse driver who has offered to take them over
the 'Grenze' may wake them with the words 'Alles ist verloren,
wir kommen nicht mehr über die Grenze!' but the children know
differently: 'Wir sind schon darüber' (p. 80). Again, were it not for
the essentially symbolic nature of the text, we could read this as
the children's self-delusion, suggesting that hope is only accessible in dreams. But the symbolic structure and Aichinger's later
comments about 'Kindheit und Spiel' as 'die Höhepunkte der
Existenz . . . Weil das Spielen und die Kindheit die Welt erträglich
machen und sie überhaupt begründen'[29] suggest that she too is
using the myth of the Romantic child who has access to knowledge and symbolizes a hope derived from a transcendent dimension.[30] This reaches a climax as Ellen runs through the battle for
Vienna, holding an imaginary conversation with Georg:

> 'Georg, die Brücke steht nicht mehr!'
> 'Wir bauen sie neu!'
> 'Wie soll sie heißen?'
> 'Die größere Hoffnung, unsere Hoffnung!'
> 'Georg, Georg, ich sehe den Stern!' (p. 269)

The work ends in a suitably ambivalent way:

Die brennenden Augen auf den zersplitterten Rest der Brücke gerichtet,
sprang Ellen über eine aus dem Boden gerissene, emporklaffende

---

[29] Manuel Esser, ' "Die Vögel beginnen zu singen, wenn es noch finster ist": Auszug
aus einem Gespräch mit Ilse Aichinger', in Samuel Moser (ed.), *Ilse Aichinger: Leben und
Werk* (2nd expanded edn., Frankfurt, 1995), 55. This element of Aichinger's work is particularly emphasized by Purdie, *'Wenn ihr nicht werdet wie die Kinder'*, 59–96.

[30] Kaiser points out that the children's ability to see reality, not realistically, but as
refracted through 'Traum' and 'Spiel', makes them a vehicle for fundamental critique
of that reality ('Ilse Aichinger', 29–30).

Straßenbahnschiene und wurde, noch ehe die Schwerkraft sie wieder zur Erde zog, von einer explodierenden Granate in Stücke gerissen. Über den umkämpften Brücken stand der Morgenstern. (p. 269)

Ellen has leapt her way through the novel,[31] giving her the air of an other-worldly ethereal spirit, and, while her death is violent, the fact that it happens 'noch ehe die Schwerkraft sie wieder zur Erde zog' suggests not just its speed but a transcendence heightened by the appearance of the 'Morgenstern'. For, while this recurrence of the leitmotif might appear mocking or at least indifferent at the death of one child, it actually symbolizes the coming of Christ and thus forms a coherent climax to the novel's religious subtext, where Christian references such as Ellen's last-minute baptism of her grandmother point to the hope of eternal life.[32] This is certainly the context in which this final image of the book should be read, for the idea of eternal life is also expressed by the leitmotif of the 'Brücke' leading from one life to another.[33] The Christian context is reinforced a page earlier by the description of the morning: 'Wie Fenster am Heiligen Abend hob sich das Rot aus dem Grau. Kalt war der Morgen. Unberührt tauchten in der Ferne die Berge über das Getümmel. Diese Berge, hinter denen es blau wurde' (p. 268).

Gmeyner and Aichinger thus both exploit the Romantic myth of the child as a symbol of hope and salvation, albeit with different artistic methods and success. But the question as to whether either text can really convince remains: any temptation to believe

---

[31] Hedi Kaiser indicates the symbolic dimension to this motif, that of the 'Sprung' into the world beyond (ibid. 32).

[32] For refs. to the 'Morgenstern', see 2 Petrus 1: 19 and Offenbarung 2: 28. Purdie points out that Venus is both the evening and the morning star and therefore symbolizes death and new life (' Wenn ihr nicht werdet wie die Kinder', 69). She considers the integration of Jewish and Christian elements to be a key feature of Aichinger's work and discusses especially the near drowning/baptism image of ch. 2 in this light (ibid. 60). The religious aspect of the novel and its integration of Christian and Jewish ideas consistent with Aichinger's Jewish background and Catholic faith has frequently been discussed. See esp. Helga-Maleen Gerresheim, 'Ilse Aichinger', in Benno von Wiese (ed.), Deutsche Dichter der Gegenwart: Ihr Leben und Werk (Berlin, 1973), esp. 486–7 for a discussion of Ellen as a second Christ figure. Hedi Kaiser discusses the biblical allusions of the novel in 'Ilse Aichinger', 33–4.

[33] See Kaiser, 'Ilse Aichinger', 30–1. For a discussion of the bridge motif as part of the concept of 'Spiel', see Purdie, ' Wenn ihr nicht werdet wie die Kinder', 90–6. She reads this motif as Aichinger's more humane reinterpretation of a central tenet of her Catholic faith, the Last Judgment (ibid. 94).

in notions like these children overcoming the Nazis in some spiritual sense is swiftly checked by a glance at any account of the Holocaust. So why do the authors perpetuate this positive image? Are they simply adding to what Kuhn calls the 'pseudo-romantic literature of the twentieth century' where the powerful myth of the child saviour 'becomes debased and sentimentalized'?[34] To imply that the vulnerable child, unable to save herself, can nonetheless offer hope to an evil society is to endow the girls with supernatural qualities in the literary context in direct proportion to their historical victim status. We might accuse Gmeyner in particular of a sentimentality born of her desire to evade the brutal reality of this situation. This use of the child figure seems inconsistent with the uncompromising honesty that usually attends any depiction of it and its perspective.

It would be easy to make and support such accusations from our present-day perspective, but we should perhaps spare a sympathetic thought for authors writing at this time on this subject. Aichinger witnessed the persecution of the Jews at first hand and lost a number of her family in the Holocaust; in view of such an emotional battering, 1948 seems early for her to be writing on the subject at all. It is not surprising that she should adopt the child's perspective, for this allows her to present the Third Reich as an incomprehensible nightmare, while at the same time integrating an element of much-needed hope through her portrayal of Ellen. And the fact that these elements of despair and hope are so closely integrated, in both Ellen and the star motif, gives the novel the unity and coherence that *Manja* lacks: rather than the element of hope being artificially grafted onto the text, it exists at the very heart of the despair that Aichinger makes no attempt to soften.

But, while we may find *Manja* idealistic to the point of sentimentality, Gmeyner has some excuse for not portraying the full reality of the Nazi 'Judenverfolgung'. The novel covers the years 1920 to 1934 and therefore, although she gives a graphic account of the rise of Nazism and anti-Semitism, Gmeyner is not concerned with the same issues as Aichinger and Becker. *Manja* is a piece of perfectly sincere wishful thinking that portrays the values Gmeyner hopes will prevail in Germany in order to avoid catastrophe. Through the children she demonstrates her own faith in the inherent goodness of the 'kleine Mann'; significantly, her most likeable adults are also

---

[34] *Corruption in Paradise*, 53.

described so as to emphasize their childlike qualities, which recalls the Romantics' habit of referring to privileged adults as 'kindlich'. While in some cases, like Eduard Müller and Lea, the adults' child-like attributes may simply imply vulnerability, in the Heidemanns and Anna Müller they suggest the capacity for love, joy, and resilience which enables them to transcend their circumstances.[35]

At the other extreme we have Becker's works. These appeared much later than *Manja* and *Die größere Hoffnung* and have the realistic and unsentimental approach we might expect from someone who not only spent his own childhood in a ghetto and two concentration camps but whose experience of persecution was not as recent and raw as Aichinger's. However, their aims seem to have been broadly similar, since she stated 'Ich wollte zuerst nur einen Bericht schreiben darüber, wie es wirklich war. Das ist dabei herausgekommen, aber doch auf eine ganz andere Weise, als ich es mir vorgestellt habe'.[36] That the novel was rooted in Aichinger's own experience is clear from her 'Rede an die Jugend' (1988), which strongly suggests that the portrayal of Ellen and her friends is not idealization but a description of Aichinger's own lived reality.[37] And, even if we suspect her of rewriting her own past in this speech so as to make it consistent with her novel, we should still beware of dismissing her too lightly, for Aichinger is not the only person to whom Ellen owes her existence: as Kaiser points out she is also modelled in part on Sophie Scholl, the youngest of the 'Weiße Rose' student resistance group.[38] Like Anne Frank, Sophie Scholl provides us with a real-life yardstick by which to measure apparently extravagant literary idealizations. And yet reality, as we saw in the case of Anne Frank, is not invulnerable to mythologizing: especially in the context of the Third Reich we need to find heroes and hope, and, while there is no denying the moral courage of those who opposed the Nazi regime, their

---

[35] On the night Heini Heidemann is conceived his parents 'lachen . . . wie kleine Kinder' (*Manja*, 24); Eduard Müller embraces his wife Anna 'so wie ein Kind, wenn ihm etwas zugestoßen ist' (p. 41); David thinks Lea looks 'sehr kindlich' (p. 47) as she sleeps in blissful ignorance of his imminent suicide; and Anna has 'ein rundes, alterndes Kindergesicht' (p. 157).

[36] In conversation with Esser, in Moser (ed.), *Ilse Aichinger*, 50.

[37] In Moser (ed.), *Ilse Aichinger*, 20–2, esp. 21–2. Kaiser discusses the autobiographical background of the novel in 'Ilse Aichinger', 18–19.

[38] Kaiser, 'Ilse Aichinger', 19. Also Hermann Vinke, 'Sich nicht anpassen lassen . . . Gespräch mit Ilse Aichinger über Sophie Scholl', in Moser (ed.), *Ilse Aichinger*, 36–41.

activities have never lost anything in the telling, whether in literary or historical accounts. Our desire to idealize is especially powerful in the cases of 'ordinary' people like Anne Frank and Sophie Scholl, because they allow us to believe in ourselves and our own inherent goodness and capacity to resist evil. This impulse is at the very heart of the writers' and our own need to idealize children who come to represent the latent good in all of us. We need to believe in human nature as expressed in Inge Scholl's statement about the members of the 'Weiße Rose' group:

Aber kann man sie Helden nennen? Sie haben nichts Übermenschliches unternommen. Sie haben etwas Einfaches verteidigt, sind für etwas Einfaches eingestanden, für das Recht und die Freiheit des einzelnen Menschen, für seine freie Entfaltung und für ein freies Leben. Sie haben sich keiner außergewöhnlichen Idee geopfert, haben keine großen Ziele verfolgt; was sie wollten, war, daß Menschen wie du und ich in einer menschlichen Welt leben können.[39]

However, the suspicion of excessive idealization in the case of Ellen is relieved quite simply by the text's poetic form for, while it may seem absurd to equate the apparently realistically conceived Manja with the saviour, Ellen is more obviously a symbolic figure from the outset. The 'fremdes Kind' survives, at least in the literary context, as a bringer of much-needed hope.

This positive, even idealistic presentation of children is perfectly understandable in the literature of the victim; even the otherwise implausible transformation from innocent victim to bringer of universal hope is comprehensible, if only as authorial wish-fulfilment. But, given the indoctrination apparatus sketched in Chapter 1, it seems impossible for Gentile children under the Third Reich to embody similar positive potential. We cannot imagine how they could cast off the 'Sack überm Kopf' in order to see clearly, let alone how they might symbolize hope for the future. However, the positive myth proves remarkably resilient. In what follows I shall examine four texts, Anna Seghers's *Der Ausflug der toten Mädchen* (1943/4), Le Fort's *Die Unschuldigen*, Hanna Johansen's *Die Analphabetin* (1982), and Wolf's *Kindheitsmuster*, where various aspects of the myth are upheld. The authors'

---

[39] *Die Weiße Rose* (1955; 2nd edn. Frankfurt, 1990), 12.

reasons for using this myth vary, as does their aesthetic success, but they are united by the positive potential they see in the child.

ASPECTS OF THE ROMANTIC CHILD

Return to Nature? Anna Seghers's Der Ausflug der toten Mädchen

Seghers's story *Der Ausflug der toten Mädchen* is set before World War I, but it bears on our theme because it deals with childhood innocence and corruption in the Third Reich context. It posits a view of childhood as entirely innocent and indeed presents the girls in the kind of idyllic pastoral landscape that has been identified with the child's original innocence since *Émile*. They are even associated with natural phenomena in a way that recalls Romantic writers.[40] Leni has an 'Apfelgesicht' (*Der Ausflug der toten Mädchen*, 10), of Marianne we are told 'Man sah ihr ebensowenig wie einer Blume Zeichen von Herzlosigkeit an, von Verschulden oder Gewissenskälte' (p. 11), and at one point the Rhine mist obscures the girls' faces 'so daß ich die einzelnen Gesichter von Nora und Leni und Marianne und wie sie sonst hießen, nicht mehr deutlich unterschied, wie sich keine einzelne Dolde mehr abhebt in einem Gewirr wilder Blumen' (p. 14). This evocation of the girls in total harmony with the landscape reaches its zenith here:

> Wir waren alle im stillen Licht still geworden, so daß man das Krächzen von ein paar Vögeln hörte und das Fabrikgeheul aus Amöneburg. Sogar Lore war völlig verstummt. Marianne und Leni und ich, wir hatten alle drei unsere Arme ineinander verschränkt in einer Verbundenheit, die einfach zu der großen Verbundenheit alles Irdischen unter der Sonne gehörte.... Nie hat uns jemand, als noch Zeit dazu war, an diese gemeinsame Fahrt erinnert. (pp. 28–9)

Given the details of Marianne and Nora's later complicity with the events of the Nazi era, which is constantly woven into this idyllic portrayal of their younger days, it seems naive to suggest a period of such total innocence, especially since the narrator gives little psychological explanation for this complicity. Indeed, her constant expressions of incredulity at this involvement, when

---

[40] e.g. the child in Novalis's *Die Lehrlinge zu Sais*: 'Es hatte große dunkle Augen mit himmelblauem Grunde, wie Lilien glänzte seine Haut und seine Locken wie lichte Wölkchen, wenn der Abend kommt' (*Schriften*, i. 80).

juxtaposed with the pastoral idyll, make the Nazi era, rather than the far-off days of childhood innocence, seem like the product of the narrator's imagination. The days of innocence seem more immediate than the Nazi era: the sound of her teacher's voice calling her by her old name, Netty, virtually effects a physical transformation: 'Beim Klang meines alten Namens packte ich vor Bestürzung . . . mit beiden Fäusten nach meinen Zöpfen. Ich wunderte mich, daß ich die zwei dicken Zöpfe anpacken konnte: man hatte sie also doch nicht im Krankenhaus abgeschnitten' (pp. 9–10). Though she knows rationally that this life is 'unwiederbringlich verloren' (p. 9), occasional tense-slippage makes her childhood seem more immediate than the Nazi present: 'Jetzt *zogen* die beiden, Marianne und Leni, von denen eine ihres Kindes verlustig *gegangen war* durch das Verschulden der anderen, die Arme gegenseitig um die Hälse geschlungen, Schläfe an Schläfe gelehnt, aus dem Schaukelgärtchen' (p. 12, my emphases). Like the narrator's desperate (and, she acknowledges, self-deluded) belief that her schoolgirl name might make her 'wieder gesund . . . jung, lustig, bereit zu dem alten Leben mit den alten Gefährten' (p. 9), this tense-slippage suggests not just nostalgia but also a fervent desire for a reconciliation between Marianne and Leni. Like all Romantic depictions of childhood, it does not spring from a purely regressive impulse; rather, like Romantic writers, Seghers turns to childhood in an attempt to imagine an alternative, better future. The girls are presented in an overwhelmingly positive light: friendly, supportive, and unselfish, and all are extremely fond of their 'Lieblingslehrerin', the Jewish Fräulein Sichel. How they turn out in the Nazi era seems essentially a matter of chance: Marianne's betrayal of her childhood friend can only be ascribed to her marrying a high-ranking Nazi official, but there is not even this much explanation for Nora's brutality to her former favourite teacher. The only hint of an explanation is an image which might have come straight from Romantic writings: 'Die Kaffeeterrasse am Rhein war mit Rosenstöcken bepflanzt. Sie schienen, mit den Mädchen verglichen, so regelrecht, so kerzengerade, so wohlbehütet wie Gartenblumen neben Feldblumen' (p. 13).[41] At this stage

---

[41] Schaub points to the association between children and flowers in works of German Romantic writers and artists. He suggests that for them, flowers, like children, represent the golden age (*Génie Enfant*, 113).

the girls are still free to follow their own basically positive inclinations and while some continue to do so into adulthood, only to fall victim to the Nazi era, in the case of Marianne and Nora, Nazi ideology prevails. The loss of so much positive potential is perhaps best explained by a description of the girls' schooling: 'Wie viele Aufsätze auch noch geschrieben wurden über die Heimat und die Geschichte der Heimat und die Liebe zur Heimat, nie wurde erwähnt, daß vornehmlich unser Schwarm aneinandergelehnter Mädchen, stromaufwärts im schrägen Nachmittagslicht, zur Heimat gehörte' (p. 29). Again, academic education and its effects are presented as at best unimportant and at worst destructive: Seghers suggests that the feeling of unity and warmth amongst these girls contains a truly positive potential for a future political state. Certainly the state she envisages would have contrasted very favourably with the perverted conception of 'Heimat' that Hitler was to introduce some years after this pastoral idyll: 'Wie konnte dann später ein Betrug, ein Wahn in ihre [Marianne's] Gedanken eindringen, daß sie und ihr Mann allein die Liebe zu diesem Land gepachtet hätten und deshalb mit gutem Recht das Mädchen, an das sie sich jetzt lehnte, verachteten und anzeigten' (pp. 28–9). The girls represent the core of innocence and spontaneous emotional responses before they are stilted by academic learning with nationalistic overtones and, later still, sullied and perverted by a malicious ideology. This use of children seems to spring from Seghers's political convictions for, as a committed Marxist, she held a belief in human perfectibility which is perfectly expressed in the child figure. This emphasis on the positive potential of childhood is common to a number of later Socialist authors, notably Wolf, whose *Kindheitsmuster* will be discussed again later in this chapter. It finds particularly striking expression in Franz Fühmann's *Das Judenauto–Vierzehn Tage aus zwei Jahrhunderten* (1962), for although the author portrays his 9-year-old self as already corrupted by Nazism, he ends his account with the founding of the German Democratic Republic, asking:

Wann war er gekommen, der erste Anstoß zu der Wandlung, die ich erfahren hatte? Auf der Antifaschule, wo es mir wie Schuppen von den Augen fiel, da ich die Bewegungsgesetze der Gesellschaft erkennen lernte und zum ersten Mal den verschlungenen Weg der deutschen Geschichte über Weltkrieg und Stalingrad zu jener deutschen Republik, die nun meine Heimat war? Gewiß, dort war jene Wende vollzogen

worden, ihr Anstoß aber mußte tiefer liegen. Als ich zum ersten Mal
Lenin las? Als ich die zertrümmerte Muschel Noworossijsk über dem
brackigen Wasser des Hafens erblickte? Als ich durch die Wälder Böh-
mens hetzte? Als ich auf der Pritsche lag und aus dem Lautsprecher die
Stimme aus Stalingrad dröhnte? Oder tiefer, noch tiefer? Ich wußte es
nicht, und ich weiß es auch heut nicht; vielleicht ist es so, daß der
Mensch sein Leben lang auf dem Weg zu dem Wesen ist, das er sein
könnte, und das er vielleicht zum ersten Mal mit den staunenden Augen
des Kinds im spiegelnden Grün des Kachelofens gesehen.[42]

This image of the 3-year-old reflected in the stove tiles is Fühmann's first memory and appears at the beginning of his account.
For him, as for Seghers, childhood is a source of positive potential,
both morally and politically, the inner core of human values of
which Seghers writes in *Das siebte Kreuz* (1942): 'wir fühlten auch,
daß es im Innersten etwas gab, was unangreifbar war und unver-
letzbar'.[43] Given the time when *Der Ausflug der toten Mädchen* was
written, we can understand how reluctant Seghers was to relin-
quish this belief in the positive potential of childhood.

The Child Saviour: Gertrud von Le Fort's Die Unschuldigen

If Seghers uses children to suggest a political ideology, Le Fort's
Die Unschuldigen also uses Romantic motifs to raise the argument
to a universal level. Again, the child narrator is the principal embodiment of moral integrity and simple fellow-feeling. He instinctively dislikes his uncle who, it turns out, had ordered the
Oradour massacre during the war. The 11-year-old only learns the
full details of his uncle's guilt at a relatively late stage of the narrative but, even while he lacks all factual evidence for disliking
Eberhard, he is unshakeable in his intuition. He formulates this in
the ambivalent terms of an unknowing child who needs an emotional image to convey his dislike but one who had also experienced the horrors of bombing raids at a very young age: 'Er lacht
gerade so wie unser Barry [their dog], aber er ist viel böser als
Barry, ich glaube, daß er Bomben werfen kann' (*Die Unschuldigen*,
432). At this stage he does not even know why he mentions bombs
and this intuition marks his kinship with what Grylls calls

---

[42] In *Das Judenauto; Kabelkran und Blauer Peter; Zweiundzwanzig Tage, oder, Die Hälfte des Lebens* (Rostock, 1993), 171–2.   [43] *Das siebte Kreuz* (Zurich, 1949), 368.

'old-fashioned children' whose uncanny powers of perception disturb the adults around them.[44] The boy's frequently unchild-like diction, as when he talks about 'diese Welt' and 'der liebe Gott' (pp. 436–7), suggests that he functions as a mouthpiece for the author's religious ideas. Le Fort clearly intended to go beyond a discussion of mere social or political injustice: the world order, divided into those capable of inhuman actions and those with fellow-feeling and integrity, is discussed through this boy, whom she identifies with the Christ child. This is first hinted at in the boy's description of the bombing raid that was such a defining experience for him, for he reports that his mother cried 'Maria, nimm mein Kind in deine Arme' (p. 418), an exhortation repeated on his deathbed (p. 457). Indeed, the child himself thought his mother was the Virgin Mary when the raid had passed, 'denn Mammis Gesicht war so schwarz wie das Bild der Gottesmutter von Altöt-ting' (p. 418). He is also identified with one of his child ancestors who went on a crusade to the Holy Land as depicted in the castle chapel, for the boy likes to believe 'daß er lebte und ein heiliges Kind gewesen ist' (p. 451). Most significantly of all he buys his mother a figurine of the 'Christuskind von Prag' for Christmas, a depiction of the Christ child with crown, sceptre, and orb 'wie ein richtiger kleiner König'. Heini had refused to buy a mere 'Krip-penkind' which 'lag arm und bloß in der Krippe'; instead, he says, 'Ich möchte ein mächtiges Christuskind haben, denn Mammi muß jetzt beschützt werden' (p. 435). The identification of Heini with the child saviour is a Romantic trait, but it is significant that in the dual figures of the Christ child Le Fort emphasizes two very different aspects of its nature: the apparent impotence and inno-cence of the child and the majesty and strength of the king and saviour. This sense of power in apparent impotence is one of the main features of myths of 'das göttliche Kind' as identified by Jung and Kerényi (1939/40).[45] The tension between these two

[44] Grylls sees the old-fashioned child as an extension of the Romantic tradition of the child's innate wisdom (*Guardians and Angels*, 36).

[45] See *Das Göttliche Kind* (1939/40) in id., *Einführung in das Wesen der Mythologie: Das Göttliche Kind, Das Göttliche Mädchen* (4th revised edn., Zurich, 1951). Kerényi points to the deep meaning of myths of the divine child as 'das Sichenthüllen der Gottheit in der paradoxen Einheit des Tiefsten und des Höchsten, des Allerschwächsten und des Allerstärksten' (ibid. 52) and Jung refers to the myth of the Christ child and St Christo-pher where the child appears in the typical form of 'Kleiner als klein und größer als groß' (ibid. 116).

apparently irreconcilable opposites is what gives this work its pe-
culiar force, even though initially it is the impotence of childhood
that is most emphasized.

As the title indicates, childhood innocence is a basic tenet of
this narrative. The various children mentioned in the text are frequently seen not only as innocent but also as victims, whether in
the Oradour massacre, the story of a similar event during the
Thirty Years War, or the biblical Slaughter of the Innocents as
represented in the castle chapel. In all these episodes they are victims of the adult world and, although Le Fort emphasizes that not
all Germans were arrant Nazis by juxtaposing Eberhard with his
brother, who committed suicide rather than carry out an inhuman
order, all the adults of this narrative are implicated in some way in
the guilt of the war. Heini's mother, for all her sympathy for the
war's victims and horror at Eberhard's actions, appears unable to
break free of the fascination he exercises over her; and the boy's
grandmother not only attempts to close her eyes to Eberhard's
guilt, but even manages to come to terms with the massacre on the
grounds that it was permitted by God (p. 439). She acquiesces in
the suffering of innocents through an almost bigoted faith, telling
her daughter-in-law: 'die Schuldigen trifft nur die gerechte Strafe,
aber der Anblick der unschuldig Leidenden macht die Herzen
weich—auch Christus hat unschuldig gelitten. Solange du das
nicht annimmst, kannst du keine Christin sein'. Le Fort's ambivalent attitude towards this tenet of Christian doctrine can be assessed from Heini's mental response to his grandmother's words:
' "Es klang eigentlich schön und geheimnisvoll, was Großmama
da sagte—warum will es Mammi denn nicht annehmen?" Dann
aber fiel mir ein, wie Herr Unger neulich zu ihr sagte: "Woran
liegt es nur, daß man den frommen Leuten ihre Frömmigkeit heut
nicht mehr glaubt?" ' (p. 440). This suggests that the child's instinctive morality is preferable to the rigid religious doctrine of his
'fromme, harte Großmamma' (p. 446), whose love for her son
makes her determined not to accept the truth about the past. The
natural order has been perverted and when the child attempts to
point this out he is himself made mad: he tries to call down divine
justice on Eberhard by ringing the cursed Frederizia bell, but ironically, instead of affecting Eberhard, the sound of the bell sends
Heini himself into a delirium. We cannot know how much of his
description of what happens at the church is true and how much

is a product of his fever, but Le Fort clearly suggests that the adult world represented by Eberhard cannot be made worse by the ringing of the Frederizia bell. Innocence and moral integrity, natural and humane values, are relegated to the marginalized status of madness by this post-war society whose members are trying to put the war behind them and deny any responsibility for it. Childhood innocence can find no place in this environment and so succumbs first to madness and then to death. Le Fort is apparently subscribing to the idea of childhood prevalent in the early decades of the twentieth century, itself a perversion of Romanticism in its dead-end mentality.

Despite Le Fort's assertion of the innocence of childhood, which is rooted in her religious convictions and, we suspect, in her desire to find some element of hope in a dark era, *Die Unschuldigen* appears to be one of the more pessimistic works to uphold the Romantic myth of childhood. Even the child saviour to whom Heini had entrusted his mother is apparently negated: initially she does not recognize the child, and even when her son tells her who it is, her response is deeply disappointing: ' "Armes, kleines Christuskind," sagte sie, "hast du jemals etwas Grausames verhindern können?" ' (p. 437). Nor do Heini's intuitive morality and clear-sightedness seem to lead anywhere: their positive potential is snuffed out by his premature death. Of course, we might say the same of *Manja* and *Die größere Hoffnung* where the religious subtext is clearly intended to imply a transcendent hope, but there is a difference between these texts in that *Die Unschuldigen* is an explicit discussion of the Christian faith at a time when recent events suggested its values had failed. The grandmother's apparent ability to come to terms with the Oradour massacre by means of her faith is chilling and implies a critique of a certain type of religious belief. The mother's faith on the other hand has been shaken by the idea of innocent suffering (p. 440).

Yet *Die Unschuldigen* is not apparently intended to be negative: the voice of conscience embodied in Heini and in the 'fremdes Kind', a ghost of times past, eventually forces Eberhard's departure and the mother is saved from him. Moreover, it is at her son's deathbed that she appears to recover her lost faith, since she is suddenly able to pray again: in effect he redeems her and so casts a more positive light even on his grandmother's comments about the suffering of the innocent. Without Christ's death there can be no redemption and the identification of these two figures is made clear by the mother's final exhortation to the Virgin and the implication that Heini has escaped 'diese Welt' for something better. However, there is a certain tension here: the boy's redemptive death may be intended to reassert Christian values in a world that has lost them, an overtly positive message with the child symbolizing the triumph of humane values, but the whole point of Christ's sacrifice was to give the human race redemption for all time, and this emphasizes the waste of a young life. The death of a child 'too good for this world' does not now have the popular appeal that it had at the beginning of the century and the deathbed scene recalls the likes of Gerhart Hauptmann's *Hanneles Himmelfahrt* (1893) which, for modern tastes, may be embarrassing rather than moving. While the image of the Romantic child seems once again to have responded to its author's needs and those of its time, it does not necessarily transfer well to our own era. However, the Romantic child has also persisted into more recent writings about the Third Reich, where the authors' own needs are not so evident and the presentation is therefore more convincing.

Ignorance is Bliss?: Hanna Johansen's Die Analphabetin

The title of Johansen's story makes it clear that her 5-year-old narrator conforms to one aspect of the Romantic myth of childhood, for her inability to read places her on the fringes of the adult world. She is one of the pre-socialized type whose natural spontaneity and fantasy life have not yet been stifled by academic training and this impression is reinforced by the idyllic landscape in which she is presented. Johansen felt that the work might in fact have become too idyllic, but this fear is dismissed by Hein, who contends that the ' "revolutionäre Idylle" . . . zeigt an, was der Mensch alles zu verlieren hat'.[46] The sense of imminent loss pervades *Die Analphabetin*, for if the idyll of *Der Ausflug der toten Mädchen* is seen to be threatened in retrospect, Johansen's childhood paradise is under more immediate threat: the story is set in summer 1944 and the main reason the child spends so much time in the countryside is to escape the bombing raids. The precarious

---

[46] 'ATLANTIS-Lesung: Hanna Johansen, *Die Analphabetin*', *Die Woche* (14 Oct. 1982).

nature of the idyll is perfectly expressed by the proximity of the 'Gärtnerei' where she spends so much of her time and the 'Friedhof', for as Pulver points out, the flowers now have only one purpose: funeral wreaths.[47] Johansen walks a fine line between presenting the idyll of childhood innocence and the horrors of war, for she does not move beyond the limited perspective of her protagonist. Because she is unable to read, the child is dependent on adults for information, and frequently they shield her from the worst knowledge. However, she is not totally dependent on them: her distinctive view of events is thrown into relief by the blind man, who tells her: 'Die Sehenden . . . sehen nichts aus Vorsicht. Und aus Rücksicht sehen sie nichts. . . . Ihre Augen gebrauchen sie zum Lesen. Sie wissen, daß das Gedruckte mit der Wahrheit nicht viel zu tun hat. Und sie lesen es doch. Andere Wege, die Wahrheit zu erfahren, beschreiten sie nicht mehr' (*Die Analphabetin,* 10). Under these circumstances it seems a positive advantage for the child not to be able to read: if the Romantics were concerned that learning repressed the child's natural spontaneity, then how much more is to be feared from an era when the reading matter available is mainly heavily slanted propaganda. As it is, the child picks up the language of propaganda parrot-fashion from adult conversations, as when she spontaneously uses the term 'feindliche Flugzeuge'. Nevertheless, her basic ignorance is clear from the rest of the conversation:

Wer ist in den Flugzeugen? Menschen?
Es sind Engländer drin.
Feindliche Flugzeuge, denke ich. Und warum sind die Engländer unsere Feinde? Das muß man doch wissen.
Sie sind es nicht. Wir haben sie dazu gemacht.
Wir? Was für ein Wort. Noch verwirrender als andere. (p. 44)

The child's ethical concern is clear from her questioning of the word 'wir', for this echoes Rousseau's determination to bring Émile up to be an 'homme' not a 'citoyen'.[48] The girl's inability to ally herself with the interests of a nation state is another positive advantage, a means of preserving her instinctive emotional and moral responses from adult bigotry. This lack of political bias is

---

[47] 'Kein Kinderreim auf die Welt', *Aargauer Tagblatt* (8 Jan. 1983).
[48] *Émile,* 9.

evident in her moral reasoning here:

Warum schicken sie [die Engländer] Flugzeuge mit Bomben?
Warum fragst du mich, sagt er.
Ja, sage ich.
Das mußt du jemand anders fragen.
Warum wollte er es nicht sagen? Wußte er nichts darüber? Das kann ich
mir kaum vorstellen. Schließlich wußte sogar ich das schon.
Das weiß doch jedes Kind, sagte ich.
... Weil unsere Flugzeuge bei ihnen Bomben werfen, sagte ich. (pp. 88–9)

The limits of the child's reasoning are obvious, but her instinctive
refusal to make black and white judgements on the basis of adult
propaganda testifies to an intuitive moral response, a desire for a
truth beyond national interests.[49]

However, as in the case of Hofmann's children, this child's
moral vision is not just a product of the curiosity that prompts awkward questions. Her ongoing game with the tin soldiers symbolizes her powerlessness and incomprehension regarding the real
war, for not only is she not allowed to change the position of the
soldiers (p. 30), but she is also unclear as to the details of the battle,
as we see from her conversation with her 'Freund', the stone frog:

Wer wird gewinnen? sagt er.
Das weiß man erst nachher. Jetzt kämpfen sie noch.
Und zu wem soll ich halten?
Er will, daß die Guten siegen. Und ich kann ihm nicht sagen, wer die
Guten sind. (p. 166)

These comments clearly refer to more than just the child's game:
Johansen allows for a certain ambiguity when the child promises
the frog 'Ich werde dir alles über den Krieg erzählen' (p. 83)
and says that he knows nothing 'über den Krieg . . . außer dem,
was ich ihm erzähle' (p. 166). But while her moral impulse, however simplistically expressed here, may be frustrated by lack of

---

[49] The apparently paradoxical manner in which this child both assimilates propaganda verbatim and yet retains an ability to question it is not as surprising as it may
seem. It recalls Robert Coles's work on children's understanding of politics, where he
suggests that, while children clearly absorb the political views expressed around them
and in some instances parrot them word for word, even those in totalitarian countries
retain a certain open-mindedness and ability to question what they have been taught.
See esp. Coles's discussion of his conversation with the 11-year-old Nicaraguan
Alfredo in id., *The Political Life of Children* (Boston and New York, 1986), 147–51.

knowledge, this is compensated for by her imaginative and emotional responses, which in true Romantic tradition are accorded great significance. This is particularly clear when she and Robert play with the tin soldiers. Robert, the adult, sets up a realistic 'Hunnenüberfall', complete with burning house and human chaos, but the child is dissatisfied:

Kann man das nicht anders aufstellen?
Man kann schon, sagt er. . . .
Man muß sich dann eben eine neue Geschichte ausdenken für das brennende Haus. Die Leute laufen weg, um die Nachbarn zu holen, daß sie den Brand löschen. Die Hunnen kommen zu Hilfe.
Er findet diese Geschichte zum Lachen. Ich nicht.
Du meinst wohl, du könntest was ändern, sagt er hustend.
Nein.
Das weiß ich selber, daß ich nichts ändern kann. Das braucht man mir nicht zu sagen. Bloß für mich ist das kein Grund, auf bessere Geschichten zu verzichten. (pp. 104–5)

As Moser points out of the last sentence, 'Kein Kind kann einen so vernünftigen Satz sagen', but 'Noch weniger . . . kann es ein Erwachsener'.[50] Such imaginative impulses, the refusal to accept reality as fixed, belong to childhood, and the fact that these impulses are not confined to the world of play is underlined later when the child passes houses where English bombers have scored a direct hit:

Wenn ich dort wohnen würde, so würde alles, was ich besitze, zu Asche verbrennen, jetzt, in diesem Augenblick. . . .
  Muß man nicht doch etwas tun? Man kann nicht bloß zuschauen. Hinrennen und die Flammen ersticken, wäre das nicht das mindeste? Wäre es den Flammen gleich, wenn ich käme, um sie zu ersticken? Oder sie werden böse, wenn du dich ihnen in den Weg stellst. Sie greifen nach dir, um dich zu verschlingen. Und selbst, wenn es so wäre, wäre es nicht das mindeste? (pp. 198–9)

The way she anthropomorphizes the flames is typical of an imaginative child and significantly it makes them a direct personal challenge: for her there is no such thing as an impersonal, amoral force, an act of God, or an unavoidable catastrophe. Her fantasy

---

[50] 'Geschüttelt von Unwissenheit: Hanna Johansens Fragen und Kinderfragen aus dem Kriegssommer 1944', *Süddeutsche Zeitung* (26/7 Mar. 1983).

life thus protects her from the worst of adult sins: resignation and indifference.

Of course, the girl does not exist in a vacuum: some of the details of the Nazi environment necessarily impinge upon her consciousness. She is occasionally alarmed by overheard adult conversations, for example: 'Ich hatte aber ganz gut verstanden, daß man zwei Eheleute zum Tode verurteilt hatte, weil sie geplündert hatten. Und ich habe mir geschworen, nie im Leben etwas mitzunehmen, was mir nicht gehört' (p. 89). Later she fears that she will be 'abgeholt' if she does 'etwas Verbotenes' (p. 168). However, it is significant that these worries are woven into the daily concerns of the average 5-year-old, for example, whether Herr Sliwinski is allowed to keep the two screws he has found on the street (p. 88), or whether it is 'verboten' for her to have written on the wall (p. 168). The 'values' of Nazi society simply reinforce her already well-developed moral sense; as for the abuses of propaganda, she is apparently preserved from these by her ignorance (the 'negative' side of innocence) and her imagination, which provides her with emotional and moral responses (the positive aspect of innocence which provides hope for the future).

Significantly the child herself worries about the possible loss of that fantasy life when in conference with the frog:

Für ihn ist die Zeit der Könige und Prinzessinnen vorbei.
Das war einmal, sagt er.
Ich lache ihn aus. Dann mußt du für immer ein Frosch bleiben. Willst du das?
Warum nicht, sagt er. Das ist keine schlechte Lösung. Weißt du was Besseres für mich?
Was sollte ich sagen? Ich war darauf nicht vorbereitet. Ich wußte nur, daß ich ihn eines Tages an die Wand werfen mußte, um ihn zu erlösen.
Und nun? Der Frosch will gar kein Prinz werden. Es gefällt ihm nicht.
Wie kann man ihn dann an die Wand werfen?
Und ich? Was wird aus mir, wenn es nichts ist damit? (pp. 159–60)

This might be the eternal lament of the child faced with the necessity of growing up, but given the particular importance of this child's fantasy life it is more than that: it is a question of how the spontaneous emotional and moral responses of childhood can be retained in adulthood, a question we shall see addressed by those novels that treat the process of growing up (see Chapter 3, below).

Instinctive Morality?: Christa Wolf's Kindheitsmuster

The survival of the Romantic child in the texts discussed above
might be explained by the fact that none of these protagonists
come under systematic Nazi indoctrination as children: while the
girls of *Der Ausflug der toten Mädchen* are fertile ground for this ideology because they have apparently been subject to a nationalisti-
cally slanted education, the protagonists of *Die Unschuldigen* and
Die Analphabetin are too young to have been indoctrinated as described in Chapter 1. Nelly Jordan is a quite different case. I have
already discussed Wolf's presentation of daily indoctrination
under the Nazi regime and suggested how difficult it is for the
child to gain any insight into an alternative value system; this emphasis seems consistent with Wolf's aims in writing the book for,
as Kuhn points out, it was written in reaction against books where
the heroes 'eigentlich schon während des Faschismus zu ziemlich
bedeutenden und richtigen Einsichten kommen, politisch, menschlich'.[51] Critics have tended to emphasize the extent to which
Nelly's character is deformed by the indoctrination to which she
is subjected; Barnett, for example, emphasizes Wolf's positive
perception of children, saying that for her they embody 'spontaneity, imagination and empathy', whereas the adult world is the
'damaging agent' that suppresses these qualities.[52] She then goes
on to look at the most extreme example of that damaging agent,
the Nazi regime, contrasting its effects on Nelly and Christa T.
and suggesting that while Christa manages to 'preserve [her]
childhood authenticity undamaged', Nelly succumbs to 'distorting influences that all but destroy' her.[53] While Barnett concedes
that there are a few moments when Nelly's inner life seems to be
in conflict with the values imposed upon her, she suggests that
'The few tentative signs that the corruption process has not been
total do not create any sense of revitalisation'.[54] Various critics including Colin E. Smith, Anna K. Kuhn, and Robert K. Shirer had
previously looked at those tentative signs and also came to quite
negative conclusions about them. Smith contends that Nelly

---

[51] *Christa Wolf's Utopian Vision: from Marxism to Feminism* (Cambridge, 1988), 109.
Wolf's comments are from ead., 'Erfahrungsmuster: Diskussion zu *Kindheitsmuster*', in
Die Dimension des Autors: Essays und Aufsätze, Reden und Gespräche 1959–1985, 2 vols. (repr.
Frankfurt, 1990), ii. 807.
[52] 'Perceptions of Childhood', 65.   [53] Ibid. 70.   [54] Ibid. 69.

becomes so adept at concealing and suppressing her 'natural moral instincts' that 'moral awareness never had the chance to develop'; he only allows her the 'moral awareness of the artist' after her time in hospital.[55] Kuhn instances episodes such as Nelly's reaction to the *Kristallnacht* and to the suspension of Gerda Link from the JM simply as proof of how effectively Nelly is able to deny and repress her true feelings.[56] Shirer concedes the positive potential of Nelly's responses in two of the incidents I shall discuss, the *Kristallnacht* and the 'Judenjunge' episode, but contends that it is natural for the narrator to prefer to recall such positive incidents, a comment which might be taken to suggest that the narrator has exaggerated their importance.[57]

I would not wish to deny that Wolf wanted to show the pernicious effects of Nazi indoctrination on Nelly. Nonetheless, it seems that even in *Kindheitsmuster* the Romantic child survives in exceptional moments of what we may call instinctive moral insight. Of course, we follow Nelly's career over a much longer period than the narrator of *Die Analphabetin*, and therefore there is considerably more time for her to become involved in and indoctrinated by the state mechanism; as we saw in Chapter 1, by the end of the war Nelly is immersed in the values of the Nazi era. But this has not always been the case. The younger Nelly is credited with flashes of instinctive perception and insight which suggest an alternative value system within the child herself, despite Wolf's assertion that 'moralische Instinkte nicht angeboren sind'.[58] Certainly Wolf is hard pressed to explain what caused 'dieses Zurückzucken bei einigen wenigen, scharf in die Erinnerung eingeritzten Gelegenheiten';[59] her only possible explanation is that even her earliest childhood reading, for example Grimms' *Märchen*, played its part in creating a moral being but, although Nelly reads such works, it is difficult to trace any literary influence in the momentary flashes of insight cited below.[60]

---

[55] *Tradition, Art and Society: Christa Wolf's Prose* (Essen, 1987), 191 and 195.

[56] *Christa Wolf's Utopian Vision*, 129–30.   [57] *Difficulties of Saying 'I'*, 157–62, 170–1.

[58] 'Lesen und Schreiben', in *Dimension des Autors*, ii. 475.   [59] Ibid.

[60] Many authors cite the important role played by literature in enabling them to see through the Nazi era, though they are often referring to 'verbotene Literatur' that came their way as adolescents. See e.g. Hensel, *Sack überm Kopf*, 122–3; Siegfried Lenz, *Kurze Hose und halblange Söckchen*, 169 and 175–6; and Dieter Wellershof, *Ein Allmachtstraum und sein Ende*, 157: all in Reich-Ranicki (ed.), *Meine Schulzeit*.

These flashes of insight are sporadic and are certainly not idealized. Nor do they lead to any action that could be described as concrete resistance to the indoctrination imposed on Nelly. However, they occur frequently enough to suggest an original innocence, which is only gradually tainted by her circumstances. The first occurs when the narrator describes Nelly's reaction to Leo Siegmann's story about the Jewish boy in his school class, whom she knows she would have been unable to hit:

Sie nimmt Anlauf, weiß: Sie muß vorbei, sie muß es tun, es ist ihre Pflicht. Sie strengt sich sehr an. Sie läßt den Film schneller laufen. Aber niemals, nicht ein einziges Mal in der ganzen Zeit, da sie den Judenjungen gut kennenlernt, alles weiß, was er denkt–vor allem, was er über sie denkt–, nicht ein einziges Mal gelingt es ihr, an ihm vorbeizukommen.– Immer reißt im entscheidenden Augenblick der Film. Immer wird es dunkel, wenn sie ganz dicht vor ihm steht, er schon den Kopf hebt, die Augen leider auch. Sie erfährt nicht, ob sie imstande wäre, ihre Pflicht zu tun. Was sie erfährt, aber lieber nicht wissen will, ist: Sie möchte nicht in die Lage kommen, ihre Pflicht tun zu müssen. Jedenfalls nicht bei diesem Jungen, den sie so genau kennt und daher nicht hassen kann. Das ist ihr Fehler. 'Blinder Haß', ja, das ginge, das wäre das einzig Richtige. Sehender Haß ist einfach zu schwierig. (*Kindheitsmuster*, 199–200)

At this point, despite the emphasis on her 'Pflicht', her mental processes have not been entirely taken over by political indoctrination. The emphasis on the pictorial nature of her perceptions suggests a non-analytical vision and essentially Nelly is still governed by her feelings. Her ability to identify so closely with a figure she has imagined produces an essentially moral response, like those in *Die Analphabetin*. However, the different emphasis in *Kindheitsmuster* is clear from the filmic image which suggests an externalization of self-aware moral action. In contrast with Johansen's 5-year-old, Wolf's narrator is recalling her childhood in retrospect; hence there is more room for analysis than in works which consciously restrict themselves to the child's present. Smith emphasizes this aspect in his reading of the film imagery in *Kindheitsmuster*, for he notes that it makes the narrator the 'director/censor of her memories'.[61] But this analysis is not always just retrospective: it spills over into Wolf's conception of the child

[61] *Tradition, Art and Society*, 188–9.

herself. Nelly's inner vision is not the hysterical emotionalism we
will see later in Walli Sawatzki (Grass, *Hundejahre* (1963)): the tone
is cool and restrained as in 'die Augen leider auch' and her reflections on 'blinder Haß' intellectualize the problem without sound-
ing inconsistent with the child's vision.

   This tone persists later in the novel when Nelly is confronted
with a real instance of injustice towards the Jews: the *Kristallnacht*.
Here, too, the visual aspect is emphasized. First, the pictorial nature of her vision guarantees its authenticity for the narrator, who
notes 'Gäbe es diese Leute nicht–ein inneres Bild, dessen
Authentizität unleugbar ist–, würdest du nicht mit dieser Sicherheit behaupten können, daß Nelly, ein Kind mit Phantasie, an
jenem Nachmittag bei der Synagoge war' (p. 236). Secondly, this
non-analytical perspective is synonymous with the child's unfalsi-
fied vision and integrity. To maintain this we find other brief snip-
pets of her original impression of the scene scattered throughout
the passage, some in the present tense to give them extra immediacy ('Man kann also in rauchende Trümmerhaufen unter
Umständen noch hineingehen', (p. 236), others simply capturing
the objective 'falseness' or naivety which is nonetheless true to the
child's original vision ('Die Juden, in Nellys Erinnerung beinlos
wegen ihrer langen Kaftane', p. 237). This non-analytical vision is
essential in shaping Nelly's moral responses to the scene:[62] the
strange sentence 'Die Sonne bekam zu tun' (pp. 236–7), whose
brevity and slightly odd structure break the narrative flow and so
suggest a moment's intense vision, even revelation, on the child's
part, is significant because it breaks the darkness which character-
izes both the Jews ('schwarze[n] Käppis'; 'schwarze[n] lange[n]
Mäntel[n]', p. 236; 'lange[n] Kaftane[n]', p. 237) and Nelly's position in a 'dunklen Torweg' (p. 235). This sudden enlightenment allows her to see the Jews as fellow human beings rather than as the
monsters of political propaganda, an example of uncorrupted
child's vision: 'Die Juden, alte Männer mit grauen Bärten, wohn-
ten in den kleinen armseligen Häuschen am Synagogenplatz. Ihre
Frauen und Kinder saßen vielleicht hinter den winzigen Fen-
sterchen und weinten'. The fact that she refers to them simply as

----

[62] On the contrast between child and adult perception in Wolf's work, ibid. 181.
Quernheim highlights the 'Erkenntnisprinzip' associated with vision in Wolf's work in
Moralische Ich, 53.

'Männer' and 'Frauen und Kinder' again suggests that Nelly is finally seeing the Jews as real human beings and her vocabulary here, especially her 'unwillkürlich' use of the verb 'retten' shows she instinctively feels these people are victims. However, this instinctive sympathy, referred to with obvious adult-narrator irony as 'eine unpassende Empfindung' is swiftly juxtaposed with sentences which stress that these people are the contemptible Jews of political propaganda: 'Die Juden sind anders als wir. Sie sind unheimlich. Vor den Juden muß man Angst haben, wenn man sie schon nicht hassen kann. Wenn die Juden jetzt stark wären, müßten sie uns alle umbringen' (p. 237). The brevity and simplicity of these sentences suggest that the child has not only absorbed political indoctrination but also reformulated it in her own terms and it is significant that, while in the earlier incident, where she was dealing only with an imaginary child, her personal feelings were too strong to be overcome by political indoctrination, by this stage, even though she is witnessing the tragedy of real people, political indoctrination seems eventually to prevail. This is suggested especially by the emphatic use of the present tense which shows the child proving to herself that what she has been taught is valid. Thus while she is allowed a momentary human insight, its very brevity indicates how difficult it is to maintain her innocent eye under the prevailing conditions.

This is a constant pattern of the narrative: while Nelly still has moments after this when personal feelings and considerations intrude briefly upon her political conciousness, rarely do we find passages like the one about the Jewish boy when her mental processes are so painfully detailed for us. In the case of the 'Jungmädel' suspended from the organization for theft, Nelly again gives way to pity, but by now she is setting out from the premiss of what she knows it would be correct for her to feel: 'Nach ihrer eigenen Überzeugung hätte sie Abscheu gegen Gerda Link fühlen müssen, nicht dieses weichliche Mitleid, und Begeisterung über die Gradlinigkeit der Führerin anstatt eben Angst. Wie öfter schon handelte es sich um die Unmöglichkeit, sich Klarheit zu verschaffen' (p. 284). By now Nelly has been so thoroughly indoctrinated that she really believes that her received ideas are her 'eigene Überzeugung'. This difficulty in distinguishing between natural instinct and learned behaviour has already been prefigured by the narrator's earlier ironic use of the word 'instinktiv' when she says that Nelly was soon able to avoid asking awkward question ' "instinktiv" wie man gerne sagt' (p. 105); this shows just how complete the political deformation of a character can be and how deeply Nelly's true responses lie buried. The contempt inherent in the words 'dieses weichliche Mitleid' is clearly her youthful exasperation against herself rather than the kind of narratorial irony by which 'Mitgefühl' was earlier dismissed as an 'unpassende Empfindung' (p. 237). The fever she succumbs to after this event apparently results from her determination to repress this form of questioning, for she is only able (and willing) to return to the JM after Gerda has been reinstated. Her illness allows her to regard her sympathy for the other girl as a delirium, a physical weakness, and so absolves her from any responsibility for her treacherous thoughts. She need not even pursue them since she is not being confronted by Gerda's absence at JM meetings. And in fact, once this incident has been dealt with, Nelly has no qualms about becoming a 'Führerinanwärterin', even 'gegen den erklärten Widerstand der Mutter' (p. 285), for this apparently corresponds to her present ideals. Gradually then, the child begins to reject her moments of instinctive sympathy until, when reading about the 'Lebensborn' institutions, her brief 'Das nicht' (p. 327) might be interpreted as an expression of the most minimal of moral responses.[63]

But, while it is clear that Nelly is becoming progressively more indoctrinated, it should also be clear that the brevity of this response, undiluted by any contradictory considerations of 'Pflicht', by no means indicates that her integrity has been lost. That very brevity does not just indicate the residual nature of her instinctive response; it also highlights and intensifies it. Indeed, it is this moment's insight that the narrator comments on most fully and regards as most significant:

Es war eine jener seltenen, kostbaren und unerklärlichen Gelegenheiten, bei denen Nelly sich in bewußtem Widerspruch zu den geforderten Überzeugungen sah, die sie doch gerne geteilt hätte. Das schlechte Gewissen, wie so oft, prägte ihr den Augenblick ein. Wie sollte sie ahnen, daß das Ertragen eines schlechten Gewissens unter den waltenden

---

[63] The importance of this moment is highlighted in Kuhn, *Christa Wolf's Utopian Vision*, 132.

Verhältnissen eine notwendige Bedingung zur inneren Freiheit war? (p. 327)[64]

That 'innere Freiheit' is an important concept, for it suggests the child's ability to retain an inner space untouched by the indoctrination to which it is exposed; interestingly, it is also one of the qualities Wolf claims a writer needs.[65] But the child's inner space is not merely a tabula rasa, for, as we have seen, it is the place where instinctive critical responses appear and Nelly's individuality asserts itself. It is not clear by what means such a space is created or preserved under the conditions of Nazism; indeed, this mysterious instinctive morality recalls an earlier writer who had much more obvious reasons for his belief in it: Jean Paul. In *Levana* he stated: 'nie kann ein Kind für zu unschuldig und gut gehalten werden',[66] and the combination of these two adjectives suggests not merely the 'negative' innocence discussed in Chapter 1, but positive moral goodness.[67] His autobiographical work *Selberlebensbeschreibung* (1818/19) shows some analogies with Wolf's *Kindheitsmuster*, for Jean Paul too refers to his child self in the third person and like Wolf's narrator he too stresses the importance of the moment when he discovered his individual identity:[68]

Nie vergeß' ich die noch keinem Menschen erzählte Erscheinung in mir, wo ich bei der Geburt meines Selbstbewußtseins stand, von der ich Ort und Zeit anzugeben weiß. An einem Vormittag stand ich als ein sehr junges Kind unter der Haustüre und sah links nach der Holzlege, als auf einmal das innere Gesicht 'ich bin ein Ich' wie ein Blitzstrahl vom Himmel vor mich fuhr und seitdem leuchtend stehen blieb: da hatte mein Ich zum ersten Male sich selber gesehen und auf ewig. Täuschungen des Erinnerns sind hier schwerlich gedenkbar, da kein fremdes Erzählen in eine bloß im verhangnen Allerheiligsten des Menschen vorgefallne Begebenheit, deren Neuheit allein so alltäglichen Nebenumständen das Bleiben gegeben, sich mit Zusätzen mengen konnte.[69]

---

[64] Wolf also comments on this episode in 'Lesen und Schreiben', 475–6.

[65] In a conversation with Joachim Walther, 'Unruhe und Betroffenheit', in *Dimension des Autors*, ii. 752.   [66] *Werke*, v. 581.

[67] For a detailed discussion of Jean Paul's conception of childhood, to which I am indebted here, see Ewers, *Kindheit*, 97–137: at 108.

[68] This parallel is suggested by Bernhard Greiner, 'Die Schwierigkeit, "ich" zu sagen: Christa Wolfs psychologische Orientierung des Erzählens', *DVjs* 55 (1981), 323.

[69] In *Werke*, vi. 1061.

The similarities between this and Wolf's description of the same experience are striking:

Frühere Entwürfe fingen anders an . . . als Fallen in einen Zeitschacht, auf dessen Grund das Kind in aller Unschuld auf einer Steinstufe sitzt und zum erstenmal in seinem Leben in Gedanken zu sich selbst ICH sagt. . . . Du aber hast eine wenn auch abgegriffene Original-Erinnerung zu bieten, denn es ist mehr als unwahrscheinlich, daß ein Außenstehender dem Kind zugesehen und ihm später berichtet haben soll, wie es da vor seines Vaters Ladentür saß und in Gedanken das neue Wort ausprobierte, ICH ICH ICH ICH ICH, jedesmal mit einem lustvollen Schrecken, von dem es niemandem sprechen durfte. Das war ihm gleich gewiß. (p. 16)

In both cases the child is outside the domestic context ('unter der Haustüre'; 'vor des Vaters Ladentüre'); the experience is too intimate to be revealed to anyone else; it is described so as to suggest a combination of delight and fear ('Blitzstrahl'; 'lustvollen Schrecken'); and the name by which the child is to be known is given for the first time directly after the discovery of the 'ich'. The moment of self-discovery is significant to both writers in a moral sense: Jean Paul was a minister's son and his descriptions of the moment of self-discovery are infused with religious implications; Richter notes that this passage is 'ganz der mystisch-pietistischen Bildsprache der "Erleuchtung" verpflichtet'.[70] In Levana Jean Paul refers to this moment as the point 'wo . . . zum erstenmal das Ich plötzlich aus dem Gewölke wie eine Sonne vorbrach' bringing both a 'Gewissen' and a 'Gott', 'das ganze Reich der Wahrheit und des Gewissens, das ohne Ich nichts ist'.[71] As Ewers points out, this 'Ich' is referred to in Jean Paul's Vorschule der Ästhetik as the 'überirdische Engel des innern Lebens',[72] the inextinguishable element of 'das Göttliche' present in every human being.[73] This idea is central to Jean Paul's theory of the child as representing an alternative spiritual and moral dimension, and while the education described in Levana was consciously to foster this sense of otherness, aiming at an 'Erhebung über den Zeitgeist',[74] the fact that education alone achieves nothing is also made clear: 'Diese Idealität ist von keiner Erziehung zu lehren–denn sie ist das

[70] Fremde Kind, 319.   [71] Werke, v. 553 and 564.   [72] Ibid. 61.
[73] Ewers, Kindheit, 101.   [74] Jean Paul, Werke, v. 567.

innerste Ich selber—aber von jeder vorauszusetzen und folglich zu beleben'.[75]

Wolf does not uses religious images but her conception of Nelly reads almost as a humanist transcription of Jean Paul. There has been much critical discussion of the significance of this moment for Nelly; Barnett focuses on the fact that both Christa T. and Nelly have the same experience of self-discovery but suggests that it has different implications for them, since for Christa the discovery of her 'Anderssein' is the first step on the road to individual self-realization whereas for Nelly the moment is associated with guilt feelings and leads only to the idea promoted by the Nazi era that ' "we" are different and thus, by definition, superior'.[76] But this identification with the masses comes some time later; initially Nelly's moment of self-discovery, like that of Christa, makes her feel distinct from and independent of her immediate environment: although she is 'ans Gehorchen gewöhnt' (p. 17) when her mother calls her she goes 'langsamer als gewöhnlich, denn ein Kind, das zum erstenmal in seinem Leben einen Schauder gespürt, als es ICH dachte, wird von der Stimme der Mutter nicht mehr gezogen wie von einer festen Schnur' (p. 18). But while her first stirrings of independence are in the domestic context, as she grows up it is Nelly's capacity for resistance to political ideology, the 'Zeitgeist', that is emphasized. Significantly there are echoes of her 'Selberlebensbeschreibung' in all the moments of instinctive insight I have cited. These are most obvious in the scene at the 'Synagogenplatz': she is again alone, beyond the domestic context and the rules that govern it ('Geh hin! hat niemand zu Nelly gesagt, . . . Eher wurde das eindeutige Verbot ausgesprochen', p. 235); her feeling of 'Staunen und Schrecken' (p. 236) when she first sees the Jews recalls 'lustvollen Schrecken' (p. 16); and the darkness-to-light transition implies a coming to consciousness as in Jean Paul's 'Blitzstrahl'. However, her self-discovery reverberates

---

[75] Ibid. 784. For a discussion of Jean Paul's ideas on education see Ewers, *Kindheit*, 108–11.

[76] 'Perceptions of Childhood', 63–4. For a psychoanalytic interpretation of Nelly's moment of self-discovery and its implications, see Christel Zahlmann, *Christa Wolfs Reise 'ins Tertiär': Eine literarpsychologische Studie zu 'Kindheitsmuster'* (Würzburg, 1986), 29–103; also Quernheim, *Moralische Ich*, esp. 93–136. Quernheim contends that because Nelly is not allowed to articulate this moment of self-discovery she tends to repress her true feelings and feel guilty when they assert themselves, which makes her easy prey for Nazi ideology (ibid., esp. 105–6 and 111–12).

through the other incidents too: in the 'Judenjunge' episode her eavesdropping is brought to an abrupt end by her mother ordering her off to bed, an interruption which recalls Charlotte's voice calling her out of her reverie on her 'ich' (p. 17). Nelly's silence and continued reverie about the 'Judenjunge' parallel her significantly slower obedience after the 'ich' experience: in both instances the child's external obedience is coupled with more subversive thoughts, here 'Auch sie wird ihm also "eine reinhaun"'. Oder vielleicht nicht?' (p. 199). Her discomfort at the Gerda Link episode is underlined by the fact that the other girl's judgement is preceded by a reading of the poem 'Vom Ich zum Wir' (p. 281); again Nelly's own 'ich' reasserts itself powerfully, even though it is not something she can articulate. Her response to the 'Lebensborn' report is the most complex of these incidents: her desire to conform is suggested by the fact that she is in the home and reading the specifically Nazi paper *Das Schwarze Korps*, yet by reading this 'verbotene Zeitung' (p. 326) she is breaking her parents' rule. Moreover, by her very deliberate and self-conscious mental formulation of the words 'Das nicht' (p. 327) which recalls her equally deliberate repetitions of the word 'ich' (p. 16) she again asserts her self over the demands of the state.

Wolf does not explain how these moral instincts survive and certainly not in the metaphysical terms Jean Paul uses, yet the similarities between their descriptions of the 'Ich' experience suggest that both are working from a similar assumption, that of an innermost being which is inherently innocent and 'other' from the society of which it forms a part. This may only indicate muted optimism in Wolf, for she certainly does not soften the presentation of Nazi indoctrination and its effects on Nelly; however, the Romantic subtext implies at least a belief in the child's potential for 'otherness' and this makes *Kindheitsmuster* the most obvious example of the clash of historical reality and myth, just as it makes Wolf simultaneously the most realistic and optimistic of the writers considered here.

The four works considered above all present the idea of childhood as 'other' from society even in the face of Hitler's perversion of the Romantic myth of childhood. Obviously this myth has particular appeal when set against the dark days of the Third Reich; just as in Gmeyner and Aichinger's accounts the children here are not so much innocent (that is, gullible), passive victims as symbols for values which may combat and overcome inhumanity and evil. Again, by implication, these values are at the heart of every human being since childhood is universal. The myth is upheld for a number of reasons, personal, political, and religious, but what strikes us is its universality. Loss of faith in this myth implies a loss of faith in humanity itself and this is not a loss these writers can afford.

BETWEEN SCEPTICISM AND NOSTALGIA: OTHER
MANIFESTATIONS OF THE ROMANTIC CHILD

Political Animals?: The Children Of Günter Grass's Hundejahre

Of course, not all post-war German writers are as convinced of the positive potential of childhood as those I quote above. Indeed, given the political abuse of childhood under the Third Reich and the generally more sceptical assessment of the child as fundamentally different from the adult initiated by Freud, it would be astounding if no more sceptical voices were to be heard. Perhaps the most notable of all the sceptics on this topic is Grass, who not only adopts the Freudian perception of the child as a sexual being, but takes it to grotesque lengths. If Freud's *Drei Abhandlungen zur Sexualtheorie* blurred the distinction between the child and the adult, then the parallels Grass establishes between children and adults sometimes make the children look even more repulsive than their elders, simply because the image he presents contrasts so starkly with our preconceptions about childhood.

Even if we exclude Oskar Matzerath from our considerations on the grounds that he is too obviously deviant, there are many other sexualized, politicized children in Grass's works. Tulla Pokriefke's grotesque character is emphasized precisely by her basically normal physical appearance, which stands in contrast with Oskar. But even as a child she is described more as a predatory female with an overwhelming sexual drive, as when Harry Liebenau describes her prominent 'Schneidezähne' (*Hundejahre*, 285) and her tendency to become 'hart, starr und böse' (p. 288). She is 'mehr ein Etwas als ein Mädchen' (p. 287), and her own attitude towards childhood and its supposed innocence is apparently one of contempt and desecration, as when she spits into Jenny Brunies's empty pram (p. 300). Moreover, while her retreat into Harras's kennel after her brother's death may indicate violent grief, Grass is apparently parodying the myth of children's intuitive understanding of nature and animals. The 'Naturkind' Effi Briest has a close relationship with her dog, but despite her father's approval of 'die Kreatur' there are obvious limits to this relationship between the human and the animal.[77] Tulla, on the other hand, positively identifies herself with Harras: she sleeps in his kennel, eats his food (p. 312), and there is almost surprise in Harry's tone when she finally re-emerges: 'Zuerst kroch sie auf allen vieren, richtete sich dann *wie ein richtiger Mensch* auf' (p. 322, my emphasis). Such a close identification between child and animal can no longer be seen as positive, especially given that Harras is also ascribed a political role. Tulla uses him as a means of victimizing both Felsner-Imbs and Jenny, and Walter Matern actually refers to the animal as a Nazi (p. 435). In Grass's work political events in the adult world are constantly reflected in the activities of even the youngest children: in *Die Blechtrommel* Stephan Bronski is beaten up at his Kindergarten by a boy of the same age because he is a 'Pollack' (*Blechtrommel*, 82) and Tulla's victimization of Jenny, culminating in the snow sequence, is paralleled by Matern's treatment of Amsel.

Tulla may be an extreme example of Grass's new myth of childhood, but even Harry conforms to some extent to this myth when we see him acting the role of innocent child in a manner quite as self-conscious as the young Oskar:

Mir brachte Harras Schülerruhm. Ich mußte nach vorne an die Tafel kommen und erzählen. Natürlich durfte ich nicht vom Decken, Belegen, vom Deckschein und dem Deckgeld, von der im Zuchtbuch vermerkten Deckfreudigkeit unseres Harras und der Hitze der Hündin Thekla sprechen. Drollig kindlich mußte und vermochte ich vom Vater Harras und der Mutter Thekla, von den Hundekindern Falko, Kastor, Bodo, Mira und Prinz zu plappern. (*Hundejahre*, 324)

This is typical of Grass's portrayal of children and adolescents as 'knowing' in the pejorative sense. They are political animals (almost literally!) with powerful sexual instincts, and this new mythology apparently leaves little or no room for Romantic ideas of childhood innocence or its affinity with God and nature.

---

[77] *Effi Briest*, in Fontane, *Werke*, iv. 315.

But while this seems a very negative image of childhood, there is a fundamental tension in Grass's work between this modern myth of the child and nostalgia for childhood innocence. This is particularly evident in Tulla's relationship with Jenny, who is something of an outsider in the child population of Danzig. She is not only a 'Findelkind' (p. 277), but is further distinguished by being named Jenny 'obgleich in unserer Gegend nie jemand Jenny hieß' (p. 282). She was supposedly found 'auf wunderbare Weise' (p. 286) and, although Harry claims that he and Tulla never believed 'daß Zigeuner und Störche mitspielten, als Jenny gefunden wurde' (p. 285), he later tries to convince Jenny of her exotic gypsy heritage (p. 475). She is a repository for any belief in the myth of childhood 'otherness', innocence and vulnerability, as demonstrated by her adoptive father, the old-fashioned humanist Brunies. He apparently wants to protect her from the outside world by keeping her in her pram well beyond the normal age (ostensibly because she has difficulty in walking) but his plans are doomed: the pram's old-fashioned appearance (p. 291) and the way it shakes and trembles under his hands (p. 302) suggest that the conception of childhood as alien and vulnerable is not only outdated but under actual threat as embodied in Tulla.

Yet there is no simple antithesis between the Romantic child Jenny and the Freudian child Tulla.[78] Jenny does have attributes of the Romantic child: her otherness as a 'Findelkind' and her artistry, for she is both musically gifted and a dancer. The description of her dance in front of the Gutenberg memorial reads like a natural rite, with her as a wood spirit in the midst of nature (p. 408). But this only happens after her transformation in the snow; before this, Grass had been at pains to counter the ethereal, other-worldly associations Jenny might evoke by emphasizing her less than agile physique. She is described as 'das pummelige

---

[78] Critics have tended to see these figures in antithetical terms. In Wilhelm Johannes Schwarz, *Der Erzähler Günter Grass* (2nd expanded edn. Bern and Munich, 1971) Schwarz notes that at the end of *Hundejahre* Grass speaks disparagingly of Jenny, thus preventing 'jegliche Dickens'sche Verklärung und Romantisierung' (ibid. 35), yet later he appears to fall into that trap when he says of her 'sie wirkt wie ein Fremdling, ein Besucher dieser Erde . . . Sie ist der genaue Gegenpol Tullas, . . . (ibid. 55). Harscheidt also portrays the girls as antithetical beings, with Tulla representing 'materia' and Jenny 'ecclesia' (*Günter Grass, Wort–Zahl–Gott: Der 'phantastische Realismus' in den Hundejahren* (Bonn, 1976), 458–503). For Harscheidt Tulla's fascination with Jenny results simply from the attraction good exercises over evil (ibid. 490–1).

Geschöpf' (p. 331), and as presenting 'den Anblick eines rosa Schweinchens, das zur schwerelosen Sylphide werden wollte' (p. 350). Conversely, descriptions of Tulla occasionally suggest a being from another dimension: her greater agility makes her 'zu einem immer laufenden, springenden, kletternden, insgesamt fliegenden Etwas' (p. 288), a description that recalls that 'fremdes Kind' Mignon, the hermaphrodite who comes from a 'springenden und tanzenden Gesellschaft'.[79] Moreover, Tulla is associated with natural phenomena through her name, derived 'von dem Koschnäwjer Wassergeist Thula' (p. 282). This combination of mockery applied to the more obviously Romantic child and the insinuation of Romantic elements in the Freudian child suggests Grass's fascination with the literary myth of positive childhood potential even in the midst of his scepticism, particularly when we consider the way that his mockery of Jenny's dancing is relativized by the description of her second dance at the Gutenberg memorial; here the sylphide that the 'rosa Schweinchen' wanted to become is evoked by the wooded setting and moreover Jenny is specifically referred to as 'schwerelos' (p. 408). That the antithesis between Tulla and Jenny is more apparent than real is suggested by Tulla's wary fascination with Jenny after her transformation. Tulla pursues the other girl at a distance, so creating a 'wanderndes Loch' (p. 420) even in the busiest streets, and this suggests not so much an unbridgeable gulf as an inherent and powerful connection. Significantly, only one person invades that space: 'der Sohn des Kolonialhändlers hielt sich winzig und stämmig bald neben Tulla bald neben Jenny. Manchmal tat er, was sonst niemand wagte: er schob sich in die menschenleere Distanz' (p. 421). This constellation of children throws retrospective light on Oskar, a figure where Grass had oscillated between Freudian and Romantic conceptions of childhood and where his nostalgia for the latter had been evident. As I shall show later, in him the tension between Tulla and Jenny is embodied in a single figure.

Tulla's fascination with Jenny after the snow sequence and her gratitude at being allowed to carry her dancing shoes may seem inconsistent with her earlier spitting into the pram, but this contradiction merely mirrors her creator's own ambivalent position, for Grass constantly cites the Romantic myth of childhood only in

---

[79] *Wilhelm Meisters Lehrjahre*, in Goethe, *Werke*, vii. 91.

order to deny it. Interestingly Tulla is associated with another character who harks back to the idea of childhood as 'other': she alone can communicate with her deaf-mute brother Konrad, 'Der lautlose Lacher, Mitsinger, Allesversteher' (p. 303) who without her would have been unable to communicate with the adult world, one of the features Kuhn ascribes to the 'enigmatic child'.[80] And her retreat to Harras's kennel after his death, cited earlier as evidence of her animal nature, could also be interpreted more positively: she, Konrad, and Harras had formed an inseparable trio, and thus it might seem natural for her to cling to the dog in her grief. It is only in its exaggeration that this becomes a return to the animal and instinctual, a perversion of the Romantic conception of childhood.

Hundejahre reverberates with the tension between Grass's fascination with the Romantic image of childhood and his realistic straining away from it. Konrad is a case in point: the fact that he is not developed but killed off could suggest Grass dispensing with a character whom he could not develop realistically and for whom there was no place in his animalistic conception of childhood. On the other hand this premature death also fits into the earlier twentieth-century tradition of killing children off before they could be tainted, the logical continuation of the Romantic tradition that we observed in Mignon. Jenny does not suffer this fate, but her magical transformation into a 'Strich' (p. 405) is equally ambiguous.[81] Her emergence from the snowman and transformed appearance accompanied by church bells evokes the

---

[80] For a full discussion of the enigmatic child, see Kuhn, *Corruption in Paradise*, 16–64: at 60.

[81] In *Günter Grass* (2nd rev. and expanded edn., Stuttgart and Weimar, 1992), 93, Volker Neuhaus points out the close parallels between the depiction of Jenny and Grass's essay 'Die Ballerina' (1956). Jenny's career is significant since for Grass ballet is an ideal, 'eine der unnatürlichsten und damit formvollendetesten aller Künste' ('Die Ballerina', *Werkausgabe*, ix. 14). Grass's nostalgia for the form of childhood she represents can also be linked to his feelings about art: his nostalgia for the more straightforward realistic linear narrative of the past where the distorting devices of parody and the grotesque would not play such a significant part as they do in his work. But just as the Romantic conception of childhood is not appropriate to Grass's own time, so a new art form is required to reflect a new reality and the artist's relationship with it. For a stimulating discussion of 'Die Ballerina', see Ann L. Mason, *The Skeptical Muse: A Study of Günter Grass's Conception of the Artist* (Berne and Frankfurt, 1974), 17–27. Mason discusses the tension between parody and nostalgia in this essay as an expression of Grass's search for a new art form.

Resurrection, and her dance around the Gutenberg memorial might recall the scene when Wilhelm Meister watches Mignon's 'Eiertanz' with the same absorption that Harry watches Jenny.[82] Moreover, as part of his argument suggesting that Jenny represents 'ecclesia', Harscheidt quotes Zacharias's 1962 book *Ballett– Gestalt und Wesen*, which refers to ballet training as a crucifixion and performance as a resurrection.[83] However, the child saviour motif is not developed in Jenny's case and the fact that her transformation only occurs due to an utterly unrealistic event casts the possibility of the Romantic child in an ironic light. Nonetheless, the Mignon echoes in the three otherwise contrasting child figures Tulla, Konrad, and Jenny suggest that Grass is very much in the thrall of the German image of childhood as described by Hagen.[84]

The adults in *Hundejahre* frequently exhibit nostalgia for the Romantic notion of childhood and the innocence associated with it; Brunies is the obvious example, but Tulla's later desire for a child whom she would have called Konrad (p. 532) suggests a similar impulse. Her miscarriage seems the ultimate proof that the world Grass is depicting has no place for this ideal, an idea cruelly underlined by the *Märchen* 'Es war einmal ein Abortus' (p. 533). However, there is something more powerful than mere nostalgia at work in this novel. The positive aspect of adult nostalgia is that it can be exploited so as to make children a far harsher critical instance, as in the 'Wunderbrille' episode.

The very name 'Wunderbrille' appeals to adult nostalgia, for 'dieser Name, so märchenhaft er anklingen mag, ist mehr für die Erwachsenen, die das Portemonnaie haben, bestimmt' (p. 698). By trading on this, Brauxel & Co's representatives can provide the youngsters with 'Erkennungs-' or 'Erkenntnisbrille', so enabling them to see 'die Vergangenheit der Eltern in wechselnden Bildern' (p. 701). The glasses are thus a far more subversive and threatening form of enlightenment than the adults imagine: they make the Nazi past 'durchschaubar' (p. 698) and this, together with the essentially pictorial element, points to the non-analytical and yet penetrating vision associated with the often inarticulate child. There is no analysis of what these children see; rather, like

---

[82] *Wilhelm Meisters Lehrjahre*, 115–16.
[83] Harscheidt, *Günter Grass*, 485. The significance of the ballet motif is discussed ibid. 475–86.   [84] Hagen, *Kinder*, 15–35.

Walli Sawatzki, those who try out the 'Wunderbrille' get an intense emotional shock which can result in illness or even suicide (p. 702).[85] This emotional and moral reaction depends not on academic knowledge but on basic integrity and fellow-feeling which are obvious when Walli stammers something

vom vielen Schnee und vom Blut, das in den Schnee fällt, von Zähnen, die gleichfalls, vom armen lieben dicken Mann, den Papa und Onkel Walter und andere Männer, die alle grausig aussehen, schlagen, immerzu schlagen mit Fäusten, am meisten Onkel Walter, immerzu den lieben dicken Mann, der nicht mehr steht, sondern im Schnee, weil ihn Onkel Walter... (p. 703)

Significantly she allies herself with the 'armen lieben dicken Mann' whom she does not know, rather than with her father and uncle: once presented with simple visual evidence of injustice and brutality, the child's response is not analytical but emotional, and that sympathy for the victim immediately reveals a core of moral integrity and innocence. Of course, one might argue that, since Walli is not old enough to have been subjected to Nazi indoctrination, her reaction to what she sees is quite natural. However, as became clear in our discussion of *Kindheitsmuster*, the ethical aspect of the child's pictorial, non-analytical vision has more far-reaching implications for, although Nelly has been thoroughly indoctrinated, her moments of non-analytical vision also facilitate an emotional and moral response.

In his depiction of the 'Wunderbrille' Grass is exploiting the age-old tradition that allows children to see things more clearly than adults by endowing them with visual rather than analytical perception, intuitive rather than learned responses. Walli has not been initiated into the corrupting adult world: she is only of an age to buy the 'Wunderbrille' because she enjoys Kohl's 'Gnade der späten Geburt'. But Grass is not simply introducing an incongruous magical element to restore our faith in the wondrous intuitive moral vision of the child, a ray of hope which is instantly negated by its fantastic nature. If he were, then we would argue that the

---

[85] Beyersdorf highlights the fact that this critical vision does not lead to any revolt of youth against the adult world and draws a contrast between German youth as presented in *Hundejahre* and in *Örtlich betäubt* ('The Immaturity Theme in the Post-War German Novel' (unpublished doctoral thesis, University of New England, 1974), 100–1). However, this does not negate the potential Grass sees in childhood per se.

Romantic tradition was simply being parodied, for Walli's moral vision is not innate: like Jenny, she takes on the attribute of the Romantic child only after a highly improbable procedure has been imposed on her. But in fact, as ever, Grass's parody is not so much a rejection of tradition as a critical adaptation of it, for the 'Wunderbrille' episode contains a paradox, highlighted by the way it is sold: the salesman 'ruft nicht, er flüstert: "Wunderbrillen zum Aufsetzen, Wunderbrillen zum Durchgucken"' (p. 698). The furtive sales technique suggests that it is forbidden knowledge that is on offer: once initiated, the children are 'fallen' in the sense discussed in Chapter 1. They too are confronted with events they are too young to understand, but nonetheless their peace of mind is gone. While it is the innocence, humanity, and fellow feeling associated with childhood that fuels Walli's response to what she sees, her new knowledge means that she too is denied any return to the paradise of childhood innocence/ignorance.

Grass uses the 'Wunderbrille' to show that there is in fact moral vision even after the 'fall', the non-analytical vision of childhood.[86] But the fact that this can exist without recourse to such devices is clear from the way Tulla contemplates the 'Knochenberg': well before the 'Wunderbrille' is marketed, she is able both to see and articulate the truth about this object (p. 516) and so prefigures the child whom Grass cites in one of his political speeches, 'Des Kaisers neue Kleider' (1965), who can tell the truth because, in contrast to the adults, the child is uninhibited by the taboos which come with full socialization (*Werkausgabe*, ix, 118). This suggests that Grass believes in the innate potential of childhood: its innocence, its enquiring and thus penetrating vision, and its fearless articulation of the truth. The grotesque and improbable elements he weaves around this fundamental belief do not merely imply his awareness that a belief in childhood innocence is no longer unproblematic cultural currency; they also force us to examine more critically the myth being parodied in order to see just how much of it he has in fact adopted. We are faced here with a paradoxical, even a contradictory, situation for, while on the one hand Grass

[86] For a stimulating discussion of the 'Wunderbrille', see Alan Frank Keele, '. . . Through a (Dark) Glass Clearly: Magic Spectacles and the Motif of the Mimetic Mantic in Postwar German Literature from Borchert to Grass', *GR* 57 (1982), esp. 52–9. Keele interprets the 'Wunderbrille' as representing Grass's desire to enlighten the younger generation about the Third Reich.

perpetuates the Freudian myth of childhood, on the other he presents us with children who are not restricted or corrupted by adult modes of thought and thus possess an unprejudiced vision and instinctive insight that recalls, albeit in a grimmer context, Wordsworth's 'Eye among the blind'. It seems that, whilst accepting the physical implications of Freud's theories, Grass is unable completely to deny children's innocence as moral and intellectual beings.

Grass thus occupies an ambiguous position for, while he by no means offers us an unproblematic image of the Romantic child, equally he does not subscribe wholeheartedly to the Freudian myth: if his overall conception of the child seems to be that it is a fallen being, this simply reflects the changes in the general perception of the child during this century. The tensions inherent in the children of *Hundejahre* suggest that Grass wants to believe in the child's positive intellectual and moral potential; within every Grass child, no matter how apparently monstrous, a Romantic child is struggling to get out.

The Deviant Child

The most obvious example of a Romantic child encased in a grotesque shell is, of course, another of Grass's creations, Oskar Matzerath. But before we turn to him it may be helpful to look at another deviant child who throws some retrospective light on Oskar's position: Siggi Jepsen in Lenz's *Deutschstunde*.

The Child Within: Siegfried Lenz's Deutschstunde

It is only a slight paradox to conclude this chapter on childhood innocence with these two apparently deviant figures, for they are the ultimate expression of the child as 'other', inhabiting an alternative dimension from society. That this dimension is represented by institutions for the deviant, a borstal and a mental asylum, is merely a sign of the times: they are judged to be deviant by a deviant society and this actually suggests a form of innocence.[87] Siggi may have been imprisoned for stealing pictures but

---

[87] Hanspeter Brode, *Die Zeitgeschichte im erzählenden Werk von Günter Grass: Versuch einer Deutung der 'Blechtrommel' und der 'Danziger Trilogie'* (Frankfurt and Berne, 1977), 123; on Oskar, see ibid. 105. Beyersdorf discusses both Oskar and Siggi in terms of Herbert Marcuse's 'Great Refusal'. The immature person's refusal to join a negatively perceived society is seen as positive ('Immaturity Theme', esp. 74 and 136).

he never regards himself as a thief: his description of his 'crime', 'ich hab Bilder in Sicherheit gebracht, denen mein Alter nachstellte' (*Deutschstunde*, 537) indicates that it was made necessary by political circumstances. Given the perverted conception of political 'normality' children held under the Third Reich, his only crime is not being able to adjust to the new political realities of the post-war era. Nor is he alone in this: his father (less excusably since he has known other value systems by which to measure Nazi reality) suffers from the same problem. No wonder Siggi feels that he is 'stellvertretend hier für meinen Alten, den Polizeiposten Rugbüll' (p. 539). Like the narrator of *Unsere Eroberung*, Siggi is a case of the sins of the father being visited on the son: he has been implicated in adult guilt, his psychologist noting 'daß man ihn wie einen Erwachsenen behandelte' (p. 322). He has been exploited by his father and taken into the painter's confidence, but significantly he chooses the painter above family loyalty. This is understandable: while Nansen's gruff affection for Siggi is evident, the Jepsen household is emotionally cold. Siggi's mother is a silent, frigid figure and his father demands only unquestioning obedience: 'Du brauchst nicht mehr zu verstehn, als du gesagt bekommst, das genügt: hast du mich verstanden? . . . Brauchbare Menschen müssen sich fügen' (p. 71). His only contact with Siggi is when giving orders or demanding information and at least linguistically the boy always makes the right submissive gestures, even when attempting to deceive his father so as to protect Nansen. Siggi thus has no one with whom he can share his feelings or vivid fantasy life. This repression of an intelligent, imaginative child is clear from his thoughts when his father beats him:

Ich schlug auf dem Tisch auf und stemmte mich leicht ab. Unter meinem Gesicht lag die blaue Meereskarte aus Leinwand, dehnten sich die Ozeane, über die ich träumerisch herrschte, wenn ich die großen Seeschlachten nachspielte: hier hatte ich mein Lepanto, mein Trafalgar geschlagen, hier hatten sich Skagerrak wiederholt und Scapa Flow und Orkney und die Gefechte von Falkland: schiffbrüchig trieb ich jetzt in den Gewässern meiner erträumten Triumphe, mit gestrichenen Segeln. (p. 69)

Given this environment it is hardly surprising that the boy should transfer his allegiance to the painter.

. Siggi and his family exist very much on the fringes of political events: the 'Malverbot' from Berlin might almost have come from another planet. Not even Hitler is mentioned by name in Siggi's account:[88] as is consistent with the child's point of view, he sees only what happens on his own limited horizon. Yet he sees enough. It may be that he is only able to articulate the emotional coldness of his home so well because he is older at the time of writing, but his perceptions of his parents are clearly those of a small child. Even at a young age he can observe his father's helplessness when he is 'ohne Auftrag' (p. 70) after beating Siggi in accordance with Gudrun Jepsen's expectations, and this domestic scene says a lot about the Jepsens's politics. Jens is merely the 'Mitläufer', the man who does his 'Pflicht' to the point of obsession but needs someone else to dictate it to him, whereas Gudrun is the committed Nazi of the family. The family dynamics reflect those of the Nazi state and Siggi's instinctive repulsion from them is another instance of the moral instinct at work in the child.

That Siggi is ruled mainly by his emotions and imagination is clear from the way he reacts to one of Addi's epileptic fits: 'Addi war tot. Er lag auf dem Rücken. Eine Sturmmöwe hatte ihn getötet, oder zehn Heringsmöwen und neunzig elegante Seeschwalben. Sie hatten ihn durchlöchert, durchbohrt' (p. 56). As ever, the impression is followed by the child's emotional response and urgent desire to put things right. His fear and concern for Addi are evident, but, as soon as he is assured that the young man is all right, this gives way to the need to avenge him: 'ich focht für Addi. Ja. Ich kämpfte eine Kompaßrose frei. Mit Ausfallsschritten, mit Sprüngen, mit Würfen aus dem Handgelenk setzte ich mich gegen die Vögel zur Wehr' (p. 57). This is the moral impulse that makes the child ally itself with the victim and can be compared with the narrator's wish to fight the flames in *Die Analphabetin*. The fact that these thoughts are based on ignorance does not detract from the original impulse. This response compares very favourably with that of the adults, especially Siggi's mother, at a later similar incident:

die andern kamen von allen Seiten heran, drängten näher, bildeten einen Kreis aus Betroffenheit, aus Staunen und wohl auch Furcht, denn sie sagten nichts, stießen sich nicht einmal an, sondern wechselten nur

---

[88] See Peter Russell, 'Siegfried Lenz's *Deutschstunde*: A North German Novel', *GLL* 28 (1974/75), 405–17. Russell points out that Hitler is mentioned by name only in Mackenroth's account of Nansen's earlier career (ibid. 412).

Blicke über Addi hinweg, . . . Und hoch aufgerichtet, weniger betroffen als in herrischer Gleichgültigkeit, stand meine Mutter etwas außerhalb des Rings (p. 94)

Paradoxically the adults, who might be expected to know what epilepsy is, show greater 'ignorance' than the truly ignorant child. Their knowledge has made them fearful and inhibited and provided them with a set of prejudices and taboos, whereas the child's ignorance allows him to act spontaneously, following his emotions rather than social taboos. In Gudrun Jepsen's case ignorance is exacerbated by her Nazism: 'Wir brauchen keinen Kranken in der Familie' (p. 103).

It is a tragic irony that Siggi, whose values have been so conditioned by a perverted conception of normality, is unable to adapt to post-war conditions. His imprisonment paradoxically becomes the ultimate proof of his innocence, for the delinquent product of a delinquent society seems by definition to be innocent. Moreover, this explains Siggi's deep reluctance to return to 'normal' life after his sentence has ended, for the man whose behaviour has forced him to continue his career as an art thief has not changed: Jens Jepsen is still conditioned by Nazi values and this is what forces Siggi to act in the same way. It is significant that the pressure to leave the 'Anstalt' increases after his twenty-first birthday, for the guilt bound up with the adult condition is clearly expressed when he says: 'Ab heute muß ich mir also Volljährigkeit nachsagen, muß mir vorwerfen lassen, erwachsen zu sein' (p. 421). His devotion to his 'Strafarbeit' is a subconscious ploy to delay his release and so remain within the value system of childhood and its rebellion against conventional social values. For even within the 'Anstalt' Siggi is isolated: the essay 'Die Freuden der Pflicht', with its unpleasant resonances of the Nazi era, is clearly intended to bring him into line, and his apparent refusal to complete it marks him (again) as a delinquent within a delinquent society.[89] The fact that he ends up writing about 'Die Freuden der Pflicht' at such compulsive length has generally been seen as a victory for the island authorities and indeed for the ethos that produced Siggi's father: Beyersdorf suggests that he has been 'infected by the same

---

[89] Various critics have noted that the borstal appears to propagate the values of the Nazi era; see Hans Wagener, *Siegfried Lenz* (2nd edn., Munich, 1976), 57–8 and Peter Russell, 'The "Lesson" in Siegfried Lenz's *Deutschstunde*', *Seminar*, 13 (1977), 46 and 52.

virus [as his father] and could not rest until he had satisfactorily completed his task'.[90] However, this idea that Siggi is unconsciously following in his father's footsteps does not explain the boy's refusal to end the 'Strafarbeit' even when Himpel, the authority who had imposed it, tries to persuade him to do so. His excessive compliance with his punishment is actually a form of defiance, and paradoxically this is the logical extension of the positive, active innocence described earlier in this chapter; rather than writing the eulogy expected of him, he produces a damning criticism of a society dominated by the 'Pflicht' ethos. If imprisonment is the proof of his innocence, his 'Strafarbeit' is the proof of his continued integrity into adulthood, his loyalty to the child within.

Nostalgia for Innocence: Günter Grass's Die Blechtrommel

The idea of the innocent delinquent also informs Grass's *Die Blechtrommel*, with its seemingly very non-innocent hero. Oskar is Grass's most obviously grotesque child figure: his physique is only one aspect of this, although it was perhaps the most immediately repellent to a German readership fed on idealized conceptions of childhood.[91] However, his mental processes too are extremely disconcerting, for this pseudo-child assumes the apparent ignorance of childhood to distance himself from events around him, disclaiming all knowledge and responsibility. His account of the *Kristallnacht* stands in stark contrast to Nelly Jordan's, for while she is capable (albeit momentarily) of empathizing with a group of Jews who are strangers to her, Oskar is apparently incapable of pitying Sigismund Markus, whom he knows very well. His main concern at this scene of devastation seems entirely selfish: 'Als man ihm den Spielzeughändler nahm und des Spielzeughändlers Laden verwüstete, ahnte er, daß sich gnomhaften Blechtrommlern, wie er einer war, Notzeiten ankündigten' (*Blechtrommel*, 243). This same lack of concern for others who are close to him appears in his account of the defence of the 'polnische Post' where, again, the human implications of

---

[90] 'Immaturity Theme', 133. See also Theo Elm, *Siegfried Lenz–'Deutschstunde': Engagement und Realismus im Gegenwartsroman* (Munich, 1974), 28–38 for a useful discussion of the various forms of 'Pflicht' ethos represented by the main characters of this novel. Elm too sees Siggi's compulsive devotion to his duty as mirroring that of his father (ibid. 36).   [91] See Hagen, *Kinder*, 34 on Oskar as 'Anti-Mignon'.

these events apparently come second to his need for a new drum (pp. 282–4).

Oskar's self-centred attitudes can be taken as a parody of contemporary adult attitudes as much as an expression of ignorance or amorality: there are plenty of references to the infantilism of the Nazi 'Mitläufer', that 'ganzes leichtgläubiges Volk' which believes in Father Christmas (p. 244) and whose 'entertainment' at the Nazi party rally is paralleled with Oskar's visit to the 'Däumeling' pantomime.[92] However, it is misguided to see Oskar only as an embodiment of Nazi values, an image of Hitler, or indeed as somehow complicit with the Nazi regime. Brode points out the extent to which Oskar can be regarded as a representative of the era in which he is brought up, but notes that at the same time Oskar can be seen as a victim of that era and an accuser of it.[93] Grass may seem to be vigorously debunking the Romantic myth of childhood innocence in this novel, but not so that he can create a Nazi child in its stead. The Nazi myth of childhood with its emphasis on a 'kerngesunder Körper' is also undermined here, for Oskar lives in constant danger of being dispatched to an 'Anstalt' where he would fall victim to the 'Euthanasie-Programm'. By debunking both these myths Grass creates in Oskar a kind of 'open space' unconstricted by any preconceptions or taboos, and in this he seems to have precisely the same prerequisites for an unbiased, clear-sighted view of events as the Romantic child. This is particularly evident in the Nazi rally episode, for there is no sense of Oskar going to the rally for political reasons. His indifference is clear:

Sie werden sagen, mußte es unbedingt die Maiwiese sein? Glauben Sie mir bitte, daß an Sonntagen im Hafen nichts los war, daß ich mich zu Waldspaziergängen nicht entschließen konnte, daß mir das Innere der Herz-Jesu-Kirche damals noch nichts sagte. Zwar gab es noch die Pfadfinder des Herrn Greff, aber jener verklemmten Erotik zog ich, es sei hier zugegeben, den Rummel auf der Maiwiese vor; auch wenn Sie mich jetzt einen Mitläufer heißen. (p. 135)

---

[92] Noel Thomas suggests that Oskar's 'carnival of amorality and infantilism . . . is paralleled by the grim saturnalian eruption of National Socialism and in the hedonism of the post-war economic miracle' (*The Narrative Works of Günter Grass: A Critical Interpretation* (Amsterdam and Philadelphia, 1982), 79).

[93] *Zeitgeschichte*, 31–46. Brode also discusses Oskar as a caricatural presentation of Hitler (ibid. 47–53).

However, as various critics have pointed out, if Oskar is indifferent to Nazism then his breaking up of the Nazi rally is not due to any belief in a sound political alternative: he objects to it not out of moral or political conviction but on the grounds of instinctive aesthetic dislike, for he is repulsed by the rigid symmetry of the tribune and its ranks.[94] This aesthetic rather than moral objection to Nazism might appear to be a feature of Oskar's generally perverse and amoral stance, but in fact it is not difficult to find accounts of Third Reich childhoods much more normal than Oskar's where we see the same kind of political indifference. Here König describes her decision not to join the BdM in terms that recall Oskar's statements and attitudes:

Ich war durchaus bereit, dazuzugehören, und ich hätte auch dazugehört, wenn nicht zweierlei mich davon abgehalten hätte: das erste waren die sehr rhythmischen Lieder, die den Verstand benebelten, ein Effekt, der mich erst stutzig und dann widerspenstig machte: ich wollte diesen Zauber nicht, ich hatte ja gerade erst mein Hirn entdeckt. Der zweite Punkt war der schier unaussprechliche Öde, die von den 'Heimabenden' ausging und mich beängstigte. Ob es um völkische Ideale, Rassendenken oder Führertreue ging—das Ganze strömte einen Geruch selbstgerechter Bravheit aus, der mir zutiefst widerstrebte; ich ging nicht mehr hin.[95]

The way König expresses willingness to belong to the movement without any statement of enthusiasm for what it represents suggests the kind of indifferent 'Mitläufertum' Oskar refers to, while her reference to the 'rhythmischen Lieder' recalls Oskar's aversion to the martial rhythms of the rally (p. 140). König clearly does not make her decision for moral or political reasons: her offhand list of sacred Nazi ideals, finally reduced to 'das Ganze', does not suggest strong feelings for or against Nazi ideology. Her aversion to the movement is apparently instinctive; like Oskar's, it is rooted more in the aesthetic, for the songs intended to stifle her individuality and make her part of the group repel her. This attempt by the Nazis to regulate individuals by aesthetic means is something Reed notes when she quotes Heinrich Böll's decision not to

---

[94] Beyersdorf points out that Oskar's protest against the adult world is non-ideological: his drumming is directed not just against Nazism but against society and its organizations as a whole ('Immaturity Theme', 75). See also Donna K. Reed, *The Novel and the Nazi Past* (New York and Frankfurt, 1985), 72.

[95] *Die verpaßte Chance*, 136.

join the Hitler Youth. This decision was taken 'nicht nur aus moralischen Gründen (weil ich zu wissen glaubte, wohin die Entwicklung führte), nicht nur aus politischen Gründen, auch aus ästhetischen: ich mochte diese Uniform nicht, und die Marschierlust hat mir immer gefehlt'.[96] Although I agree with Reed that there is a strong contrast between the way Böll and Grass express their aesthetic revolt against Nazism in their novels,[97] what seems clear is that the attitudes expressed by Oskar are not so far removed from those felt by 'normal' children and adolescents under the Third Reich: while Grass's mode of expression may differ in his use of parody and the grotesque, he too is celebrating the child's vision, instinctive and untrammelled by adult prejudices.[98] As Reed points out,[99] Oskar's view from behind and beneath the tribune is radically different from that of adults. Oskar asks the reader:

Haben Sie schon einmal eine Tribüne von hinten gesehen? Alle Menschen sollte man—nur um einen Vorschlag zu machen—mit der Hinteransicht einer Tribüne vertraut machen, bevor man sie vor Tribünen versammelt. Wer jemals eine Tribüne von hinten anschaute, recht anschaute, wird von Stund an gezeichnet und somit gegen jegliche Zauberei, die in dieser oder jener Form auf Tribünen zelebriert wird, gefeit sein. (pp. 138–9)

But it is only Oskar's childhood that allows him this freedom of access: he seems to be suggesting that, if the child's vision/self can be retained into adulthood, then the adult's integrity too can be preserved from influences like those of Nazism. Once again the ideas of retaining elements of childhood into adulthood and of the child representing a dimension beyond that of the adults clearly refer back to the Romantic myth of childhood.

This may seem a surprising reading of *Die Blechtrommel*, given the critical emphasis that has been placed on Oskar's childish amorality. While Volker Neuhaus cites a number of critics who have taken a more positive view of Oskar as an embodiment of

---

[96] 'Zu Reich-Ranicki's *Deutsche Literatur in West und Ost*' (1964), in Heinrich Böll, *Essayistische Schriften und Reden,* ii. 1964–1972, ed. Bernd Balzer (Cologne, 1979), 20. Quoted in Reed, *The Novel and the Nazi Past,* 55.

[97] *The Novel and the Nazi Past,* 81.

[98] Reed comments that Grass 'counters the ecstasy and hysteria intended in Nazi ritual with a child's common sense; the mystical unity and collective will engendered by their propaganda with a heretical, eternally unaffiliated individualism; and their illusory art of indoctrination with anti-illusionist views from the rear' (ibid. 80).

[99] Ibid. 79–80.

moral and humane principles that are far superior to those of his society, he notes that no other German literary figure has been subjected to so many 'Verbalinjurien' as Oskar.[100] Nor indeed would I wish to claim that mine is the only possible interpretation of Oskar: perhaps the only thing on which critics of *Die Blechtrommel* agree is that its narrator is an extremely elusive entity and my reading can only be one amongst many. By setting him in the context of the Romantic child and emphasizing the positive aspects of his childlike features I may be reading against the grain, for Oskar himself emphasizes his childhood amorality, indeed, evil: after all, he accuses his younger self of murdering Agnes, Jan, Roswitha, and Matzerath. But, if we accept Barstow's contention that it is the adult narrator rather than the child protagonist who occupies the foreground of Grass's novel, we may have to revise our opinion of this child self.[101] It is after all a critical commonplace that Oskar is an unreliable narrator; why then should we believe what he says about the child Oskar and his motives? The murders are a case in point, for while Oskar may be a contributory factor in these deaths, in the cases of Agnes and Roswitha his role is minimal. It is more substantial in the cases of Jan and Matzerath, but even so, essentially these figures are destroyed by greater military and historical forces.[102] As Barstow points out, the guilt is the narrator's, not the child's: it is something in which he becomes ever more involved through the sheer intensity of his narration.[103] The question is why Oskar should go to such lengths to blacken his child persona, and the answer may lie in a perverse twist of Grass's nostalgia for childhood innocence as discussed earlier. Even in the most trivial incidents, Oskar refuses to allow his child self the benefit of the doubt. Here, for example, Jan has bought him a new drum for his birthday: 'Und während Jan das müde Blech, ich das frische faßten, blieben Jans, Mamas, Matzeraths Augen auf Oskar gerichtet–fast mußte ich lächeln–ja

---

[100] *Günter Grass*, 56–7.

[101] Jane Missner Barstow, 'Childhood Revisited and Revised: Perspective in the First Person Novels of Dickens, Grass and Proust' (unpublished doctoral thesis, University of Michigan, 1973), 43.

[102] Neuhaus completely dismisses the idea that Oskar can be held responsible for the four deaths he claims. He explains Oskar's insistence on his guilt as an expression of his hatred of life itself and as a means of concealing his real guilt which is that he alone sees society's flaws, yet withdraws from society to save himself (*Günter Grass*, 59).

[103] 'Childhood Revisited and Revised', 44.

dachten die denn, ich klebte am Althergebrachten, nährte Prinzip-
ien in meiner Brust? (p. 76) We might consider Oskar's preference
for a new toy over an old and broken one to be quite natural, yet the
narrating Oskar apparently encourages us to see this incident as
proof of a kind of unnatural amorality. However, it is also possible
that this very deliberate blackening is intended to create an impression of him being too hard on his child self and so encourage reader
sympathy with him or at the very least the sense that 'he can't be as
bad as all that'. This is the ultimate in adult nostalgia for innocence
when they know they are living in a fallen world. There is no doubt
that Oskar longs for innocence: so much is clear from his initial
attachment to his 'weißlackiertes' bed (p. 6) and his request for
'unschuldiges Papier' (p. 8). Like Grass in *Hundejahre*, he thus
expresses a longing for innocence whilst apparently denying the
possibility of it. This paradoxically becomes a means of emphasizing and reasserting innocence. Oskar recalls the Romantic child
almost by force of contrast, for he presents the negative side of its
transcendence.[104] His refusal to grow up and his incarceration are
parodic literalizations of the Romantic child's agelessness and the
way it inhabits a separate dimension. Like the classic 'fremdes Kind'
he does not belong in any social context, but operates on a plane
above/below it as an observer and implied means of criticism: his
paradoxical position is perfectly expressed in Grass's comment that
he is an 'umgepolter Säulenheiliger' (*Werkausgabe*, ix, 627). And also,
like the Romantic child, he cannot be treated as a flesh-and-blood
character: Mason sees him as 'a realized contrivance, built on a
number of other abstract ideas about the artist'.[105]

Of course, as in *Hundejahre*, the liberal use of parody and
the grotesque in *Die Blechtrommel* reflects Grass's realization that
childhood 'innocence' is no longer an unproblematic cultural
assumption, and there are many instances where we are repelled
by Oskar's apparent refusal to accept the full implications of events

[104] Barstow suggests that critics oversimplify Oskar's case when they refer to Grass
rejecting Romanticism completely and presenting a new myth of the evil child in him:
she suggests that he embodies both positive and negative aspects of the child myth
prevalent in the 20th cent. (ibid. 106). While I would agree with this, I would question
her contention that his nature is made up of 'a set of mutually exclusive paradoxes'
(ibid. 109) because this suggests a duality where the two halves exist independently of
each other: in fact if Oskar sees himself as Jesus and as Satan these visions are mutually
dependent, for his deep consciousness of evil leads to his nostalgia for innocence.
[105] *Skeptical Muse*, 28.

around him. In 'Glaube Hoffnung Liebe', for instance the fairy-tale structure and bitter refrain 'Es war einmal' produces a powerful reaction in the reader, whose violent rejection of Oskar's account is precisely the kind of moral response Grass was doubtless seeking.[106] The very phrase 'es war einmal' is ambivalent: it can be taken as the opening of a fairytale and therefore as a means of denial, but it can also be read literally as emphasizing that these events really did happen. This phrase demonstrates the fine tightrope Oskar walks between his desire to deny these events, even (or indeed especially) to himself, and Grass's aim, which is to force the contemporary reader (who may be just as keen as Oskar to repress memories of these events) to see them as they really were. Grass's use of parody is rather like Oskar's own linguistic bravado: there is a sense in which both are simply 'protesting too much' and the pain of what they express is felt by the reader not despite but precisely because of the linguistic defiance that attempts to mask it. Oskar is not just the totally unfeeling brat he can appear,[107] as we see in this extraordinary passage just after his mother's death:

Mama konnte sehr lustig sein. Mama konnte sehr ängstlich sein. Mama konnte schnell vergessen. Mama hatte dennoch ein gutes Gedächtnis. Mama schüttete mich aus und saß dennoch mit mir in einem Bade. Mama ging mir manchmal verloren, aber ihr Finder ging mit ihr. Wenn ich Scheiben zersang handelte Mama mit Kitt. Sie setzte sich manchmal ins Unrecht, obgleich es ringsherum Stühle genug gab. Auch wenn Mama sich zuknöpfte, blieb sie mir aufschlußreich. Mama fürchtete die Zugluft und machte dennoch ständig Wind. Sie lebte auf Spesen und zahlte ungerne Steuern. Ich war die Kehrseite ihres Deckblattes. Wenn Mama Herz Hand spielte, gewann sie immer. Als Mama starb, verblaßten die roten Flammen auf der Einfassung meiner Trommel etwas; der weiße Lack jedoch wurde weißer und so grell, daß selbst Oskar manchmal geblendet sein Auge schließen mußte. (p. 194)[108]

---

[106] Thomas sees this kind of provocation as characteristic of Oskar's perspective (*Narrative Works of Günter Grass*, 28).

[107] John Reddick identifies two main aspects of Oskar, 'Brainbox Oskar' and the 'Tears persona' and suggests that the vulnerability inherent in the latter is as much a part of Oskar as the apparently superconfident picaro figure (*The 'Danzig Trilogy' of Günter Grass: A Study of The Tin Drum, Cat and Mouse and Dog Years* (London, 1975), 59–82). Barstow also emphasizes the positive value of Oskar's vulnerability and tears ('Childhood Revisited and Revised', 111).

[108] The importance of this passage and the way Oskar's speech betrays his true feelings is pointed out in Neuhaus, *Günter Grass*, 59.

Although this passage begins with four very simple, unaffected sentences which perfectly translate the feelings of an emotionally numbed child, it moves quickly into the linguistic virtuosity typical of Grass, the puns and wordplay of a narrator who is trying desperately to build up a flippant façade to conceal his true feelings. But the final sentence with its hints at pain and tears clearly shows the crack in that façade, and it is significant that this pain is associated with the drum, the object most closely linked with Oskar's childhood. We might argue that the drum is merely an essential prop for Oskar's performance as a child. But there is more to it than that: Barstow suggests that the drum functions as a comfort blanket[109] as we see after Herbert Truczinski's death when Oskar comments that he 'fand . . . wie immer wenn ihm etwas verlorenging, zu seiner Trommel zurück' (p. 234). The drum is Oskar's means of obtaining information because it allows him to pose as a child, but it is simultaneously a defence mechanism, a way of denying that same knowledge when it distresses him. Moreover, it is his medium of recall when in the sanatorium, when the pain and distress that various chapters cause him can be assessed from the volume of noise he inflicts on the other inmates.

The drum allows both Oskar and those listening to his drumming to perceive the world 'aus dem Blickwinkel der Dreijährigen' (p. 660). That this implies an emotional response is clear when Oskar notes in 'Im Zwiebelkeller': 'Nur weniger, ganz bestimmter Takte bedurfte es, und Oskar fand Tränen, die nicht besser und nicht schlechter als die teuren Tränen des Zwiebelkellers waren' (p. 655). This emotional and thus ethical dimension of Oskar's art recalls what has already been said about the instinctive emotional response of the Romantic child (and of course Oskar's presentation as an artist also places him within the Romantic tradition).[110] Grass apparently parodies this notion not only in recognition that the myth of the innocent child can no longer be allowed to go unchallenged, but also as an expression of nostalgia for that very notion. Reddick's suggestion that in Oskar

---

[109] 'Childhood Revisited and Revised', 108.

[110] The positive ethical value of this episode is pointed out by Brode, *Zeitgeschichte*, 113–14. Kuhn recognizes Oskar's Romantic inheritance when he refers to the chapter 'Im Zwiebelkeller' as 'a variation on a favourite theme of the German romantics' namely 'the reversion to childhood as the goal of the artist-magician' (*Corruption in Paradise*, 63).

'Grass manages brilliantly to have it both ways' by burlesquing the traditions to which Oskar is also the serious heir is as valid for the tradition of the Romantic child as the other traditions he cites.[111] Grass's defiant 'protesting too much' that the Romantic child does not exist thus becomes an affirmation of that myth's power over our author.[112]

One of the most obvious echoes of the Romantic myth of childhood in *Die Blechtrommel*, and one where Grass's ambivalent attitude to the myth becomes most apparent, is the self-identification between Oskar and Jesus. We have already noted identifications between the child figure and the infant saviour in the work of Novalis and also in *Manja, Die größere Hoffnung*, and *Die Unschuldigen* but, whereas in these works the authors created an association between the child protagonist and the saviour, Grass's more ambivalent attitude is suggested by the fact that it is Oskar himself who creates the identification. This allows Grass to maintain a certain distance from the myth and so escape Kuhn's charge of writing 'pseudo-romantic' literature where the topos of the saviour child is 'debased and sentimentalized'.[113] Moreover, Grass's ambivalent attitude towards the myth is paralleled by Oskar's ambivalent attitude towards Jesus. To begin with he clearly believes in the Christ child's powers, for otherwise he

---

[111] *'Danzig Trilogy'*, 76.

[112] For a fuller discussion of Oskar's mythical background, see Erhard M. Friedrichsmeyer, 'Aspects of Myth, Parody and Obscenity in Grass's *Die Blechtrommel* and *Katz und Maus*', *GR* 40 (1965), 240–50. Friedrichsmeyer argues that Oskar is a compound of the various divine child mythologems discussed in *Das göttliche Kind in mythologischer und psychologischer Beleuchtung* by C. G. Jung and K. Kerényi. He suggests that this becomes particularly clear when 'we strip some of Oskar's characteristics of the obliquity of parody' (ibid. 241). While I agree with Friedrichsmeyer's main point, I see the parodic aspect of *Die Blechtrommel* as reinforcing rather than obscuring the parallel between Oskar and these myths. See also Ueding, 'Verstoßen in ein fremdes Land', 356, where it is suggested that the myth of the 'göttliche Kind' has been revived even in the 'Deformationen' Ueding refers to. He cites Oskar as an example of the way modern literature is more concerned with the 'destruktive Komponente im Charakter des Erlöserkindes'.

[113] Kuhn, *Corruption in Paradise*, 53. Oskar's relationship with the Christ child is discussed by Dimler S J, 'Simplicius Simplicissimus and Oskar Matzerath', esp. 120–34. For a discussion of Oskar as a Christ figure for our time, see Hans-Gernot Jung, 'Lästerungen bei Günter Grass', in Manfred Jurgensen (ed.), *Grass: Kritik–Thesen–Analysen* (Berne and Munich, 1973), esp. 82–5. Brode discusses Oskar's self-identification with Jesus as part of Grass's caricatural presentation of Hitler (*Zeitgeschichte*, 49–50). For a discussion of Grass's ambivalent attitude to religion and the Catholic Church and the way it is expressed in his work, see Volker Neuhaus, 'Das christliche Erbe bei Günter Grass', in Heinz Ludwig Arnold (ed.), *Günter Grass: Text + Kritik*, i (6th edn., Munich, 1988).

would not be so disappointed when he tries in vain to force a miracle from the figure in the Herz-Jesu-Kirche (p. 170). This initial belief becomes more complex later when he repeats his experiment, but says: '[ich] hoffte also nicht blöd auf ein Wunder, wollte vielmehr die Ohnmacht plastisch sehen' (p. 438). This defensive statement, pre-empting any new failure on Jesus's part, recalls Grass's own use of parody as he presents a grotesque form of the Romantic child, while nonetheless wanting there to be some saving grace in the myth. But Oskar's surprise and delight when the miracle happens soon turns sour: he addresses the Christ child thus: 'Jesus . . . so haben wir nicht gewettet. Sofort gibst du mir meine Trommel wieder. Du hast dein Kreuz, das sollte dir reichen' (p. 439). Oskar's drum or art is thus made an implicit form of salvation, which recalls the favourite Romantic myth of the artist as divine messenger or saviour. This is despite the fact that in his 'conversation' with Jesus (p. 440), a parody of that between Jesus and Simon Peter (John 21: 15–20), Oskar fervently rejects him. For the fact that these biblical references are firmly enough rooted in his subconscious for him to be able to form this kind of projection suggests that he is as saturated in this Christian mythology as Grass is in the Romantic myth of childhood. In both cases their violent rejection of the myth only seems to point to a deep-seated need to affirm its power; hence Oskar's grudging 'Jesus hatte eventuell einen Nachfolger' (p. 441) and his subsequent identification with him throughout the 'Stäuber' chapters and his trial, the 'zweite Prozeß Christi' (p. 469).

Oskar does eventually reject the redeemer role, for he is appalled by Vittlar's suggestion that he should 'mein Bett verlassen, Jünger sammeln, nur weil ich dreißig Jahre zähle' (p. 717). This seems odd given that earlier he had referred to the 'Stäuber' as his disciples (p. 441). But it is not as contradictory as it seems, for if Oskar sees hope or redemptive value anywhere then it is in the childlike. He rejects the adult representations of Christ in the Herz-Jesu-Kirche (p. 163–4) in favour of the infant Christ, and equally he rejects the idea of taking on the Christ role as an adult. For although he had introduced himself to the police officers who arrested him as Jesus (p. 729) it is only on his thirtieth birthday that he seems to accept his own adulthood, observing: 'Als Dreißigjähriger ist man verpflichtet, über das Thema Flucht wie ein Mann und nicht wie ein Jüngling zu sprechen' (p. 717) and 'Mit dreißig Jahren darf man nicht mehr weinen' (p. 723). This reluctant recognition of his adult status negates any positive potential, as we see from his reference to the 'Buckel' which has resulted from his belated resolve to grow: 'Wenn Jesus einen Buckel gehabt hätte, hätten sie ihn schwerlich aufs Kreuz genagelt' (p. 725). This rejection of the adult Christ and his redemptive role makes clear what has been implicit throughout: while Oskar finds it hard to accept the act of redemption embodied in the adult Christ, let alone see himself in that role, he is nonetheless fascinated by the *potential* for redemption embodied in the infant. By thus allowing Oskar to be both attracted and repelled by Christian mythology, Grass points up his own ambivalent attitude to the Romantic myth of childhood, his nostalgia for it and yet his scepticism: in Oskar's own words 'getreu der Regel: wer zweifelt, der glaubt, wer nicht glaubt, glaubt am längsten' (p. 442).[114]

Oskar's fascination with the infant rather than the adult Christ also suggests that he sees hope for himself only in preserving his child status: even if he cannot play this role indefinitely, he at least hopes to remain in the protective atmosphere of the 'Anstalt'. Importantly he is an 'innocent delinquent' in that he has not actually committed the crime for which he has been imprisoned and yet, like Siggi Jepsen, he fears nothing more than being released. He too feels safe in a value system he knows: staying in the institution allows him to cling to his pretence of childhood unknowing, to stay safe in the 'endlich erreichtes Ziel' of his 'Anstaltsbett' (p. 6) and thus escape from the society he has rejected no less than it has rejected him. His is the paradox not only of an inner space of emotion and childlike vulnerability within a grotesque shell but also of a madman who is judged to be so by a mad society.[115] His 'Anstalt' is merely the external space that corresponds to the internal space of emotion and ethical responses created by his art, his drumming: it is both his imprisonment and his freedom, a place of regression where he no longer has to face the world's corrupting influences. This regressive urge in Oskar is clear from the depiction of his birth onwards; it is apparently only the prospect

---

[114] See also Reddick's comments on Oskar's 'dual and overwrought attitude to the faith' which he believes reflects Grass's own at the time of writing (*'Danzig Trilogy'*, 72).

[115] There is an apparently unlikely parallel between Oskar and Heini in *Die Unschuldigen*, for Heini too is rendered mad by the madness of the adult world and so withdraws from it, not into an institution but into death.

of having his own tin drum that prevents him 'dem Wunsch nach Rückkehr in meine embryonale Kopflage stärkeren Ausdruck zu geben' (p. 49) and his later desire for a refuge beneath his grandmother's skirts and his predilection for hiding under tables and in cupboards express the same regressive urge. This all suggests, however parodistically, that the world is no place for an innocent child, the sentiment that dominated the early twentieth century's view of childhood; moreover, it suggests that it is only Oskar's art that makes his existence bearable at all. Of course, we may argue that this emphasis on regression runs directly counter to the forward-looking potential of the myth of the Romantic child. However, as Chapter 3 will demonstrate, one main feature of the Romantic myth of childhood ensures this forward-looking element: the identification of the child with the artist. In this respect too, Oskar conforms (albeit in his own way) to type.

It should by now be clear that German writers, even those dealing with the Third Reich, are deeply saturated with the Romantic myth of childhood that has dominated German thinking on the subject for over two centuries. Whether they adopt this cultural myth as a means of consolation, like Gmeyner, or for ideological reasons, as in the case of Seghers and Le Fort; whether they accept and exploit it as part of their cultural heritage or whether they strain desperately away from it, only to affirm it ever more powerfully through the very process of denial, it is clearly an orientation point for all of them. In view of the historical reality of Third Reich childhood described in Chapter 1, this continued belief in the child's positive potential seems remarkable. And children's potential is not limited to what they are in the present: in *Levana* Jean Paul calls them 'die ganze Nachwelt . . . in die wir, wie Moses ins gelobte Land, nur schauen, nicht kommen'.[116] They represent hope for a future and perhaps more humane way of life: perhaps equally importantly, in the parallel with the artist they hint at the possibility of a clear-sighted and humane form of future art. If art and life itself are seen as dependent on the myth of the Romantic child, it is no wonder that German writers have been so reluctant to abandon it.

---

[116] *Werke*, v. 533.

3

'SOLLTEN ALLE KINDER DICHTER SEIN?':[1] THE CHILD AS ARTIST

ORIGINS OF A MYTH

The idea that the child bears certain similarities to the artist achieved widespread literary recognition towards the end of the eighteenth century, and so coincided with the new perception of the child's original innocence. But as Schaub points out, the child/artist topos has a longer history: he cites the example of Kallimachos, a Greek poet of the third century BC, who referred to his writing activities as 'childlike play' and his poems as a 'game'.[2] Nor did this revival of the older myth at the end of the eighteenth century owe anything to Rousseau, for his conception of the child excludes any idea of it as the source of poetry.[3] Schaub suggests that Hamann was the first German writer to recognize the child-like element in the artist and that Herder was influenced by him in this respect.[4] Herder's intellectual inheritance was mixed; as Ewers indicates, his early work was influenced by the primitivism of Rousseau, which he adapted in such a way as to suggest the poetic nature of an earlier stage in human civilization and of the child whom he saw as an embodiment of this poetic potential.[5] The idea of the childlike artistic mentality becomes more explicit in Schiller's *Über naive und sentimentalische Dichtung*, but it is not confined to the late eighteenth century. Schaub cites individual nineteenth-century authors who also subscribed to this idea, Schopenhauer in *Vom Genie* (1819) and Baudelaire in *Le peintre de*

---

[1] Wolf, *Nachdenken über Christa T.*, 145. [2] *Génie Enfant*, 11.

[3] This becomes very clear in Ewers's deliberations on Rousseau's view of child-hood, and esp. in the contrasts he draws between Rousseau and Herder (*Kindheit*, 77–9). Ewers notes that Rousseau does not wish to overstimulate Émile's imaginative or emotional facilties and that he expects him to talk in plain language without any rhetorical ornament (ibid. 45 and 47).

[4] *Génie Enfant*, 12.

[5] Herder's conception of childhood is discussed in Ewers, *Kindheit*, 59–96. Ewers stresses that for all Rousseau's influence on the young Herder's thought, Herder's image of childhood is diametrically opposed to that of Rousseau (ibid. 59).

la vie moderne (1863), but goes on to state that it only resurfaced in full force in the late nineteenth and early twentieth centuries.[6] Ironically Freud, who has done most to destroy one myth of childhood, that of its 'innocence', emphasizes the connections between the child and the poet in *Der Dichter und das Phantasieren* (1908). This highlights the fact that the two principal modern myths of childhood, its innocence and its artistry, are not mutually dependent, an important point for any discussion of the theme as it appears in the twentieth century.

At first glance the idea of a parallel between the child and the artist may seem absurd, for if we consider objectively the child and the artist we can hardly imagine two more different beings. While there have been many child prodigies down the ages, as Boas points out, they are the exception rather than the rule, which is why they attract so much attention.[7] Great art is not the preserve of the average child; even at its apparently most naive and spontaneous, art is usually the product of self-conscious and self-disciplined work, and even that most famous child prodigy, Mozart, could not have produced his works without first learning the tools of his trade. Moreover, art has a permanent end product in view, not something we usually associate with children's efforts.

However, the Romantic myth does not claim that the child *is* an artist but that it embodies artistic potential, another example of adults assuming qualities of childhood and building myths on it, rather than looking at real children. Ewers points out that Herder's conception of childhood is based on the idea that individual children, like primitive peoples, reflect the childhood stage of the human race; both are seen as close to nature and therefore to the source of all things, including language.[8] Indeed, Herder's comments on education in *Journal meiner Reise im Jahr 1769* emphasize the benefits of children learning language as though they were savages in the wilderness:

Weg also mit Grammatiken und Grammatiker! Mein Kind soll jede tote Sprache lebendig und jede lebendige so lernen, als wenn sie sich selbst erfände. . . . Und wer seine Muttersprache so lebendig lernte, daß jedes Wort ihm so zur Zeit käme, als er die Sache sieht und den Gedanken hat: welch ein richtiger, philosophisch denkender Kopf, welch eine junge, blühende Seele! So waren die, die sich ihre Sprache selbst erfinden

---

[6] *Génie Enfant*, 15.　　[7] *Cult of Childhood*, 17–18.　　[8] *Kindheit*, 67–8, 77–8.

mußten, Hermes in der Wüste und Robinson Crusoe. In solcher Wüste sollen unsre Kinder sein, nichts als Kindisches zu ihnen reden! Der erste abstrakte unverstandne Begriff ist ihnen Gift, ist wie eine Speise, die durchaus nicht verdaut werden kann, und also, wenn die Natur sich ihrer nicht entledigt, schwächt und verdirbt. . . . Welche Methode, Sprache beizubringen![9]

The primitive language is not a matter of intellectual concepts and abstractions, but of experience, physical sensations, and emotions. Ewers suggests that in Herder's eyes the child's language was therefore more powerful, flexible, and poetic than that of adults in that it makes greater use of onomatopoeia and images.[10] Thus, according to Herder, children are fully equipped with the potential to be artists.[11]

At this point the emphasis is still on the child's artistic potential, but writers of our own era have pointed out closer associations between the activities of the child and the artist. Widlöcher points out that not only psychologists but also adults in general are interested in children's drawings precisely because the category 'adult drawings' does not exist: 'Der Erwachsene zeichnet nicht, wenn er kein Künstler ist'.[12] Similarly, for Freud, the child and the artist are the two categories of people who are not ashamed of using their imaginations:

Das Phantasieren der Menschen ist weniger leicht zu beobachten als das Spielen der Kinder. Das Kind spielt zwar auch allein oder es bildet mit anderen Kindern ein geschlossenes psychisches System zum Zwecke des Spieles, aber wenn es auch den Erwachsenen nichts vorspielt, so verbirgt es doch sein Spielen nicht vor ihnen. Der Erwachsene aber schämt sich seiner Phantasien und versteckt sie vor anderen, er hegt sie als seine eigensten Intimitäten . . .

Sie vergessen nicht, daß die vielleicht befremdende Betonung der Kindheitserinnerung im Leben des Dichters sich in letzter Linie von der Voraussetzung ableitet, daß die Dichtung wie der Tagtraum Fortsetzung und Ersatz des einstigen kindlichen Spielens ist.[13]

---

[9] In *Herders Werke*, ed. Wilhelm Dobbek, 5 vols. (repr. Berlin and Weimar, 1969), i. 181–2.   [10] *Kindheit*, 78.
[11] The idea of the child's poetic language is discussed ibid. 77–9.
[12] *Was eine Kinderzeichnung verrät: Methode und Beispiele psychoanalytischer Deutung*, trans. Annette Roellenbleck (Frankfurt, 1993), 11.
[13] *Der Dichter und das Phantasieren*, in id., *Studienausgabe* ed. Alexander Mitscherlich et al., 11 vols. (Frankfurt, 1969 –1975), x. 173 and 178.

The only place where this theory falls down is in his rather utilitarian analysis of why children play in the first place:

Das Spielen des Kindes wurde von Wünschen dirigiert, eigentlich von dem einen Wunsche, der das Kind erziehen hilft, vom Wunsche: groß und erwachsen zu sein. Es spielt immer 'groß sein', imitiert im Spiele, was ihm vom Leben der Großen bekannt geworden ist.[14]

For, if this imitation of adult roles is a large part of play, it is certainly not the sole driving force behind it;[15] if it were, it would be difficult to explain why some children go through months of 'being' variously animals, vehicles, and other inappropriate 'role models'. Play can in fact be as gratuitously non-utilitarian as art, a simple 'bubbling over' of the child's fantasy life. The only real difference is that artists produce something permanent; yet, as Widlöcher says of children's drawings: 'Das Kind ist vor allem an dauerhaften Spuren interessiert.'[16] This is borne out by Cohen and MacKeith's study of 'paracosms', children's imaginary worlds which are often fully documented with maps, chronicles, and architects' plans.[17] The classic example of children involved in such activities is the Brontë children, but unlike them most of the children in Cohen and MacKeith's study did not grow up to be artists.[18]

This all suggests that the idea of the child embodying artistic potential is less ridiculous than it might initially appear; in all but rare cases the child simply grows out of this potential. But why should the myth of the child as artist have acquired such common currency in the twentieth century?

A TWENTIETH-CENTURY MYTH?

The twentieth century may have gone some way towards debunking the ideal of the child's unequivocal innocence, but the myth of the child as artist and conversely the artist as child has flourished.[19] This separation of two of the main elements of the

---

[14] Ibid. 173.

[15] Coe refers to Freud's rather functional conception of play and contrasts it with that of Johan Huizinga in *Homo Ludens* (1938) (Coe, *When the Grass was Taller: Autobiography and the Experience of Childhood* (New Haven and London, 1984), 243–8).

[16] *Was eine Kinderzeichnung verrät*, 32.

[17] *The Development of Imagination: The Private Worlds of Childhood* (London and New York, 1992).   [18] Ibid. 3–4.

[19] See Boas, *Cult of Childhood*, 79–102 and Schaub, *Génie Enfant*, 15–17.

Romantic myth is not as contradictory as it may appear, first because these elements did not originate together and secondly because 'aesthetic' innocence, the ability to see a thing as if for the
first time, is not necessarily a moral attribute, even though moral
and aesthetic innocence do frequently coincide in accordance
with Schiller's dictum in *Über naive und sentimentalische Dichtung*.
'Seine Naivität allein macht es zum Genie, und was es im In-
tellektuellen und Ästhetischen ist, kann es im Moralischen nicht
verläugnen' (*Werke*, xx. 424). While we recognize that the child's
talents are unlikely to be equal, let alone superior, to those of an
adult artist, writers still regard the childlike vision as a prerequisite
for art.

In making this statement, the emphasis is definitely on the word
child*like*. If we look at Rilke's depiction of the child in his essay
Über Kunst (1898), for example, we have to agree with Boas, who
notes that this image of the child cannot be considered a 'contri-
bution to scientific psychology'.[20] Rilke is not so much interested
in the child as in finding a means to evoke the nature of aritistic vision, and so he portrays the child's delighted but undiscriminating
enjoyment of the beauty around him as the prerequisite for creativity. If the 'Fülle der Bilder' the child collects at this time is not
unduly stifled by education, then the child may mature 'einfach
ruhig weiter von tiefinnen, aus seinem eigensten Kindsein heraus,
und das bedeutet, es wird Mensch im Geiste *aller* Zeiten:
Künstler'.[21] The child's vision is the basis of artistic creativity, but
we have no indications of actual artistry.

The tension between the child's artistic ability (or the lack of it)
and vision is evoked in Reiner Kunze's poem 'Der blitz in unserem namen' where the speaker's amusement at his child's artistic efforts is suddenly checked:

> ... Der künstlerstolz deiner fünf jahre
> wollte die schöpfung signieren
> Vertieft in die grellbunte mühsal
> fragtest du plötzlich:
> Und wann kommt der blitz?

---

[20] *Cult of Childhood*, 78.
[21] In Rilke, *Sämtliche Werke*, v. 430. Boas quotes Rilke's description of the child as a
forerunner of Dada and surrealism (*Cult of Childhood*, 77–9), though this seems to
ignore Rilke's emphasis on a certain maturity.

Wir staunten
Was für ein blitz?
Du sagtest:
Na, der blitz!?
Wir liessen das kunstwerk uns bringen
Du meintest
Das z in unserem namen

Wirklich, zum erstenmal sahen wir
In unserem namen
den blitz
Wann hatte er eingeschlagen?
Sicher, als wir nicht zuhause waren
Ein glück—
der name ist nicht abgebrannt
O kind, was werden wir alles erst sehen
mit deinen augen[22]

Neither Rilke nor Kunze credit the child with creative ability, but both follow the Romantic tradition of the 'Eye among the blind', whereby the child's effortless, naive vision allows him or her to perceive the world in a way that is alien to the average adult. It is this vision that the child-artist has to retain into adulthood.

The idea of the child's vision maturing in the adult artist is upheld in Joyce Cary's *Charley is my Darling* (1940), in the very face of the local artist's self-serving distortion of the Romantic myth.[23] When the children first visit Lommax's home 'They looked about them with expressions of awe, which in simple and frank minds answers every revelation of power, whether in religion or beauty'.[24] Charley is most moved of all.

And yet Charley is a far cry from the children of Rilke and Kunze, for their authors are interested in their vision rather than their psychological make-up. Charley is a fully rounded individual, one who clearly exemplifies the modern disjunction between the myths of childhood innocence and artistry. His artistic sensibility and delinquency are symbiotic, for his habit of telling tall stories forces him into extravagant criminal acts to make good his assertions, and his 'best' works of art are well-executed crudities which would be thoroughly offensive to his unwitting models.

---

[22] In *Gespräch mit der Amsel* (Frankfurt, 1984), 26.
[23] *Charley is my Darling* (London, 1990), 156–62.   [24] Ibid. 155.

Eventually society's perception of him as a delinquent prevails, for he finishes up in a remand home. However, in an essay on this novel Carey comments 'that every ordinary child is by nature a delinquent'[25] and goes on to make a connection between artistry and delinquency:

The suddenness of temptation or, rather, inspiration, which, (like many that come to an artist) is so quick that he doesn't even notice it, it leaves no moment for reflection. . . . You can watch this happen with any good talker, and you can see such inspired talkers carried suddenly away into brutalities. They drop bricks. That is to say, they are whirled into delinquency before they know it.[26]

This association of the child, the delinquent, and the artist gives a new twist to the constellation of child, saviour, and artist discussed with reference to the Romantic era. German literature has consistently presented children as not belonging in the everyday world: in the Romantic era they existed on a transcendent plane; in the *Bildungsroman* they lived on the fringes of society until such time as they had become socially conformist adults; in the early twentieth century they were social misfits and consequently victims; and we saw in Chapter 2 the way that a positive myth of the child as representative of another dimension has been maintained into the later twentieth century, where even children presented as victims of the Third Reich represent transcendent values. By the time we reach the post-war era, new knowledge of child psychology has taken authors beyond presenting children as silent victims of the adult world: the latter half of the twentieth century has seen a great increase in the numbers of child narrators and focalizers and even the child's most delinquent acts can be seen as its justifiable defence against an uncomprehending adult environment. The child is now the misfit who fights back, often with our full approval and sympathy. And if the idea of the child as saviour seems to have vanished from our more secular society and its literature to be replaced by the delinquent, then this too is understandable. By the post-war era social secularization had reached a point where the idea of salvation had to be thrust under a reader's nose: the prime example of this is Oskar Matzerath's self-identification

---

[25] 'Prefaratory Essay written especially for the Carfax Edition of CHARLEY IS MY DARLING', app. to *Charley is my Darling* (London, 1990).   [26] Ibid.

with the infant Christ. This resulted in the new myth of the delinquent and of the secular saviour: the artist.

This new myth underlies Josef Ippers's story *Zacharias Zachary*. While at kindergarten the protagonist entertains the other children with a strange cocktail of stories and characters drawn from the books he has had read to him at home, ranging from the biblical Samson through Red Riding Hood to Hitler. At this stage his storytelling is positively encouraged by the kindergarten staff for 'ich sorgte für Ruhe'.[27] But when he gets to school this gift is no longer acceptable: his imaginings are branded lies by his teacher, who, together with his mother, tries in vain to crush the boy's fantasy life: 'Bald konnte ich auf das mündliche Lügen verzichten, das mir bloß Schläge eintrug; ich konnte es mir abgewöhnen. Nachdem der Lehrer mir das Schreiben beigebracht hatte, schrieb ich meine Lügengeschichten auf Papier. Ich begriff, das verlieh ihnen sogar Dauer.'[28] The fact that the boy himself refers to his stories as lies emphasizes his own socially conditioned perception of himself as a delinquent and stresses the link between artistry and social nonconformity: for this 'Arbeiterjunge' to show any interest in reading and writing is already a sign of deviance and forces him to do both in secret: 'Die Bücher mußte ich stehlen...'.[29] He thus goes from merely transgressing the conventions of his social class to criminal acts, hence his imprisonment in various institutions for young offenders:

Dennoch beharrte ich weiter eigensinnig auf meiner Randexistenz, . . . Ich bin ein *freier* Schriftsteller. Das ist einer, der sich nicht darum kümmert, was seine Nachbarn von ihm halten. Ich stehe wieder—oder immer noch—dort, wo ich zu erzählen angefangen habe, in einer Ecke mit dem Rücken zur Wand.[30]

Significantly that final pose is that of his kindergarten days, 'die einzige glückliche Phase meiner Kindheit',[31] when his creativity had been encouraged, but although this visual echo suggests the inner continuity between the child and the adult artist as envisaged by Wordsworth, this position is described in an entirely different tone, that of the social critic and indeed the rebel that

---

[27] In Böll (ed.), *Niemands Land,* 110.
[28] Ibid. 111. This desire for permanence recalls Widlöcher, *Was eine Kinderzeichnung verrät,* 32.   [29] *Zacharias Zachary,* in Böll (ed.), *Niemands Land,* 111.
[30] Ibid. 118–19.   [31] Ibid. 110.

society has forced him to be. In this he recalls Oskar Matzerath and Siggi Jepsen, whose delinquency is not only a means of social protest and of protecting their 'innocence' as discussed in Chapter 2, but also part and parcel of their artistry.

THE GERMAN ARTIST: ANOTHER DEBASED MYTH?

But, before we return to Oskar and Siggi as examples of a new type of artist, we should consider why it was that the favourite German myth of the artist as the sensitive, superior outsider, sometimes victimized, but usually vindicated by his artistic activity, had taken on these rather harsher contours. As with so many treasured cultural myths, the Third Reich had forced a radical reassessment of it and its reverberations can still be felt in the literature of our own era.[32] It was not just that Hitler's regime suppressed any form of artistic activity that could not be coerced into glorifying its aims: there is also the problem that Hitler himself embodied a perversion of the artist. In *Mein Kampf* he promoted a romanticized image of himself as an artist as he emphasized his struggle against his family and the educational establishment;[33] significantly he also presented himself as Germany's saviour, which had obvious implications for the Messianic myth of the poet earlier promoted by the Expressionists.[34] Thomas Mann turned his attention to this image of the Führer in his essay *Bruder Hitler*, where he noted a number of 'Märchenzüge' (*Gesammelte Werke,* xii. 847)[35] in the story of Hitler's rise, another example of the debasement of Romanticism noted in Chapter 1, and went on to write about the Führer as a perverted 'Erscheinungsform des Künstlertums' (p. 848). We can only agree with Mann when he comments: 'das Motiv der Verhunzung und der Heruntergekommenheit spielt eine große Rolle im gegenwärtigen europäischen Leben' (p. 847); just as the Romantic myth of the child was perverted by the Nazis, so the idea of the artist was also irrevocably damaged by this era. From having been indulgently tolerated eccentrics, artists suddenly found themselves forced into the role of

---

[32] For a discussion of the debasement of the German myth of the artist under the Third Reich and the difficulties writers had in coming to terms with their post-war role, see Mason, *Skeptical Muse,* 9–16.   [33] *Mein Kampf,* i. 6–8, 15–20.
[34] Mason, *Skeptical Muse,* 15.   [35] This essay is discussed ibid. 55–6.

delinquents, compelled either to keep their opinions to themselves—indeed sometimes to express opinions which were clearly
not their own in order to survive—or to go into exile with all its attendant difficulties. The artist's resultant loss of self-confidence is
understandable and helps to explain the more sceptical post-war
attitude towards this figure. Certainly he is unlikely now to be
seen in terms of a saviour figure as in the nineteenth and earlier
twentieth centuries; indeed, we may consider Adrian Leverkühn
as the precise opposite of that myth and as more symptomatic of
this generation.

Adrian is an extreme example, but there is ample evidence of a
more sceptical attitude to the artist persisting into our own era,
even when the writer is saturated with the earlier myth. Artists appear almost as frequently as children in Hofmann's works and,
like the myth of childhood, that of the artist is treated with a certain scepticism.[36] The actor of *Unsere Eroberung* and the grandfather in *Der Kinoerzähler* (1990) are both vain men who use their art
as a means of self-aggrandizement and the grandfather loves his
'art' so much that he would collude with Nazism in order to save
it. Both men are 'Mitläufer' who fail miserably to uphold Thomas
Mann's ideal of an innate critical element in art's interaction with
society.[37] Hofmann also uses the grandfather to parody the
Messianic myth of the artist; Karl Hofmann occasionally quotes
Christ in utterly bathetic contexts, and yet ironically he refuses to
act as a model for a picture of the Crucifixion 'weil er als Christus
hätte nackt sein müssen'.[38] This suggests what his behaviour towards the Nazi regime has suggested all along: despite the artistic
airs he gives himself, he does not want the responsibilities that go
with serious artistry. *Der Blindensturz* (1985) is a rather more com-
plicated case for, although the 'Maler' appears initially a very inadequate figure, there are also indications that suggest he might
represent the saviour. He shares the fate of his models, for he is
going blind; nonetheless, this does not affect his aspirations, for he

---

[36] For a more detailed discussion of Hofmann's artist figures, see Schede, *Gert Hofmann*, 336–86.

[37] 'Der Künstler und die Gesellschaft': 'Und doch ist es wahr, daß dem eingebore-
nen Kritizismus der Kunst etwas Moralisches anhaftet, das sich offenbar von der in der
Welt des Ästhetischen und des Sittlichen gleicherweise beheimateten Idee des
"Guten" herleitet' (*GesammelteWerke*, x. 392).

[38] Gert Hofmann, *Der Kinoerzähler: Roman* (Munich, 1990), 186.

wants to paint the ultimate picture 'des menschlichen Schreis'.[39] This sounds a despairing project but could refer to the Crucifixion, where Christ 'schrie laut' just before he died.[40] The fact that the painter is suffering the same fate as his models but is trying to paint the picture to end all pictures, the ultimate act of salvation, suggests that while Hofmann cannot see the artist in the light of the omnipotent creator God, he can humanize him into the suffering saviour, a much more ambivalent image. This ambivalence suggests that as in the case of the child, positive myths are not easily dispensed with, however much irony writers may bring to them.

THE DELINQUENT ARTIST: AN ENFORCED POSITION?

As we saw in Chapter 2, Oskar Matzerath and Siggi Jepsen continue the Romantic myth of childhood, despite all the indications to the contrary: they too are outsiders alienated from society like their early twentieth-century counterparts. However, the emphasis is different: the likes of Hanno Buddenbrook, Hans Giebenrath (in *Unterm Rad*), and Karl Gruber (in *Die Turnstunde*) are unable to make valid connections with adult reality and their authors are forced to let them die if they are to escape the existential dilemma of growing up. In contrast, in the novels dealing with the Third Reich the child figures are alienated by specific social and historical conditions and thus Oskar and Siggi withdraw into asylums for the lunatic and the criminal rather than into death.

But, as we saw in the Introduction, this too places them in a literary tradition. Ziolkowski notes the prevalence of the madness theme in post-war German literature, asserting that we are often asked to share the madman's view of society, but he also indicates that this preoccupation with insanity was inherited from the Romantics.[41] Nor is madness the only or worst form of deviance associated with the artist figure, for there is also a German tradition of seeing the artist not merely as an outsider but also as a criminal, a point Mason makes when she suggests Mann's Felix Krull as one of Oskar's literary forefathers.[42] There are clearly similarities

---

[39] Id., *Der Blindensturz: Erzählung* (Darmstadt and Neuwied, 1985), 98.
[40] Markus, 15: 37.   [41] *Dimensions of the Modern Novel*, 343.
[42] *Skeptical Muse*, 31 and 35.

between these figures, but equally we can contrast them so as to highlight the positive aspects of Oskar's art, for Krull is simply a petty thief and swindler unable to do anything but imitate others, albeit fluently. Oskar is clearly a more grotesque figure, but his 'art' is at least original to him and can be construed as a form of social protest and means of creating awareness. While Krull's society may often appear ridiculous, it is not morally wrong as that of Oskar and Siggi is: while all Krull's attempts to exculpate himself by pointing to his particular circumstances fall rather flat, in Oskar and Siggi we feel that their isolated position is to at least some extent a sign of their integrity.

It is their isolation, their enforced (yet desired) withdrawal from society, that allows these delinquents the opportunity to write. Siggi is initially under the compulsion of a 'Strafarbeit' whilst Oskar wishes to write. However, although they only become literary artists when isolated from mainstream society, their artistic tendencies and their probable consequences have been evident since early childhood.[43] The chapter of *Die Blechtrommel* entitled 'Der Stundenplan', for example, may be a conscious parody of the school chapter in *Buddenbrooks*: the musician Hanno is replaced by the drummer Oskar, who evidently regards his drumming as high art. Like Hanno, Oskar shows the potential to be a writer in his acute observations of his teacher. Not only does she apparently feel 'durchschaut' by him (another echo of *Buddenbrooks*) but he also notes that her inner life contains 'Erzählenswertes genug für drei unmoralische Kapitel' (*Blechtrommel*, 89). As before, the child is an outsider figure in the classroom, this time due to his grotesque physique as well as his artistic activities. He regards this isolation as a mark of natural superiority, referring to the other children as 'das Volk' (p. 86), 'die Bande hinter mir' (p. 88) and 'eine Horde Grimassen schneidende, völlig

---

[43] For other interpretations of Oskar as an artist see Henry Hatfield, 'Günter Grass: The Artist as Satirist', in Robert R. Heitner (ed.), *The Contemporary Novel in German: A Symposium* (Austin, Tex. and London, 1967), 119–23 and Klaus Stallbaum, *Kunst und Künstlerexistenz im Frühwerk von Günter Grass* (Cologne, 1989). See also Hannelore Mundt, *'Doktor Faustus' und die Folgen. Kunstkritik als Gesellschaftskritik im deutschen Roman seit 1947* (Bonn, 1989), 74–7, for a discussion of Oskar as a parody of the bourgeois artist. Mason discusses the connections between Freud's metaphor of the child as artist and the way Oskar is presented (*Skeptical Muse*, 28–31); Oskar's dual status as a representative of the Nazi artist and the kind of artist persecuted by the Nazi regime (ibid. 41–9); and the moral import of his artistic fantasy (ibid. 77–86).

überdrehte Rüpel' (p. 87). In contrast to them he sits quietly (at least to start with) with his artistic medium, his drum. However, as with Hanno, the artistic individual suffers a hard fate in the conformist classroom environment: instead of being appreciated as he thinks fit, Oskar is forcibly silenced by his teacher. It may seem an over-interpretation to see in Oskar the marginalized and finally repressed artist but other later indications support this view. In 'Madonna 49', for example, the description of the 'Rosenmontag' carnival suggests that Grass is consciously identifying his own role with that of Oskar. As in the school chapter, Oskar is isolated from his contemporaries. He dresses as a Fool in a costume made of 'Stoffreste' so as to enjoy the carnival on equal terms with his peers but, while his costume recalls the pagan roots of the carnival tradition, the rest of the 'Wiederaufbau' society refuses to indulge in anything but a rather tame version of the same event.[44] As in the school chapter, Oskar imagines that he is amusing his contemporaries, and yet gradually he realizes 'daß ich das Volk, alles was da als Cowboy und Spanierin das Büro und den Ladentisch verdrängen wollte, nicht zum Lachen brachte, sondern erschreckte' (pp. 575–6). Grass was later to suggest a parallel between the 'Hofnarr' and the writer[45] and this, together with the significant 'verdrängen', may make us equate the carnival 'Volk' (an echo of the school chapter) with the 'Bürger' of 1959 who were so shocked by Grass's portrayal of their recent past and present society in *Die Blechtrommel*. In the carnival sequence Oskar assumes and indeed exaggerates the people's own irresponsibility and desire to repress the past. He thus unconsciously forces them to contemplate themselves and their behaviour, the effect Grass was consciously aiming at in *Die Blechtrommel*.

Oskar is very much an artist of the 'Wiederaufbau' period, as the satirical chapter 'Im Zwiebelkeller' demonstrates.[46] The

---

[44] On Oskar and the image of the fool and carnival in post-1945 German literature, see Richard Sheppard, 'Upstairs-Downstairs: Some Reflections on German Literature in the Light of Bakhtin's Theory of Carnival' in id. (ed.), *New Ways in Germanistik* (New York, Oxford, and Munich, 1990), 309–13, esp. 309.

[45] In 'Vom mangelnden Selbstvertrauen der schreibenden Hofnarren unter Berücksichtigung nicht vorhandener Höfe', in *Werkausgabe*, ix.

[46] Grass later revised this conception of the artist. In 'Vom mangelnden Selbstvertrauen der schreibenden Hofnarren' he attempts to define a position between the myth of the German 'Dichter' or 'Genie' of the 19th century and the self-conscious 'engagierter Schriftsteller' of his own day. (For a discussion of this essay, see Mason,

'Volk' of the 'Wirtschaftswunder' is unable to grieve unless helped to catharsis by the suitably bathetic onions. Oskar, however, belongs to an elite, those 'die noch ohne Zwiebel zu Tränen kommen konnten' (p. 655). His art enables him to remain in touch with his own emotions and with the childhood self who still wants to mourn his mother, Jan Bronski, and Matzerath.[47] That art is described quite specifically as childlike, for Oskar 'spielte . . . nicht, was ich konnte, sondern was ich vom Herzen her wußte. Es gelang Oskar, einem einst dreijährigen Oskar die Knüppel in die Fäuste zu drücken' (pp. 659–60). It is the childlike nature of this art that reduces his audience in the 'Zwiebelkeller' to the status of young children. This episode has been assessed negatively by some critics, who see Oskar as encouraging his audience's escapism.[48] Nevertheless, Grass's positive conception of the child's spontaneity and lack of inhibitions might suggest that the activities of the 'Zwiebelkeller' guests could at least lay the basis for a new perception of themselves and their society. As Botheroyd indicates, this achievement is prefigured in the school chapter when Oskar observes that Fräulein Spollenhauer's attempts to clap along to his beat make her 'menschlich . . . das heißt kindlich, neugierig, vielschichtig, unmoralisch' (p. 89).[49] Such art creates an inner space of emotion against which the horrors of the Nazi period and the *Wiederaufbau* can be measured, and it is no coincidence that Oskar should need his drum as a stimulus for writing while in the 'Anstalt'. This medium allows him to feign a childlike

Skeptical Muse, 113–16.) His use of parody and the grotesque in his depiction of Oskar is a first step in the process of demystifying the German conception of the 'Dichter'. Nonetheless, in 1959 Oskar's asocial and uncompromising nature exemplified exactly what was required from art; he is an image for his creator and his determination not to allow the Nazi past to be comfortably forgotten. His art has both shock and therapeutic value, but it is an art that is only appropriate to this particular season.

[47] Brode sees this ability to remember and to grieve as a sign of Oskar's morality when compared with the rest of the 'Wirtschaftswunder' society (*Die Zeitgeschichte*, 113–14).

[48] See Elizabeth Boa, 'Günter Grass and the German Gremlin', *GLL* 23 (1969/70), 149; Mason, *Skeptical Muse*, 44; and Thomas, *Narrative Works of Günter Grass*, 75, where he suggests that Oskar 'encourages the public in its immaturity and escapism' after 1945. While Thomas sees the drum as a barrier between the individual and his reality, whether past or present, in fact Oskar's drumming allows him access to his innermost feelings ('Im Zwiebelkeller') and facilitates an account of the Third Reich whose shock value seems far from escapism.

[49] *Ich und Er: First and Third Person Self-Reference and Problems of Identity in Three Contemporary German-Language Novels* (The Hague and Paris, 1976), 60.

incomprehension of events in the main narrative, a device which functions almost as a defence mechanism against the painful insights which that same art has allowed him. The drum's role in his narrative thus parallels its role in his life: it allows him to play the uncomprehending child, and thus to observe and understand more of adult society than the adults realize. It is left to the reader to enter the emotional space created by Oskar's art and to complete depictions of events which are too painful for him to record in their undistorted reality. And given his ability to force us to confront unpleasant truths in this way, we might ask whether Oskar himself seeks the 'Anstalt' as a refuge, an external space to match the inner one created by his art, or whether society, seeing in him a dangerously subversive element who reveals more about it than it wants to know, simply wants him suppressed, if necessary by force, as in the schoolroom.

The same question can be asked of Siggi Jepsen. His fate is clearly identified with that of Nansen, whose art is seen symbolically as the only form of hope in the dark days of the Third Reich: the light from his workshop during the blackout is 'das erste Licht, das sich seit Jahren in der Ebene zeigte' (*Deutschstunde*, 202) and when the policeman attempts to suppress this light, Nansen's response, 'gleich schaff ich euch die Dunkelheit, die ihr haben wollt' (p. 206), is clearly symbolic. Siggi is associated literally with the artist in his friendship for the man and his willingness to help him, but their association goes beyond this. The boy's vision is paralleled with that of the artist, for his narrative is made up of vividly described but often silent pictures:[50]

Ich linste durch die Scheiben. Sie waren allein im Atelier. Sie standen vor Doktor Busbecks Geschenktisch. Ich legte meine Hände neben meinem Gesicht auf die Scheibe, und jetzt, da die Blendung aufhörte, sah ich, daß sie vor dem Bild standen, auf dem Segel sich in Licht auflösten, und ich merkte, daß ein zäher Prozeß um das Bild geführt wurde: fordernd stieß der Zeigefinger meines Vaters auf das Bild herab, worauf

---

[50] The role played by 'gefrorene Bilder' is pointed out by Elm, *Siegfried Lenz–'Deutschstunde'*, 67–9. See also Wilhelm Johannes Schwarz, *Der Erzähler Siegfried Lenz* (Berne and Munich, 1974), 78–9. Schwarz observes that many scenes in *Deutschstunde* recall silent films, though he attributes this, perhaps over-literally, to the natural taciturnity of the people Lenz is describing. For the idea that the child's attempts at drawing are usually narrative rather than strictly representational or aesthetic, see Widlöcher, *Was eine Kinderzeichnung verrät*, esp. 220.

der Maler sich mit seinem Körper davorstellte, da wurde beansprucht und verweigert, begehrt und zurückgewiesen—alles lautlos, in erregtem Aquariumschweigen (p. 93)

As in the case of Walli Sawatzki this vision is essentially childlike in that whilst vivid it is wholly non-analytical. The child simply notes what he sees, as is suggested by the quantity of verbs of visual perception,[51] and this emphasis on the visual over the linguistic runs through the text. The pictorial narrative is a means of retaining the child's intense vision without over-intellectualizing it, a frequent dilemma of childhood narratives. However, it also helps to avoid a language which Lenz sees as tainted by the political abuses of the Nazi era. For, while language is an intellectual convention which can be corrupted when it falls into the wrong hands, vision forms an organic part of a person's make-up and is therefore not so easy to repress, as Nansen points out:

Diese Wahnsinnigen, als ob sie nicht wüßten, daß das unmöglich ist: Malverbot. Sie können vielleicht viel tun mit ihren Mitteln, sie können allerhand verhindern, mag sein, aber nicht dies: daß einer aufhört zu malen. . . . Sie brauchen doch nur nachzulesen: gegen unerwünschte Bilder hat es noch nie einen Schutz gegeben, nicht durch Verbannen, auch nicht durch Blendung, und wenn sie die Hände abhacken ließen, hat man eben mit dem Mund gemalt. Diese Narren, als ob sie nicht wüßten, daß es auch unsichtbare Bilder gibt. (p. 41)

The vision of the child and the artist are paralleled in that both are untainted by events around them. The artist may understand more about political realities than the naive child, but although Siggi's vision is incomplete because it is frequently blocked by physical obstacles (the window panes, the door which only stands ajar, or the fear of being seen), which all symbolize his less developed intellectual status, this apparently incomplete perspective is actually made complete by his artistic sensibility. This becomes clear in the chapter 'Das Porträt', which describes an encounter between Nansen and the policeman when the artist rips up his own painting for, although Siggi is not actually present at this encounter, he assumes total narrative omniscience when narrating it. Manfred Durzak highlighted this break in narrative perspective in conversation with Lenz but, while the critic clearly regarded

---

[51] Schwarz, *Erzähler Siegfried Lenz*, 78–9.

this as a formal fault, Lenz defended his right to step outside his self-imposed limitations.[52] In fact, 'Das Porträt' has even wider implications than Lenz allowed for in this conversation since it highlights the close parallel between Siggi's vision and Nansen's creative process. The boy effectively pieces together the encounter between his father and Nansen just as he pieces together the ripped painting, an analogy between pictorial and literary art that is made explicit when Siggi refers to the bits of canvas as 'Kapitel, die nun geordnet werden mußten' (p. 223) and ends his description of the argument with the words 'so mal ich es mir aus' (p. 206). This is one of the most obvious examples of Siggi following Nansen's dictum: 'man beginnt zu sehen, wenn man aufhört, den Betrachter zu spielen und sich das, was man braucht, erfindet' (p. 402).[53] As for Oskar, art for Siggi is a means not only of understanding and coming to terms with his own experience, but also of creating a distance between himself and the corruption which could derive from those experiences, a means of retaining his childlike and uncorrupted vision and nature. For, while the island authorities are apparently trying to force him into accepting values suspiciously akin to those of a previous Nazi generation ('Die Freuden der Pflicht'), his essay bursts the bounds of an academic exercise intended to bring him into line and instead becomes a substantial part of the work of art we are reading, one which preserves the child's untainted, non-analytical vision. Once again the child has proved at least to some extent inviolate against the influences of his time, a space where values other than those of the prevailing social and political realities can survive.

THE CHILD AS AN AUßENSEITER

Oskar and Siggi may be seen as innocent victims of a society which in both *Die Blechtrommel* and *Deutschstunde* is portrayed in the most unflattering terms. Their resistance is extreme and gets them put away. Nelly Jordan is apparently a very different case. We saw in Chapter 1 how clearly the banality of daily indoctrination and its

---

[52] *Gespräche über den Roman* ... (Frankfurt, 1976), 180–4.

[53] Todd Kontje suggests that Nansen's theories as expounded in the chapter 'Sehen' can be applied globally to Siggi's perspective ('Captive Creator in Siegfried Lenz's *Deutschstunde*: Writer, Reader and Response', *GQ* 53 (1980), 460).

effects on the child's receptive consciousness are demonstrated in *Kindheitsmuster*. However, the moments of apparently instinctive moral insight and the parallels with Jean Paul indicate that Wolf's conception of the child comes close to that of the Romantics. This also holds true of the Romantic perception of the child as artist, or at least as embodying artistic potential, as is clear if we look at the short story *Juninachmittag* (1965).[54] Like the child of Kunze's 'Der blitz in unserem namen', the 8-year-old here is not artistically adept; there is something faintly comic in her 'verbissen' attempts to produce some recognizable object from a piece of bark, using a 'stumpfes Messer', and the fact that the intended object keeps changing (it mutates from a 'Schiff' to an 'Ul' by way of a 'Dolch' and a 'Regenschirm')[55] shows the same realistic assessment of the child's ability as Kunze. But here too, the child's value is not so much in what she produces as in the perspective she suggests for, as Smith points out, her activities remind the adults of 'the potential for change and development' and 'the value of shifting perspectives, looking at a well-known object from a fresh angle'.[56] Her capacity for playing with open possibilities is seen later in the linguistic game she initiates, where the aim is to produce the most original compound nouns.[57] This spontaneous creation compares very favourably with the earnest attempts of the young technocrat to play the game, for he ruins it with his use of ideologically correct state vocabulary.[58] The reactions of the narrator's two daughters to this young conformist again highlight a Romantic element in Wolf's conception of childhood. The way the elder daughter is attracted to him and her irritation when her parents seem not to be taking her own political convictions seriously make it clear that it is not only in the physical sense that the narrator could note 'daß es kein Kind mehr war, was da vor uns saß'.[59] The younger daughter on the other hand is 'ganz verwirrt' by the engineer's

---

[54] For stimulating discussions of this story, see Anne Tanner, 'Wendepunkt: Christa Wolfs *Juninachmittag*', in Manfred Jurgensen (ed.), *Wolf: Darstellung–Deutung–Diskussion* (Berne and Munich, 1984) and William H. Rey, 'Christa Wolfs *Juninachmittag*: Vorspiel zu den letzten Erzählungen', *WB* 38 (1992), 85–103. Tanner discusses the child as an embodiment of Wolfs multi-faceted conception of the imagination ('Wendepunkt', 63–5); Rey too acknowledges the child's positive potential but emphasizes her 'Hang zum Grausigen' when bored ('Christa Wolfs *Juninachmittag*', 94).

[55] Wolf, *Juninachmittag*, in ead. *Gesammelte Erzählungen* (repr. Berlin and Weimar, 1990), 46–7.   [56] *Tradition, Art and Society*, 131.

[57] *Juninachmittag*, 59   [58] Ibid. 59–60.   [59] Ibid. 57.

attempt at playing her favourite game.[60] It is significant that she is referred to throughout as 'das Kind' and 'es', in a way consistent with Romantic ideas on childhood; she is both innocent (that is, asexual) and untainted in the political/ideological sense. She is thus able to be open and spontaneous in her responses in a way that recalls the artist. And she is not the only child artist in Wolf's work: Christa T. responds to a short story written by her daughter with the words 'Sollten alle Kinder Dichter sein?'.[61] Wolf thus apparently subscribes to two of the Romantics' main articles of faith regarding children: first to the idea of their original innocence which is only corrupted later by social influences and secondly to their identification with the artist.

Certainly in *Kindheitsmuster* Nelly's more obviously moral responses, as for example in the 'Judenjunge' incident, seem to be a product of her artistic sensibility, the kind of imaginative and emotional responses we noted in Johansen's 'Analphabetin'. When Nelly watches the aftermath of the *Kristallnacht* the visual, indeed pictorial, nature of her perception is emphasized, as is her ability to empathize with the women and children whom she has never met but whose distress she is well able to imagine. Such moments of moral insight are a symptom of the 'innere Freiheit' (*Kindheitsmuster*, 327), discussed in Chapter 2. The child is only marginally involved in the events of the Nazi era, but this marginal involvement allows her opportunities to observe and criticize as when her cousin Astrid is hypnotized at their confirmation tea. Nelly considers the possibility of imitating her cousin, whose acts under hypnosis clearly mirror the behaviour of indoctrinated youngsters under the Third Reich. However, 'Zugleich wußte sie: Das war ihre Sache nicht. Ihre Sache war, die eine [Astrid] zu beobachten und ein wenig zu beneiden, den anderen [the hypnotist] zu durchschauen. Und alles–die geheime Sehnsucht, den Neid, das Gefühl von Überlegenheit–vor jedermann zu verbergen' (p. 395). This description, with its echoes of Mann's *Tonio Kröger*,[62] is not merely a description of the child; it also character-

---

[60] Ibid. 60.

[61] *Nachdenken über Christa T.*, 145. Barnett quotes this child amongst others to demonstrate the 'imaginative capacity' that Wolf sees in childhood ('Perceptions of Childhood', 62–3).

[62] Smith points out this allusion in his discussion of *Kindheitsmuster* as an aesthetic *Bildungsroman* (*Tradition, Art and Society*, 189–200, esp. 196).

izes Wolf's perception of the artist's role in a capitalist society.[63] And, indeed, when Wolf refers to the child's 'innere[n] Freiheit', it does not only echo her comment that one of the qualities required by the artist is 'eine gewisse innere Freiheit':[64] this phrase has a number of different resonances, for the child's marginal involvement in the Nazi era may also recall the 'innere Emigration' of certain intellectuals who claimed to have kept an inner critical space unsullied by outside influences even while they were not allowed to publish their true thoughts and feelings. Nelly's 'innere Freiheit', perhaps like theirs, is only bought at the price of a 'schlechtes Gewissen'; this mental state is externalized for Siggi and Oskar in their respective institutions.[65]

We know from the narrative framework of *Kindheitsmuster* that Nelly is to grow up to be a writer, but there are already plenty of indications of her artistic tendencies in her childhood experience, for example her ability to empathize with characters of her own creation and her powers of imagination which, as in Siggi's case, are extremely visual.[66] But while Siggi's vision is largely non-analytical, in Nelly the child's untainted vision apparently demands a moral response, as in the synagogue scene. Wolf seems to suggest that the child functions as a potential moral yardstick (note her preoccupation with Bobrowski's question 'Wie muß die Welt für ein moralisches Wesen beschaffen sein?'[67]) since, even beneath layers of political indoctrination, she possesses a core of innocence or instinctive moral responses. However, Wolf's conception of the child as identified with the artist, rather like that of

---

[63] Her conception of the artist's role under Socialist rule is completely different, for although she stresses his/her distinct way of life, she adds: 'Der Autor, von dem wir reden, läßt sich also trotz seiner merkwürdigen Lebensweise nicht in eine Außenseiterposition drängen, die fast alle bürgerlichen Autoren heftig beklagen' ('Lesen und Schreiben', 498).   [64] 'Unruhe und Betroffenheit', 752.

[65] Barbara Saunders seems to advance rather too positive a view of Nelly's 'innere Freiheit' in her analysis of the *Mario und der Zauberer* allusion (*Contemporary German Autobiography: Literary Approaches to the Problem of Identity* (London, 1985), 120). While I agree with her that this episode shows Nelly's capacity for occasional resistance, it also seems to allude to her broader failure to resist the Hitler regime as a whole.

[66] Saunders notes other aspects of the young Nelly that suggest a continuity between her and the adult writer, referring to the child as 'intellectually curious, suspicious and independent' (ibid. 113), but in the light of Ch. 1, above, this description looks rather too positive.

[67] 'Unruhe und Betroffenheit', 765, and 'Subjektive Authentizität: Gespräch mit Hans Kaufmann', in *Die Dimension des Autors*, ii. 804–5.

Grass and Lenz, tells us something about their conception not only of childhood, but also of literature as another 'space' where moral and humane values may be preserved. This seems a particularly plausible explanation for the Hammurabi incident in *Nachdenken über Christa T.*, when Christa's loutish pupil bites the head off a toad and Christa is apparently unable to handle this 'nackte, wahre Wirklichkeit' other than by writing a 'möglicher Schluß', where the cook tells her of Hammurabi's distress after the incident, concluding: 'jetzt heult er wie ein kleines Kind'.[68] Just as fiction provides a moral ending, so the fictional regression to a childlike state suggests the possibility of redemption for Hammurabi.

The narrator sees this episode as proof of Christa's wishful thinking and inability to deal with real life. But it is significant that Wolf shows Christa reconstructing the moral values associated with the Romantic image of childhood in literature when she is not able to find them in reality. For, although we have noted a wealth of positive moral and cultural potential symbolized in children, to say that they embody hope purely because they represent or are to grow into artists is a rather pessimistic and limiting conclusion. We saw in Chapter 2 that, however optimistic the tone of narratives dealing with Jewish children as symbols of hope and spiritual freedom, the symbolic moral weight of one child seems pitifully little to pit against the Nazi regime when we step out of literature and into the cold light of historical reality. Similarly, the future looks bleak for Oskar, Siggi, and the 'kleine Imbachs'; the only real hope in their accounts exists not for them personally but in the testaments they have produced. This raises the thorny question as to whether writers are simply taking the most readily available symbol and asking it to bear a burden too heavy for its young shoulders, especially given the extent to which the myth of the artist itself has been discredited.

CHILD = ARTIST = HOPE: A PESSIMISTIC EQUATION?

But it would be wrong to suggest that children represent hope only because they represent the artist, even if this is what the authors themselves subconsciously want to suggest. If we take *Manja*

---

[68] *Nachdenken über Christa T.*, 110.

as possibly the most optimistic example of writing about children, we may be surprised at how little we see of the girl's artistic activity. Given the novel's emphasis on heredity, we might expect all her parents' frustrated artistic potential to blossom in her but, although she plays the piano, we never actually see her playing; instead, we hear reports about it and about the effect it has on her and others. These reports suggest that the most important aspect of her art is the feelings it produces, but these are not the preserve of art alone: they are produced by such diverse experiences as a butterfly landing on one's hand, reading, talking to people, and the sound of rain on the windows. Gmeyner suggests that such experiences are essentially childlike: 'Die Worte waren wie Geheimnisse, die nur geheimnisvoller wurden, indem man sie aussprach. Hinter ihnen stand das unbeschreibbare Erlebnis, gemischt aus Vergehen und Dauer, aus Strom und Stille, Schreck und Beruhigung, das zu vergessen ein Teil des Erwachsenwerdens ist' (*Manja*, 237).

Manja's art is not a matter of technical virtuosity and she does not regard herself as an artist. Only once does she consider this as a potential career, and then only because of the new laws regarding marriages between Jews and Aryans: ' "Wenn ich Künstlerin werde," sagte Manja unerwartet, "braucht mich keiner zu heiraten" ' (p. 329). Becoming an artist would simply be a means of guaranteeing her independence, a way of life rather than an artistic vocation. Her piano playing is not an end in itself: it is a means of expressing feelings too deep to be articulated otherwise. Indeed, if we are to regard the most childlike form of art not as a need to present reality in a realistic way but to express feelings, then music, the least referential of the arts, is also perhaps the most childlike. The diverse moments that Heini and Manja long to preserve suggest that these children are not associated so much with art as with moments of transient and inexplicable joy, such as we can feel at apparently quite banal causes. Manja calls these 'Augenblicke . . . in denen eigentlich gar nichts geschieht' (p. 237) which makes them sound insignificant. But in fact these non-utilitarian, transient moments are of the same stuff as imagination, dreams, and play; they are also the stuff artists long to preserve for posterity. Manja is not an artist; she simply wants to remember the beauty of those inexpressible moments. Gmeyner is celebrating the fact that this vision is at the origins of human nature because, as long as she can still believe that every child that comes into the world has this potential, she can still see hope for the future. The fact that Manja could equally represent the 'Eye among the blind', the basis of artistic creation, is in a sense incidental.

However, we might argue that Manja possesses quite enough positive qualities without necessarily having to represent artistic potential as well. She is an idealized figure who stands in the Romantic tradition of childhood innocence and redemptive potential. Significantly, when we are dealing with children who have been more obviously affected by the Nazi era, the idea of the child embodying artistic potential emerges more strongly. The Romantic myth thus survives even in the frankly non-idealizing *Unsere Eroberung* and *Veilchenfeld.*

As we saw in Chapter 1, these works feature basically ignorant, amoral children. Whereas Manja is characterized by her ability to empathize with others, her warmth and humanity, Hofmann's children function mainly as laconic observers who show little emotional involvement in the events they narrate. The highly artificial 'wir' construction of *Unsere Eroberung* effectively precludes any sense of a 'real' character and Hans too has been described as an 'anonymisierte Aufzeichnungsfläche der Reden und des Geredes der anderen'.[69] However, this very depersonalization suggests the more symbolic function of the Romantic child, and while Hofmann's children may not be obvious symbols of the artist, they are at least as artistically active as Manja: the 'wir' too has had piano lessons and Hans enjoys drawing. But, as in *Manja,* it is not their overt artistic activities that are most important; in *Veilchenfeld* these activities are a symbol for Hans's perceptions as narrator, for when looking at pictures with Veilchenfeld he tells him 'welche mir gefielen und welche nicht, konnte aber nicht sagen warum' (*Veilchenfeld,* 48). This non-analytical approach corresponds precisely to his narrative: as in *Unsere Eroberung* the emphasis is on 'sich umschauen'. This unprejudiced vision is the first prerequisite for art. The second is imagination, which in both *Unsere Eroberung* and *Veilchenfeld* appears in the form of grim flights of fancy. These produce almost poetic images for the horrors of the Nazi regime: in *Unsere Eroberung* there is the meeting of death and culture in the piano lessons at the 'Schlachthof'; in *Veilchenfeld*

---

[69] Steinlein, 'Gert Hofmanns Erzählung "Veilchenfeld"', 110.

Hans dreams that Veilchenfeld is unable to wave to him because the neighbours have cut off his 'Schreibarm' (p. 115). The child's uncertainty as to whether he is actually dreaming (pp. 115–16) suggests how close to his everyday reality this surreal image is and, while Grünzweig cites this as an example of the child's unconscious mental processes being manipulated by euphemistic adult speech, the boy's horrified reaction suggests that such brief moments have a revelatory function rather than merely demonstrating the corruption of Hans's thought processes.[70] Nor is the narrators' imaginative facility merely a matter of unconscious day-dreaming, as the narrator's attempts to reconstruct the 'Vaterverbrechen' in *Unsere Eroberung* (p. 150) demonstrates. The same can be said of Hans, who makes a conscious decision to reconstruct the events surrounding the philosopher's death: 'und mache meine Augen zu und stelle mir lieber alles vor' (*Veilchenfeld*, 18). Hartmann considers this narrative construction implausible and suggests that *Veilchenfeld* is actually an authorial narrative with Hans acting as a mere pretext, since what he narrates often goes beyond what a 9-year-old could know or imagine.[71] However, we might compare this construction with Siggi's virtual omniscience in 'Das Porträt' and suggest that in both cases the author is making an implicit statement about the imaginative facility of childhood and its implications. Even as a child Hans embodies the moral impulse that compels writers of Hofmann's generation to continue writing about the Third Reich—the refusal to allow oneself, or others, to forget: 'Und denken, frage ich, darf ich an ihn [Herrn Magirius] denken? Nun, das kann ich dir nicht verbieten, aber lieber wäre es mir schon, wenn du nicht so viel an ihn dächtest, sagt der Vater. Aber wenn man an jemand nicht mehr denkt, vergißt man ihn ja, sage ich' (p. 17). His reconstruction of Veilchenfeld's story, which results in the suicide of the old philosopher's pupil and friend Magirius, is thus in direct opposition to his father's command and suggests again that the child's vision and moral and creative impulses are the basis for the adult's art.

In the works examined in this chapter children play a dual role: on the realistic level they can appear as traumatized victims of the Third Reich, but the fact that they may have been psychologically

---

[70] 'Vergebliche Enttrümmerung', 65.
[71] 'Auf der Suche nach dem Autor', 122.

damaged does not prevent them representing the artist or at least his potential if this is the only way for writers to suggest some glimmer of hope. It is not difficult to see the attraction of the child figure for post-war German writers: it offers the possibility of a new beginning, fresh vision, perspective, and language—all of which were desperately needed by writers in a morally bankrupt country, whose very language had been tainted by political abuse. Nor is it difficult to see why they should have wanted to associate it with the artist in view of that figure's dwindling reputation and loss of self-confidence. But what is clear is that the child figure is not used in a glib attempt to suggest some form of innocence which did not exist; there is too much emphasis on the guilt feelings suffered by Oskar, Siggi, Nelly, and the 'kleine Imbachs' for that. Rather, it indicates the horror of political indoctrination and its potentially corrupting effect on receptive minds, thus mourning an innocence which has to some extent been lost, while at the same time looking forward to a clear-sighted and humanitarian art of the future. Oskar, Siggi, Nelly, and Hofmann's children may be repressed but their creators are not: by exploiting the child's vision they escape the conformity to which their protagonists are subject and so produce an artistic form which is both childlike in the best sense and highly sophisticated and subversive. As protagonist the child represents hope for future life; as narrative focus it represents a clarity and integrity of vision which will become those of the artist. Our modern authors are perhaps too realistic to see potential for a new golden age in the child figure: for all her refusal to give up her 'bessere Geschichten', even Johansen's 'Analphabetin' knows that she cannot change anything (*Die Analphabetin*, 105). Nonetheless, it is clear that, despite the many superficial differences between them, twentieth-century writers have inherited much of their conception of childhood from their Romantic predecessors, and indeed have retained an equally ideological conception of it. The extreme circumstances of the Third Reich generated a need for extreme solutions, both moral and aesthetic, and the child figure apparently responded admirably to both needs. As in the Romantic era it was a figure for its time.

4

THE INADMISSIBLE WITNESS?

In Chapter 3 we considered the child as a symbol for the artist in post-war literature; as we saw, the literary parallel between these two figures has a long history. But in more recent literature authors do not merely use the child as a symbol of the artist; the child has in fact become artistically active, for we hear its voice narrating. Modern authors are very conscious of the limitations and difficulties imposed by using the child's perspective and voice, and the fact that they do not shy away from this challenge places them firmly within the modern tradition as expressed by D. H. Lawrence: 'This struggle for verbal consciousness should not be left out in art. It is a very great part of life. It is not superimposition of a theory. *It is the passionate struggle into conscious being*.'[1] By using the child figure, writers highlight their own struggle with language and thus contribute to the myth of the child as a symbol of the artist, albeit in a new sense. For, if the nineteenth century saw the child's fresh vision feeding the artist's more laborious creative process, our own era both develops this line and points to the child's inadequacies so as to emphasize the artist's creative struggle. In what follows I shall look in more detail at some of the problems implied by using the child's perspective and voice, especially to describe the Third Reich, and ask what solutions authors have found.

THE CHILD'S TESTIMONY: A CASE OF IGNORANCE AND INCOMPETENCE?

'*I* don't know nothink.' This is the frequently repeated assertion of Jo, the illiterate crossing sweeper boy in Dickens's *Bleak House* (1852–3).[2] Jo's only knowledge comes from experience: 'He knows that it's hard to keep the mud off the crossing in dirty

---

[1] Foreword to *Women in Love*, pub. as an app. to *Women in Love* (Harmondsworth, 1995), 486.
[2] In Charles Dickens, *The Authentic Edition*, 21 vols. (London and New York, 1901), xi. 185.

weather, and harder still to live by doing it. Nobody taught him, even that much; he found it out'.[3] His ignorance and uneducated speech make him entirely unacceptable as a witness at the inquest where the coroner's middle-class disapproval is evident: ' "Can't exactly say" won't do, you know. We can't take *that*, in a Court of Justice, gentlemen. It's terrible depravity. Put the boy aside'.[4] Ironically though, Jo's inadmissible evidence would help resolve the mystery of Nemo's death, just as he later resolves the other mysteries of the novel.

Jo's dismissal seems profoundly unjust; the fact that he 'knows it's wicked to tell a lie'[5] without having any recollection of being told as much, and expects to be punished if he did, suggests a strong innate sense of justice and truth which contrasts favourably with one of Dickens's adult witnesses, who is prepared to swear 'in a general way, anythink'.[6] Why then is the child so unacceptable?

Dickens has a fairly straightforward explanation: the smug middle classes object to the boy because his presence suggests the inadequacies of the social system they have created for their own convenience. His very existence is an implied reproach. However, his speech also seems to be objectionable and this combination of ignorance and an unacceptable mode of expression suggests the technical problems faced by authors who narrate a story from the child's perspective.

Like most nineteenth-century child figures Jo is a peripheral figure rather than a narrator. But, by allowing the child to bear a greater narrative burden, either as narrator or focalizer, later authors create more substantial practical problems for themselves. As in Jo's case, the child usually has little knowledge or experience to draw on, and this ignorance makes the term 'child narrative' inherently contradictory for, as Hayden White points out, the word narrative derives from 'the Latin *gnarus* ("knowing", "acquainted with", "expert", "skilful" and so forth) and *narró* ("relate", "tell") from the Sanskrit root *gnâ* ("know")'.[7] Any author who chooses to flout this etymological definition of narrative and write from the child's perspective does so at the risk of descending

---

[3] Ibid.   [4] Ibid. 125.   [5] Ibid.

[6] *Great Expectations* (1861), in Dickens, *Authentic Edition*, xiii. 132.

[7] 'The Value of Narrativity in the Representation of Reality', in W. J. T. Mitchell (ed.), *On Narrative* (Chicago and London, 1981), 1.

into the banal and trivial.[8] Moreover, the child is frequently still acquiring linguistic skills, and writers are thus faced with the paradox of a verbally incompetent child 'writing' a narrative. Their dilemma then is to decide what language best conveys the child's experience.[9] If they choose to use an adult language they can be accused of falsifying the child's experience by over-intellectualizing it. On the other hand, if they choose to simulate the child's own language, they face the charge of intellectual dishonesty and at the same time add a superficial stylistic simplicity to a narrative which by the nature of childhood experience may already seem insignificant.

Moreover, while children may love stories, they need not necessarily be very good at telling them, even when asked to relate their own recent experiences. The interview between the lawyer Mathias and the children in Hughes's *A High Wind in Jamaica* degenerates into chaos as the younger children join in Edward's onomatapoeic but totally false version of events and then dwell on irrelevant details like the monkey being drunk. We may sympathize with Mathias, but he is wrong when he considers the children 'strangely unobservant of what went on around them':[10] their eye for detail proves it is not their observation that is at fault. Rather, they are incapable of distinguishing trivia from main event and of constructing a coherent narrative. The reader may find it incredible that these disjointed and often false bits of information should be all they have 'remembered' of their adventures. Nor can we explain this failure by the time lapse since the events occurred: even when first rescued, the children give only the most disjointed and often inaccurate version of events, Emily for fear that the truth about the murder will come out, Edward because he is unable to distinguish reality from his vivid imaginings, especially when in front of an admiring audience.

There are thus three major technical problems involved in writing a child narrative: the potential unreliablity of the witness, narrative coherence, and achieving the register appropriate to the

---

[8] Coe, *When the Grass was Taller*, p. xii.

[9] This dilemma is discussed in Rosemary Lloyd, *The Land of Lost Content: Children and Childhood in Nineteenth-Century French Literature* (Oxford, 1992), 24–31. See also Laurie Ricou, *Everyday Magic: Child Languages in Canadian Literature* (Vancouver, 1987), 1–13 for a discussion of the issues surrounding child language and its literary transcription.

[10] *A High Wind in Jamaica* (repr. Harmondsworth, 1971), 181.

child. Few writers would be content to write 'a suite in goo-goo'[11] but how are they to translate the child's distinctive vision if not in the child's language?

THE CHILD'S LANGUAGE: A LITERARY POSSIBILITY?

Various critics have suggested it is impossible to write an extended piece of narrative in the authentic tones of childhood and criticized those who have tried for creating sentimental and irritating approximations to the child's lisp.[12] Nevertheless, despite the obvious difficulties of rendering it, writers' fascination with the child's language remains. As Coe points out, the perceived intensity of childhood experience derives to a great extent from the fact that everything is felt rather than verbalized, analysed, and categorized, yet the only means writers have to convey this stage of non-verbal intensity is precisely language.[13] Nothing they attempt is ever likely to come close to the private language the child makes up so as to ' tell A Story, Every Story, everything all at once, not anything in particular that might be said through the words I know',[14] for this language implies a natural poetic all-inclusiveness, a deeper resonance, and more implications for the individual than the functional language into which the child is later socialized. The paradise of this poetic childhood language, the linguistic 'fall', and the rediscovery of the child's individual language by the adult poet is beautifully evoked in the fifth of Seamus Heaney's *Glanmore Sonnets* (1979) where he describes his childhood experience of the 'boortree':

> . . . It is shires dreaming wine.
> Boortree is bower tree, where I played 'touching tongues'
> And felt another's texture quick on mine.[15]

There is something sad about his comment 'And elderberry I have learned to call it', for this suggests the loss of all the associations which inform the child's linguistic invention 'boortree'.[16]

---

[11] A telling phrase from Theodore Roethke's comments on his poem 'The Flight', quoted in Ricou, *Everyday Magic*, 2.   [12] See Coe, *When the Grass was Taller*, 83.
[13] Ibid. 253; on the compromises that result from this dilemma, ibid. 83–5.
[14] Eva Hoffmann, *Lost in Translation: A Life in a New Language* (repr., London, 1995), 11.
[15] In *Field Work* (London, 1979), 37.   [16] Ibid.

Appropriately the poem ends with an evocation of childhood experience, showing how this feeds the adult's poetry:

> So, etymologist of roots and graftings,
> I fall back to my tree-house and would crouch
> Where small buds shoot and flourish in the hush.[17]

Coe discusses this idea of the child's individual language with reference to Eugene Ionesco, who believed that concepts precede thought and therefore language is a logical outcome of the desire to communicate those concepts; whilst the child is still making up its own words to express those concepts it remains a poet but, as it becomes socialized and accepts 'given' words, it loses that creativity.[18] However, if the concept of childhood and the child's language are universals, then paradoxically there is nothing more individual than the individual child and its language; Ricou warns against adopting the idea of a universal child language when he lists factors which affect any individual child's speech at any one time: 'age, social class, context (school, playground and home), culture (multilingual or monolingual)'.[19] For any sense of that individuality to be conveyed in a work of art accessible to all, there has to be some degree of compromise: otherwise we would be faced with the linguistic equivalent of Kuhn's 'self-enclosed, non-referential system'[20] which would have little artistic success.

This qualitative difference between the child's language and that of the adult is one of the difficulties in putting the child's language on paper. The other problem is less insuperable, for it is based rather shakily on the idea that because the child is not yet master of verbal, let alone written, language, its voice cannot be transposed into the 'poetic' sphere of literature. Yet most adults' spontaneous speech would be as inappropriate in a written context as the average child's.[21] Thus all literary language is in some sense a convention, whether it represents that of a child or an adult. Moreover, linguists have argued that spoken language can

---

[17] Ibid.
[18] See Coe, *When the Grass was Taller*, 253–4. He traces the idea of pre-linguistic memory back beyond Ionesco as far as Thomas Traherne, 253–8. Ricou also points to the metaphorical quality of children's earliest language in *Everyday Magic*, 6–7.
[19] *Everyday Magic*, 4.   [20] *Corruption in Paradise*, 60.
[21] See Norman Page, *Speech in the English Novel* (2nd edn., Basingstoke and London, 1988), esp. 3–7 for a discussion of spontaneous speech and its transformation into written dialogue.

be as well structured and exhibit as many elements of what we might call formal rhetorical devices as a literary text; therefore, the dividing line between informal spoken language and formal written language is less rigid than it first appears.[22] According to conventional definitions, the problem of translating the informality of spoken language into a written context is exacerbated in the case of the child's language; however, such conventions have been relaxed in the modern era by experiments with free indirect speech and stream-of-consciousness narration.[23] As we try to see the world from the point of view not only of its 'mainstream' representatives but also of more marginal elements, so narrative conventions have to change to keep pace with this desire for new vision.

Consciousness of the language problem will lead to various strategies, ranging from an adult voice rendering a child's perceptions, as in *What Maisie Knew*, to the attempt to render the child's language mimetically, as at the beginning of James Joyce's *A Portrait of the Artist as a Young Man* (1916). Neither method is unproblematic for, if Coveney approves Joyce's opening, saying that 'even where the style is most deliberately childlike, there is no sense of straining after effect',[24] Lloyd contends that 'for all their brilliance', if the style of these pages were to be sustained for any longer it would soon 'induce in the reader a sense of irritation or boredom, without thereby capturing the reality of the child's experience'.[25] Coe takes a middle line, referring to the opening of this novel as 'an *impression* of early childhood', adding that 'an impression is as much of over-literal reality as the genre can absorb'.[26] But, while Lloyd expresses reservations about the opening of Joyce's novel, she does not regard the linguistic polish of *What Maisie Knew* as unproblematic either, though she cites

---

[22] See Mary Jane Hurst, *The Voice of the Child in American Literature: Linguistic Approaches to Fictional Child Language* (Lexington, 1990), 6. Hurst cites Page, *Speech in the English Novel*; Mary Louise Pratt's *Toward a Speech Act Theory of Literary Discourse* (Bloomington, Ind. 1977), and the work of the sociolinguist William Labov to suggest that there is not such a gulf between spontaneous and literary language as had conventionally been assumed.

[23] Lloyd emphasizes the relationship between an interest in the child in 19th cent. French literature and the experiments in narrative voice and literary language taking place at the same time (*Land of Lost Content*, 241–2).

[24] *Image of Childhood*, 308.   [25] *Land of Lost Content*, 26–7.

[26] *When the Grass was Taller*, 84.

James's preface to the novel to indicate that this narrative strategy was the only way to render the full range of the inarticulate child's perceptions.[27] In view of these difficulties, it is hardly surprising that some authors try to escape this dilemma altogether; in *Unsere Eroberung*, for example, Hofmann steps outside the terms of the problem by using the artificial 'wir' construction.[28] However, for authors who want to use a more obviously 'real' child as their medium the problem remains: the child has no authentic literary voice because real children are in every sense pre-literary. And yet, as the case of Jo demonstrates, the fact that a child does not have an acceptable voice does not mean that it has nothing to say.

According to Kuhn, one of the main features of the 'enigmatic child' is that 'communication between the child and the adult is virtually impossible. This is symbolized by the linguistic deficiency of so many of these children'.[29] But the children he examines are not usually narrators and consequently he does not deal with the implications of this communications block for narrative itself. This is an important omission because child narratives are frequently intended for an adult audience and, although many of the children I deal with would not necessarily be classed as 'enigmatic' by Kuhn, there is nonetheless a concern on the part of writers like Wolf and Härtling that childhood is inaccessible to them. Although in *Kindheitsmuster* and *Nachgetragene Liebe* the authors are reaching back into their past lives and one might assume that their childhood and adult selves form part of one psychic whole, this is not necessarily the case. They feel alienated from their own childhood and the concept of the child's language (or the lack of it) plays a substantial part in this sense of alienation. While Härtling tries to adhere to the child's perspective without the support of documentary evidence, he finds the child's linguistic deficiencies frustrating: 'meine alt und schlau gewordene Sprache widersetzt sich seiner Sprachlosigkeit'.[30] *Nachgetragene Liebe* therefore alternates between passages confined to the child's limited perspective, often couched in the present tense to create added immediacy, and more retrospective passages where the adult

---

[27] *Land of Lost Content*, 25–6.
[28] Hartmann, 'Auf der Suche nach dem Autor', 119.
[29] *Corruption in Paradise*, 60.
[30] *Nachgetragene Liebe*, 36. This point is made by Werner Brettschneider in *'Kindheitsmuster': Kindheit als Thema autobiographischer Dichtung* (Berlin, 1982), 89.

narrator analyses his child self and especially his relationship with his father. The language of both types of passage is uniformly adult. Wolf too knows that she would be unable to write as a child: her only choices are 'sprachlos bleiben oder in der dritten Person leben' (*Kindheitsmuster*, 13) and she chooses the lesser of the two evils.

THE GERMAN POST-WAR VOICE

There is a further complicating factor in these and other authors; namely, the child's experience of the Third Reich. If the child per se has no authentic literary voice, then this is doubly so of the child traumatized by this era. In Gerd Fuchs's *Stunde Null* (1981), 15-year-old Georg Haupt is left mute by the shock of the German capitulation and his individual dilemma is placed in a wider context by his elder brother's question: 'Jedenfalls interessieren mich Wörter nicht mehr, . . . In welcher Sprache sollte man denn reden?'[31] This was widely perceived as a literary concern after World War II. There seemed to be no language capable of dealing with the horror of events and the shock writers had experienced, hence the notions of 'Kahlschlag' and 'Stunde Null': a fresh beginning was needed, but one which would allow for a confrontation with the past.

In the early pages of *Kindheitsmuster* Wolf's narrator rehearses the methods she intends to use in presenting her own and her country's past. Her primary material is Nelly's recollection of events, but she soon modifies this; Nelly is virtually inaccessible to her and therefore she is also reliant on documentary material and the input of her daughter Lenka. She emphasizes the inaccessibility of both her child self and the information she needs: when she wants to consult her old school textbooks she goes to the 'Haus des Lehrers' where they are kept, 'als Gift sekretiert, nur gegen Vorlage einer Sonderbescheinigung entleihbar' (*Kindheitsmuster*, 20). Especially in the GDR, where the whole process of recognizing and dealing with the Nazi past started much later than in the west, the period is still taboo, alien, and inaccessible.[32] This is reflected in the behaviour of the child self who seems to be running

---

[31] (Hamburg, 1987), 12.
[32] Wolfgang Emmerich, *Kleine Literaturgeschichte der DDR: Erweiterte Neuausgabe* (repr. Leipzig, 1997), 317–22. Emmerich regards *Kindheitsmuster* as the first piece of GDR literature to deal with the experience of everyday Nazism.

away from the narrator: 'Das Kind, Nelly, biegt um die Ecke, steigt die drei Stufen hoch und verschwindet hinter seiner Haustür' (p. 18). Given these conditions it is remarkable that the book ever came to be written.

Yet the explosion of interest in the child's perspective in post-war German literature, despite all the difficulties attendant on it, suggests that this figure answered deeply felt needs on the part of writers dealing with the Third Reich. As I suggested in the Introduction, there are various possible explanations for this. Perhaps the most convincing is that the child not only mirrored the artists' incomprehension and the inadequacy of their language to describe events but also presented the possibility of a new language which would be up to this difficult task. However, the tension is obvious: is an interest in presenting the psychological reality of the child's limited knowledge and linguistic register compatible with presenting the full complexities and horror of the Third Reich? In what follows I shall discuss a variety of texts and the solutions they offer to this problem.

Representing the Child's Language: Helga M. Novak, Die Eisheiligen

Reviewing Helga Schütz's novel *Mädchenrätsel* (1978),[33] Martin Gregor-Dellin made much of the fact that, although written 'in einer zurückgenommenen Sprache', it is *not* an example of naturalistic child's language: 'Helga Schütz weiß, daß man den Mangel an Worten, die Entbehrung von Glück und Liebe nicht in Stottern oder Brüllen ummünzen kann, sondern daß ein Roman, der fast nur aus Bildern und dem Geruch und Geschmack einer grauen Zeit erzählt, auf sprachliche Sensibilität besonders angewiesen ist.'[34] He is apparently contradicted by Brettschneider, who asks whether adult speech is able to reflect the true nature of the child's inner life and perspective and cites the attempts of Helga Schütz, Diana Kempff, Tilman Moser, and Helga M. Novak 'die Sprache des Kindes mit literarischen Mitteln nachzubilden'.[35] But the contradiction between Gregor-Dellin's

---

[33] Originally published in the GDR as *Jette in Dresden* (1977).
[34] 'Mädchenrätsel in Dresden: Helga Schütz erzählt von einem Kind und einer Großmutter', *Frankfurter Allgemeine Zeitung* (18 Aug. 1978).
[35] '*Kindheitsmuster*', 109–10.

emphasis on 'sprachliche Sensibilität' and Brettschneider's interest in 'die Sprache des Kindes' is more apparent than real: Brettschneider's 'mit literarischen Mitteln' highlights his awareness that he is dealing with literary conventions rather than naturalistic child language. Neither *Vorgeschichten oder Schöne Gegend Probstein* (1970) nor *Jette in Dresden* (1977) are narrated directly by Schütz's child protagonist Jette; instead, these third-person accounts of the war and the post-war period respectively are written in a spare and simple style which creates a sense of the child's self-contained world whilst still reflecting historical reality.[36] But these texts do not answer the question whether a child narrator, using the child's language, can adequately reflect the reality of the Third Reich.

This question can be posed with reference to Helga M. Novak's *Die Eisheiligen* (1979) which attempts to render the immediacy of the child's experience and the development of its language as it grows older.[37] The novel covers the years 1939 to 1950, beginning with the narrator's first memory in the summer of 1939, and the earlier chapters are made up of brief, largely unconnected scenes reflecting the momentary but intense nature of the child's experience. Novak frequently attempts to mirror the linguistic patterns of childhood, as here:

wie es dröhnt und prasselt auf dem Rückweg von der Kugelbake zurück zurück die Seen schlagen über die Mole schlagen an die Steine an die seitlichen Befestigungen schlagen über uns hinweg die See rollt über meinen Kopf hinaus so naß so stark so weich klatscht es mir ins Gesicht ich habe Schaum im Gesicht und sehe nichts mehr Concordia hält mich an der Hand die rutscht ihr dauernd weg dann hält sie mich am Arm zieht mich und die Seen treiben uns an den Rand der Mole Concordia hält mich fest und zurück wir laufen nicht mehr wir waten wir treiben wir stoßen gegen die Wassermengen vor es peitscht mal hoch mal tief vorwärts wir sind selber schon ganz Wasser fliegendes Wasser am Strand liegen alle Körbe auf dem Rücken und keine Spur mehr von einer Burg (*Die Eisheiligen*, 10)

A number of features reflect the child's phase of linguistic development and so add to the intensity of her experience. The present tense suggests, however improbably, that this is a simultaneous transcription of the event and conveys the fleeting nature of childhood experience. The total lack of punctuation, apart from

---

[36] Ibid. 24–5.   [37] Ibid. 80.

imitating a child's breathless chatter, also evokes her dynamic perception of the natural scene and the use of repetition is significant, the 'so naß so stark so weich' all conveying the child's exhilaration, while the 'wir waten wir treiben wir stoßen' vividly expresses the physical effort required of her.

Nor is it only the way the child speaks that is evoked; her experience of other people's speech is also conveyed when the author records speeches which read more like verbal assault. For example, her mother at the dinner table:

aufessen
aufessen
der Teller wird leergegessen bis zum letzten Happen
rein in den Mund und schlucken
schlucken
schlucken nicht vergessen
kau nicht ewig auf derselben Kartoffel herum
bitte
nimm den Schieber nicht in den Mund
zum Essen ist der Löffel da
mit dem Schieber wird das Essen auf den Löffel geschoben
rein in den Mund
kauen
schlucken
ich bleibe so lange neben dir sitzen bis der Teller leer ist (p. 8)

In this episode the lack of punctuation performs a different function from in the first passage. There is no respite from this onslaught for, while the almost poetic layout seems to allow pauses for the mother to draw breath, its most notable feature is the amount of white space left on the page. These are the silences where we might expect the child to respond, but no response is forthcoming. This is typical of the early phase of the text: the child is simply the object of a language whose violence often leads to physical abuse.

The girl is remarkably silent in the early stages of the text, partly because she is still acquiring oral competence, but also because she is a victim of verbal repression. It is significant that she has a speech impediment, possibly a result of her mother's constant nagging and bullying. While this is not made explicit, what is clear is that written language is not deemed a suitable means of

self-expression for the child either: she is thrilled when Kaltesophie gives her twenty exercise books to practise her handwriting,
but the joy of these books is soon tainted when Kaltesophie imposes lines to be written in them (p. 61). The child is linguistically
repressed and yet we have the paradox, as in so many childhood
narratives, of a predominantly silent child 'writing' a book. Writing becomes an assertion of her individual identity: the silent and
nameless child's need to carve her name everywhere she goes
seems transformed into the adult's need to write a book which will
have her name on the cover, an assertion of her individuality.

However, while lack of oral competence is clearly reflected in
the style of the early parts of the novel, it is significant that the
main emphasis in these early chapters is on her personal concerns, especially her relationship with her adoptive mother; these
are perhaps best expressed in the child's own language. And,
even at its most 'artless', this language is still based on literary
conventions rather than a mimetic representation of a child's language. For example:

Und die Wärme des Hauses, in dem wir ein Zimmer haben
und die Wärme der Heuschober, wo ich meine Arme reinstecke
und die Wärme des Kuhstalls, wo ich mich verkrieche
und die Wärme in den Milcheimern, wo heimlich meine Hände unter-
tauchen
und die Wärme der Wasserlachen, wo ich bei Ebbe drin sitze
und die Wärme der Modderpampe am Strand
und die Wärme, wie Concordia ankommt, extra von Berlin uns be-
suchen kommt und mich hochnimmt und mich auf den Brunnenrand
setzt
die große Concordia ist da
Concordia, alt, riesengroß, dünn, grauhaarig, in einem langen geblümten
Kleid
Concordia in Knopfstiefeln
und die Wärme, wenn sie mich ins Bett bringt und vorsingt. (pp. 8–9)

While the repetition and the apparently artless use of 'und' might
suggest a child's language, this passage has an almost liturgical
quality derived precisely from that biblical 'und' and the repetition. Moreover, the movement from the free association of different sensations of physical warmth to the emotional warmth of
Concordia's arrival is too sophisticated a leap for a child of this

age, even if she apparently returns to mere physical warmth when describing the bedtime scene. The child evoked here may be largely silent, passive, and aware only of physical sensation, but the description itself clearly betrays the hand of an adult writer.

Thus, even in these early chapters, there is a tension between the desire to render the child's experience in her own terms and the conscious artistry of the adult manipulating her material. While the frequent use of the present tense, uncommentated adult conversation, and non-literary language create an impression of the child's immediate experience and inadequate understanding, there are also passages where the vocabulary and structures seem inconsistent with the child's stage of development. Of her first day at school she writes:

Später folgen wir Fräulein Mammert in unser zukünftiges Klassenzimmer, wo sie uns einzeln aus dem Gedränge ruft, uns unseren Namen sagen läßt–'Lauter!'–und uns gründlich mustert. Angst? Scheu? Still? Sie weist uns Plätze an, und ich gelange nach vorn in die zweite Reihe, Mittelgang. Ziemlich dicht am Lehrerpult. (p. 40)

While the present tense and the direct quoting of the teacher lend this scene immediacy, the vocabulary and structures are hardly those of a 6-year-old.

However, despite such discrepancies, the vision evoked in these early chapters is clearly that of a child, as demonstrated particularly by the political references. Although the girl is living through a momentous era, the first four chapters contain only minimal references to the Third Reich and the war, and these are entirely consistent with her own concerns and understanding. The bald statement 'Es gibt keine Bananen mehr' is explained only by Kaltesophie's 'Das liegt am Krieg' (p. 13) and other instances of the Third Reich's effect on her life are usually integrated with other concerns of the moment:

Wir werden in Zweierreihen zum Badehaus geführt und lernen, wo rechts und wo links ist.
Rechts ist die Hand, mit der ich den Löffel halte.
Rechts ist der Fuß, mit dem ich den Ball anstoße.
Rechts ist die Hand, die ich hochheb beim Grüßen. (p. 29)

She does occasionally cite familiar wartime phrases, for example 'Pst! Feind hört mit' (p. 80), but we do not see the placard bearing the words 'Juden verboten!' (p. 78) in the grocer's window until we have had adequate proof of her reading ability, a clear indicator that we are being restricted to the child's perspective. In the early chapters the war seems above all to provide a temporal reference point ('Im zweiten Kriegswinter stand zu Weihnachten ein langer Schlitten halb aufgerichtet an der Wohnzimmerwand', p. 32) and this laconic treatment is consistent with what was said earlier about children accepting these conditions as their normality. In the early chapters the war is merely the unremarkable background to the child's experiences at home and school, which are generally described in greater detail because they are of more immediate importance to her. Paradoxically her language becomes more obviously simple and childlike when dealing with the war: her comments are brief and non-analytical, for example, 'Berlin ißt heute sein Eintopfgericht' (p. 66) (a phrase which could well have been picked up parrot fashion from adult propaganda) and 'Concordia ist ausgebombt' (p. 78), phrases set apart from the rest of the text so as to give them extra emphasis and perhaps allow us to consider the implications the unknowing child does not detail for us.

Even when the war begins to impinge to a greater extent on the girl's existence, Novak continues to maintain an impression of the child's vision and language. In the Christmas bombing raid, for instance, the emotional impact on the child is very clear from her language: 'Die Nacht vor Heiligabend, und wieder raus und wieder runter. Ich bete und bete und bete und bete. . . . Wenn ich darum bitte, daß es niemanden erschlägt, meint das Gebet auch mich, und ich bin gerettet' (p. 83). The abrupt opening of this account, the missing verb in the first sentence, suggesting the rush of getting to the cellar and the childlike repetition of 'bete' all convey that sense of individual panic. There is a certain plasticity to the child's account in that it focuses directly on her experience without analysis, sometimes homing in on details that an adult narrator might consider irrelevant. For example,

An der Ecke, wo wir in die Friedrichstraße einbiegen, liegt ein totes Pferd. Das war das Pferd von Bolles Milchwagen, und das da unter der Decke? Kann nur der Milchmann selber sein.
    Komm weiter, nicht stehenbleiben! . . . Mal sehen, wie es am Ende der Straße aussieht, entsetzlich, womit haben wir das verdient. (p. 98)

This book is essentially about personal experience, whether domestic or the personal implications of historical reality, and it is therefore appropriate for Novak to maintain the literary illusion of the child's perspective and language. The mother–daughter relationship gains a certain savage intensity through their virtually uncommentated speech, just as the air raids become doubly terrifying when presented through the unknowing consciousness and simple language of a child. And yet there are clearly disadvantages to these self-imposed limitations, for they do not allow Novak to reflect on the wider context of the war. This becomes glaringly obvious when she allows her narrator to step outside the temporal frame to describe the first 'Heimkehrer':

Zur selben Zeit trafen Überlebende aus deutschen Gefängnissen und KaZets ein, so blaß wie unser Licht im April. . . .
    Die alte ausladende zerfahrene, sandige Heerstraße hat in dem Jahr viel Fußvolk gesehen und viel Reiterei. Aber so weit sind wir noch nicht. Es ist April und zwar genau der zwanzigste. (p. 130)

The past tense and the very matter-of-fact reference to concentration camps indicate that this is written with hindsight rather than from the child's perspective. To see just how different a first reference to these camps as rendered from the child's point of view could be, we have only to look at Christian Grote's *Für Kinder die Hälfte* (1963), where the experience of seeing a group of concentration camp prisoners is focalized directly through the unknowing child. This results in a detailed, plastic description without any hindsight or explanation:

Aus der Kurve der Straße kamen einzelne Menschen, alle in gleichen Kleidern, langsam, wie eine Herde von Tieren, sich verbreiternd, sich zusammenziehend. Um sie herum Soldaten mit eckigen Waffen in den Händen. Die Herde kam die Straße entlang auf die Reihe zu, die das Gesicht, wie er, in die gleiche Richtung hielt. Alles wurde still. Die Stille ging auf die Reihe zu, einzelne Gesichter waren in der Gruppe nicht zu erkennen, die Kleider wurden deutlich, blaugrau gestreifte, lose Jacken, lange über die Schuhe fallende Hosen. Die Streifen schoben sich auf der Fläche ineinander, nur an schnellen Bewegungen waren einzelne Menschen zu sehen. Manche trugen runde Mützen. Die Schritte klangen hölzern, sie kamen sehr langsam.[38]

This immediacy of presentation also implies a more direct evocation of the child's emotional response. While his feelings are not

---

[38] *Für Kinder die Hälfte: Ein Bericht* (Frankfurt, 1963), 235.

analysed, his physical sensations after the group has passed are described so as to suggest a powerful emotional reaction: 'Er bemerkte seinen Atem, fühlte die harte Mauer neben sich, seine Hände im Eisen des Gitters'.[39] While this may not deal with the wider issues of persecution under the Third Reich, it does confront the horror more directly than Novak. Perhaps she doubted the possibility of dealing with such issues through the child's perspective and language, yet felt unable to leave them unmentioned. It is true that as the narrator grows up her increasing verbal proficiency, seen in her interaction with her parents, is reflected in the style of the text and her increasing sophistication allows her to reflect more on political issues and become politically independent. This is the obvious advantage of following a child's perspective over some time, for it rescues the text from possible charges of banality and self-indulgent introspection. However, the question whether the wider political and moral issues raised by the Third Reich can be dealt with through the child's perspective and language has still not been answered.

The Tainted Voice: Hubert Fichte's Das Waisenhaus

Hubert Fichte's *Das Waisenhaus* (1965) is presented very differently from *Die Eisheiligen* and therefore offers different possibilities for reflecting the child's political reality.[40] First, the narrative is concentrated within a single day as Detlev waits for his mother to collect him from the Catholic orphanage, though Fichte's use of flashbacks within the child's consciousness creates an impression of a much longer time span, and this reflects the intensity of the child's experience. Secondly, the narrative is in the third rather than the first person. However, it is still possible to consider *Das Waisenhaus* as an instance of child language because, although Detlev does not tell his own story, paradoxically he is not as silent as the narrator of *Die Eisheiligen*. He is frequently presented in conversation with the other children and with his mother and his

---

[39] Ibid. 236.
[40] In *Kinder*, 95–102, Hagen discusses the issue of presenting events from the child's perspective with reference to *Das Waisenhaus*, Grote's *Für Kinder die Hälfte*, and Monique Wittig's *L'Opoponax*.

speech has all the simplicity of a real 7-year-old. For example, when looking at a photograph of himself he says:

'Meine Lippen sind dick'.
'Ich habe eine Locke im Haar'.
'Ich bin weiß im Gesicht'.
'Mein Kinn steht nicht vor'. (*Das Waisenhaus*, 8)

This spare simple style is to some extent carried over into the main body of the text, which is clearly filtered through Detlev's perspective despite the third-person narrator. For example, whilst waiting for his mother, Detlev accidentally puts his hand in some bird droppings:

Detlev hebt die Hände. Der Vogelkot fällt nicht ab. Detlev reibt die Hände gegeneinander. Detlev verschränkt seine Finger und reibt. . . .
   Detlev zerquetscht den Kot zwischen seinen Fingern. Detlev legt die Handflächen gegeneinander. Er will den grünen Schleim wegreiben, ohne daß die Waisenhauszöglinge es bemerken. . . .
   Detlev verschmiert den Kot an den Händen. Er legt die Hände mit ausgestreckten Fingern übereinander. Er kreuzt die Daumen. (p. 15)

The present tense again evokes the momentary nature of the child's experience, while the constant repetition of Detlev's name suggests his burning embarrassment at being the focal point of all eyes, his sense that the others are talking about him and relishing his predicament. However, while Fichte, like Novak, clearly wants to create a dominant impression of the child's perspective through language, there are passages where the adult creator is very much in evidence:

Detlev steht abseits von den anderen auf dem Balkon. Die Waisen-hauszöglinge warten, daß Schwester Silissa und Schwester Appia in den Eßsaal treten, daß sie in die beiden tiefen Suppentöpfe gucken, aus der ver-borgenen Tasche des schwarzen Habits zwei Eier holen, die Eier am Topfrand zerschlagen, Eiweiß und Eigelb in die Suppe fallen lassen, die zwei Hälften der Schalen mit dem Finger auswischen, daß sie die rascheln-den Schalen in den Abfalleimer neben dem Kanonenofen werfen und mit den Kellen Eigelb und Eiweiß schnell vor dem Gerinnen verrühren. (p. 7)

Although this work is largely made up of conversations between the children and perceptions filtered through Detlev's conscious-ness, this opening passage makes it clear that an adult narrator is at work for, if the first sentence is brief and simple enough to have come from a child, the second is definitely not. Fichte thus recognizes that, while children do have a language of their own (at least when they are not verbally repressed as in *Die Eisheiligen*), it is not a literary language.

The attempt to render the child's perspective through an approximation to the child's language is again appropriate here because much of the turmoil Detlev goes through results from being separated from his mother and placed in the unfamiliar surroundings of the orphanage. But Fichte also reflects political realities through the children's language, despite the fact that they are safely away from the main events of the war. The ideology of the period is reflected through Detlev's consciousness and the children's conversation. Some of the comments Detlev makes have clearly been picked up verbatim from adults without him understanding their subtext. For example, ' "Frieda ist ein richtiges Vorbild. Ihre blonden Zöpfe. Ihre Augenfarbe. Ihre Ohren sind nicht zu groß", hat Schwester Appia gesagt' and ' "Frieda ist ein arischer Typ", hatte die Mutter zu Schwester Appia gesagt' (p. 12). The children's language is coloured by the political ideology that informs the adults' speech, as in this conversation which unconsciously reflects adult concerns:

Dann wurde vom Kriegel erzählt, der die Polen im Rathauskeller mit einer Peitsche voller Stahlsterne prügelte, daß man ihr Schreien bei der Heiligen Messe hören konnte.
'Die Polen sollten den Kriegel selbst einmal durchprügeln'.
'Das dürfen sie nicht, weil er Gendarm ist. Sie sind Kriegsgefangene'.
'Wenn sie es trotzdem tun?'
'Wir sollten dem Kriegel Brandgeld hinlegen: Da, Herr Kriegel, wir haben Ihnen Geld auf die Fensterbank gelegt. Wenn er's aufnimmt, verbrennt er sich die Finger, daß er keinen Polen mehr durchprügeln kann'.
'Und anschließend würden die Schwestern verhaftet, weil sie die Verantwortung haben für alles, was wir tun. Die Heilige Katholische Kirche ist in diesen Jahren großen Nachstellungen ausgeliefert'.
'Die Polen schneiden in Polen die deutschen Kriegsgefangenen mit der Brandsäge entzwei'.
'Wir müssen wählen zwischen Endsieg oder bolschewistischem Chaos'.
(p. 32)

The children are obviously aping their elders in an attempt to make themselves feel important. Detlev is especially vulnerable to linguistic indoctrination for, although initially he is not aware of it, he is half-Jewish and cannot afford to attract attention. His mother tells him: 'Sag: Die Polen haben selbst schuld. Warum arbeiten sie nicht? Sag: Wer arbeiten will, der hat zu essen und der wird nicht mit der Peitsche geprügelt' to which the child answers simply 'Das stimmt' (p. 42) because he still believes in his mother's integrity. But this is not the only form of linguistic indoctrination to which he is subject: Catholic conformity also affects his language when he tells his mother 'Ich hab dich lieb wie die Jungfrau Maria im Himmel oben' (p. 43). Those who have been in the orphanage for some time are very conversant with the language of Catholicism, without necessarily understanding its concepts. Anna tells Detlev that he cannot become a Catholic because that would be 'die Erbsünde', but it is clear that she does not know what 'die Erbsünde' is (p. 63). And when the two discuss the Passion it becomes clear that Anna's conventional version of that event has become muddled with events in her own time:

'Du kannst gar nicht alles wissen, was der Herr Jesus Christus für unsere Schuld leiden mußte. Sie haben ihn Judenkönig genannt. Sie haben geschrien: Dem Judenhund, dem Judenschwein geschieht es ganz recht.–Sie haben Fingernägel ausgezogen, unter Wasser gesteckt, Füße zerstampft. Sie haben ihn an eine Elektrisiermaschine gebunden'. (pp. 65–6)

In view of these varied forms of indoctrination, we may ask whether these children have an authentic voice at all.

But while the children may appear to be simply uncritical reflectors of their society without sufficient knowledge, either empirical or linguistic, to rebel against it, Fichte actually uses their 'inadequate' perspective to deal with wider political and moral issues, thus expressing his own criticism.[41] This is particularly obvious in the Jewish motif, first mentioned when Detlev recalls a school punishment: ' "Deine Ohren sind so groß wie Judenohren", sagte die Lehrerin, ehe sie ihm mit dem gespaltenen Rohrstock über die Finger schlug' (p. 8). There is no mention of why he was being punished and this suggests that the uncomprehending child had simply been made a scapegoat because of his appearance. The children are also quick to use the word 'Jude'

---

[41] Grünzweig makes a similar point about Hofmann's *Unsere Eroberung* when he notes the implicit criticism of National Socialism which manifests itself mainly as 'Sprachkritik' ('Vergebliche Enttrümmerung', 58–61).

in negative contexts. Twice when Detlev uses unfamiliar vocabulary he is asked 'Bist du ein Jude?' (p. 115), 'Bist du wirklich kein
Jude?' (p. 122) but, although Detlev says he does not know what a
Jew is, his interlocutors do not enlighten him, apparently because
they do not know themselves. This all-pervasive ignorance exposes the irrational prejudice that has led Detlev to the orphanage: obviously the children are parroting their elders, who
doubtless have no better reasons for their prejudices. This is emphasized when Detlev finally asks his mother what a Jew is. She
answers: 'Ein Jude ist jemand, der sich nicht gerne wäscht, der un-
ordentlich ist und mit schlürfendem Gang geht, der sich nicht ge-
radehält, Detlev, und der beim Sitzen die Fußspitzen nach innen
kehrt–sagen sie' (p. 186). This shows how far the political reality of
these years was determined by a state-imposed language. The
children's largely uncritical acceptance of this vocabulary both
reflects and criticizes the way that the adult world had adopted
these ideas and thus the 'limitations' of the child's language are
exploited so as to deal with wider political and moral issues than
we might have thought possible.

The Survival Of The Child's Language: Hanna Johansen's
Die Analphabetin

Of course, children are dependent on the adult world for information and when, as in the Nazi era, a whole new language has
evolved out of political concerns, it is not surprising that children
should take on the language of adults together with the information they desire. The literary child is thus doubly handicapped, for
it is dependent on linguistic skills both to acquire information and
to transmit it. This is a main theme of Johansen's *Die Analphabetin*
where the emphasis on language is clear from the title. The story
is a first-person narrative covering the summer of 1944. This limited time span means there is no sustained linguistic development: Johansen restricts herself mainly to the perspective and
language of the 5-year-old. The story has three main modes. First,
the child is frequently seen in conversation with other people and
with animals and inanimate objects, and here the tone is generally
realistically childlike. Secondly, her mental processes are also
presented and these too tend to be framed in a simple style made
up of brief sentences and lots of questions such as those she asks of

the adults. The third mode is narrative/descriptive and here Johansen finds it more difficult to adhere strictly to the child's register. However, the three modes are quite fluid and the whole text is characterized by predominantly present-tense narration, short sentences, and simple syntax, which create an impression of the childlike throughout.

The self-imposed limitations of the child's perspective are considerable: like Dickens's Jo, the 'Analphabetin' is a witness with limited knowledge and language. She sees little of the main events of the war, for she lives on the outskirts of the city, and the newspapers are of little use to her since the adults refuse to read her anything but the most innocuous pieces of information. As in *Die Eisheiligen* and *Das Waisenhaus*, the child's language seems particularly appropriate to her personal concerns rather than those of the war, as when she indulges in this moment of spontaneous fantastical flight:

Fliegen. Das müßte man können. Ich kann es. Das heißt, ich kann es noch nicht. Ich übe. Ein paarmal ist es gegangen. Es kann nicht mehr lange dauern. Bald ist es soweit. Dann kann ich mich auf die Bäume wagen. Und von da aus sind die Wolken nicht mehr weit. Es ist wegen der Wolken, daß man fliegen muß. Sie sind anders nicht zu erreichen. (*Die Analphabetin*, 16)

However, of the authors considered so far in this chapter Johansen is perhaps the most concerned with showing not just the child's emotional life but also her perception of the war. So what are the advantages of limiting herself to a restricted perspective and language?

The child may have difficulty gaining access to information, but like the children of *Das Waisenhaus* she has nonetheless absorbed the vocabulary of the period: she produces the word 'Volksschädling' (p. 13) apparently apropos of nothing and without knowing what it means, and the term 'feindliche Flugzeuge' (p. 44) is familiar to her, despite the ignorance she displays in the rest of this conversation (see Chapter 2, above). These words have been picked up parrot-fashion and thus appear devoid of coherent context. Her question 'Aber was ist ein Volksschädling' appears between her contention that 'Bleifederspitzmaschine' is 'das merkwürdigste Wort, das ich je gehört habe' and her comment 'Maschen, denke ich. Auch so ein Wort' (p. 13). She is at that stage of linguistic discovery where all language is open to question, as we see when she says 'Ein unbegreiflicher Name. Warum heißt der Frosch Frosch?' (p. 93). The realization that there is no inherent connection between an object and its name is a fairly common one, but the fact that it is applied equally to everyday objects and the abstract vocabulary of political ideology is highly disconcerting, for it reduces these political terms with their far-reaching consequences to the status of merely puzzling words: 'Wilfried hat ein neues Wort. Es heißt Neurüstung' (p. 178). This alienating technique makes the reader pause to consider the implications of these glibly produced yet incomprehensible words, thus opening up the language of an era.

The child is essentially alienated from the adult world by her inadequate linguistic skills: not only is she unable to read, but she also gets little information from the radio since it seems her family listen mainly to the British station. Even when she quotes the news that the invasion has begun, she seems to have little idea of what this means. But when she says 'Ich verstehe die Stimmen des Radios nicht. Es ist, als sprächen sie nicht meine Sprache' (p. 54) it is more than a reference to the voices possibly speaking a foreign language: the adult world per se has a different language from that of the child. Nor is this simply a question of her linguistic skills being inadequate: they are qualitatively different, an extension of the Romantic idea that the child is not merely an incomplete adult but has qualities in its own right. By the end of the work the girl does not see her different linguistic register as a handicap; rather, she is content to accept it as different: 'Hölle, dieses Wort, denke ich, wie es sich auflöst, wenn man es sagt. Der Himmel tut das auch. Kein besseres Wort. Man braucht es nur auszuprobieren. Oder ist das nur bei mir so, und bei den anderen bleiben die Wörter ganz?' (p. 198). For all her parroting of adult vocabulary her language is not as secure, as 'fixed' as that of adults, but this is largely because children and adults use language for very different reasons. The adults in these novels, even if not politically active, use a largely functional language in order to communicate information and instructions. This is exacerbated by the state-imposed language of the Nazi era, which allowed little room for personal feeling and judgement. The child's language is new and therefore less stable but more flexible: children lack knowledge, but this can also imply a lack of preconceptions and prejudices built into the adults' political terminology. Children frequently use their language in a much more reflexive way: having less in the way of information to impart and certainly no instructions to give, their speech mode is one of questions and open-ended statements as well as reflections on their own feelings, something to which the adults in these novels are certainly not prone.

The combination of the narrator's inadequate comprehension and questioning attitude to language can open up new perspectives for the reader. Quite apart from the alienation which results when she isolates elements of political terminology, a kind of moral insight can be achieved through her linguistic incomprehension. When the gardener tells her that 'wir' have made the British their enemies, her 'Wir? Was für ein Wort. Noch verwirrender als andere' (p. 44) highlights a word most adults would pass over without further thought, and by so doing poses questions about identifying with a nation state and collective responsibility. Similarly she uses the standard phrase 'in den Krieg gehen' of some lorries, but apparently does not grasp that 'Krieg' is a state rather than a place: 'Man kann nicht in den Krieg gehen, denke ich, und nach ein paar Metern wieder umkehren' (p. 53). This linguistic misapprehension again opens up questions of individual moral responsibility for the reader.

The deliberately restricted perspective and language of *Die Analphabetin* clearly fulfil an important aesthetic and moral purpose for the active reader: while the child's knowledge, like Jo's, is limited, she too has an instinctive morality which bears comparison with any adult in the book and it is she who registers the emotional impact of events. She is a prime example of how the child's perspective provides the underside of history. This apparently subjective and restricted perspective can be used to deal with the serious issues behind events and so this child moves from the periphery, where Jo stands, to centre stage.

Nevertheless the limitations of a work like *Die Analphabetin* are obvious. The attempt to render everything from the child's point of view makes the adult reader identify with the child, thus opening new and disconcerting perspectives. However, the child's horizon is necessarily limited; it can be compared with Hanno's in the school chapter of *Buddenbrooks*, where society is seen through the medium of the child's own environment. When the child's view is rendered as if its thoughts and feelings were being transcribed simultaneously, we are too close to the material to take in a broad canvas. That is why so many of our writers favour retrospective analysis, where the child's perspective is complemented by the adult's later considerations.

Recreating the Child and its Language: Christa Wolf's Kindheitsmuster

Perhaps the best example of this is *Kindheitsmuster*, whose highly self-conscious retrospective element is far removed from the limited perspective and language of narratives like *Die Analphabetin*. Wolf makes no attempt to tell Nelly's story in the child's own words; in fact she presents the child as largely silent and to some extent unknowing, as symbolized in the 'Schaukel' dream (*Kindheitsmuster*, 249–50). Again we are dealing with a 'witness' but, whereas in Jo's case the child's evidence is dismissed, here there is an attempt to force information out of a 'kleinen, mißgestalteten Mann' (p. 249) who clearly represents the narrator's child self.[42] Obviously the narrator imagines the child's evidence will be valuable, for she goes to some lengths to prise information from it, and this dream expresses her frustration in exaggerated form. The dream suggests the new attitude to childhood in the modern era for, if earlier writers were content to portray children as silent enigmas, which implies not only a lack of interest in real children and their experience but also a respect for what they are assumed to represent, in our own era writers have become so interested in the individual child's experience that they are willing to force information from it. But the attempt fails, for the man is not only inarticulate–'Dieser Mann konnte nicht sprechen, er hatte keinen Mund'–but he is also unknowing. The incomprehensible grunts he emits are enough for the narrator: 'Das schlimmste aber war, du verstandest ihn: Er wisse nichts' (p. 250).

Kindheitsmuster presents certain parallels with *Die Eisheiligen* for, although Nelly's mother is frequently quoted verbatim, which reflects the adult's inherent right to speech, Nelly is often merely the recipient of that language. Charlotte's comments to her

---

[42] This point is made by Zahlmann, *Christa Wolfs Reise 'ins Tertiär'*, 81–2; also by Quernheim, *Moralische Ich*, 153.

daughter, usually quoted in direct speech, are often met by silence or answers which are merely given in indirect speech or implied, for example: 'Was hast du denn. Ist dir was? Was heißt hier Kopfschmerzen. Zeig mal her. Na also: Fieber. Das Kind hat ja Fieber. Das Kind muß ja stehenden Fußes ins Bett' (p. 93) or 'Sie [Nelly] leugnete, daß Horst Binder sie jemals nach der Akkordeonstunde belästigte. Hat er dich denn wieder belästigt? Das ist doch einfach unglaublich. Laß dich bloß nicht mit diesem dummen Bengel ein, Kind' (p. 299). Actual conversation between Charlotte and Nelly is rare and brief, and this implies a linguistic power relationship between the generations. This contrasts with the relationship between Lenka and her elders, which is characterized by extended passages of conversation, often in direct speech, implying a certain parity. Charlotte's language, like that of the mother in *Die Eisheiligen*, is largely functional and conventional: mainly instructions, information, and trite clichés. Nelly is comparatively silent because she too is to some extent linguistically repressed. She is not allowed to use language to express her true feelings, for

Es lag ihr [Charlotte] nicht daran, zu erfahren, wie sie [Nelly] in ihrem innersten Innern war. . . . Wörter wie 'traurig' oder 'einsam' lernt das Kind einer glücklichen Familie nicht, das dafür die schwere Aufgabe übernimmt, seine Eltern zu schonen. Sie zu verschonen mit Unglück und Scham. Die Alltagswörter herrschen: iß und trink und nimm und bitte danke. (p. 42)

One of the narrator's main problems in creating Nelly is that of language. She describes the child she is creating thus:

Es bewegt sich, geht, liegt, sitzt, ißt, schläft, trinkt. Es kann lachen und weinen, Sandkuten bauen, Märchen anhören, mit Puppen spielen, sich fürchten, glücklich sein, Mama und Papa sagen, lieben und hassen und zum lieben Gott beten. Und das alles täuschend echt. Bis ihm ein falscher Zungenschlag unterliefe, eine altkluge Bemerkung, weniger noch: ein Gedanke, eine Geste und die Nachahmung entlarvt wäre, auf die du dich beinahe eingelassen hättest. (p. 18)

The clichéd attributes ascribed to the child, especially her ability to say 'Mama' and 'Papa', evoke an animated doll rather than a real child and the narrator is all too aware of the artificiality of this construct. Hence the impossibility of creating a child's language and speaking in the first person. The child is only accessible to her through the third-person narrative.[43]

Not only does Wolf apparently dismiss the idea of using a child's language, but the child's knowledge is also occasionally portrayed as suspect. Nelly is explicitly described as a witness when the narrator refers to 'Zeiten, die Nelly überhaupt nicht oder als so kleines Kind erlebt hat, daß ihr Zeugnis kaum brauchbar ist' and goes on to comment on the 'nachlässige Gedächtnis der Kinder' (p. 109). The most radical doubts as to the child's knowledge are expressed in the 'Schaukel' dream.

Even when Nelly is old enough for her 'Zeugnis' to be 'brauchbar', we might see it as limited in its usefulness for, like the 'Analphabetin', she is too close to events to grasp their wider political, social and moral implications: for Nelly the fire at the synagogue is an isolated event, associated with the 'Rohrsesselbrand' instigated by her younger brother, and it calls forth powerful emotions before she is able to repress them. But, while Johansen might have been content to evoke this emotion, Wolf supplements the child's impression with later documentary material in order to bring out the full implications of the event. This is a consistent pattern in *Kindheitsmuster* which allows it to go beyond the self-imposed limitations of *Die Analphabetin*. However, the technique also invites questions for, while the authors examined earlier in this chapter apparently found inherent value in the child's perspective and language as a means of reflecting both the intensity of the child's experience and political reality, Wolf seems to adopt the child's perspective only to struggle constantly against its limitations. Does her self-conscious retrospective technique expose her to the

---

[43] Kuhn, *Christa Wolf's Utopian Vision*, 104. Third-person autobiographical writing is not a new departure in German literature. In *Fremde Kind*, 315, Richter points out that a certain distance between the narrating and the described self was a feature of autobiographical writing around 1800, instancing Johann Heinrich Jung's *Heinrich Stillings Jugend* (1777), Karl Philipp Moritz's *Anton Reiser* (1785–94), Goethe's *Dichtung und Wahrheit* (1811) and Jean Paul's *Selberlebensbeschreibung*. Brettschneider ('*Kindheitsmuster*', 29 and 50) suggests that the third person served Jung's didactic and Moritz's psychological purposes since it allowed them a certain distance from their subject. It also allows them to retreat behind a self-effacing mask, so escaping charges of self-indulgent introspection, for it suggests the potential universality of their experience. Greiner emphasizes that Wolf's use of the third person is rather different, for the narrator does not simply disappear behind a mask: her constant presence is emphasized by the 'du' address ('Schwierigkeit, "ich" zu sagen', 332).

danger of over-intellectualizing the child's experience, so failing to capture its intensity? And, if the child's limited knowledge is so frustrating, why does Wolf choose to use her perspective at all?

It is obviously possible to create a sense of the child's independent universe without necessarily using the child's own language. In *Jette in Dresden* Schütz achieves this by using mysterious chapter headings which refer to everyday elements of Jette's reality but are baffling to the reader, for example, 'Ich bin die Eule. Eure Jette'.[44] The reader's puzzlement at the beginning of each chapter preserves a sense of the child's independent universe. In *What Maisie Knew*, as Paul Theroux points out, James achieves this by using appropriately childlike imagery, for example, 'eyebrows arched like skipping-ropes' or focusing on details Maisie would be more likely to notice than the adults because of her size, like the legs of the people she sees in France.[45]

Wolf does something similar in *Kindheitsmuster*. In the synagogue scene she emphasizes Nelly's inarticulateness: 'Es war die erste Ruine, die Nelly in ihrem Leben sah. Vielleicht kannte sie das Wort noch nicht' (p. 235) and 'Das verkohlte Bauwerk machte sie traurig. Sie wußte aber nicht, daß es Trauer war, was sie empfand, weil sie es nicht wissen sollte' (p. 236). However, this inarticulateness does not hamper the accuracy or the immediacy of Nelly's perceptions, many of which are given in the present tense to suggest their fleeting but intense nature. The objective 'falsity' of some of these impressions only reinforces our sense of their immediacy, and this makes Nelly an eloquent witness to the suffering of the Jews despite the fact that she is inarticulate. Her powerful emotional response ('Staunen und Schrecken') could not be vocalized at the time, but subsists as an 'inneres Bild' (p. 236) for the adult narrator to articulate.

But if Nelly's vision has a childlike immediacy and intensity, when she does find words her language is as tainted as that of the children in *Das Waisenhaus*. While she clearly feels intense sympathy with the Jews, her first response is repressed by the words of a song: '(Blut, Blut, Bluhuhut, Blut muß fließen knüppelhageldick . . .) Die Juden sind anders als wir. Sie sind unheimlich.

---

[44] *Jette in Dresden* (Berlin and Weimar, 1979), 10.
[45] In his introd. to *What Maisie Knew* (Harmondsworth, 1985), 13. Quotations from text, pp. 50 and 187.

Vor den Juden muß man Angst haben, wenn man sie schon nicht hassen kann. Wenn die Juden jetzt stark wären, müßten sie uns alle umbringen' (p. 237). This is a clear example of political indoctrination repressing the child's authentic voice, for none of Nelly's other thoughts when contemplating this scene are recorded so directly: her vague feeling of sadness is nameless, for her feelings are almost as inaccessible to the child as they are to the adult attempting to recreate her. It is easier for the narrator to remember the public language of the time than the private, non-verbalized language of feelings.

Language clearly plays an important role in political indoctrination, and its form can be as important as its content. According to the appendix to Orwell's *Nineteen Eighty-Four* the ever-shrinking vocabulary of 'Newspeak' is intended to cancel out whole areas of thought and thus supposedly renders any revolt literally 'unthinkable'.[46] Nazi indoctrination was a different process in that it imposed a new language rather than reducing the old one, but the same kind of simplification is at work in that both languages are apparently intended to reduce the room for free thought and individual initiative. But that being said, how is it that Winston Smith finds it in himself to revolt and that Nelly feels that subconscious disquiet and nameless 'Trauer' before the pat answers of Nazi doctrine rescue her from her uncertainty? Admittedly, the concept of Newspeak has not been fully realized in Winston Smith's generation and therefore he does still have another language to think in. But there are no such clear-cut explanations for those who have been 'hineingeboren' into the Third Reich.

The answer to this puzzle may lie in Steven Pinker's concept of 'mentalese', for while Pinker quotes Orwell's idea that deviance from the principles of Ingsoc will be 'unthinkable' once the changeover to Newspeak is complete, he highlights Orwell's own caveat 'at least so far as thought is dependent on words'.[47] Pinker suggests that thought is not in fact dependent on words and this allows him to make a series of optimistic predictions for 2050, according to Orwell the year when 'Newspeak' was to have been

---

[46] 'Appendix: The Principles of Newspeak', in *Nineteen Eighty-Four* (repr. Harmondsworth, 1984), 257.

[47] *The Language Instinct: The New Science of Language and Mind* (Harmondsworth, 1995), 55–6. The concept of 'mentalese' is discussed ibid. 55–82.

the only language available. The most important of these predictions for our purposes is that, given that thought is not dependent on words, mental life would go on independently of language, which would assure the continued existence of concepts like freedom and equality even if those thinking them were unable to name them.[48] It is perhaps in the inner space of mentalese that Nelly's nameless 'Trauer', based on her inadmissible, instinctive sympathy for the Jews, is located. Her feelings are at variance with the language she has learned: 'Wörter wie "traurig" . . . lernt das Kind einer glücklichen Familie nicht' (p. 42). Feelings are not easily expressed; the language of political indoctrination on the other hand is much more straightforward and concrete: it comes ready vocalized and thus intrudes easily on the child's consciousness, followed by a simplified version of the political propaganda she has heard. The language of propaganda is more than a match for the flash of moral insight involuntarily articulated in the word 'retteten' (p. 237) and the role played by language in this work is thus an extremely unelevating one.

Nevertheless, like the 'Analphabetin' Nelly can adopt political vocabulary without necessarily understanding it or applying it to her own existence. Nothing Leo Siegmann says about the 'Judenjunge' can make her even imagine herself hitting a Jewish child. As we saw in Chapter 3, this refusal can be attributed partly to her latent artistic ability, but interestingly this sense of humane values does not appear in her childhood writings. Her literary output too is apparently influenced by the political language of her time, for example the intensely nationalistic poem of which Herr Warsinski comments admiringly 'Das hast du doch nicht selber gemacht! Das hast du doch aus der Zeitung abgeschrieben' (p. 192). Her 'creativity' is thus merely an imitation of the propaganda that surrounds her. It is clear when the children are asked to write essays about their personal experience that all have been linguistically repressed, although significantly Nelly performs rather better than the others:

Nicht daß Nelly versagt hätte: das war beim Deutschaufsatz nicht zu erwarten, Julia verlor kein Wort darüber. Wie kam es aber, daß viele über 'Volk ohne Raum' oder 'Nordischer Geist in antiker Dichtung' flüssig

---

[48] Ibid. 82.

schreiben konnten, ein so einfaches Thema wie 'Der erste Schnee' aber ganz und gar nicht bewältigten? Nelly wußte es nicht, und was sie vermutete, hätte sie nicht ausdrücken können: daß es um vieles schwieriger ist, über sich selbst zu schreiben als über allgemeine Ideen, die einem geläufig sind. (p. 329)

This passage suggests that the spontaneous inner life of these children has been repressed because they are constantly having to regurgitate the ideology of their era; it recalls the patriotic essays of *Der Ausflug der toten Mädchen* (see Chapter 2, above). But, though Nelly has apparently managed to write something from personal experience, she is still uneasily aware that her true self has not been conveyed in writing: 'Über jeder Zeile lag ein Hauch von Unwahrhaftigkeit, sie hatte ihre Familie eine Spur zu idyllisch, sich selbst um mehr als eine Spur zu brav geschildert'. What hope there is for Nelly lies in her awareness that this is not a totally honest description; this awareness is the starting point for her later, writing self who is on a quest for her true identity. The narrator continues '(Die Heuchelei und daß sie ihr schwach bewußt blieb, ebenso wie die Sehnsucht nach Aufrichtigkeit: Vielleicht war das eine Art von Rettung? Ein Rest von Eigenleben, an den sie später anknüpfen konnte?)' (p. 329). Thus it is not simply that the girl is writing which suggests her later literary activity, but also the fact that she is self-conscious about her literary efforts.

But for all this awareness, during the Nazi era there is no part of Nelly's writing that is not affected by the prevalent political language. Even her diary, the most private means of self-expression open to her, is seen by Charlotte as a politically incriminating document: she makes her daughter burn the diary, for 'Wenn der Russe das bei uns findet, sind wir erledigt, dumm und offenherzig, wie du bist!' (p. 332). There is a paradox here: Charlotte's words suggest that the diary is full of Nelly's most intimate emotions, and yet the only thing we actually know that goes into her diary is 'ihr[en] Entschluß . . . dem Führer auch in schweren Zeiten unverbrüchliche Treue zu bewahren' (p. 442). This statement, which reads almost as a declaration of love, shows how far the languages of personal feeling and political ideology have merged. The insidiousness of this linguistic indoctrination cannot be overestimated. Much earlier in the novel the child's comic incomprehension of the phrase 'der polnische Korridor' shows how political ideology, just like middle-class morality, can be transmitted almost imperceptibly through language:

All diese nicht alltäglichen Vorkommnisse hatte man sich inmitten des Polnischen Korridors vorzustellen, der wegen der bekannten polnischen Wirtschaft niemals aufgeräumt sein konnte wie ihr eigener deutscher Korridor, in dem man seine schmutzigen Schuhe nicht abstellen durfte, weil Korridor und Badezimmer nun mal die Visitenkarte einer Wohnung waren. (p. 98)

As in *Das Waisenhaus* and *Die Eisheiligen* we are left wondering whether the child actually has an authentic voice. Indeed Nelly seems a more mute figure than the young protagonist of *Die Eisheiligen*, although they are subject to similar linguistic repression. Here the protagonist of *Die Eisheiligen* describes coming home from school to find that Kaltesophie has searched her room and found her poems: 'Nun stehe ich vor ihr in der Küche und sie liest mir meine Reime vor.... Die meisten Verse sind über Kaltesophie. Ich stehe vor ihr, rot vor Scham und Wut. Sie zieht die Herdringe vom mittleren Feuerloch und stopft die Hefte ins Feuer' (pp. 244–5). These poems are clearly more the expression of personal sentiments and inner life than Nelly's diary, and the young poet's impotent rage at this destruction contrasts starkly with Nelly's almost total indifference to the destruction of her diary: 'du hast es nicht über dich gebracht, die Vernichtung dieses unersetzlichen, aber gewiß entlarvenden Dokumentes wirklich zu bedauern' (p. 333).

Like the children in *Das Waisenhaus* and *Die Analphabetin*, many of Nelly's linguistic experiences are intimately bound up with the transmission of political ideology, and consequently she has no authentic voice as a child. The narrator's alienation from this inarticulate child is expressed by the third-person narrative, and this problem is not even resolved at the end of the novel for, just as Nelly increasingly accepts Nazi values as she grows older, so presumably her language too is ever more ideologically tainted. Small wonder then that the narrator doubts whether she has found a language that can express her identity both past and present when she writes: 'Und die Vergangenheit, die noch Sprachregelungen verfügen, die erste Person in eine zweite und dritte spalten konnte—ist ihre Vormacht gebrochen? Werden die Stimmen sich beruhigen? Ich weiß es nicht' (p. 594).

And yet Wolf's faith in the child and its potential survives in the linguistic as well as in the moral context. For, while the narrator seems to reject the idea of using the child's own language and expresses her distance from the child self by using the third person, paradoxically this is also an attempt at approaching the child self, since she notes: 'Ein dreijähriges normal entwickeltes Kind trennt sich von der dritten Person, für die es sich bis jetzt gehalten hat' (p. 19). By returning to a linguistic stage before she was able to think of herself in the first person, and certainly before she came under the systematic verbal indoctrination of the Nazi era, the narrator is actually identifying herself with the vulnerability and innocence of the young child. And other elements of Wolf's style also suggest a recourse to the child's relationship with language. We see a certain affinity with the way the 'Analphabetin' questions language in Nelly's attempts to understand ideological 'Glitzerwörter' by applying her limited linguistic knowledge: 'Was sind Geschlechtskranke? . . . Friedrich der Große aus dem Geschlecht der Hohenzollern. Weißes Emailleschild in der Richtstraße: Facharzt für Haut- und Geschlechtskrankheiten. Es kam also vor, daß ein ganzes Geschlecht erkrankte, und dadurch heiratsunfähig wurde' (pp. 96–7). This presents parallels with the way the narrator examines language, especially the words that shaped her childhood: 'Endlösung' (p. 341), 'Hypnose' (p. 368), and 'Verfallen' (p. 420).[49] The narrator's questioning occurs on a more intellectual level than that of her childhood self; nonetheless, this parallel suggests a desire to return to the child's critical relationship with language, if not to the child's language itself.

The third-person narrative implies that the linguistic potential Wolf sees in the children of her era derives from a very early stage of development: the 'kleinen, mißgestalteten Mann' (p. 249, my emphasis) suggests that the child's values and language had been deformed from an early age, a point made explicit in 'Über Sinn und Unsinn von Naivität' where Wolf refers to childhood as the

---

[49] Smith discusses the way Wolf analyses language in *Tradition, Art and Society*, 180–4. Manfred Jurgensen suggests that women authors use the child as an orientation point for their literary style, and discusses this aspect of *Kindheitsmuster* (*Deutsche Frauenautoren der Gegenwart* . . . (Berne, 1983), 108–11). However, he emphasizes more the change from the linguistically conformist Nelly who becomes 'taub und unwissend' (*Kindheitsmuster*, 106) to the more critical narrator, so implying that the narrator is trying to break out of her childhood linguistic patterns rather than return to them. As we shall see below, this different emphasis depends largely on precisely what stage of Nelly's childhood the narrator is deemed to be using as her orientation point.

source of writing:

Nun ist die Prosa ja eine derjenigen Gattungen, die, auf Nüchternheit und Souveranität angewiesen, für Naivität keine Verwendung zu haben scheinen. Zugleich aber lebt sie, wie alle sogenannte Kunst, aus jenem Vorrat an ursprünglichem Verhalten, für das in der Kindheit der Grund gelegt wird. Ihre Bedingungen sind spontanes, direktes, rücksichtsloses Reagieren, Denken, Fühlen, Handeln, ein unbefangenes (eben doch 'naives') ungebrochenes Verhältnis zu sich selbst und zu seiner persönlichen Biographie–genau das, was wir eingebüßt haben.[50]

While Wolf clearly recognizes that her generation's childhood was perverted, it is also clear that Nelly's sensitivity to language, like her moments of instinctive moral insight, survives up to quite a late stage of her development. In fact, these two attributes are closely associated for, while Nelly's naive attempts at getting at the meaning of 'Glitzerwörter' by means of association are confined to Chapter 3, there is something instinctive about her later response to the word 'Medium': 'Damals hat Nelly das Wort "Medium" zum erstenmal gehört und sofort begonnen, ihm zu mißtrauen' (p. 380). Given the earlier allusion to *Mario und der Zauberer* (p. 358), this ironically points up the potential power of Nelly's instinctive insight since she knows it is not her place to succumb to Andrack (p. 395), yet it also highlights her wider failure to resist the Hitler regime itself. Wolf's rediscovery of these elements of childhood, as suggested by the passage from 'Über Sinn und Unsinn von Naivität' above, does not just provide her with a subject but also with the means to write about it, a perhaps surprising conclusion to draw from so resolutely intellectual and self-conscious a writer.

Kindheitsmuster tackles the same problem as *Das Waisenhaus* and *Die Analphabetin*, that of giving the indoctrinated child a voice but, superficially at least, Wolf's solutions are radically different from those of Fichte and Johansen, because she is trying to find a language for the adult abused as a child as well as for the child herself. Nonetheless, Wolf too is clearly trying to find her way back into the child's relationship with language in order to investigate the linguistic indoctrination to which Nelly was subject. The narrator is attempting to break through childhood repression and

---

[50] In Wolf, *Die Dimension des Autors*, i. 52.

indoctrination almost by jumping over her shadow, trying to return to a point before these experiences had taken place. This is a more complex procedure than was attempted in *Das Waisenhaus* or *Die Analphabetin*, where there is no adult presence. This is reflected even in the relative lengths of the texts for, while the brevity of *Das Waisenhaus* and *Die Analphabetin* reflect the child's limited knowledge and linguistic skills, the very expansiveness of *Kindheitsmuster* suggests that the mute child is accompanied by a rather more articulate adult.

Language against the Odds: Siegfried Lenz's Deutschstunde

'Expansive' is also an appropriate word for *Die Blechtrommel* and *Deutschstunde*, and expansiveness is at least as paradoxical in these texts as it is in *Kindheitsmuster*. In both, the narrator's written expansiveness stands in powerful contrast to the physical restraint to which he is subject, though paradoxically this very restraint allows him the opportunity to write. In Siggi's case his written expansiveness makes a mockery of the task imposed upon him. His 'Strafarbeit' takes a very specific and conformist form, that of the 'Deutschaufsatz': this punishment is not merely intended to bring his behaviour into line, but should also keep his written style within certain limits as described by Hannes Heer:

immer will er [der Deutschaufsatz] Sprachwildwuchs beschneiden, un-geordneten Gedankenfluß kanalisieren, Wahrnehmung und Auswahl von Wahrgenommenem lenken. Diese Wirkung wird verstärkt durch die Sprache, die er verlangt: Stilkundendeutsch, Redewendungen von Erwachsenen, Spruchweisheiten. Sich dieser Form unterwerfen, heißt Verzicht auf Unmittelbarkeit und Originalität, heißt das Extreme der Ereignisse ins Normale zu pressen, bedeutet auch fast immer einen Ver-lust an Wahrhaftigkeit.[51]

But Siggi's essay bursts the bounds of the school-imposed exer-cise. His almost compulsive excess of language springs from his childhood experience for, if children learn to speak by imitating

---

[51] *Als ich 9 Jahre alt war, kam der Krieg: Ein Lesebuch gegen den Krieg* (Reinbek, 1983), 226. Interestingly Heer suggests that the Nuremburg schoolchildren who were asked to write the essays in this collection in Nov. 1946 might not have been able to speak about their experiences of the war at all had it not been for the 'objektivierten Sprachgestus' of the German essay.

their parents, especially the mother, it is amazing that Siggi ever learned to speak at all, given Gudrun Jepsen's taciturnity. Moreover, language and its withdrawal are used as a punishment: if the child of *Die Eisheiligen* suffers under a torrent of violent language, then Siggi suffers from a different form of linguistic abuse. When his father finds him at Nansen's 'Hütte' during the storm the child is more frightened by his father's silence than by anything else: 'Wenn er mir nur eine geschmiert hätte, als er mich aus der Hütte riß! ... Aber mein Vater schwieg auf der ganzen Fahrt, er strafte mich mit einem Schweigen, das die endgültige Strafe erst ankündigte, das war so üblich bei ihm' (pp. 66–7). Härtling describes something similar in *Nachgetragene Liebe*, where the boy's father punishes him by refusing to speak to him for over a week. This infects the whole family and becomes much more than a simple lack of verbal communication; the child experiences it as an attempt to negate his very existence.[52] This childhood punishment has long-term effects: 'Manchmal, Vater, kehren Sprichwörter in ihre gelebte Bedeutung zurück. Seit dieser stummen Kur kann ich den Satz "Er schweigt ihn tot" nicht mehr lesen, geschweige denn schreiben, ohne daß es mich schaudert'.[53]

As its title suggests, Härtling's book is an attempt to re-establish communications between himself and his father. Siggi's work, too, seems to be largely compensatory: not only does it allow him a kind of sanctioned defiance against the island authorities, but it also enables him to use the words he so rarely used in childhood. As in *Kindheitsmuster*, it is the adults who have an inherent right to speech in *Deutschstunde*. Adult conversations are frequently quoted in direct speech, but the child is only rarely and minimally involved in such conversations and, on those occasions when he is, it is generally as a result of being asked a direct question; he does not usually initiate conversation with adults. This again implies a power relationship for, as in *Kindheitsmuster*, the adults' language, especially that of Siggi's parents, is largely functional. The narrator Siggi frequently quotes adults in virtually uncommentated direct speech in order to show rather than tell the reader what went on in Rugbüll under the Third Reich; while the opening paragraph of his 'Strafarbeit' refers to 'ein in Berlin beschlossenes Malverbot' (p. 23) which suggests narrative

---

[52] *Nachgetragene Liebe*, 22.   [53] Ibid. 23.

hindsight, the conversation between Jens and Max when the 'Malverbot' is delivered suggests Siggi is reliving rather than merely relating the scene, once more a silent and uncomprehending child watching events unfold. His first attempt to write the essay required him to return to the immediacy of childhood experience and vision, for he writes that he thought himself 'noch näher heran, . . . ließ mich auf den Gepäckträger des Dienstfahrrades setzen und fuhr einfach mit nach Bleekenwarf' (p. 12).

Thus while Siggi's language may be that of the 20-year-old, his vision is often quite consciously limited to that of the child. This becomes particularly obvious in the examples of pictorial narrative noted in Chapter 3, for it can result in a rather oblique portrayal of the Nazi era and its implications. For example, when the runaway Klaas is brought home injured, Siggi observes the encounter between his father and the doctor from a very limited perspective:

Ich schlich zur Tür und linste durch das Schlüsselloch. Doktor Gripp saß auf der Couch, neben ihm stand mein Vater. Die Decke lag auf dem Boden. Ich sah in das Gesicht meines Vaters, es war verkniffen von Neugierde und Schmerz, seine Lippen waren aufgesprungen. Doktor Gripps Rücken verdeckte Klaas. Mein Vater fragte etwas, und Doktor Gripp schüttelte den Kopf. Mein Vater fragte laut genug, so daß ich es verstehen konnte: Warum geht das nicht? und der riesige Arzt, auf meinen Bruder niederblickend: Das geht nur im Lazarett, wir müssen ihn sofort ins Lazarett schaffen, dazu deutete er mit flacher, gleitender Hand auf Klaas, so als wolle er zu seiner Behauptung den sichtbaren Beweis anbieten. Wieder stellte mein Vater eine Frage, worauf Doktor Gripp seine abwärts gleitende Hand hob und sie geöffnet, etwa in Schulterhöhe, für sich sprechen ließ. . . . Jetzt trat mein Vater neben ihn, ich sah nur ihrer beider Rücken, vermutlich erläuterte der Arzt da etwas, machte meinem Vater etwas begreiflich, was dieser Mühe hatte einzusehen. (pp. 254–5)

Siggi seems unaware of the full implications of these fragments of conversation; indeed, even when he quotes more fully from the subsequent conversation between Jens and Nansen, when Nansen states 'Sie werden ihn holen . . . für den Pfahl werden sie ihn gesund machen' (pp. 256–7), the boy does not seem to grasp the full implications of what is happening. Like Maisie, he registers considerably more than he understands, and it is this self-consciously limited perspective that Siggi the narrator offers his reader.

It is true that the adolescent Siggi sometimes almost casually completes the perspective of his younger self: when he describes the way Nansen is taken away for questioning, he refers merely to the arrival of an 'Auto' and 'zwei Ledermäntel' (p. 267) suggesting the child's immediate experience; only later does Siggi specify 'daß Max Ludwig Nansen im Polizeiauto abgeholt worden war' (p. 281). Grote uses a similar technique in *Für Kinder die Hälfte*, where the child's account of an elderly Jewess being taken away is given without retrospective knowledge: although the scene is described in detail, right down to the bolts on the lorry doors and the bars on the windows, the child's limited knowledge is expressed by neutral vocabulary such as 'ein Lastwagen', 'ein Mann', and 'die alte Dame'.[54] The scene is put into context by the adult conversations before and after the event, with their references to 'Jüdin', 'den gelben Stern', and the 'Postkarte' informing the woman of her imminent departure.[55] In a sense Siggi's original perspective, like that of the unnamed child in Grote's book, achieves what Hofmann was later to do quite consistently in *Veilchenfeld*, where Hans is much closer to the events he is narrating. Critics have noted that, while the everyday reality of anti-Semitism is clearly rendered in this book, the word 'Jude' itself never appears.[56] By using the childhood perspective Lenz, Grote, and Hofmann can avoid the all-too-familiar language used to tell us about the Third Reich and instead present it in its concrete immediacy, a challenge to the active reader, especially when there is no retrospective level of narration.

There are clear parallels between *Deutschstunde* and *Kindheitsmuster* for, while both Lenz and Wolf use retrospective comment and an essentially adult language to evoke a Third Reich

---

[54] *Für Kinder die Hälfte*, 108.   [55] Ibid. 106, 107, 109.

[56] See Schmid, 'Hänsel und Gretel, 1938', 170; Schumacher also notes a total absence of the political terminology of the Third Reich in *Veilchenfeld*. ('Gert Hofmann, *Veilchenfeld*', 291). Ralph Gehrke expands on this point by suggesting that *Veilchenfeld* is not so much about the historical phenomenon of the Holocaust as a universal fable against racism and prejudice (' "Es ist nicht wahr, daß die Geschichte nichts lehren könnte, ihr fehlen bloß die Schüler . . ." "Veilchenfeld": Gert Hofmanns Lehrstück über Auschwitz und Fremdenhaß und sein Bezug zur Gegenwart', *Der Deutschunterricht*, 44/3 (1992), esp. 99–100). Ernestine Schlant on the other hand thinks this strategy allows Hofmann to emphasize that Jews in Nazi Germany became non-persons long before they were physically destroyed and forces the reader to consider them as human beings rather than as an ethnic group (*The Language of Silence: West German Literature and the Holocaust* (New York and London, 1999), 184).

childhood, both attempt to find their way back to certain aspects of childhood in order to write at all: Wolf is concerned with rediscovering the child's vision and its spontaneous relationship with language, Lenz wants to rediscover the child's non-analytical vision as a means of producing a fresh perspective on events and this naturally affects his linguistic register to some extent, as in the 'Ledermäntel' passage quoted above. Moreover, Siggi's childhood relationship with language is also reflected in his written work. The fact that the predominantly silent child does not usually take the initiative in speech with adults is reflected in his literary activities; although he was good at 'Bildbeschreibungen' while at school (p. 321) (a prominent feature of his present narrative), there is no indication that he had ever wanted to write at greater length. It is only when the adult world imposes the 'Strafarbeit' on him that he realizes how much he has to say, rather like Jo, who would never have appeared as a witness of his own accord. Significantly too, his written expansiveness parallels Nansen's eloquence when Siggi quotes his aesthetic theories verbatim, with scant regard for plausibility. This passage in 'Sehen' is the longest example of one person's direct speech in this novel. This is significant, not just because it is attributed to Nansen, suggesting what a profound impact he has had on the boy, but also because Siggi recognizes that any audience is irrelevant to him, for the questions he asks 'galten ihm selbst mehr als einem Anwesenden' (p. 402). This is paralleled when one of the psychologists asks Siggi 'Wem erzählst du das alles da?' and he responds 'Mir' (p. 184). But, although his story may be limited to a personal crisis, it also has a representative quality that makes it an uncomfortable testimony for the adults: 'Ich bin stellvertretend hier für meinen Alten, den Polizeiposten Rugbüll. . . . Vielleicht sind sogar alle Jungen stellvertretend für irgend jemand hier. . . . Aber etwas möchte ich fragen: warum gibt es nicht eine Insel und solche Gebäude für schwer erziehbare Alte?' (p. 539). Siggi sees his own predicament as part of a more general malaise and, although in the narrative of his childhood there are very few overt references to historical events, the emotional impact of events on him is very clear. His art is almost as unwelcome to present-day society as Nansen's during the Nazi era for, although it would be a misinterpretation to see Nansen as a 'Widerstandskünstler', his paintings clearly register the emotional impact of the regime. The very fact that Siggi's character has been corrupted to such a degree by 'normality' under the Nazis is a clear implicit criticism of that past society and makes him a very uncomfortable witness to his present one. The smug psychologists try to categorize him but they refuse to accept any responsibility for his condition. Again this presents parallels with Jo's case. Siggi's second meeting with an international team of psychologists has a similar comic element to Jo's encounter with the pomposity of Chancery, for although the psychologists are supposed to assess Siggi's inner life and motivation, they do not even read the best clue they have, namely his 'Strafarbeit' thus far:

Der Besucher aus Cleveland, Ohio, Mr. Boris Zwettkoff, lieh sich von Himpel meine Hefte aus, ließ die beschriebenen Seiten schnurrend über den Daumen laufen und war im Bilde; desgleichen verrieten der Herr aus Zürich, ein Carl Fouchard jr., und der Herr aus Stockholm, ein Lars Peter Larsen, unbekannte Fähigkeiten der Durchdringung und Aneignung eines Stoffes, indem sie die Hefte zwar hier und da öffneten, vornehmlich aber in der Hand wogen und auch so zu einem Urteil kamen, das ausreichte. (p. 182)

Siggi's evidence is dismissed; his story is told by Himpel, and this is exclusively the story of how his punishment came about rather than any detailed account of his past career. These psychologists are looking at symptoms without examining their root causes, just as in Jo's case the coroner simply sees a dirty, uneducated child without asking why the child is like that in the first place. For the psychologists Siggi's evidence is unacceptable because the boy is in an institution for young offenders: they cannot believe that he will have anything valid to say to them.

This episode may well reflect how Lenz thought his novel would be received by critics and the reading public. Certainly he did not expect *Deutschstunde* to be the great commercial success it was, perhaps partly because of the necessary limitations of the child narrative.[57] But if in some ways, notably perspective, Lenz deliberately adopts those limitations, then his use of retrospect, like Wolf's, allows him not only to use an essentially adult

---

[57] See Siegfried Lenz, 'Interview mit Marcel Reich-Ranicki' (1969), in *Beziehungen: Ansichten und Bekenntnisse zur Literatur* (Hamburg, 1970), 287. Here Lenz offers a more obvious reason for his doubts about the novel's success, the central theme of the 'Malverbot'.

language but also to suggest the wider implications of the child's account. In this text the adult character's skill is as necessary to art as the child's vision.

A Single Language? Günter Grass's Die Blechtrommel

Although *Die Blechtrommel* is the earliest of the texts dealt with in this chapter, I have kept it to the end because of the particular difficulty of establishing Oskar's true status and voice. We can distinguish a number of different personae in whose name he speaks. First there is the little boy in Danzig who is only very occasionally heard in speech. Then there is the older boy who apparently refuses to leave this linguistic register except when with social outsiders like Bebra, whom he addresses in an adult, even precocious, tone. There is the 30-year-old in a mental institution who also occasionally uses the child's language to heighten our impression of his ignorance and lack of responsibility. And there is the 30-year-old narrator who uses a perfectly adult written style, complete with virtuoso wordplay, but whose writing, paradoxically enough, is couched in a conversational tone with frequent references to an implied interlocutor, 'Sie'. Yet all these apparent shifts and developments are undercut by two stabilizing elements: first, Oskar's claim that he belongs to 'den hellhörigen Säuglingen, deren geistige Entwicklung schon bei der Geburt abgeschlossen ist' (*Die Blechtrommel*, 46) which suggests a uniform level of perception from birth onwards and, secondly, his static narrative situation which we might also expect to imply a uniform tone.

Oskar uses child language far less often than we might imagine: we get so used to him feigning childlike ignorance that we assume he constantly uses an appropriate linguistic register to support it. In fact there are very few instances of genuine child language or at least the literary transcription of it. Oskar is an almost unnaturally silent child, at least verbally: his main means of 'communication' are his drum and his destructive scream, both non-verbal 'languages'. There are very few examples of him communicating in direct speech and even fewer in an apparently 'genuine' child's register: ' "Rapupin!" schrie ich oder auch: "Raschuschin!" Zeitweilig tat ich ganz und gar albern: "Raschu, Raschu!" hörte man Oskar plappern' (p. 103). And even here the 'tat ich' makes it quite clear that this is merely a linguistic act. Other examples of direct speech make it very clear that he is role-playing when he speaks as a child: these occur either with the midgets, with the Christ child, or with Jan whilst in the 'polnische Post'. Thus he drops the child's linguistic mask only when he knows either that he is among his own kind, the social misfits, when he is unobserved, or when he knows there is little chance of being betrayed afterwards.

Conversely though, he sometimes uses an approximation to the child's language in his written narrative, for instance when describing the full-length portrait taken on his third birthday:

Da habe ich sie, die Trommel. Da hängt sie mir gerade, neu und weißrot gezackt vor dem Bauch. Da kreuze ich selbstbewußt und unter ernst entschlossenem Gesicht hölzerne Trommelstöcke auf dem Blech. Da habe ich einen gestreiften Pullover an. Da stecke ich in glänzenden Lackschuhen. Da stehen mir die Haare wie eine putzsüchtige Bürste auf dem Kopf, da spiegelt sich in jedem meiner blauen Augen der Wille zu einer Macht, die ohne Gefolgschaft auskommen sollte. Da gelang mir damals eine Position, die aufzugeben ich keine Veranlassung hatte. (pp. 63–4)

Of course this is only an approximation for, if the brief opening sentence and the heavy repetition of those that follow ('Da ... Da ... Da') give a linguistic impression of the childlike to translate the visual image, this is only a light gloss to cover more obviously adult structures and vocabulary. This is even more evident in the 'polnische Post', when the experiencing Oskar is considerably older and more linguistically competent but the narrating Oskar persists in using the same approximation to the child's language:

–da klirrte es, wie vielleicht Engel zur Ehre Gottes klirren, da sang es, wie im Radio der Äther singt, da traf es nicht den Bronski, da traf es Kobyella, da hatte sich eine Granate einen Riesenspaß erlaubt, da lachten Ziegel sich zu Splitt, Scherben zu Staub, Putz wurde Mehl, Holz fand sein Beil, da hüpfte das ganze komische Kinderzimmer auf einem Bein, da platzten die Käthe-Kruse-Puppen, da ging das Schaukelpferd durch und hätte so gerne einen Reiter zum Abwerfen gehabt, da ergaben sich Fehlkonstruktionen im Märklinbaukasten, und die polnischen Ulanen besetzten alle vier Zimmerecken gleichzeitig–da warf es endlich das Gestell mit dem Spielzeug um: und das Glockenspiel läutete Ostern ein, auf schrie die Ziehharmonika, die Trompete mag wem was geblasen haben, alles gab gleichzeitig Ton an, ein probendes Orchester: das schrie, platzte, wieherte, läutete, zerschellte, barst, knirschte, kreischte, zirpte ganz hoch und grub doch tief unten Fundamente aus. Mir aber, der ich mich, wie es zu einem Dreijährigen paßte, während des Granateinschlages im Schutzengelwinkel des Kinderzimmers dicht unterm Fenster befunden hatte, mir fiel das Blech zu, die Trommel zu–und sie hatte nur wenige Sprünge im Lack und gar kein einziges Loch, Oskars neue Blechtrommel. (pp. 282–3)

Again, there are a number of features that recall the child's language: the heavy repetitive structure of the opening, the list of verbs with no logical or syntactical connection, the insistent use of toys as props to mask grim realities, and the final reference to himself in the third person. But Oskar overplays his hand here: the element of role-play evident in his 'wie es zu einem Dreijährigen paßte' is as obvious in his language as in his actions. He uses the child's tone to help him avoid any suspicion of knowledge or responsibility.

Oskar's language is thus unstable and entirely disorientating to read. He refuses to adopt the literary convention of a child 'writing' in a uniformly adult tone but nor does he write in a child's language that develops logically with age. He further disorientates the reader by referring to himself as both 'ich' and 'Oskar' (sometimes within the same sentence) and, although sometimes there seems to be a clear criterion for this shift, analogous to the technique used by Wolf in *Kindheitsmuster,* with 'ich' referring to the 'erzählendes ich' and 'Oskar' to the 'erlebendes ich', this distinction is not consistently maintained. Indeed, he frequently refers to himself as Oskar in the narrative present, which may be the narrator playing with the conventions of childlike speech in order to create an illusion of innocence and harmlessness around the madman, or indeed of madness itself.[58]

Clearly Oskar's relationship with language is extremely mendacious. His determination to read so as to get precisely the

---

[58] For further discussion of this point see Botheroyd, *Ich und Er.* Botheroyd rejects both the temporal distinction and the child narrative argument as inadequate explanations of Oskar's apparently arbitrary use of the first and third person (ibid. 52–3). He suggests that Oskar uses the third person for three reasons: to create an effect of mock pathos as a part of Oskar's narrative posture; to refer to the child in Danzig and to the permanent child 'Oskar', cases where there is a strong sense of his role for others, whether characters in the novel or the reader; and when referring to the fixed image of 'Oskar', e.g. in photographs (ibid. 53).

information he wants has to be kept secret from the adults, for his apparent inability to read is part of his façade of childhood, like his pretence of not understanding what is going on around him as he affects a childlike tone to deny all knowledge and responsibility. The prime example of this is in the 'Es war einmal' of the *Kristallnacht.* This narrative strategy is made doubly artificial by our knowledge that Oskar does not read fairy tales: he prefers Goethe and Rasputin. The use of a childlike convention thus emphasizes the fact that he does in fact know what is going on, as in the 'polnische Post' episode.

There are, however, moments when Oskar's language reveals a much more childlike self, usually when there is apparently no attempt to produce the conventional language of childhood. This is especially true at moments of extreme crisis, as after his mother's death in the 'Mama konnte sehr lustig sein' (p. 194) passage (see Chapter 2, above). The movement from the unaffected, numbed quality of the first four sentences through brilliant defensive wordplay back to the very real sense of pain at his loss is clearly not an example of conventional literary child language, but it is no less evocative for that. It is significant that the drum appears here, for it is his means of childhood communication and importantly it is non-verbal. The drum is the true language of Oskar's childhood and, as Kuhn points out, it is also what enables him to bring about communication between the adult and child in 'Im Zwiebelkeller': Kuhn sees this as Grass's tentative solution to the problem of finding an adequate language to evoke childhood.[59] As we have seen, Oskar's use of a conventional written child language is simply that: following certain literary conventions which are necessarily artificial since the child has no authentic literary voice. We might therefore see his language as a parodic exaggeration of the concerns faced by the authors discussed earlier in this chapter. To communicate with the reader at all Oskar has to use those conventions, but they are merely a transcription of an almost Proustian earlier stage in the creative process, that of reattaining his childhood through a non-verbal medium. Certainly, the drumming is very closely associated with childhood, but its most remarkable effect is that it can transport other people back to their own childhood, whether Fräulein Spollenhauer or the guests

---

[59] *Corruption in Paradise,* 62.

'im Zwiebelkeller' where Oskar's artless drumming 'machte die Welt aus dem Blickwinkel der Dreijährigen deutlich' (p. 660).

In 'Im Zwiebelkeller' Oskar's drum appears to be an adequate means of communication. For him it also has a therapeutic effect, since it allows him access to his inner self. This movement beyond the façade into his true feelings is reflected in the pronouns used:

Wie aber verhielt es sich mit Oskar? Oskar hätte Grund zum Weinen genug gehabt. Galt es nicht, die Schwester Dorothea, eine lange vergeb-liche Nacht auf einem noch längeren Kokosläufer davonzuspülen? Und meine Maria, bot sie mir nicht Anlaß zur Klage? Ging ihr Chef, der Stenzel, nicht ein und aus in der Bilker Wohnung? Sagte das Kurtchen, mein Sohn, nicht zu dem Feinkosthändler und nebenberuflichen Karnevalisten zuerst 'Onkel Stenzel', dann 'Papa Stenzel'? Und hinter meiner Maria, lagen sie da nicht unterm fernen lockeren Sand des Friedhofes Saspe, unterm Lehm des Friedhofes Brentau: meine arme Mama, der törichte Jan Bronski, der Koch Matzerath, der Gefühle nur in Suppen ausdrücken konnte?–Sie alle galt es zu beweinen. (p. 655)

There is a significant movement from the third person of the opening two sentences through the impersonal 'galt es' into the first person, which, as in the 'Mama konnte sehr lustig sein' (p. 194) passage, is the language of true feeling. He then reverts to the impersonal 'galt es' and finally to the third person again. It is as if the drum enables him to find his way back to 'die eigene nackte Sprache' (p. 650) which so astounds the guests of the 'Zwiebelkeller'. It is always by going back to the linguistic simplicity, even the non-verbality of childhood that Oskar achieves his most vibrant use of language. The virtuoso wordplay seems to spring forth from those numbed opening sentences of the 'Mama konnte sehr lustig sein' passage (p. 194) as if by returning to the purity and gen-uine feeling of childhood Oskar is able to free his present-day lan-guage. This, like the return to the drum before writing, is a kind of individual 'Stunde Null'. Oskar's aim apparently parallels Wolf's later attempts to find a language in which 'ich, du und sie' will become one coherent unity again and, if he fails to achieve it, then it is for similar reasons: the language of childhood is largely non-verbal, one of sensation, but one which can only be transmitted to us by literary description.

Oskar is forced to use a language which is not naturally his own, but in a rather different way from Siggi or the narrator of *Kindheitsmuster*. In both those works the authors chose to adopt an essentially adult tone to convey the vision and perspective of childhood, possibly because they feared the charge of intellectual dishonesty which greets any attempt to write in the authentic language of the child. Oskar, paradoxically, is at his least genuine when he attempts to use the literary conventions of the child's language, and this perhaps implies Grass's realization that there *is* no literary language of childhood, but that childhood has its own language of sensation and emotion. It is not simply that Oskar is a pseudo-child in every way, an adult writer who attempts to maintain the illusion of the child's limited perspective and language, yet also deliberately shatters that same illusion: through him Grass also exposes the artificiality of literary conventions regarding the portrayal of childhood.

Grass has a very different agenda from most of the authors in this chapter, for while they show a genuine concern to retain the integrity of either the child's vision, the child's language or both, and sometimes a 'realistic' concern to show linguistic development, Grass treats these concerns in a very cavalier manner, preferring the parodic and the grotesque modes. Moreover, *Die Blechtrommel* differs from conventional child accounts in that it records momentous historical events like the *Kristallnacht* and the attack on the 'polnische Post' rather than sticking realistically to the child's usually limited horizon. These stylistic and thematic points indicate that, unlike the other children, Oskar is principally a means rather than an end: whereas in the other narratives there is a psychological interest in the children as well as in the events they experience, we cannot talk about Oskar as a character. His language, like everything else about him, is an artificial construct created for a specific literary purpose, namely to shock and to alienate the reading public in order to confront them directly with the events of the Third Reich.[60] With Oskar Grass both asserted the possibility of portraying the Third Reich through the child's perspective and went further than any of his successors. For while later narratives using the child's perspective and language may leave suggestive gaps for the attentive reader to fill, Oskar's

---

[60] For an alternative reading of Oskar's ludic nature, see André Fischer, *Inszenierte Naivität: Zur ästhetischen Simulation von Geschichte bei Günter Grass, Albert Drach und Walter Kempowski* (Munich, 1992), 95–213. Fischer regards Oskar's grotesque, naive perspective as a means of undermining traditional modes of writing about history as though it had some inherent meaning.

defiant 'ignorance' provokes the reader into providing the missing information. It is no wonder he met with such a mixed reception from the reading public of 1959: not only did he apparently subvert the idealized image of childhood to which German readers had been accustomed since the Romantic era, but his language accused and disorientated the reader in almost equal measure. His frequent addresses to his public and the haunting refrain of the 'schwarze Köchin', 'Du bist schuld und du bist schuld und du am allermeisten' (p. 730) not only held up a mirror to the public, but also accused them of creating him in their image, just as Siggi Jepsen was to do later. This is Kuhn's menacing child par excellence,[61] and certainly he is not the kind of witness to whom an audience could listen without being shaken out of their 'Wirtschaftswunder' complacency. Like Jo, Oskar is the living proof that there has been something very rotten in this state.

I began this chapter with a child witness from English literature, and will end with another who is an ironically extreme case, the apparently quite acceptable child witness Emily, in Hughes's *A High Wind in Jamaica*. What none of the adults at the trial knows is that Emily is actually guilty of the murder for which the accused are being tried. They therefore attribute the 10-year-old's reluctance to testify to a lack of memory and to the affection which has grown up between her and her erstwhile captors. Her lawyer says frankly: 'It's bad enough having a child in the box anyway . . .– You can never count on them. They say what they think you want them to say. And then they say what they think the opposing counsel wants them to say too–if they like his face'.[62] To overcome this difficulty Emily is trained to give the appropriate responses as in a 'Shorter Catechism' and, while Mathias thinks she is 'a most valuable witness', this is largely due to the effect his words will have when they come out of her mouth.[63] The pirates are wrongly convicted of murder on her evidence, and her value as a witness, in saying precisely what the adults want her to say, is confirmed. Even when her authentic voice breaks through in her

---

[61] *Corruption in Paradise*, 30–44. These children tend to be silent enigmas with whom the adult world cannot communicate. This alone can make them menacing, but the examples Kuhn quotes also demonstrate flaws in the adult world.

[62] *High Wind in Jamaica*, 185.   [63] Ibid. 187.

hysterical, almost incoherent sobbing under cross-examination, her hysterics are misinterpreted by those in the courtroom. None of the adults really want to hear the truth of Emily's experience: they hear what they want to hear, partly because it does not occur to them that a child can be less than innocent, partly because they have a fixed agenda they want to complete. The child witness is putty in the hands of the adult court. The child narrators we have examined differ from Emily in that they refuse to be manipulated in this way: whether their testimony is given in the authentic tones of childhood or not, it is an accurate reflection of their experience. However, it is for the reader to decide whether the witness is 'valuable' or whether it should be 'put aside'. Perhaps as far as child witnesses are concerned, the jury is still out.

5

CONCLUSION

Der Mensch spielt nur, wo er in voller Bedeutung des Worts
Mensch ist, und *er ist nur da ganz Mensch, wo er spielt.*

Schiller, *Über die Ästhetische Erziehung des Menschen*
(*Werke*, xx. 359)

When Adrian Leverkühn expresses doubts about becoming a
composer 'weil ich mir die robuste Naivität absprechen muß, die,
soviel ich sehe, unter anderem, und nicht zuletzt, zum Künstler-
tum gehört' (*Mann, Doktor Faustus*, 178) he is aligning himself with a
modern artistic mentality. As Robertson points out, this statement
echoes Schiller's *Über naive und sentimentalische Dichtung*, an essay
whose influence can be traced in Mann's *Schwere Stunde* (1905) as
well as *Doktor Faustus*.[1] There are similarities between Mann's depiction of Schiller and Adrian: both are essentially intellectual
and self-disciplined artists and Adrian's desire for 'robuste Naivität' is prefigured by Schiller's envy of the ultimate 'naiv' poet *'den*
dort, in Weimar, den er mit einer sehnsüchtigen Feindschaft
liebte...' (*Werke*, viii. 377). But it is clear that Adrian has gone
beyond the creative process evoked in *Schwere Stunde*. Mann
clearly admires Schiller's intellectual rigour and self-discipline
which look forward to Adrian, but the demonic pact clearly
invests Adrian with a different and more ambiguous dimension.

Initially Adrian uses modernist techniques to produce an art
which despises the concept of mere inspiration and does not
derive from any ethical impulse. Inspiration can only be restored
to him by his disease/pact with the Devil, but this restoration of
one aspect associated with 'robuste Naivität' clearly does not
restore the other element associated with it, namely ethical or
humane values. The pact heralds an artistic breakthrough, but the

---

[1] 'Accounting for History: Thomas Mann, *Doktor Faustus*', in David Midgley (ed.),
The German Novel in the Twentieth Century: Beyond Realism (Edinburgh and New York,
1993), 131. Mann greatly admired Schiller's essay; see T. J. Reed, *Thomas Mann: The Uses
of Tradition* (2nd edn., Oxford, 1996), 139.

whole basis of Adrian's life and art is questioned as powerfully as it is briefly by the arrival of his nephew Echo.

Echo is a curious figure. Zeitblom's description of his arrival at Pfeiffering already invests him with an other-worldly aura, and while we can easily dismiss the villagers' reactions to the boy as those of uneducated peasants[2] and Zeitblom defensively refers to his own perception of the child as 'Schwärmerei' (*Doktor Faustus*, 619) this does not account for the way the much more reserved Adrian is captivated by the child, nor indeed for Mann's own reference to the 'Geschichte des Gotteskindes' (*Gesammelte Werke*, xi. 162). Mann's letter of 6 May 1943 to Bruno Walter[3] and the references to his grandson Frido in *Die Entstehung des Doktor Faustus* (1949) make it clear that Echo is drawn from life, though as Hagen points out, it is life as viewed by an adoring grandfather.[4] As Pütz indicates, there are perfectly rational explanations for Echo's quaint speech and other-worldly behaviour: his archaic speech has been influenced by his father's 'mit stehengebliebenaltdeutschen Ausdrücken von eigentümlich feierlichem Klange durchsetzte schweizerische Redeweise'; his self-possession and unconscious confidence in his power to charm his elders can be attributed to the fact that he is the indulged youngest of four children; his quiet manner and delicate appearance go back to his severe bout of measles; and his attractive physical appearance seems to be a genetic benefit from his parents, who have produced four 'schmucke Geschöpfe' (*Doktor Faustus*, 247).[5] Yet the boy's arrival in Pfeiffering is described so as to evoke a 'Besuch aus niedlicher Klein- und Feinwelt' (p. 611), a sphere beyond the human. We might attribute this simply to Zeitblom's tendency to myth-making but, as Hagen points out, Zeitblom was not present when Echo arrived;[6] he notes 'Adrian hat mir die Szene geschildert' and goes on to say 'Trotzdem war einem bei seinem

---

[2] Peter Pütz notes that the villagers' reactions to Echo are ironized (*Kunst und Künstlerexistenz bei Nietzsche und Thomas Mann: Zum Problem des ästhetischen Perspektivismus in der Moderne* (2nd edn., Bonn, 1975), 141).

[3] In *Blätter der Thomas Mann Gesellschaft*, ix (Zurich, 1969), 24–5.

[4] See *Kinder*, 111–15 for a discussion of Thomas Mann's and Victor Hugo's literary presentation of their respective grandchildren. Hagen contends that Mann only took those elements from real life that fitted his 'Kinder-Klischee' (ibid. 114) and that his presentation of this child shows him at his least realistic.

[5] *Kunst und Künstlerexistenz*, 143.   [6] *Kinder*, 29.

Anblick nicht anders, als sähe man ein Elfenprinzchen' (p. 611). This is ambiguous, for it is not clear how far Zeitblom is quoting Adrian and how far he is embellishing his friend's account; however, the detail and the tone of this description suggest that even the reserved Adrian was immediately captivated by the child's other-worldly nature. Echo is the direct antithesis of his uncle, whose evident affection suggests a nostalgia for childhood innocence. Moreover, his comments about 'robuste Naivität' suggest a longing for the kind of art associated with it.

As long as Echo survives there is hope for both Adrian's soul and his art: for Zeitblom the boy recalls the Christ child (p. 619) and Adrian notes the way his prayers intercede for others (p. 626). And it is only when his nephew is dying that Adrian finally rejects the bourgeois-humanist canon and all it represents when he announces to Zeitblom that he intends to 'zurücknehmen' the ultimate symbol of 'das Menschliche', Beethoven's Ninth Symphony (p. 634). The child's death thus apparently sets the seal on Adrian's fate: it both suggests his damnation and apparently confirms him in a conception of art that has no ethical or humane basis.[7]

Doktor Faustus occupies an important place in post-war German literature: not only was it one of the first major novels to appear after the war, but it also reflects consciously on the role of art. As Robertson points out, it presents an interaction of myth, modernism, and realism: the modernist artist Adrian plays out a version of the Faust myth within Zeitblom's realist narrative.[8] To these categories I should like to add that of the 'naive' represented by Echo. This might suggest a rather sorry state of German art; as Robertson points out, myth had been discredited by the way it had been exploited by the Nazis and Adrian's modernist ideas are suspect for, as a manuscript note makes clear, Mann saw a possible link between them and the political catastrophe against which *Doktor Faustus* is set.[9] Nor does the conventional realist narrative fare much better, for Zeitblom, at least initially, is a sadly inadequate narrator when faced with such events. As for Echo, he, like other children, is 'aus zartem Stoff . . . gar leicht für giftige Einflüsse empfänglich...' (p. 633). The question being posed

---

[7] This connection between Echo and the artistic tradition is pointed out in Pütz, *Kunst und Künstlerexistenz*, 147.   [8] 'Accounting for History', 128.
[9] Ibid. Reed, *Thomas Mann*, 374.

in 1947 was apparently whether art was still possible. The fact that Mann had written *Doktor Faustus* in the first place suggests his own answer; as he wrote to Kerényi in 1947:

Klage ist ja ein recht aktueller Ausdrucksgehalt, finden Sie nicht? Es sieht böse aus . . . Und doch, ein Werk, und sei es eines der Verzweiflung, kann immer nur den Optimismus, den Glauben ans Leben zur letzten Substanz haben—wie es ja mit der Verzweiflung eine besondere Sache ist: sie trägt die Transzendenz zur Hoffnung schon in sich selbst.[10]

But Mann also referred to *Doktor Faustus* as a 'novel to end all novels' (*Gesammelte Werke*, xi. 205).[11] The fusion of different forms indicated by Robertson shows that the novel had gone beyond the traditional realistic form[12] and therefore a second question still remained: if art was still possible, then what *kind* of art?

If Echo represents an artistic category, then his fate might suggest that the childlike or the naive has no place in post-war German fiction. And this may seem valid in an age when more traditional critics have bemoaned the extreme self-consciousness and unnecessary complexity of the modern novel, some going so far as to 'unravel' the plots for bewildered readers.[13] Yet the concept of the childlike is central to post-war German writing, and not just because the child is a prominent figure in post-war literature.[14] The state of being childlike or approaching reality from a childlike perspective is also much to the fore, as Bance points out when he notes the predominance of childlike characters in post-war fiction who, 'by their quest for self and for values, re-assert a positive acceptance of life'.[15] This suggests a similar situation to that in the Romantic era, when the state of being 'kindlich' was as important to writers as actually being a child. Moreover, Bance implicitly recognizes a fundamental duality to the post-war use of the child figure when he notes that it represents the artist's sense of

---

[10] Quoted from Christa Wolf, *Voraussetzungen einer Erzählung: Kassandra: Frankfurter Poetik-Vorlesungen* (1983; Frankfurt, 1988), 105.

[11] See Reed, *The Novel and the Nazi Past*, 97 on this point.

[12] Robertson, 'Accounting for History', 128.

[13] Mary E. Stewart makes this point of Uwe Johnson's *Mutmaßungen über Jakob* whose publication was followed by 'a rash of "keys" and chronologies . . . trying to disentangle who said what and when!' ('A Dialogic Reality: Uwe Johnson, *Mutmaßungen über Jakob*', in Midgley, *German Novel in the Twentieth Century*, 165.)

[14] See Jens, 'Erwachsene Kinder'. Bance picks up this point with specific reference to German literature in *German Novel 1945–1960*, 30–1 and 40.   [15] Ibid. 30.

'frustration and powerlessness with regard to the world around him';[16] as in the Romantic era, then, the child seems to embody both the problem and the solution.

An author's idea of the childlike need have very little to do with real children: so much has been clear from *Über naive und sentimentalische Dichtung* onwards.[17] And in taking *Doktor Faustus* as my starting point I am not proposing quite such a simplistic schema as Adrian the modernist v. Echo the naive for, as Kuhn indicates, Echo's reflexive name suggests a degree of self-consciousness as does 'sein selbstverständlich von Koketterie und Wissen um seinen Zauber nicht ganz freies Lächeln' (*Doktor Faustus*, 611).[18] This is no real surprise, for we have seen the child used in several very self-conscious novels in this study. German literature immediately after the war may seem obviously childlike to the point of simplistic: the 'Stunde Null' and 'Kahlschlag', simply the desire to start again, reducing everything, language included, to its barest essentials and limiting art to the description of concrete detail as in the short stories of Borchert and Böll. But such *Trümmerliteratur* was an aesthetic necessity rather than a virtue and writers had to move beyond it into a world where all could not be described in such black and white terms. The child perspectives on the Third Reich that we have examined vary enormously as regards the degree of their naivety, but they are united in their ethical dimension. The child itself does not have to be an obviously moral figure, as Oskar Matzerath makes clear: its complete acceptance of Nazism as normality is usually enough to show rather than tell us that the Third Reich was an evil period. But while Nazism and the immediate post-war era had provided a moral focal point on which writers could agree, the social and moral issues of the later post-war era were less clear cut. Helmut Heißenbüttel touched on this problem in his essay 'Schwierigkeiten beim Schreiben der Wahrheit 1964', an answer to Brecht's earlier 'Fünf Schwierigkeiten beim Schreiben der Wahrheit' (1935). Brecht had argued that literature's function was to assert 'Wahrheit' against 'Unwahrheit' where the 'Wahrheit' is repressed by political conditions, but Heißenbüttel argued that social conditions had now changed: 'Heute, wo alles gemischt erscheint, läßt sich nicht einfach mehr

---

[16] Ibid. 40.

[17] Boas, *Cult of Childhood*, 72.

[18] Kuhn, *Corruption in Paradise*, 189–90.

sagen, daß ich die Wahrheit schreibe, wenn ich die Unwahrheit bekämpfe'.[19] Moreover, the emphasis in what people are writing about has changed: many are more interested in discovering the truth about themselves than in social systems and, whatever people choose to write about, there is also the problem of 'richtiges Schreiben überhaupt', 'der Zweifel, ob überhaupt noch sagbar ist, was gesagt werden kann'.[20] The social and thus the literary climate had changed: the moral certainty regarding the Third Reich had given way to the uncertainty of writers confronted with more contentious political and social events.

This uncertainty is mirrored in many novels of the post-war era, an age when the individual faced large, impersonal social systems. The consequent sense of vulnerability is clear from the choice of narrators and focalizers, who often frankly admit that they are unsure about the events they are presenting. It is clear that many of these adult narrators are more aware of their unreliability than the child narrator of the Third Reich who knows of no other value system. What links the two types of narrator, however, is a degree of ignorance, whether it is perceived by the character or only by the reader, and by the sense of vulnerability that attends this lack of certainty. The titles speak for themselves: Johnson's *Mutmaßungen über Jakob* (1959), *Das dritte Buch über Achim* (1961), and *Zwei Ansichten* (1965) all suggest the impossibility of any one person or book presenting the complete truth about a person, event, or political system; Böll's *Ansichten eines Clowns* and Wolf's *Nachdenken über Christa T.* have the same tentative ring; and *Amanda: Ein Hexenroman* (1983) is ostensibly only written because the narrator, Beatriz de Dia, does not believe Morgner has given a full presentation of Laura Salman's character in the earlier *Leben und Abenteuer der Trobadora Beatriz* (1974). Most of these novels have an open form to match their tentative titles, and the preference for an episodic form, as seen especially in Wolf and Morgner, or a fragmentary, polyphonic narrative where the authority of the narrative voice is substantially reduced, as in Johnson, again reflects post-war writers' more questioning approach to reality and their

---

[19] In Otto F. Best and Hans-Jürgen Schmitt (eds.), *Die deutsche Literatur: Ein Abriß in Text und Darstellung*, xvi. *Gegenwart*, ed. Gerhard R. Kaiser (rev. and expanded edn., Stuttgart, 1983), 33.

[20] Ibid. 34.

interest in an individual, subjective truth rather than something universally valid. The political and aesthetic climate might be summed up by that most forward-looking of Fontane's characters, Dubslav von Stechlin: 'Unanfechtbare Wahrheiten gibt es überhaupt nicht, und wenn es welche gibt, so sind sie langweilig'.[21]

As we saw in the Introduction, the defamiliarizing perspective is not confined to the child narrative and nor is the naive perspective an invention of the post-war period. The naive character and his or her point of view have been used for centuries to point up flaws in the social and moral order. It is clear from the cases of Parzival and Simplicissimus that naivety had implied exclusion or withdrawal from mainstream society well before Rousseau; however, Rousseau's work consolidated the perception of society as a corrupting influence and created an image of the child as the pure individual who is deformed by it. Schiller's later definition of naivety as 'eine *Kindlichkeit, wo sie nicht mehr erwartet wird*' (*Werke*, xx. 419) meant that any naive or unsocialized perspective could be associated with the childlike, as for example in Goethe's *Die Wahlverwandtschaften* (1809) where Ottilie is frequently referred to as 'das Kind', both by other characters and the narrator, and her pre-socialized mode of thought gives her a distinctive view of the moral entanglements she is involved in. Given that naivety is virtually defined by an exclusion from society it is no surprise that authors presenting the Nazi era and the 'Wirtschaftswunder' frequently use the perspective of characters who have either been sidelined by society or have refused to accept its mores: hence the frequency with which the prison and the madhouse appear in this literature.[22]

The perspective from 'outside' or 'beneath' the normal social environment became more frequent as the novel freed itself from earlier constraints. This relatively young genre had for a long time been regarded as a second-rate form: Schiller had referred to the 'Romanschreiber' as the poet's 'Halbbruder' (*Werke*, xx. 462). Thus nineteenth-century novelists tended to use traditional forms and techniques, apparently aimed at enhancing the artistic and moral respectability of the genre. These included the omniscient

---

[21] *Der Stechlin*, in *Werke*, v. 10.
[22] See Ziolkowski 'View from the Madhouse', in *Dimensions of the Modern Novel*, 332–61.

narrator, a figure who was usually, as in the case of Fontane, well integrated in his society and reflected its mores; the traditional form of the *Bildungsroman*, which was supposed to improve as well as entertain its reader; and the epistolary novel, which was usually prefaced with a note certifying its complete authenticity and so exculpating it from any suspicion of fantasy or indeed lies. The twentieth century, however, has seen a process which we might call a 'democratization' of the novel, by which a number of new narrator types have been enfranchised. Naturalism had made the widespread literary use of the working class possible and by 1929 Döblin was breaking new ground with *Berlin Alexanderplatz*, focalized through the perspective of a proletarian, indeed criminal. Even before that, Mann's *Buddenbrooks* had demonstrated the flexibility of narrative focalization by moving from omniscient narration reminiscent of the nineteenth century to Hanno's perspective. In the post-war novel these earlier tentative experiments begin to blossom as women, antisocial elements, and children start to emerge as focalizers and narrators. As early as 1961 Jens noted a disturbing element in this more flexible approach to narrative perspective when he mourned the death of the 'positiver Held', asking 'spiegeln nicht nur noch der Blinde, der Irre, der Krüppel, der Roboter und Décadent als verläßliche Zeugen die aus den Fugen geratene Welt?'[23] This shift may be due in part to historical events: as we saw in *Doktor Faustus*, the old style of bourgeois-humanist narrative is not in itself adequate to describing the events of the Third Reich. There is a rebellious, even subversive, spirit abroad in post-war German writing: Donna K. Reed suggests that the way political authority had been discredited by recent events had a knock-on effect in the aesthetic realm immediately after World War II, with authors tending to opt for open literary forms as a rebellious response to the ideological indoctrination they had suffered.[24] It was time for a new beginning but, more than that, for a view of recent German history from a different perspective, that of the victims. We see this strategy in Borchert's *Draußen vor der Tür*, where the 'Gasmaskenbrille' motif makes it clear that we are seeing everything through the delirium of Unteroffizier Beckmann, or in Böll's short stories, for example the collection *Wanderer*,

[23] *Deutsche Literatur der Gegenwart: Themen, Stile, Tendenzen* (Munich, 1961), 36.
[24] *The Novel and the Nazi Past*, 110–11.

kommst du nach Spa... (1950). And while Jens may have regarded some of the later manifestations of the 'alternative' perspective as somewhat disturbing, the emphasis on the child is not merely an extreme but also a very positive example of this syndrome.

But the defamiliarizing perspective that appears so frequently in the post-war novel as a means of social criticism is not the only feature of post-war writing to recall the child, for social critique has not been the novel's only function. To an extent the very tone of many modern novels is childlike: one of the novels that most resoundingly endorsed the female narrative perspective, *Leben und Abenteuer der Trobadora Beatriz*, is a prime example in its initial fairy-tale motif (the magic sleep of Dornröschen) and its refusal to conform to any traditional concept of realistic plausibility. The same may be said of Grass's *Der Butt* (1977), an imaginative reworking of the Grimms' *Märchen* 'Von dem Fischer un syner Fru' where the Protean narrator travels in time from the Stone Age to the present in a series of role plays which read like the transcription of a child's game.[25] The *Märchen* element is important because this form is traditionally the repository of oral culture and therefore gives the 'underside' of history; equally of course it is the literary form most readily associated with children. Such novels demand readers who are prepared to 'mitspielen', rather than to interpret,[26] to enter an independent reality where the only limits are set by the author's imagination. Nor is this self-contained quality confined to fantastic narratives. Uwe Johnson wrote of the representation of reality in his novels: 'Es ist nicht eine Gesellschaft in der Miniatur, und es ist kein maß-stäbliches Modell. Es ist auch nicht ein Spiegel der Welt und weiterhin nicht ihre Widerspiegelung; es ist eine Welt, gegen die Welt zu halten.'[27]

---

[25] See Bance, *German Novel 1945–1960*, 40 on the rediscovery of art as play (quoted in the Introduction, above). Jens had made a similar point about the impotence of art when he highlighted the importance of parody in contemporary literature, referring to the 20th cent. as 'die hohe Zeit des Stil-Esperantos', where authors try out all sorts of styles but cannot settle on a single one: 'Es ist alles verfügbar; nie war die Kunst so ohnmächtig-mächtig wie heute' (*Deutsche Literatur der Gegenwart*, 14).

[26] Bruno Hillebrand makes this distinction with reference to the post-modern reader's response to Italo Calvino's novel *Se una notte d'inverno un viaggiatore* (1979), in *Theorie des Romans: Erzählstrategien der Neuzeit* (3rd expanded edn., Stuttgart and Weimar, 1993), 478.

[27] 'Vorschläge zur Prüfung eines Romans', in Eberhard Lämmert et al. (eds.), *Romantheorie: Dokumentation ihrer Geschichte in Deutschland seit 1800* (2nd edn., Königstein/Ts., 1984), 402–3.

This quality of Johnson's work recalls the child narrative for, although their polyphonic and lacunary nature may suggest uncertainty and ignorance, his texts are complete in their own terms. This is the more self-conscious playfulness for which Echo seems such an appropriate symbol: the narrators or focalizers may be naive to varying degrees, but the art itself clearly is not.

Even before such fantastic novels as *Leben und Abenteuer der Trobadora Beatriz* and *Der Butt*, however, German-speaking writers had been turning away from the idea of literature as purely a means of social critique, a mood swing exemplified by the provocative titles of Peter Handke's essays 'Die Literatur ist romantisch' (1966) and 'Ich bin ein Bewohner des Elfenbeinturms' (1967). Having railed against the 'Beschreibungsimpotenz' of the Gruppe 47 at its 1966 Princeton meeting,[28] Handke went on to make his position abundantly clear when he wrote: 'Es interessiert mich als Autor übrigens gar nicht, die Wirklichkeit zu zeigen oder zu bewältigen, sondern es geht mir darum, *meine* Wirklichkeit zu zeigen.'[29] During the 1960s authors like Handke and Peter Weiss had been experimenting with literary possibilities in a way which may now seem childlike in the least positive sense of the word. Weiss's *Der Schatten des Körpers des Kutschers* (1960), for example, is written in 'Registrationsprosa' from a self-consciously very limited perspective, with the most minute details of everyday activities recorded so as to produce a defamiliarizing slow-motion effect. But while this novel and parts of Handke's *Die Hornissen* (1966) with its minute description of such everyday activities as getting dressed may be fascinatingly defamiliarizing, there is clearly a limit to how far one can go with such essentially self-contained narrative, and indeed to its interest for the reader.[30] Handke himself later assessed *Die Hornissen* very negatively[31] and moved on to use different techniques in line with his dictum: 'Eine Möglichkeit besteht für mich jeweils nur einmal. Die Nachahmung dieser Möglichkeit ist dann schon unmöglich. Ein

---

[28] See 'Zur Tagung der Gruppe 47 in USA' (1966), in Handke, *Ich bin ein Bewohner des Elfenbeinturms* (Frankfurt, 1972).

[29] Title essay, in *Ich bin ein Bewohner des Elfenbeinturms*, 25.

[30] Id., *Die Hornissen: Roman* (Frankfurt, 1966), 65–7.

[31] Gretel A. Koskella, *Die Krise des deutschen Romans 1960–1970* (Frankfurt, 1986), 97.

Modell der Darstellung, ein zweites Mal angewendet, ergibt keine Neuigkeit mehr, höchstens eine Variation'.[32]

However, the preoccupation with literature, not as a description of external reality but as a linguistic construct, was to remain dominant for some time. In Weiss and Handke the concern with language, while expressed very differently, was intimately bound up with the search for and development of the individual identity; like Max Frisch's Stiller, they are intent on finding a 'Sprache für meine Wirklichkeit'.[33] Weiss's linguistic concerns may be traced to his exile experience during the Third Reich, which caused a lasting preoccupation with 'die Sprache, die ich am Anfang meines Lebens gelernt hatte, die natürliche Sprache, die mein Werkzeug war, die nur noch mir selbst gehörte, und mit dem Land, in dem ich aufgewachsen war, nichts mehr zu tun hatte', that of his childhood.[34] However, this interest is generally expressed thematically rather than technically. Handke is more interested in illuminating language itself,[35] in defamiliarizing both it and the reality it seeks to describe in order to experience both in a more authentic and personal way. His preoccupation with a fresh and spontaneous language appears mainly on the level of characters like Bloch in *Die Angst des Tormanns beim Elfmeter* (1970) and Keuschnig in *Die Stunde der wahren Empfindung* (1975) who both attempt to build a new relationship with language and thus with reality. Bloch and Keuschnig both reach a point where society's language is meaningless to them; this is reflected in the way Handke puts inverted commas around perfectly comprehensible words in *Die Angst des Tormanns beim Elfmeter* or capitalizes similarly self-evident words in *Die Stunde der wahren Empfindung*.[36] Eventually Bloch's alienation from conventional language reaches such a pitch that at one point his view from the window is transcribed in a series of pictures.[37] These strategies recall those used

---

[32] Title essay, in *Ich bin ein Bewohner des Elfenbeinturms,* 20.

[33] *Stiller: Roman* (repr. Frankfurt, 1973), 84.

[34] *Fluchtpunkt,* in *Werke,* ii. 293–4. See also his essay *Laokoon oder über die Grenzen der Sprache* (1965), in id., *Rapporte* (Frankfurt, 1968).

[35] For a detailed discussion of this theme, see Gunther Sergooris, *Peter Handke und die Sprache* (Bonn, 1979).

[36] *Die Angst des Tormanns beim Elfmeter: Erzählung* (Frankfurt, 1970), 117; and *Die Stunde der wahren Empfindung* (Frankfurt, 1975), 78–80.

[37] *Angst des Tormanns,* 117.

in the child narratives we have examined: the inverted commas or capital letters to highlight words reminds us of the way Gert Hofmann uses italics for words that are comprehensible to an adult reader but not to the child narrator, while the use of pictures is an extreme form of the kind of pictorial narrative used by the likes of Lenz. However, while in Lenz's work it is used as a sign of linguistic inadequacy, in Handke's work it is a return to the beginning in the hope of being able to start afresh.

Handke is thus caught in a similar trap to the writers of child narratives as discussed in Chapter 4 for, while his characters apparently doubt that society's language can adequately express their personal experiences, Handke cannot transcribe Bloch's experiences in pictures any more than Joyce could write all of *A Portrait of the Artist as a Young Man* in the child's own language. Both writers need an idiom which is comprehensible to their public in order to communicate, and thus even the most sceptical writer implicitly affirms the power of conventional language as he writes.[38]

This concern with an individual language is closely linked to the discovery of the self. The fact that language can be used to indoctrinate and facilitate mob-thinking had been amply demonstrated by the Third Reich, but even the ordinary socialization process as effected through language began to be portrayed as pernicious, for example in Handke's play *Kaspar* (1967), where the pre-socialized figure is used to demonstrate the powerful socializing effect of language. By this time writers were particularly interested in the individual and its subjective truth. Thus began the search for the self at its most intrinsic, as exemplified in Wolf, Weiss, Handke, and particularly in Frisch. For, although his narrator in *Mein Name sei Gantenbein* (1964) states that this is not the era for 'Ich-Geschichten',[39] Frisch's novels *Stiller* (1954), *Homo Faber* (1957), and *Mein Name sei Gantenbein* all seem to concentrate on the possibilities evoked in the second half of that same statement: 'Und doch vollzieht sich das menschliche Leben oder verfehlt sich am einzelnen Ich, nirgends sonst'.[40] In *Homo Faber* modern man is landed unceremoniously in the wilderness and has to cope without the props of modern civilization to lend him an identity; in *Stiller* and *Mein Name sei Gantenbein* the narrators play with

---

[38] Sergooris, *Peter Handke*, 86.
[39] *Mein Name sei Gantenbein: Roman* (repr. Frankfurt, 1975), 62.   [40] Ibid. 62.

different fictional identities in an attempt to find the intrinsic self before it was conditioned by society. Stiller longs to withdraw into a pre-socialized state where society cannot impinge on his personality and where his acts have no consequences for anyone else; like Oskar and Siggi, he is only 'free' to enjoy this state, and then only to a limited degree, when in prison. The search is for the child within, who, like the gypsy child Christa T. so admires, can say 'ICH bin anders'.[41] This is the ultimate Romantic understanding of the self, implying not arrogant belief in one's own superiority but a belief in the inherent difference and therefore value of the individual. It takes us back to Rousseau's 'Si je ne vaux pas mieux, au moins je suis autre'.[42]

Quite apart from the number of children who appear in its pages, post-war German literature seems to be preoccupied by the childlike, both thematically and technically. Of course, the idea of art being childlike is not confined to the post-war era: Boas and Schaub both point to the prevalence of this idea in the earlier twentieth century and the epigraph to this chapter shows that it has a longer history than this.[43] Boas is sceptical about the critical acclaim given to primitivist artists who exploit the 'child's' or 'innocent' eye, asking 'with what crime has the adult artist been charged?'[44] However, German writing of the post-war era is not childlike in the primitivist sense he is discussing: the predominance of the childlike is hardly an escape into a false simplicity, an attempt to evade the real issues of the post-war world, for just as novels with child narrators can confront us with the reality of Third Reich, so these novels are often anything but simple. The interest in the childlike can be explained by the association between the artist and the child, for the child is symbolic of the artistic tenor of the post-war era just as it is of the Romantic period. Its vulnerability and uncertainty and its difficulty in expressing itself and discovering its true identity unencumbered by adult prejudices, taboos, and restrictions are reflected in many modern novels narrated by adults. But this picture need not be as depressing as it seems for, if the problems faced by the modern writer are

---

[41] Wolf, *Nachdenken über Christa T.*, 28.
[42] *Les Confessions*, ed. Ernest Seillière, 3 vols. (Paris, 1929), i.1.
[43] Boas, *Cult of Childhood*, esp. 94–102; Schaub, *Génie Enfant*, 1.
[44] *Cult of Childhood*, 92.

neatly expressed in the child figure, then so are the solutions. I have frequently referred to writers' belief in the child's extraordinary resilience, its ability to retain moral integrity and clear-sightedness even under unfavourable conditions, and its capacity for resisting the constraints and taboos of the adult world, positive ideals which writers also claim to pursue. This too can be traced back to the Romantics: as Kind points out, in Schlegel's *Lucinde* (1799) the narrator excuses the 'Freyheit und Frechheit' of his writings by using the example of 'die unschuldige kleine Wilhelmine',[45] whose uninhibited, spontaneous behaviour is the 'Ideal, welches ich mir stets vor Augen halten will'.[46] Schlegel argues that his novel is like a child whose excesses are excusable as mere high spirits, and this image is echoed in the twentieth century by Uwe Johnson's contention that the novel must entertain us like 'ein spielendes Kind'.[47] The emphasis seems to be on exuberance and, in Schlegel's image, a 'beneidenswürdige Freyheit von Vorurtheilen', on the child's daring and readiness to accept a challenge simply because it is not constrained by adult prudence.[48] Both the negative and the positive connotations of the child figure traced above in the Romantic era seem to characterize novels of our own age and to point a way forward for literature even at a time when the German social and political climate looked so unstable. The child can embrace artists' feelings of uncertainty and vulnerability and yet provide a sense of certainty and set of values beyond them. It is this mentality that allows art to continue even under the most difficult social and political conditions.

The childlike element in modern German literature is important in a very broad sense for, if the reassertion of the positive myth of childhood reaffirms the German belief in the artist, then the dominance of the childlike in literature reasserts the belief in culture as a means of preserving human values. All art may be childlike in a purely aesthetic sense, but the post-war preoccupation with the child and the childlike carries ethical implications

---

[45] *Lucinde: Vertraute Briefe über Lucinde von Friedrich Schleiermacher*, ed. Rudolf Frank (Leipzig, 1907), 61.

[46] Ibid. 64. This passage is discussed in Kind, *Kind*, 37–8. Like Echo, Wilhelmine should not be taken as a symbol of the purely 'naive'. For a discussion of the way she embodies Schlegel's poetology, esp. his conception of irony, and his attitude towards it, see Simonis, *Kindheit in Romanen um 1800*, 197–210.

[47] 'Vorschläge zur Prüfung eines Romans', 403.   [48] *Lucinde*, 65.

which go back to the conception of naivety in *Über naive und sentimentalische Dichtung*. The Romantic myth of the child equated it with both the artist and the saviour; equally, German culture, which had been no less dragged through the mud by the Nazis than the myth of the child, had previously been considered the great guarantor of humane values. Writers felt the need to begin again after World War II, not just because the Nazis had perverted their culture, but because the cultural life of which they had been justifiably proud had failed to prevent this political catastrophe in the first place. In Peter Weiss's novel *Die Ästhetik des Widerstands* (1975; 1978; 1981) Funk sums up this disillusionment with German art when he evokes the heady years of the Weimar Republic:

Es waren nicht nur die Werke eines Piscator, Brecht, Weill und Eisler, eines Grosz, Dix, Schlemmer, Nolde, Beckmann und Klee, eines Döblin, Musil, Broch, Jahnn oder Benjamin, es war die gesamte Atmosphäre aus Vitalität, aus unbegrenzter Phantasie, aus Lust am Experimentieren, die das kulturelle Leben ausmachte, . . . Wie aber konnte geschehn, . . . daß zugleich mit diesem kulturellen Aufstieg das Niedrigste, das es im Wesen der Menschen gab, zu einer Ausbreitung kam, die sich innerhalb weniger Jahre stärker erwies als alle Klarsicht. Wie konnten sich diese Meilensteine auf dem Weg zu einem bessern und gerechtern Leben so einfach von der Verdummung umstürzen lassen, wie konnte sich dieser kritische und poetische Geist vom Pöbel vertreiben lassen.[49]

This is a possible answer to Boas's question as to what crime the adult artist has been charged with. In Germany at least it was a crime of omission: authors had seen political catastrophe overtake their country in spite of its cultural inheritance. Even if they were not personally implicated in that failure, it weighed on them like an 'Erbsünde'. The positive values of that culture therefore had to be reasserted, as in *Die Ästhetik des Widerstands* which, although it is a form of political *Bildungsroman,* clearly suggests that political convictions and personal feelings are not enough to resist the evils of the Nazi regime: 'Die Erfahrungen im Lager, die schweren Foltern, die Ermordung nächster Freunde, fachten wohl den Haß an, wie er benötigt wird für den Aufstand, ließen ihn [Boysen]

---

[49] In *Werke*, iii /3. 84–5.

aber nicht vergessen, daß es die wissenschaftlichen Entdeck-
ungen waren, die seine Haltung bestimmten'.[50] The members of
this Communist group regard art and culture as the foundation
stone of human and political resistance to evil; hence Hodann's
comment that 'Kunst sei gleichbedeutend mit Humanität'.[51] The
prominence of the child and the childlike in our own era may be
seen as an attempt to redeem artist and art alike.

But this is only one somewhat oversimplified position. Just as
the twentieth century is not able to regard the child as unequivocally innocent, so the ethical values of culture have also been
questioned, not least by Thomas Mann, who refused to subscribe
to any straightforward antithesis between the goodness and
humanity of culture and the evil of politics. For him the abuses of
the Nazi era derived from the irrationalist elements of German
culture: in 'Deutschland und die Deutschen' (1945) he contended
'daß es nicht zwei Deutschland gibt, ein böses und ein gutes, sondern nur eines, dem sein Bestes durch Teufelslist zum Bösen aus-
schlug' (*Gesammelte Werke*, xi. 1146). This idea is central to *Doktor
Faustus*. But this does not imply a rejection of culture on Mann's
part: as I suggested above, the publication of *Doktor Faustus* was in
itself an affirmation of the possibility, indeed necessity, of art after
1945. To some extent the novel corresponds to Adrian's *Doktor
Fausti Weheklag* for, although the cantata results from Adrian's
despair when Echo is dying, Zeitblom sees in it the possibility of a
'Hoffnung jenseits der Hoffnungslosigkeit, die Transzendenz der
Verzweiflung' (*Doktor Faustus*, 651). This is a formulation that cost
Mann some time and trouble; he referred to *Doktor Faustus* as 'ein
Buch des Endes' (*Gesammelte Werke*, xi. 162) and, although 'nach
all der Finsternis', he clearly wanted to create a sense of 'Hoffnung' and 'Gnade', achieving the right balance between despair
and hope proved difficult (xi. 294). The cantata's ambivalence becomes obvious in its main structural motif, the 'Echo', for although
this motif sounds like a lament (*Doktor Faustus*, 644) it also recalls
the child whom Adrian considers powerful enough to overcome
evil, even if only beyond death (pp. 632–3). As Pütz points out,
Echo is presented as physically vulnerable even before he comes
into contact with Adrian;[52] symbolically this makes him easy prey

---

[50] Ibid. 185.   [51] Ibid. 134.   [52] *Kunst und Künstlerexistenz*, 143.

for the demonic forces surrounding his uncle. Yet while this suggests the potential ease with which a child can be perverted, even destroyed, Echo's death is relieved by features that suggest a potentially more positive interpretation of this figure.[53] Adrian's defiant speech to the Devil as his nephew is dying suggests where that hope lies: 'Nimm seinen Leib, über den du Gewalt hast! Wirst mir seine süße Seele doch hübsch zufrieden lassen müssen, und das ist deine Ohnmacht und dein Ridikül, ... ich werde doch wissen, daß er da ist, von wo du hinausgeworfen wurdest, Dreckskerl' (pp. 632–3). This is not merely defiant wishful thinking, the need to believe that Echo has escaped this world for something better: his death scene is too harrowing for this to be much consolation. Mann rejected Bruno Walter's idea that the episode with the child would function as a piece of light relief or 'Allegretto moderato', saying that his friend did not know 'welche Unmenschlichkeit das Buch des Endes kalt durchweht–, und daß ich gehalten sein würde, die Geschichte des Gotteskindes in ganz anderem Geist zu erzählen als in dem des Allegretto Moderato' (*Gesammelte Werke*, xi. 162). But, while the child may not physically survive the attack of evil forces, Adrian's '*mir* seine süße Seele' (*Doktor Faustus*, 632, my emphasis) suggests that the idea of the child and what he represents will survive through his uncle: Echo may be 'aus zartem Stoff' (p. 633) but he represents a 'robuste Naivität' (p. 178) and this suggests the survival of the culture Mann loved even beyond its perverted manifestation in Nazism. Indeed, the way Echo's final illness is described implies a good deal about Mann's feelings concerning *Doktor Faustus* and the value of traditional realist art. Particularly if we bear in mind the impersonal treatment of Hanno Buddenbrook's demise in the typhus chapter (pp. 751–4), the harrowing presentation of Echo's last hours is clearly intended to have an emotional impact. Mann noted with some satisfaction the disastrous effect that reading this

---

[53] Judith Ryan sees the possibility of some relief in the associations between Echo and Shakespeare's Ariel and the references to Ariel's release at Echo's deathbed (*The Uncompleted Past: Postwar German Novels and the Third Reich*, (Detroit, 1983), 55). However, for her this positive potential is negated by Adrian's mourning for Echo in *Dr Fausti Wehklag*. Pütz had previously emphasized the mortality that distinguishes Echo from Ariel and observed that Adrian's art, unlike Prospero's, is not dependent on his Ariel figure (*Kunst und Künstlerexistenz*, 146). I interpret Adrian's expression of mourning rather more positively (see below).

episode had on his daughter's new eye make-up (*Gesammelte Werke*, xi. 296) and wrote that he had read the chapters about Echo to another audience 'zu großer Rührung' (xi. 300). When asked by his English translator 'How could you do it?', he paralleled his own feelings with those of Adrian: 'sie möge aus Adrians Gebaren, aus seinem "Es soll nicht sein", seinem Bruch mit der Hoffnung, seinem Wort von der "Zurücknahme"–sie möge daraus ablesen, wie schwer es mir geworden' (xi. 291–2). This very open emotional commitment to the character of Echo and the realistic description of the boy's suffering powerfully suggest Mann's own continued belief in the value and power of traditional realist art and, as we shall see, this is reflected in Adrian's own motivation for writing the *Faust* cantata.

Echo's symbolic significance becomes particularly clear in the tension between him, the individual child, and the 'Engelskinder' in Adrian's *Apocalypsis cum Figuris*. There has been much critical debate about the significance of Echo: he has been variously interpreted as the innocent child saviour diametrically opposed to Adrian and as an ambiguous figure who is instrumental in his uncle's downfall.[54] Pütz in particular notes that, while the boy embodies possible salvation for Adrian, he also endangers the artist because he might alienate him from 'dem ekzentrischen, aber nur dadurch fruchtbaren und opferwürdigen Künstlerdasein'.[55] However, I would suggest that this negative element is not inherent in Echo, who represents a danger to Adrian only because of the terms of the demonic pact. In fact this child is presented in an essentially positive light whereas *Apocalypsis cum Figuris* with its 'innere Einerleiheit des Engelkinder-Chors mit dem Höllengelächter' (*Doktor Faustus*, 645) suggests a duality in the child which

---

[54] For various interpretations of Echo see Alfredo Dornheim, 'Goethes "Mignon" and Thomas Manns "Echo": Zwei Formen des "göttlichen Kindes" im deutschen Roman', *Euphorion*, 46 (1952), 315–47 which interprets the boy as a form of the 'göttliches Kind' described in Jung and Kerényi's study, but not as a traditional Christian saviour (esp. 319–20); Joachim Müller, 'Thomas Manns *Doktor Faustus*: Grundthematik und Motivgefüge', *Euphorion* 54 (1960), 262–80 which stresses the religious nature of the novel and therefore by extension of Echo (esp. pp. 276–7); Hagen, who sees Echo as a typical example of the German tendency to idealize childhood (*Kinder*, 28 and 111–15); and Kuhn who describes the boy as an enigma who may represent possible redemption through innocence but also points to an uncertain future (*Corruption in Paradise*, 189). Pütz discusses the ambiguity of this figure in *Kunst und Künstlerexistenz*, 140–8.

[55] *Kunst und Künstlerexistenz*, 142.

reflects Mann's conception of the ambivalence of German culture.[56] This ambivalence had already been prefigured in the character of Rudolf Schwerdtfeger, of whom the word 'kindisch' is used, but in combination with less positive vocabulary: 'einer absolut naiven, kindischen, ja koboldhaften Dämonie' (p. 462). Echo's childlike nature is not qualified in this way; perhaps he is presented in an overwhelmingly positive light because he is still a real child, not merely a childlike adult. His integrity as a child has not yet been compromised; he is the being of whom Schiller writes in *Über naive und sentimentalische Dichtung*:

Das Kind ist uns daher eine Vergegenwärtigung des Ideals, nicht zwar des erfüllten aber des aufgegebenen, und es ist also keineswegs die Vorstellung seiner Bedürftigkeit und Schranken, es ist ganz im Gegentheil die Vorstellung seiner reinen und freyen Kraft, seiner Integrität, seiner Unendlichkeit, was uns rührt. (*Werke*, xx. 416)

Echo represents the good of German culture before, but also beyond, its appearance 'im Unglück, in Schuld und Untergang' (Mann, *Gesammelte Werke*, xi. 1146) the good which seems to have disappeared but is in fact ever-present as a source of hope which it is still worth striving for. Thus while his death may symbolize a shattering break, it does not represent an irrevocable end.[57] This paradox is clear in that although Echo's death may be what causes Adrian finally to abandon the bourgeois-humanist tradition, in fact his rage and grief at the loss of this much-loved child is one of the stimuli for his composition; even more than the violin concerto he composed for Rudi Schwerdtfeger, this is a 'menschlich inspiriertes Werk' (*Doktor Faustus*, 579). Indeed, what more traditional and human inspiration could there be for a work of art? The tension between the boy's physical absence and Adrian's

---

[56] This duality is also noted ibid. 144 and by Kuhn, *Corruption in Paradise*, 192, but both take it to be proof of Echo's ambiguous nature.

[57] Kuhn suggests this when he refers to Echo's death as 'the harbinger of the end of the epoch of bourgeois humanism and the herald of a new stage in life' (*Corruption in Paradise*, 192), but he does not seem to see any continuity between these eras. Mundt stresses that Adrian's art is in fact dependent on the tradition he apparently despises (*'Doktor Faustus' und die Folgen*, 34–41, esp. 38–9). She also emphasizes the continuities that inform Thomas Mann's own art even after the ostensible caesura of 1945 (ibid. 41). Robertson offers a more positive interpretation of the parallels between Thomas Mann and Adrian, and the continuities that underpin Mann's work (Robertson, 'Accounting for History', 140 and 146).

preservation of what he represents is clear in the final description of the *Faust* cantata: while Zeitblom does not actually use the word 'Echo', his comments on the final note evoke the word and thus the child: 'Dann ist nichts mehr,–Schweigen und Nacht. Aber der nachschwingend im Schweigen hängende Ton, der nicht mehr ist, dem nur die Seele noch nachlauscht, und der Ausklang der Trauer war, ist es nicht mehr, wandelt den Sinn, steht als ein Licht in der Nacht' (p. 651). The emphasis on the word 'Nacht' is important, for 'Nacht' was Echo's 'Abschiedsgruß überhaupt' (p. 620). The 'Schweigen und Nacht' painfully emphasizes his physical absence, but the echo of the final note and the phrase 'ein Licht in der Nacht' suggest that his spirit persists even in his physical absence. The hope the child represents may be intangible, but its power is undeniable.

This brief conclusion could offer no comprehensive survey of the German novel since 1945, nor was this the intention. But the German preoccupation with the child after 1945 clearly derives from authors' most pressing concerns, both moral and literary. The post-war era has been one of doubt and re-evaluation on every level: the Third Reich caused political and moral shock waves which reverberated around a society rapidly becoming more secular, a society in need of values. And at a time of uncertainty and rapid social and political change the child is a perfect vehicle for suggesting openness to change while also representing certain constants of human existence and indeed of cultural and literary values. As I suggested in the Introduction, the child has a long history in German literature and that history is an overwhelmingly positive one, which implies the possibility of holding on to what is good about the past as well as looking forward to the future, both aspects of the child's symbolic potential. Certainly this is the force of Echo, who represents religious and cultural values and so embodies both past securities and more tentative future hopes. That those hopes are more tentative is inevitable: our own era has had more reason than most to be sceptical of the positive values of childhood and culture alike. And yet, as in the Romantic period, the child can both embody those uncertainties and transcend them: now, as then, it expresses the spirit of an age.

SELECT BIBLIOGRAPHY

I. PRIMARY TEXTS

1.1. Childhood under The Third Reich and in the Immediate Post-War Period

Abraham, Peter, *Die Schüsse der Arche Noah oder Die Irrtümer und Irrfahrten meines Freundes Wensloff* (repr. Berlin, 1971).

Aichinger, Ilse, *Die größere Hoffnung: Roman* (repr. Frankfurt, 1994).

Andres, Stefan, *Der Taubenturm: Roman* (Munich, 1966).

Apitz, Bruno, *Nackt unter Wölfen: Roman* (Halle and Saale, 1958).

Baer, Frank, *Die Magermilchbande: Roman* (Hamburg, 1979).

Becker, Jurek, *Jakob der Lügner: Roman* (repr. Frankfurt, 1982).

— *Die Mauer*, in id., *Nach der ersten Zukunft: Erzählungen* (Frankfurt, 1980).

Bender, Hans, *Willst du nicht beitreten?*, in Reich-Ranicki (ed.), *Meine Schulzeit*, 31–9.

Berkéwicz, Ulla, *Engel sind schwarz und weiß: Roman* (Frankfurt, 1992).

Bernhard, Thomas, *Ein Kind* (Salzburg and Vienna, 1982).

— *Auslöschung: Ein Zerfall* (Frankfurt, 1986).

Beyer, Marcel, *Flughunde: Roman* (Frankfurt, 1995).

Bienek, Horst, *Reise in die Kindheit: Wiedersehen mit Schlesien* (Munich and Vienna, 1988).

Böll, Heinrich, *Haus ohne Hüter: Roman* (Cologne, 1954).

— *Im Tal der donnernden Hufe: Erzählung* (repr. Frankfurt, 1985).

— (ed.), *Niemands Land: Kindheitserinnerungen an die Jahre 1945 bis 1949* (Munich, 1988).

Bosetzky, Horst, *Brennholz für Kartoffelschalen: Roman eines Schlüsselkindes* (Berlin, 1995).

Durlacher, Gerhard, *Drowning: Growing Up in the Third Reich*, trans. Susan Massotty (London and New York, 1993).

Edvardson, Cordelia, *Gebranntes Kind sucht das Feuer*, trans. Anna-Liese Kornitzky (repr. Munich, 1991).

Fichte, Hubert, *Das Waisenhaus: Roman* (Reinbek, 1965).

— *Die Palette: Roman* (Reinbek, 1968).

— *Detlevs Imitationen; 'Grünspan': Roman* (Reinbek, 1971).

Fischer, Karl C., *Erwachsene Kinder* (Overath, 1996).

Fitzherbert, Katrin, *True to Both My Selves: A Family Memoir of Germany and England in Two World Wars* (London, 1997).

Forte, Dieter, *Der Junge mit den blutigen Schuhen: Roman* (Frankfurt, 1995).

— *In der Erinnerung: Roman* (Frankfurt, 1998).

Frank, Anne, *The Diary of Anne Frank: The Critical Edition*, ed. David Barnouw and Gerrold van der Stoom, trans. Arnold J. Pomerans and B. M. Mooyaart-Doubleday (London, 1989).

— *The Diary of Anne Frank*, trans. B. M. Mooyaart-Doubleday, with foreword by Storm Jameson (London, 1981).

— *The Diary of a Young Girl: The Definitive Edition*, ed. Otto H. Frank and Mirjam Pressler, trans. Susan Massotty (London, 1997).

Fuchs, Gerd, *Stunde Null: Roman* (Hamburg, 1987).

Fühmann, Franz, *Das Judenauto; Kabelkran und Blauer Peter; Zweiundzwanzig Tage, oder, Die Hälfte des Lebens* (Rostock, 1993).

Gay, Peter, *My German Question: Growing Up in Nazi Berlin* (New Haven and London, 1998).

Gmeyner, Anna, *Manja: Ein Roman um fünf Kinder*, with foreword by Heike Klapdor-Kops (repr. Mannheim, 1987).

Goldschmidt, Georges-Arthur, *Die Absonderung: Erzählung* (Zurich, 1991).

Goodrich, Frances, and Hackett, Albert, *The Play of the Diary of Anne Frank* (Oxford, 1991).

Grass, Günter, *Werkausgabe*, ed. Volker Neuhaus, 10 vols. (Darmstadt and Neuwied, 1987).

Grote, Christian, *Für Kinder die Hälfte: Ein Bericht* (Frankfurt, 1963).

Grün, Max von der, *Wie war das eigentlich? Kindheit und Jugend im Dritten Reich* (1979; repr. Hamburg and Zurich, 1988).

Haider, Edith, *Guckuck-oder die Kreise der Menschlichkeit* (Krems, 2000).

Hannsmann, Margarete, *Der helle Tag bricht an: Ein Kind wird Nazi* (Munich and Hamburg, 1982).

Harig, Ludwig, *Weh dem, der aus der Reihe tanzt: Roman* (Frankfurt, 1994).

Härtling, Peter, *Krücke: Roman* (Weinheim and Basle, 1986).

— *Nachgetragene Liebe* (Frankfurt, 1988).

— *Zwettl: Nachprüfung einer Erinnerung* (Frankfurt, 1982).

Hensel, Georg, *Der Sack überm Kopf*, in Reich-Ranicki (ed.), *Meine Schulzeit*, 109–25.

Hermand, Jost, *Als Pimpf in Polen: Erweiterte Kinderlandverschickung 1940–1945* (Frankfurt, 1993).

Hofmann, Gert, *Unsere Eroberung: Roman* (Darmstadt and Neuwied, 1984).

— *Veilchenfeld: Erzählung* (Darmstadt and Neuwied, 1986).

— *Der Kinoerzähler: Roman* (Munich, 1990).

Horváth, Ödön von, *Jugend ohne Gott: Roman* (Amsterdam, 1938).

Ippers, Josef, *Zacharias Zachary*, in Böll (ed.), *Niemands Land*, 105–19.

Jehn, Margarete, *Niemands Land*, in Böll (ed.), *Niemands Land*, 19–32.

Johansen, Hanna, *Die Analphabetin: Eine Erzählung* (Munich and Vienna, 1982).

Kaufmann, Alois, *Spiegelgrund, Pavillon 18: Ein Kind im NS-Erziehungsheim* (Vienna, 1993).

Kempowski, Walter, *Tadellöser & Wolff: Roman* (Munich, 1978).

Kerr, Judith, *When Hitler stole Pink Rabbit*, in ead., *Out of the Hitler Time* (London, 1994).

Klüger, Ruth, *weiter leben: Eine Jugend* (Göttingen, 1992).

König, Barbara, *Die verpaßte Chance*, in Reich-Ranicki (ed.), *Meine Schulzeit*, 134–45.

Kosinski, Jerzy, *The Painted Bird* (London, 1966).

Krüger, Horst, *Das Grunewald-Gymnasium: Eine Erinnerung an die Banalität des Bösen*, in Reich-Ranicki (ed.), *Meine Schulzeit*, 40–9.

Le Fort, Gertrud von, *Die Unschuldigen*, in ead., *Erzählende Schriften*, 3 vols. (Munich and Wiesbaden, 1956), vol. iii.

Lenz, Siegfried, *Deutschstunde: Roman* (repr. Hamburg, 1969).

— *Kurze Hosen und halblange Söckchen*, in Reich-Ranicki (ed.), *Meine Schulzeit*, 169–77.

Metelmann, Henry, *A Hitler Youth: Growing Up In Germany In the 1930s* (London, 1997).

Novak, Helga M., *Die Eisheiligen: Roman* (Darmstadt and Neuwied, 1979).

Nyiri, János, *Battlefields and Playgrounds*, trans. William Brandon and the author (London, 1989).

Oberski, Jona, *Childhood: A Novella*, trans. Ralph Manheim (London, 1983).

Rehmann, Ruth, *Der Mann auf der Kanzel: Fragen an einen Vater* (Munich and Vienna, 1979).

Reich-Ranicki, Marcel (ed.) *Meine Schulzeit im Dritten Reich: Erinnerungen deutscher Schriftsteller* (4th expanded edn., Munich, 1993).

Reschke, Karin, *Memoiren eines Kindes* (Berlin, 1980).

Rosendorfer, Herbert, *Vier Jahreszeiten in Yrwental: Vier Berichte* (Munich, 1986).

Schneider, Karla, *Kor, der Engel: Ein Roman in 22 Geschichten* (Zurich, 1992).

Schumann, Willy, *Being Present: Growing Up in Hitler's Germany* (Kent, Ohio, 1991).

Schütz, Helga, *Vorgeschichten oder Schöne Gegend Probstein* (Berlin and Weimar, 1987).

— *Jette in Dresden* (Berlin and Weimar, 1979).

— *Mädchenrätsel: Roman* (Munich, 1980).

Stiller, Klaus, *Weihnachten: Als wir Kinder den Krieg verloren* (Frankfurt, 1982).

Walser, Martin, *Ein springender Brunnen: Roman* (Frankfurt, 1998).

Wellershof, Dieter, *Ein Allmachtstraum und sein Ende*, in Reich-Ranicki (ed.), *Meine Schulzeit*, 146–60.

Wilkomirski, Binjamin, *Bruchstücke: Aus einer Kindheit 1939–1945* (Frankfurt, 1995).

Wolf, Christa, *Kindheitsmuster*, in *Werkausgabe*, 12 vols., ed. Sonja Hilzinger, vol. v (Munich, 2000).

— *Blickwechsel*, in ead., *Gesammelte Erzählungen* (repr. Berlin and Weimar, 1990).

1.2. Other Accounts of Childhood Oblique from the Child's Perspective

Cary, Joyce, *Charley is my Darling* (London, 1990).

Dickens, Charles, *Oliver Twist* in id., *The Authentic Edition*, 21 vols. (London and New York, 1901), vol. iii.

Elsner, Gisela, *Die Riesenzwerge: Ein Beitrag* (Reinbek, 1964).

Golding, William, *Lord of the Flies* (London, 1954).

Hartley, L. P., *The Go-Between* (Harmondsworth, 1958).

Hauptmann, Gerhart, *Hanneles Himmelfahrt: Traumdichtung in zwei Akten*, in id., *Gesammelte Werke*, 8 vols. (Berlin, 1921), vol. ii.

Hesse, Hermann, *Unterm Rad: Erzählung* (Frankfurt, 1972).

— *Kinderseele* (Frankfurt, 1985).

Holz, Arno, *Der erste Schultag* (Berlin, 1924).

Hughes, Richard, *A High Wind in Jamaica* (repr. Harmondsworth, 1971).

Hughes, Thomas, *Tom Brown's Schooldays*, ed. and introd. Andrew Sanders (Oxford and New York, 1989).

James, Henry, *What Maisie Knew*, ed. and introd. Paul Theroux (repr. Harmondsworth, 1985).

Joyce, James, *A Portrait of the Artist as a Young Man* (Harmondsworth, 1992).

Kaschnitz, Marie Luise, *Das Haus der Kindheit*, in ead., *Gesammelte Werke*, ed. Christian Büttrich and Norbert Miller, 7 vols. (Frankfurt, 1981–9), vol. ii.

— *Das dicke Kind*, in ead., *Gesammelte Werke*, ed Büttrich and Miller, vol. iv.

Kempff, Diana, *Fettfleck: Roman* (Salzburg and Vienna, 1979).

Kipling, Rudyard, *Stalky & Co.* (London and Basingstoke, 1982).

Meyer, Conrad Ferdinand, *Das Leiden eines Knaben*, in id., *Sämtliche Werke: Historisch-kritische Ausgabe*, ed. Hans Zeller and Alfred Zäch (Berne, 1958 —), vol. xii.

Moser, Tilman, *Grammatik der Gefühle: Mutmaßungen über die ersten Lebensjahre* (Frankfurt, 1983).

Musil, Robert, *Die Verwirrungen des Zöglings Törleß* (Reinbek, 1978).

Rilke, Rainer Maria, *Die Turnstunde*, in id., *Sämtliche Werke*, ed. Ernst Zinn, 6 vols., vol. iv (Frankfurt, 1961).

Seghers, Anna, *Der Ausflug der toten Mädchen und andere Erzählungen* (Berlin, 1948).

Strauß, Emil, *Freund Hein: Eine Lebensgeschichte* (Kirchheim, 1982).

Toller, Ernst, *Eine Jugend in Deutschland* in id., *Prosa, Briefe, Dramen, Gedichte*, with foreword by Kurt Hiller (Reinbek, 1961).

Wedekind, Frank, *Frühlings Erwachen*, in id., *Werke*, ed. Ernst Weidl, 2 vols. (Darmstadt, 1992), vol. i.

Wittig, Monique, *L'Opoponax* (Paris, 1964).

Zweig, Stefan, *Brennendes Geheimnis: Erzählung* (repr. Frankfurt, 1993).

1.3. Other Primary Sources

Aichinger, Ilse, *Kleist, Moos, Fasane* (Frankfurt, 1987).

—— 'Rede an die Jugend', in Samuel Moser (ed.), *Ilse Aichinger: Leben und Werk*, (2nd expanded edn., Frankfurt, 1995).

Basedow, Johann Bernhard, *Ausgewählte pädagogische Schriften*, ed. A. Reble (Paderborn, 1965).

Baudelaire, Charles, *Le Peintre de la vie moderne*, in id., *Œuvres complètes*, ed. Claude Pichois, 2 vols. (Paris, 1975–6), vol. ii.

Blake, William, *The Poems of William Blake*, ed. W. H. Stevenson (London, 1971).

Böll, Heinrich, *Wanderer kommst du nach Spa...: Erzählungen* (repr. Munich, 1990).

—— *Ansichten eines Clowns: Roman* (repr. Munich, 1991).

—— *Billard um halbzehn: Roman* (repr. Munich, 1992).

—— 'Zu Reich-Ranickis *Deutsche Literatur in West und Ost*', in *Essayistische Schriften und Reden*, ii. 1964–72, ed. Bernd Balzer (Cologne, 1979), 18–20.

Borchert, Wolfgang, *Draußen vor der Tür*, in id., *Das Gesamtwerk*, with biographical afterword by Bernhard Meyer-Marwitz (Hamburg, 1949).

Brecht, Bertolt, *Furcht und Elend des Dritten Reiches*, in id., *Werke*, 30 vols., ed. Werner Hecht, Jan Knopf, Werner Mittenzwei, Klaus-Detlef Müller (Berlin and Frankfurt, 1988), vol. iv.

—— 'Fünf Schwierigkeiten beim Schreiben der Wahrheit', in *Werke*, ed. Hecht et al., vol. xxii/1.

Brontë, Charlotte, *Jane Eyre* (London, 1985).

Burns, Robert, *Selected Poems*, ed. Carol McGuirk (Harmondsworth, 1993).

Camus, Albert, *L'Étranger*, in id., *Théâtre; Récits; Nouvelles*, ed. Roger Quilliot (Paris, 1962).

Craig, Patricia (ed.), *The Oxford Book of Schooldays* (Oxford, 1994).

Dickens, Charles, *The Old Curiosity Shop*, in id., *The Authentic Edition*, 21 vols. (London and New York, 1901), vol. viii.

—— *Bleak House*, in id., *Authentic Edition*, vol. xi.

—— *Great Expectations*, in id., *Authentic Edition*, vol. xiii.

Döblin, Alfred, *Berlin Alexanderplatz: Die Geschichte vom Franz Biberkopf* (repr. Munich, 1990).

Flaubert, Gustave, *L'Éducation sentimentale: Histoire d'un jeune homme*, ed. Peter Michael Wetherill (Paris, 1984).

Fontane, Theodor, *Werke*, ed. Hans-Heinrich Reuter, 5 vols. (Berlin and Weimar, 1964).

Freud, Sigmund, *Drei Abhandlungen zur Sexualtheorie* in id., *Studienausgabe*, ed. Alexander Mitscherlich, Angela Richards, and James Strachey, 11 vols. (Frankfurt, 1969–75), vol. v.

— *Der Dichter und das Phantasieren*, in id., *Studienausgabe*, ed. Mitscherlich et al., vol. x.

Frisch, Max, *Stiller: Roman* (repr. Frankfurt, 1973).

— *Homo Faber: Ein Bericht* (repr. Frankfurt, 1977).

— *Mein Name sei Gantenbein: Roman* (repr. Frankfurt, 1975).

Gide, André: *La Porte étroite*, in id., *Romans; Récits et Soties; Œuvres lyriques* (Paris, 1958).

Goethe, Johann Wolfgang von, *Werke: Hamburger Ausgabe*, ed. Erich Trunz, 14 vols. (rev. edn., Munich, 1981).

— *Wilhelm Meisters Wanderjahre oder Die Entsagenden*, with afterword by Adolf Muschg (Frankfurt, 1982).

— *Wilhelm Meisters Theatralische Sendung*, with afterword by Wilhelm Voßkamp (Frankfurt, 1984).

Grimmelshausen, Hans Jakob Christoffel von, *Der Abenteuerliche Simplicissimus Teutsch* (repr. Munich, 1990).

Halamicková, Jana (ed.), *Die Kinder dieser Welt: Gedichte aus zwei Jahrhunderten* (Frankfurt, 1993).

Hamann, Johann Georg, *Fünf Hirtenbriefe*, in *Sämtliche Werke*, 6 vols., ed. Josef Nadler (Vienna, 1949–57), vol. ii.

Handke, Peter, *Die Hornissen: Roman* (Frankfurt, 1966).

— *Der Hausierer: Roman* (Frankfurt, 1967).

— *Kaspar* (Frankfurt, 1967).

— *Die Angst des Tormanns beim Elfmeter: Erzählung* (Frankfurt, 1970).

— *Die Stunde der wahren Empfindung* (Frankfurt, 1975).

— 'Ich bin ein Bewohner des Elfenbeinturms', 'Zur Tagung der Gruppe 47 in USA' (1966), and 'Die Literatur ist romantisch', in id., *Ich bin ein Bewohner des Elfenbeinturms* (Frankfurt, 1972).

Hardy, Thomas, *Jude the Obscure*, ed. with introd. and notes by C. H. Sisson (repr. Harmondsworth, 1985).

Heaney, Seamus, *Glanmore Sonnets*, in id., *Field Work* (London, 1979).

Heißenbüttel, Helmut, 'Schwierigkeiten beim Schreiben der Wahrheit 1964', in Otto F. Best and Hans-Jürgen Schmitt (eds.), *Die deutsche Literatur: Ein Abriß in Text und Darstellung*, vol. xvi. *Gegenwart*, ed. Gerhard R. Kaiser (rev. and expanded edn., Stuttgart, 1983).

Herder, Johann Gottfried von, *Journal meiner Reise im Jahr 1769*, in id., *Werke*, ed. Wilhelm Dobbek, 5 vols. (repr. Berlin and Weimar, 1969), vol. i.

— *Abhandlung über den Ursprung der Sprache*, in id., *Werke*, ed. Dobbek, vol. ii.

— *Vom Erkennen und Empfinden der menschlichen Seele: Bemerkungen und Träume*, in id., *Werke*, ed. Dobbek, vol. iii.

— *Iduna oder der Apfel der Verjüngung*, in id., *Schriften*, ed. Karl Otto Conrady (Hamburg, 1968).

Hesse, Hermann, *Das Glasperlenspiel: Versuch einer Lebensbeschreibung des Magister Ludi Josef Knecht samt Knechts hinterlassenen Schriften*, 2 vols. (Zurich, 1943).

Hitler, Adolf, *Mein Kampf*, 2 vols. (repr. Munich, 1936).

Hoffmann, E. T. A., *Das fremde Kind*, in id., *Dichtungen und Schriften, so wie Briefe und Tagebücher: Gesamtausgabe*, ed. Walther Harich, 15 vols. (Weimar, 1924), vol. vii.

Hoffmann, Eva, *Lost in Translation: A Life in a New Language* (repr. London, 1995).

Hofmann, Gert, *Die Denunziation: Novelle* (Darmstadt and Neuwied, 1987).

— *Der Blindensturz: Erzählung* (Darmstadt and Neuwied, 1985)

— *Unsere Vergeßlichkeit: Roman* (Darmstadt and Neuwied, 1987)

Huizinga, J., *Homo Ludens: A Study of the Play-Element in Culture*, trans. R. F. C. Hull (London, 1949).

Huxley, Aldous, *Brave New World*, introd. David Bradshawe (repr. London, 1994).

Jean Paul, *Werke*, ed. Norbert Miller (Munich, 1959–).

Johnson, Uwe, *Mutmaßungen über Jakob: Roman* (Frankfurt, 1959).

— *Das dritte Buch über Achim: Roman* (Frankfurt, 1961).

— *Zwei Ansichten* (Frankfurt, 1965).

— *Jahrestage: Aus dem Leben von Gesine Cresspahl*, 4 vols. (Frankfurt, 1970–83).

— 'Vorschläge zur Prüfung eines Romans', in Eberhard Lämmert et al. (eds.), *Romantheorie: Dokumentation ihrer Geschichte in Deutschland seit 1880* (2nd edn., Königstein, 1984).

Jung-Stilling, *Heinrich Stillings Jugend, Jünglingsjahre und Wanderschaft: Eine wahrhafte Geschichte von ihm selbst erzählt* (Hamburg, 1904).

Kafka, Franz, *Beim Bau der chinesischen Mauer und andere Schriften aus dem Nachlaß* (Frankfurt, 1994).

Kant, Immanuel, *Beantwortung der Frage: Was ist Aufklärung?*, in id., *Werke*, ed. Wilhelm Weischedel, 6 vols. (Wiesbaden, 1956–64), vol. vi.

Keller, Gottfried, *Sämtliche Werke*, ed. Thomas Böning, Gerhard Kaiser, Kai Kauffmann, Dominik Müller, and Peter Villwock, 7 vols. (Frankfurt, 1985–96).

Kerr, Judith, *The Other Way Round* and *A Small Person Far Away* in ead., *Out of the Hitler Time* (London, 1994).

Key, Ellen, *The Century of the Child* (New York and London, 1909).

Kleist, Heinrich von, *Über das Marionettentheater* in id., *Sämtliche Werke und Briefe*, ed. Helmut Sembdner, 2 vols. (Darmstadt, 1962), vol. ii.

Kunze, Reiner, *Gespräch mit der Amsel* (Frankfurt, 1984).

Langer, Lawrence L. (ed.), *Art from the Ashes: A Holocaust Anthology* (New York and Oxford, 1995).

Lawrence, D. H., Foreword to *Women in Love*, pub. as an app. to *Women in Love* (Harmondsworth, 1995), 485–6.

Lenz, Siegfried, *Beziehungen: Ansichten und Bekenntnisse zur Literatur* (Hamburg, 1970).

— 'Interview mit Marcel Reich-Ranicki', (1969) in id., *Beziehungen*.

Levi, Primo, *If This is a Man and The Truce*, trans. Stuart Woolf, with introd. by Paul Bailey and afterword by the author (repr. London, 1995).

— *If not now, when?*, trans. William Weaver (repr. London, 1994).

— *Moments of Reprieve*, trans. Ruth Feldman (repr. London, 1994).

Locke, John, *Some Thoughts concerning Education* (1693), ed. John W. and Jean S. Youlton (Oxford, 1989).

Mann, Heinrich, *Professor Unrat oder das Ende eines Tyrannen: Roman*, in id., *Studienausgabe in Einzelbänden*, ed. Paul-Peter Schneider (repr. Frankfurt, 1994).

Mann, Thomas, *Gesammelte Werke*, 12 vols. (Frankfurt, 1960).

— *Blätter der Thomas Mann Gesellschaft*, ix (Zurich, 1969).

Michels, Volker (ed.), *Unterbrochene Schulstunde: Schriftsteller und Schule. Eine Anthologie* (Frankfurt, 1972).

Morgner, Irmtraud, *Leben und Abenteuer der Trobadora Beatriz nach Zeugnissen ihrer Spielfrau Laura: Roman in dreizehn Büchern und sieben Intermezzos* (Berlin and Weimar, 1974).

— *Amanda: Ein Hexenroman* (Berlin and Weimar, 1983).

Moritz, Karl Philipp, *Anton Reiser: Ein psychologischer Roman*, in id., *Werke*, ed. Horst Günther, 3 vols. (Frankfurt, 1981), vol. i.

Nietzsche, Friedrich, *Also sprach Zarathustra: Ein Buch für Alle und für Keinen*, in id., *Werke: Kritische Gesamtausgabe*, ed. Giorgio Colli and Mazzino Montinari (Berlin, 1967––), vol. vi/1.

Novalis, *Schriften*, ed. Paul Kluckhohn and Richard H. Samuel, 5 vols. (2nd rev. and expanded edn., Stuttgart, 1960–88).

Orwell, George, *Nineteen Eighty-Four* (repr. Harmondsworth, 1984).

Pestalozzi, Johann Heinrich, *Wie Gertrud ihre Kinder lehrt* in id., *Ausgewählte Werke*, ed. Otto Boldemann, 2 vols. (Berlin, 1962–3), vol. ii.

Richter, Dieter (ed.), *Kindheit im Gedicht: Deutsche Verse aus acht Jahrhunderten* (Frankfurt, 1992).

Rilke, Rainer Maria, *Über Kunst*, in id., *Sämtliche Werke*, ed. Ernst Zinn, 6 vols., vol. v (Frankfurt, 1965).

Rousseau, Jean-Jacques, *Émile ou de l'éducation*, ed. François and Pierre Richard (Paris, 1992).
— *Les Confessions*, ed. Ernest Seillière, 3 vols. (Paris, 1929).
Schenzinger, Karl Aloys, *Der Hitlerjunge Quex: Roman* (Berlin, 1932).
Schiller, Friedrich von, *Über naive und sentimentalische Dichtung*, in id., *Werke: Nationalausgabe*, ed. Julius Petersen (Weimar, 1943––), xx. *Philosophische Schriften erster Teil*, ed. Benno von Wiese and Helmut Koopman (Weimar, 1962).
— *Über die Ästhetische Erziehung des Menschen*, in id., *Werke*, vol. xx.
Schlegel, Friedrich, *Lucinde: Vertraute Briefe über Lucinde von Friedrich Schleiermacher*, ed. Rudolf Frank (Leipzig, 1907).
Scholl, Inge, *Die Weiße Rose* (2nd edn., Frankfurt, 1990).
Schopenhauer, Arthur, 'Vom Genie', in *Die Welt als Wille und Vorstellung*, in *Schopenhauer's Sämmtliche Werke*, ed. Eduard Grisebach, 5 vols. (Leipzig, n.d.), vol. ii.
Seghers, Anna, *Das siebte Kreuz* (Zurich, 1949).
Solms, Wilhelm (ed.), *Begrenzt glücklich. Kindheit in der DDR* (Marburg, 1992).
Spark, Muriel, *The Prime of Miss Jean Brodie* (1st pub. 1961; Harmondsworth, 1965).
Stifter, Adalbert, *Gesammelte Werke*, ed. Konrad Steffen, 14 vols. (Basle and Stuttgart, 1962–72).
Tieck, Ludwig, *Schriften in zwölf Bänden*, ed. Hans Peter Balmes (Frankfurt, 1985–).
Tolstoy, L. N., *Anna Karenin*, trans. and introd. Rosemary Edmonds (Harmondsworth, 1978).
Voltaire, *Candide*, in id., *Romans et contes*, ed. René Pomeau (Paris, 1966).
Weiss, Peter, *Werke*, 6 vols. (Frankfurt, 1991).
— *Laokoon oder über die Grenzen der Sprache*, in id., *Rapporte* (Frankfurt, 1968).
Wolf, Christa, *Der geteilte Himmel: Erzählung* (repr. Munich, 1973).
— *Nachdenken über Christa T.* (Frankfurt, 1971).
— *Kassandra: Erzählung* (repr. Hamburg, 1986).
— *Voraussetzungen einer Erzählung: Kassandra; Frankfurter Poetik-Vorlesungen* (1983; Frankfurt, 1988).
— *Juninachmittag*, in ead., *Gesammelte Erzählungen* (repr. Berlin and Weimar, 1990).
— *Die Dimension des Autors: Essays und Aufsätze, Reden und Gespräche 1959–1985*, 2 vols. (repr. Frankfurt, 1990).
Wolfram von Eschenbach, *Parzival*, 2 vols. (repr. Stuttgart, 1992).
Wordsworth, William, *The Prelude 1799, 1805, 1850: Authoritative Texts, Contexts and Reception; Recent Critical Essays*, ed. Jonathan Wordsworth, M. H. Abrams, Stephen Gill (New York and London, 1979).
— *Selected Poems*, ed. Walford Davies (repr. London, 1990).

2. SECONDARY LITERATURE

2.1. Studies on Childhood in Literature

Andrews, Malcolm, *Dickens and the Grown-Up Child* (Basingstoke and London, 1994).

Assmann, Aleida, 'Werden was wir waren: Anmerkungen zur Geschichte der Kindheitsidee', *AA* 24 (1978), 98–124.

Barnett, Pamela R., 'Perceptions of Childhood', Ian Wallace (ed.), *Christa Wolf in Perspective*, (*GM* 30, Amsterdam and Atlanta, Ga., 1994), 59–72.

Barstow, Jane Missner, 'Childhood Revisited and Revised: Perspective in the First Person Novels of Dickens, Grass and Proust' (unpublished doctoral thesis, University of Michigan, 1973).

Beyersdorf, Herman Ernst, 'The Immaturity Theme in the Post-War German Novel' (unpublished doctoral thesis, University of New England, 1974).

Bien, Günter, 'Das Bild des Jugendlichen in modernen Dichtungen', *Deutschunterricht*, 21/2 (1969), 5–27.

Brettschneider, Werner, *'Kindheitsmuster': Kindheit als Thema autobiographischer Dichtung* (Berlin, 1982).

Coe, Richard N., *When the Grass was Taller: Autobiography and the Experience of Childhood* (New Haven and London, 1984).

Coveney, Peter, *The Image of Childhood, The Individual and Society: A Study of the Theme in English Literature* (rev. edn., Harmondsworth, 1967).

Dornheim, Alfredo, 'Goethes "Mignon" und Thomas Manns "Echo": Zwei Formen des "göttlichen Kindes" im deutschen Roman', *Euphorion*, 46 (1952), 315–47.

Ewers, Hans-Heino, *Kindheit als poetische Daseinsform; Studien zur Entstehung der romantischen Kindheitsutopie im 18. Jahrhundert: Herder, Jean Paul, Novalis und Tieck* (Munich, 1989).

Graucob, Karl, *Kindliches und jugendliches Seelenleben in deutscher Dichtung* (Erfurt, 1936).

Grolman, Adolf von, *Kind und junger Mensch in der Dichtung der Gegenwart* (Berlin, 1930).

Grotzer, Peter, *Die zweite Geburt: Figuren des Jugendlichen in der Literatur des 20. Jahrhunderts*, 2 vols. (Zurich, 1991).

Grünzweig, Walter, 'Die vergebliche Enttrümmerung beschädigter Kinderköpfe: Nationalsozialismus in den Werken Gert Hofmanns', *GSR* (1989), 55–67.

Grylls, David, *Guardians and Angels: Parents and Children in Nineteenth-Century Literature* (London, 1978).

Hagen, Rainer, *Kinder, wie sie im Buche stehen* (Munich, 1967).

Hensel, Barbara, *Das Kind und der Jugendliche in der deutschen Roman-und Erzählliteratur nach dem 2. Weltkrieg: Ein pädagogische Untersuchung* (Diss. Munich; Munich, 1962).

Howe, Patricia, 'The Child as Metaphor in the Novels of Fontane', *OGS* 10 (1979), 121–38.

Hurst, Mary Jane, *The Voice of the Child in American Literature: Linguistic Approaches to Fictional Child Language* (Lexington, 1990).

Jens, Walter, 'Erwachsene Kinder: Das Bild des Jugendlichen in der modernen Literatur', in id., *Statt einer Literaturgeschichte* (5th expanded edn., Pfullingen, 1962), 135–59.

Kincaid, James R., *Child-Loving: The Erotic Child and Victorian Culture* (New York and London, 1992).

Kind, Hansgeorg, *Das Kind in der Ideologie und in der Dichtung der deutschen Romantik* (Diss. Leipzig, Dresden, 1936).

Krebhenne, Birgit, 'Kindnahe Erzählperspektive bei Gert Hofmann: Untersuchungen zu "Unsere Eroberung", "Veilchenfeld", "Der Kino-erzähler"' (unpublished M.A. thesis, Göttingen, 1992).

Kuhn, Reinhard, *Corruption in Paradise: The Child in Western Literature* (Hanover, N.H and London, 1982).

Lathey, Gillian, *The Impossible Legacy: Identity and Purpose in Autobiographical Children's Literature set in the Third Reich and the Second World War* (Berne, 1999).

Lloyd, Rosemary, *The Land of Lost Content: Children and Childhood in Nineteenth-Century French Literature* (Oxford, 1992).

Müller, Joachim, 'Die Gestalt des Kindes und des Jugendlichen in der deutschen Literatur von Goethe bis Thomas Mann', *SSAWL*, 116/1 (1971), 1–38.

Noob, Joachim, *Der Schülerselbstmord in der deutschen Literatur um die Jahrhundertwende: Non Vitae sed Scholae discimus* (Heidelberg, 1998).

Pattison, Robert, *The Child Figure in English Literature* (Athens, Ga., 1978).

Purdie, Catherine, *'Wenn ihr nicht werdet wie die Kinder': The Significance of the Child in the World-View of Ilse Aichinger* (Frankfurt, 1998).

Richter, Dieter, *Das fremde Kind: Zur Entstehung der Kindheitsbilder des bürgerlichen Zeitalters* (Frankfurt, 1987).

Ricou, Laurie, *Everyday Magic: Child Languages in Canadian Literature* (Vancouver, 1987).

Schaub, Gerhard, *Le Génie Enfant: Die Kategorie des Kindlichen bei Clemens Brentano* (Berlin and New York, 1973).

Scherer, Alfred Charles Frederick, 'Formative Influences in the Life of the Child in German Prose Fiction of the Nineteenth Century' (unpublished doctoral thesis, University of Illinois, 1939).

Schindler, Stephan K., *Das Subjekt als Kind: Die Erfindung der Kindheit im Roman des 18. Jahrhunderts* (Berlin, 1994).

Schlör, Irene, *Pubertät und Poesie: Das Problem der Erziehung in den literarischen Beispielen von Wedekind, Musil und Siegfried Lenz* (Constance, 1992).

Simonis, Annette, *Kindheit in Romanen um 1800* (Bielefeld, 1993).

Söntgerath, Alfred, *Pädagogik und Dichtung: Das Kind in der Literatur des 20. Jahrhunderts* (Stuttgart, 1967).

Ueding, Gert, 'Verstoßen in ein fremdes Land: Kinderbilder der deutschen Literatur', *NS* 17 (1977), 344–56.

2.2. Social and Cultural History

On Childhood in General

Ariès, Philippe, *Centuries of Childhood*, trans. Robert Baldick (London, 1962).

Avery, Gillian, 'The Puritans and their Heirs', in ead. and Julia Briggs (eds.), *Children and their Books: A Celebration of the Work of Iona and Peter Opie* (repr. Oxford, 1990), 95–118.

Boas, George, *The Cult of Childhood* (London, 1966).

deMause, Lloyd (ed.), *The History of Childhood: The Untold Story of Child Abuse* (London, 1991).

Fertig, Ludwig, *Zeitgeist und Erziehungskunst: Eine Einführung in die Kulturgeschichte der Erziehung in Deutschland von 1600 bis 1900* (Darmstadt, 1984).

Higonnet, Anne, *Pictures of Innocence: The History and Crisis of Ideal Childhood* (London, 1998).

Lenzen, Dieter, *Mythologie der Kindheit; Die Verewigung des Kindlichen in der Erwachsenenkultur; Versteckte Bilder und vergessene Geschichten* (Reinbek, 1985).

Pollock, Linda, *A Lasting Relationship: Parents and Children over Three Centuries* (Hanover and London, 1987).

Rosen, Michael, *The Penguin Book of Childhood* (Harmondsworth, 1994).

Rutschky, Katharina, *Deutsche Kinder-Chronik: Wunsch- und Schreckensbilder aus vier Jahrhunderten* (Cologne, 1983).

Nazi Germany

Benz, Ute, and Benz, Wolfgang (eds.), *Sozialisation und Traumatisierung: Kinder in der Zeit des Nationalsozialismus* (Frankfurt, 1992).

Benz, Wolfgang, 'Kinder und Jugendliche unter der Herrschaft des Nationalsozialismus' in Benz and Benz, (eds.), *Sozialisation und Traumatisierung*, 11–24.

Dick, Lutz van (ed.), *Lehreropposition im NS-Staat: Biographische Berichte über den 'aufrechten Gang'* (rev. edn. Frankfurt, 1990).

Distel, Barbara, 'Kinder in Konzentrationslagern', in Benz and Benz (eds.), *Sozialisation und Traumatisierung*, 117–27.

Dwork, Debórah, *Children with a Star: Jewish Youth in Nazi Europe* (New Haven and London, 1991).

Fischer, Klaus P., *Nazi Germany: A New History* (London, 1995).

Flessau, Kurt-Ingo, *Schule der Diktatur: Lehrpläne und Schulbücher des Nationalsozialismus* (Munich, 1977).

Fricke-Finkelnburg, Renate (ed.), *Nationalsozialismus und Schule: Amtliche Erlasse und Richtlinien 1933–1945* (Opladen, 1989).

Graml, Hermann, 'Integration und Entfremdung: Inanspruchnahme durch Staatsjugend und Dienstpflicht', in Benz and Benz (eds.), *Sozialisation und Traumatisierung*, 70–9.

Grunberger, Richard, *A Social History of the Third Reich* (London, 1971).

Heer, Hannes (ed.), *Als ich 9 Jahre alt war, kam der Krieg: Ein Lesebuch gegen den Krieg* (Reinbek, 1983).

Hertling, Viktoria (ed.), *Mit den Augen eines Kindes: Children in the Holocaust, Children in Exile, Children under Fascism* (Amsterdam and Atlanta Ga., 1998).

Hohmann, Joachim S., and Langer, Hermann (eds.), ' *"Stolz, ein Deutscher zu sein..."' Nationales Selbstverständnis in Schulaufsätzen 1914–1945* (Frankfurt, 1995).

Klafki, Wolfgang (ed.), *Verführung, Distanzierung, Ernüchterung; Kindheit und Jugend im Nationalsozialismus; Autobiographisches aus erziehungswissenschaftlicher Sicht* (Weinheim and Basle, 1988).

Klönne, Arno, *Jugend im Dritten Reich: Die Hitler-Jugend und ihre Gegner* (2nd edn., Munich, 1990).

Koch, H. W., *The Hitler Youth: Origins and Development 1922–1945* (London, 1975).

Langbein, Hermann, *... nicht wie die Schafe zur Schlachtbank: Widerstand in den nationalsozialistischen Konzentrationslagern 1938–1945* (Frankfurt, 1980).

Mann, Erika, *Zehn Millionen Kinder: Die Erziehung der Jugend im Dritten Reich* (Amsterdam, 1938).

Marks, Jane, *The Hidden Children: The Secret Survivors of the Holocaust* (London, 1994).

Peukert, Detlev J. K., *Inside Nazi Germany: Conformity, Opposition and Racism in Everyday Life*, trans. Richard Deveson (repr. Harmondsworth, 1993).

Rempel, Gerhard, *Hitler's Children: The Hitler Youth and the SS* (Chapel Hill, NC and London, 1989).

Schirach, Baldur von, *Die Hitler-Jugend: Idee und Gestalt* (Berlin, 1934).

— *Revolution der Erziehung: Reden aus den Jahren des Aufbaus* (Munich, 1938).

— *Ich glaubte an Hitler* (Hamburg, 1967).

Schoenberner, Gerhard, *Der gelbe Stern: Die Judenverfolgung in Europa 1933–1945* (2nd expanded edn., Frankfurt, 1991).

Steinhoff, Johannes, Pechel, Peter, and Showalter, Dennis, *Voices from the Third Reich: An Oral History* (repr. New York, 1994).

Ziemer, Gregor, *Education for Death: The Making of the Nazi* (London, 1942).

2.3. Child Psychology

Braunmühl, Ekkehard von, *Zeit für Kinder; Theorie und Praxis von Kinderfeindlichkeit, Kinderfreundlichkeit, Kinderschutz; Zur Beseitigung der Unsicherheit im Umgang mit Kindern; Ein Lernbuch* (Frankfurt, 1993).

Cohen, David, and MacKeith, Stephen A., *The Development of Imagination: The Private Worlds of Childhood* (repr. London and New York, 1992).

Coles, Robert, *The Political Life of Children* (Boston and New York, 1986).

Dornes, Martin, *Der kompetente Säugling: Die präverbale Entwicklung des Menschen* (Frankfurt, 1993).

Erikson, Erik H., *Childhood and Society* (2nd edn., London, 1977).

Hoffmann, Edward, *Visions of Innocence: Spiritual and Inspirational Experiences of Childhood* (Boston and London, 1992).

Miller, Alice, *The Drama of Being a Child and the Search for the True Self,* trans. Ruth Ward (repr. London, 1993).

— *Banished Knowledge: Facing Childhood Injuries,* trans. Leila Vennewitz (repr. London, 1991)

— *Breaking Down the Wall of Silence to Join the Waiting Child,* trans. Simon Worrall (repr. London, 1993)

Piaget, Jean, *Le Jugement moral chez l'enfant* (4th edn., Paris, 1973).

Widlöcher, Daniel, *Was eine Kinderzeichnung verrät: Methode und Beispiele psychoanalytischer Deutung,* trans. Annette Roellenbleck (Frankfurt, 1993).

2.4. General Secondary Literature

Adler, Hildegard, 'Scham und Schuld: Barrieren des Erinnerns in Christa Wolfs und Peter Härtlings Kindheitsmustern und im psychoanalytischen Prozeß', *Deutschunterricht,* 35/5 (1983), 5–20.

Arnold, Heinz Ludwig (ed.), *Günter Grass: Text + Kritik, i (6th edn., Munich, 1988).*

Bance, A. F., 'The Enigma of Oskar in Grass's *Blechtrommel*', *Seminar,* 3 (1967), 147–56.

Bance, Alan, *The German Novel 1945–1960* (Stuttgart, 1980).

— *Theodor Fontane: The Major Novels* (Cambridge, 1982).

Behn, Manfred (ed.), *Wirkungsgeschichte von Christa Wolfs 'Nachdenken über Christa T.'* (Königstein, 1978).

Blackall, Eric A., *Adalbert Stifter: A Critical Study* (Cambridge, 1948).

Boa, Elizabeth, 'Günter Grass and the German Gremlin', *GLL* 23 (1969/70), 144–51.

Booth, Wayne C., *The Rhetoric of Fiction* (2nd edn., repr. Harmondsworth, 1991).

Botheroyd, Paul F., *Ich und Er: First and Third Person Self-Reference and Problems of Identity in Three Contemporary German-Language Novels* (The Hague and Paris, 1976).

Brode, Hanspeter, *Die Zeitgeschichte im erzählenden Werk von Günter Grass: Versuch einer Deutung der 'Blechtrommel' und der 'Danziger Trilogie'* (Frankfurt and Berne, 1977).

Clausen, Jeanette, 'The Difficulty of Saying "I" as Theme and Narrative Technique in the Works of Christa Wolf', in Marianne Burckhard (ed.), *Gestaltet und Gestaltend: Frauen in der deutschen Literatur (AB* 10; 1980), 319–33.

Dahrendorf, Malte, and Shavit, Zohar (eds.), *Die Darstellung des Dritten Reiches im Kinder- und Jugendbuch* (Frankfurt, 1988).

Dimler, SJ, G. Richard, 'Simplicius Simplicissimus and Oskar Matzerath as Alienated Heroes: Comparison and Contrast', *AB* 4 (1975), 113–34.

Durzak, Manfred, *Gespräche über den Roman, mit Josef Breitbach, Elias Canetti, Heinrich Böll, Siegfried Lenz, Wolfgang Hildesheimer, Peter Handke, Hans Erich Nossack, Uwe Johnson, Walter Höllerer* (Frankfurt, 1976).

Elm, Theo, *Siegfried Lenz–'Deutschstunde': Engagement und Realismus im Gegenwartsroman* (Munich, 1974).

Emmerich, Wolfgang, *Kleine Literaturgeschichte der DDR: Erweiterte Neuausgabe* (repr. Leipzig, 1997).

Esser, Manuel, '"Die Vögel beginnen zu singen, wenn es noch finster ist": Auszug aus einem Gespräch mit Ilse Aichinger', in Moser (ed.), *Ilse Aichinger* 47–57.

Fertig, Ludwig, *Vor-leben: Bekenntnis und Erziehung bei Thomas Mann* (Darmstadt, 1993).

Fischer, André, *Inszenierte Naivität: Zur ästhetischen Simulation von Geschichte bei Günter Grass, Albert Drach und Walter Kempowski* (Munich, 1992).

Frieden, Sandra, *Autobiography, Self into Form: German-Language Autobiographical Writings of the 1970s* (Frankfurt, 1983).

Friedrichsmeyer, Erhard M., 'Aspects of Myth, Parody and Obscenity in Grass's *Die Blechtrommel* and *Katz und Maus*', *GR* 40 (1965), 240–50.

Gehrke, Ralph, ' "Es ist nicht wahr, daß die Geschichte nichts lehren könnte, ihr fehlen bloß die Schüler..." "Veilchenfeld": Gert Hofmanns Lehrstück über Auschwitz und Fremdenhaß und sein Bezug zur Gegenwart', *Der Deutschunterricht*, 44/3 (1992), 92–103.

Gerlach, Rainer, and Richter, Matthias (eds.), *Uwe Johnson* (Frankfurt, 1984).

Gerresheim, Helga-Maleen, 'Ilse Aichinger', in Wiese (ed.), *Deutsche Dichter der Gegenwart*, 481–96.

Ghurye, Charlotte W., *The Movement towards a New Social and Political Consciousness in Postwar German Prose* (Berne and Frankfurt, 1971).

Görtz, Franz Josef (ed.), *Die Blechtrommel; Attraktion und Ärgernis; Ein Kapitel deutscher Literaturkritik* (Darmstadt and Neuwied, 1984).

Gregor-Dellin, Martin, 'Mädchenrätsel in Dresden; Helga Schütz erzählt von einem Kind und einer Großmutter', *Frankfurter Allgemeine Zeitung* (18 Aug. 1978).

Greif, Hans-Jürgen, *Christa Wolf: 'Wie sind wir so geworden wie wir heute sind?'* (Berne, 1978).

Greiner, Bernhard, 'Die Schwierigkeit, "ich" zu sagen: Christa Wolfs psychologische Orientierung des Erzählens', *DVjs* 55 (1981), 323–42.

Grünzweig, Walter, 'Gert Hofmann', in *Kritisches Lexikon zur deutschsprachigen Gegenwartsliteratur* (Munich, 1995).

Harscheidt, Michael, *Günter Grass, Wort– Zahl–Gott: Der 'phantastische Realismus' in den Hundejahren* (Bonn, 1976).

Hartmann, Lily Maria von, 'Auf der Suche nach dem Autor: Erzählstrukturen im Werk Gert Hofmanns', in Kosler (ed.), *Gert Hofmann*, 105–25.

Hatfield, Henry, 'Günter Grass: The Artist as Satirist', in Robert R. Heitner (ed.), *The Contemporary Novel in German: A Symposium* (Austin, Tex. and London, 1967), 117–34.

Hein, Helmut, 'ATLANTIS-Lesung: Hanna Johansen, *Die Analphabetin*', *Die Woche* (14 Oct. 1982).

Helbling, Hanno, ' "Unsere" Identität', in Kosler (ed.), *Gert Hofmann*, 153–5.

Hieber, Jochen, 'Die Schrecken der Welt am Tage Null', in Kosler (ed.), *Gert Hofmann*, 149–53.

Hillebrand, Bruno, *Theorie des Romans: Erzählstrategien der Neuzeit* (3rd expanded edn., Stuttgart and Weimar, 1993).

Jackson, Neil, and Saunders, Barbara, 'Christa Wolf's *Kindheitsmuster*: An East German Experiment in Political Autobiography', *GLL* 33 (1979/80), 319–29.

Jens, Walter, *Deutsche Literatur der Gegenwart: Themen, Stile, Tendenzen*, (Munich, 1961).

— *Statt einer Literaturgeschichte* (5th expanded edn., Pfullingen, 1962)

Jung, C. G., and Kerényi, K., *Einführung in das Wesen der Mythologie: Das Göttliche Kind, Das Göttliche Mädchen* (4th rev. edn., Zurich, 1951).

Jung, Hans-Gernot, 'Lästerungen bei Günter Grass', in Manfred Jurgensen (ed.), *Grass: Kritik–Thesen–Analysen* (Berne and Munich, 1973), 75–85.

Jurgensen, Manfred, *Erzählformen des fiktionalen Ich: Beiträge zum deutschen Gegenwartsroman* (Berne and Munich, 1980).

— *Deutsche Frauenautoren der Gegenwart: Bachmann, Reinig, Wolf, Wohmann, Struck, Leutenegger, Schwaiger* (Berne, 1983).

Kaiser, Hedi, 'Ilse Aichinger, *Die größere Hoffnung*' in Herbert Kaiser and Köpf (eds.), *Erzählen, Erinnern*, 18–37.

Kaiser, Herbert, 'Jurek Becker, *Jakob der Lügner*', in id. and Köpf (eds.), *Erzählen, Erinnern*, 106–24.

— and Köpf, Gerhard (eds.), *Erzählen, Erinnern: Deutsche Prosa der Gegenwart, Interpretationen* (Frankfurt, 1992).

Kaiser, Walter, *Praisers of Folly* (London, 1964).

Keele, Alan Frank, ' . . . Through a (Dark) Glass Clearly: Magic Spectacles and the Motif of the Mimetic Mantic in Postwar German Literature from Borchert to Grass', *GR* 57 (1982), 49–59.

Klapdor-Kops, Heike, ' "Und was die Verfasserin betrifft, laßt uns weitersehen": Die Rekonstruktion der schriftstellerischen Laufbahn Anna Gmeyners', *Ef* 3 (1985), 313–38.

Knoll, Renate, 'Das "Innerste Innere": Christa Wolf und die Tradition des 18. Jahrhunderts, Eine phänomenologische Skizze', *Text & Kontext*, 7 (1979), 146–65.

Kolb, Eberhard, *Anne Frank: Stimme eines Kindes im Holocaust* (Hanover, 1992).

Kontje, Todd, 'Captive Creator in Siegfried Lenz's *Deutschstunde*: Writer, Reader and Response', *GQ* 53 (1980), 458–66.

Koskella, Gretel A., *Die Krise des deutschen Romans 1960–1970* (Frankfurt, 1986).

Kosler, Hans Christian, (ed.), *Gert Hofmann: Auskunft für Leser* (Darmstadt and Neuwied, 1987).

— 'Aus den Fenstern noch einmal das Abendland begrüßen: Ein Gespräch mit Gert Hofmann', in id. (ed.), *Gert Hofmann*, 41–50.

— 'Das fremde Kunstwerk: Anmerkungen zu einem Artisten', in id. (ed.), *Gert Hofmann*, 77–92.

Kuhn, Anna K., *Christa Wolf's Utopian Vision: From Marxism to Feminism* (Cambridge, 1988).

Labov, William, *Language in the Inner City: Studies in the Black English Vernacular* (Oxford, 1977).

Lämmert, Eberhard, and Eggert, Halmut, et al. (eds.): *Romantheorie: Dokumentation ihrer Geschichte in Deutschland seit 1880* (2nd edn., Königstein, 1984).

Lee, Carol Ann, *Roses from the Earth: The Biography of Anne Frank* (London, 1999).

Lindwer, Willy, *Anne Frank: Die letzten sieben Monate, Augenzeuginnen berichten*, trans. Mirjam Pressler (Frankfurt, 1990).

Lützeler, Paul Michael, 'Gert Hofmann: Der verstoßene Sohn, Ein Werk-Porträt', in Kosler (ed.), *Gert Hofmann*, 50–8.

Mähl, Hans-Joachim, *Die Idee des goldenen Zeitalters im Werk des Novalis: Studien zur Wesensbestimmung der frühromantischen Utopie und zu ihren ideengeschichtlichen Voraussetzungen* (Heidelberg, 1965).

Mason, Ann L., *The Skeptical Muse: A Study of Günter Grass's Conception of the Artist* (Berne and Frankfurt, 1974).

Mecklenburg, Norbert, 'Faschismus und Alltag in deutscher Gegenwartsprosa: Kempowski und andere', in Wagener (ed.), *Gegenwarts-literatur und Drittes Reich*, 11–32.

Midgley, David (ed.), *The German Novel in the Twentieth Century: Beyond Realism* (Edinburgh and New York, 1993).

Miles, Keith, *Günter Grass* (London, 1975).

Mitscherlich-Nielsen, Margarete, 'Gratwanderung zwischen Anspruch und Verstrickung', in Angela Drescher (ed.), *Christa Wolf, Ein Arbeitsbuch: Studien, Dokumente, Bibliographie* (Frankfurt, 1990), 114–20.

Moser, Samuel (ed.), *Ilse Aichinger: Leben und Werk* (2nd expanded edn., Frankfurt, 1995).

— 'Geschüttelt von Unwissenheit: Hanna Johansens Fragen und Kinderfragen aus dem Kriegssommer 1944', *Süddeutsche Zeitung*, (26/7 Mar. 1983).

Müller, Joachim, 'Thomas Manns *Doktor Faustus*: Grundthematik und Motivgefüge', *Euphorion* 54 (1960), 262–80.

Mundt, Hannelore, *'Doktor Faustus' und die Folgen: Kunstkritik als Gesellschaftskritik im deutschen Roman seit 1947* (Bonn, 1989).

Neuhaus, Volker, 'Das christliche Erbe bei Günter Grass', in Arnold (ed.), *Günter Grass*, 108–19.

— *Günter Grass* (2nd rev. and expanded edn., Stuttgart and Weimar 1992).

Nussbaum, Laureen, 'Anne Frank, The Writer', in Viktoria Hertling (ed.), *Mit den Augen eines Kindes: Children in the Holocaust, Children in Exile, Children under Fascism* (Amsterdam and Atlanta, Ga., 1998), 111–21.

Page, Norman, *Speech in the English Novel* (2nd edn., Basingstoke and London, 1988).

Paslick, Robert H., 'Narrowing the Distance: Siegfried Lenz's *Deutschstunde*', *GQ* 46 (1973), 210–18.

Pinker, Steven, *The Language Instinct: The New Science of Language and Mind* (Harmondsworth, 1995).

Pratt, Mary Louise, *Toward a Speech Act Theory of Literary Discourse* (Bloomington, Ind. 1977).

Pulver, Elsbeth, 'Kein Kinderreim auf die Welt', *Aargauer Tagblatt* (8 Jan. 1983).

Pütz, Peter, *Kunst und Künstlerexistenz bei Nietzsche und Thomas Mann: Zum Problem des ästhetischen Perspektivismus in der Moderne* (2nd edn., Bonn, 1975).

Quernheim, Mechthild, *Das moralische Ich: Kritische Studien zur Subjektwerdung in der Erzählprosa Christa Wolfs* (Würzburg, 1990).

Quigly, Isabel, *The Heirs of Tom Brown: The English School Story* (London, 1982).

Reddick, John, *The 'Danzig Trilogy' of Günter Grass: A Study of The Tin Drum, Cat and Mouse and Dog Years* (London, 1975).

Reed, Donna K., *The Novel and the Nazi Past* (New York and Frankfurt, 1985).

Reed, T. J., *Thomas Mann: The Uses of Tradition* (2nd edn., Oxford, 1996).

—— 'Nietzsche's Animals: Idea, Image and Influence', in Malcolm Pasley (ed.), *Nietzsche: Imagery and Thought* (London, 1978), 159–219.

Reich-Ranicki, Marcel, *Deutsche Literatur in West und Ost: Prosa seit 1945* (Munich, 1963).

—— 'Christa Wolfs unruhige Elegie', in Manfred Behn (ed.), *Wirkungsgeschichte von Christa Wolfs 'Nachdenken über Christa T.'* (Königstein, 1978).

Rey, William H., 'Christa Wolfs *Juninachmittag*: Vorspiel zu den letzten Erzählungen', *WB* 38 (1992), 85–103.

Riordan, Colin, *The Ethics of Narration: Uwe Johnson's Novels from 'Ingrid Babenderede' to 'Jahrestage'* (London, 1989).

Robertson, Ritchie, 'Accounting for History: Thomas Mann, *Doktor Faustus*', in Midgley (ed.), *German Novel in the Twentieth Century*, 128–48.

Russell, Peter, 'Siegfried Lenz's *Deutschstunde*: A North German Novel', *GLL* 28 (1974/5), 405–17.

—— 'The "Lesson" in Siegfried Lenz's *Deutschstunde*', *Seminar*, 13 (1977), 42–55.

Ryan, Judith, *The Uncompleted Past: Postwar German Novels and the Third Reich* (Detroit, 1983).

Sampath, Ursula, *Kaspar Hauser: A Modern Metaphor* (Columbia, 1991).

Sauer, Klaus, *Christa Wolf Materialienbuch* (Darmstadt and Neuwied, 1987).

Saunders, Barbara, *Contemporary German Autobiography: Literary Approaches to the Problem of Identity* (London, 1985).

Schede, Hans-Georg, *Gert Hofmann: Werkmonographie* (Würzburg, 1999).

Schirrmacher, Frank, 'Abschied von der Literatur der Bundesrepublik: Neue Pässe, neue Identitäten, neue Lebensläufe: Über die Kündigung einiger Mythen des westdeutschen Bewußtseins', *Frankfurter Allgemeine Zeitung* (2 Oct. 1990).

Schlant, Ernestine, *The Language of Silence: West German Literature and the Holocaust* (New York and London, 1999).

Schlöndorff, Volker, *'Die Blechtrommel': Tagebuch einer Verfilmung* (Darmstadt and Neuwied, 1979).

Schmid, Thomas, 'Hänsel und Gretel, 1938', in Kosler (ed.), *Gert Hofmann*, 167–71.

Schnabel, Ernst, *Anne Frank: Spur eines Kindes, Ein Bericht* (Frankfurt, 1958).

Schu, Josef, *Kinder als Erzähler: Erwachsene als Zuhörer* (Frankfurt, 1994).

Schumacher, Heinz, 'Gert Hofmann, *Veilchenfeld*', in Kaiser and Köpf (eds.), *Erzählen, Erinnern*, 285–304.

Schwarz, Wilhelm Johannes, *Der Erzähler Günter Grass* (2nd expanded edn., Berne and Munich, 1971).

— *Der Erzähler Siegfried Lenz* (Berne and Munich, 1974).

Sergooris, Gunther, *Peter Handke und die Sprache* (Bonn, 1979).

Sheppard, Richard, 'Upstairs-Downstairs: Some Reflections on German Literature in the Light of Bakhtin's Theory of Carnival', in id. (ed.) *New Ways in Germanistik* (New York, Oxford, and Munich, 1990), 278–315.

Shirer, Robert K., *Difficulties of Saying 'I': The Narrator as Protagonist in Christa Wolf's 'Kindheitsmuster' and Uwe Johnson's* Jahrestage' (New York, 1988).

Shklovsky, Victor, 'Art as Technique', in Lee T. Lemon and Marion J. Rees (eds. and trans.), *Russian Formalist Criticism: Four Essays* (Lincoln, Nebr. 1965), 3–24.

Smith, Colin E., *Tradition, Art and Society: Christa Wolf's Prose* (Essen, 1987).

Stallbaum, Klaus, *Kunst und Künstlerexistenz im Frühwerk von Günter Grass* (Cologne, 1989).

Steinlein, Rüdiger, 'Gert Hofmanns Erzählung "Veilchenfeld" (1986) und der Nationalsozialismus im fiktionalen Jugendbuch: Überlegungen zu einer erzählstrukturellen und rezeptionsästhetischen Herausforderung', in Malte Dahrendorf and Zohar Shavit (eds.), *Die Darstellung des Dritten Reiches im Kinder- und Jugendbuch* (Frankfurt, 1988), 90–123.

Stewart, Mary E., 'A Dialogic Reality: Uwe Johnson, *Mutmaßungen über Jakob*', in Midgley (ed.), *German Novel in the Twentieth Century*, 164–78.

Tanner, Anne, 'Wendepunkt: Christa Wolfs *Juninachmittag*', in Manfred Jurgensen (ed.), *Wolf: Darstellung–Deutung–Diskussion* (Berne and Munich, 1984), 51–76.

Tanner, Tony, *The Reign of Wonder: Naivety and Reality in American Literature* (Cambridge, 1965).

Thomas, Noel, *The Narrative Works of Günter Grass: A Critical Interpretation* (Amsterdam and Philadelphia, 1982).

Urban-Halle, Peter, 'Schauplatz Menschenkopf: Wahrheit und Wirklichkeit bei Gert Hofmann', in Kosler (ed.), *Gert Hofmann*, 92–105.

Vinke, Hermann, 'Sich nicht anpassen lassen... Gespräch mit Ilse Aichinger über Sophie Scholl', in Moser (ed.), *Ilse Aichinger*, 36–41.

Viollet, Catherine, 'Nachdenken über Pronomina: Zur Entstehung von Christa Wolfs "Kindheitsmuster"', in Drescher (ed.), *Christa Wolf*, 101–13.

Vormweg, Heinrich, *Peter Weiss* (Munich, 1981).

Wagener, Hans, *Siegfried Lenz* (2nd edn., Munich, 1976).

— (ed.) *Gegenwartsliteratur und Drittes Reich: Deutsche Autoren in der Auseinandersetzung mit der Vergangenheit* (Stuttgart, 1977).

Wendt-Hildebrandt, Susan: *'Kindheitsmuster:* Christa Wolfs "Probestück"', *Seminar*, 17 (1981), 164–76.

White, Hayden, 'The Value of Narrativity in the Representation of Reality', in W. J. T. Mitchell (ed.), *On Narrative* (Chicago and London, 1981), 1–23.

Wiese, Benno von (ed.), *Deutsche Dichter der Gegenwart: Ihr Leben und Werk* (Berlin, 1973).

Will, Wilfried van der, *Pikaro heute: Metamorphosen des Schelms bei Thomas Mann, Döblin, Brecht, Grass* (Stuttgart, 1967).

Zahlmann, Christel, *Christa Wolfs Reise 'ins Tertiär': Eine literaturpsychologische Studie zu 'Kindheitsmuster'* (Würzburg, 1986).

Ziolkowski, Theodore, *Dimensions of the Modern Novel: German Texts and European Contexts* (Princeton, 1969).

— *Fictional Transfigurations of Jesus* (Princeton, 1972).

INDEX